The Outdoor Getaway Guide

for Southern California

by Steve Hymon
and Julie Sheer

1-57354-011-0

Text copyright © 1998 by Steve Hymon and Julie Sheer
Maps copyright © 1998 by Foghorn Press
All rights reserved by Foghorn Press

This book may not be reproduced in full or in part without the written permission of the publisher, except for use by a reviewer in the context of a review. Inquiries and excerpt requests should be addressed to:
Foghorn Press
Rights Department
P.O. Box 2036
Santa Rosa, CA 95405-0036
foghorn@well.com

Foghorn Outdoors' guidebooks are available wherever books are sold. To find a retailer near you or to order, call 1-800-FOGHORN (364-4676) or (707) 521-3300 or visit the Fokghorn Press web site at www.foghorn.com. Foghorn Press titles are available to the book trade through Publishers Group West (800-788-3123) as well as through wholesalers.

Although the author and publisher have made every effort to ensure that the information in this book was correct at press time, the author and publisher do not assume and hereby disclaim any liability to any party for any loss, damage, or potential travel disruption caused by errors or omissions, whether such errors or omissions result from negligence, accident, or any other cause.

Library of Congress ISSN Data:
October 1998
The Outdoor Getaway Guide for Southern California
First Edition
ISSN:1099-6575

AUTHORS' NOTE

Dear Readers:

While our information is as current as possible, changes to fees, regulations, parks, roads, and trails sometimes are made after we go to press. Businesses can close or change ownership. Fires, rainstorms, and other natural phenomena can radically alter the condition of parks, campgrounds, and hiking trails. Before you begin your adventuring, please call the phone numbers listed in this book for current information.

We always welcome your comments and suggestions about *The Outdoor Getaway Guide for Southern California.* Please write us at Foghorn Press, P.O. Box 2036, Santa Rosa, CA 95405-0036.

—*S.H. and J.S.*

ACKNOWLEDGMENTS

We would especially like to thank the many rangers and employees of the U.S. Forest Service, the National Park Service, the Bureau of Land Management, California State Parks, and the California Department of Fish and Game for their help in assembling the information in this book. Sadly, the agencies charged with managing recreation on our public lands are perpetually underfunded. Quite fortunately, however, those mentioned above can boast of having some of the most dedicated, hard-working, and caring employees you'll find anywhere.

—*S.H. and J.S.*

INTRODUCTION

Not so long ago, we arrived in Los Angeles with a wide-open country in our heads and mostly empty wallets in our pockets. Natives of the flat and featureless Midwest, where a Waffle House often passes for landscape and a trip to the mall as culture, we came running when Southern California batted her eyelashes at us.

And then, like a faceplant on L.A. concrete, reality came calling.

We had landed in a city with, seemingly, the largest and most diverse collection of freaks this side of the galaxy. Hey guys, think the Victoria's Secret catalog is exciting? Here's a suggestion: Grab a cup of coffee at the Coffee Bean in Santa Monica, where underwear is outerwear, more earrings are worn below the neck than above, and the preferred mode of transportation is a pit bull and a skateboard.

Every day brought a new lesson. We sought out Hollywood and Hollywood actually called back—with temp work in the commissary. In L.A., the City of Angels with tummytucks, we saw fellow commuters openly weep during traffic jams. No weather out here, eh? It's not every day you can watch a chunk of Topanga Canyon Boulevard fall 100 feet into a creek, thereby tripling your commute in the time it takes to say, "Let's check what's going on outside with Fritz." Hey Fritz, point your weather stick at this.

While we were coming to grips with our new city—which we now heartily endorse, by the way—we also discovered something else: Just beyond the red tiled roofs of Southern California's endless sprawl, there was paradise.

If you fold a map of California in half, the southern portion of the state would include over 600 miles of pristine coastline, five national parks, six national forests, and the highest and lowest points in the lower 48. And that's only the browsing menu.

Consider all of the things to do here. Backpacking in the John Muir Wilderness. Fly-fishing in the Owens River or chasing dorado and tuna off San Diego. White-water rafting on the mighty Kern River. Scuba diving the shipwrecks near Catalina. Rock climbing at Joshua Tree. Camping in the snow above Bishop. Skiing the local resorts, or even better, Mammoth Mountain.

That's a list so short it's almost criminal.

As you flip through the following pages, you'll find we're not experts really at anything. This book was written for other rank amateurs who want to get a taste, and possibly a mouthful, of adventure. The point is: If we can do it, anyone can do it.

Time and again, just beyond this strange city of ours, we've found a little slice of heaven tucked away in this rugged, beautiful, hard land. It's our sincere hope this book helps you find your little slice of heaven, too.

Happy trails,

Steve Hymon and Julie Sheer

ABOUT THIS BOOK

The first third of this book is devoted to the many outdoor pursuits that are available in Southern California, as well as the places to go to enjoy them. We've also included lists of commercial outfitters, so you'll find someone who will be more than glad to shove you out of the plane or push your rear end up and over a rock.

The last two-thirds of the book is organized by the counties of Southern California. In each county we write about several places to visit—with at least one primary outdoor activity to enjoy while you're there. Some of the information in the activities section is repeated in the county section. No, we're not trying to make the book take up more shelf space—we're hoping to make information more convenient for readers to find.

Please let us know about your experiences on any of these outdoor getaways. If you would like to contact us, our e-mail address is: Shymon7890@aol.com. You can also reach us at Foghorn Press, P.O. Box 2036, Santa Rosa, CA 95405-0036. We would love to hear from readers and use their anecdotes in the next edition of the book!

—*S.H. and J.S.*

HOW TO USE THIS BOOK

The Outdoor Getaway Guide for Southern California has several stylistic features designed to help the reader navigate through its contents and zoom in on useful information.

1. Hot Tips (in Activities Section only): Suggestions for how to survive in the wilderness, what equipment to take, or where the best outfitters are.

Example:

• **HOT TIPS** •

BACKPACKING READINESS
(in Chapter 1: Backpacking)

2. Top Ratings (in Activities Section only): Thumbnail descriptions of the top 5, top 12, top 20 (etc.) locations or activities in the different categories (e.g. hiking, camping, fishing).

Example:

• **TOP RATINGS** •

THE TOP 11 BIKING AND ROLLERBLADING TRAILS
(in Chapter 5: Biking)

3. Featured Trips (in County Section only): Longer descriptions of locations or activities broken down by county.

Example:

• **FEATURED TRIP** •

BIKING THE WINE COUNTRY
(in Chapter 19: Santa Barbara County)

4. Reference sections with directions, fees, contact information, locators, and featured trip references: Offset from the main text so the reader can cut to the chase.

Example:
Directions: From Ojai, take either Gridley Street or Signal Street north until it ends at Shelf Road. **Contact:** Ojai Chamber of Commerce, (805) 646-8126. **Locator:** OJAI. **See featured trip page:** 192.

5. Locators: In the reference section, the name of the nearest city, park, or other geographical locator appears in small caps. You can look directly on the map for this reference.

Example:
Locator: CARPINTERIA STATE BEACH.

6. Page numbers of a Featured Trip or a map right after the locators. (Maps are all at the **beginning** of county chapters.)

Example:
See featured trip page: 192.

or:

Example:
See map on page: 242.

TABLE OF CONTENTS

Part 1—Adventures and Activities

Chapter 1: BACKPACKING

• HOT TIPS •
Backpacking Readiness 1

• TOP RATINGS •
The Top 4 Easy
  Backpacking Trips 3

Chapter 2: HIKING

• TOP RATINGS •
The Top 4 Peaks to Hike 7
The Pacific Crest Trail 11
The Top 8 Geology Hikes 12
The Top 10 Scenic Hikes 15

Chapter 3: ROCK CLIMBING

• HOT TIPS •
Where to Rock Climb 18

Chapter 4: CROSS-COUNTRY SKIING

• TOP RATINGS •
The Top 3 Ungroomed Trails 21
The Top 5 Groomed Trails 22

Chapter 5: BICYCLING

• TOP RATINGS •
The Top 11 Biking and
  Rollerblading Trails 25
The Top 10 Places to
  Mountain Bike 27

• HOT TIPS •
Other Places to
  Mountain Bike 31
California AIDS Bike Ride 32

Chapter 6: BEACH CAMPING

• TOP RATINGS •
The Top 12 Places to
  Camp on the Beach 35

Chapter 7: SURFING

• TOP RATINGS •

The Top 12 Places
to Surf 39

Chapter 8: PICNICKING & PAINTBALLING

• TOP RATINGS •　　**• HOT TIPS •**

The Top 10 Places to Picnic .... 43　　Paintballing: The Basics 43

Chapter 9: SKYDIVING, HANG GLIDING, AND KITE FLYING

• HOT TIPS •　　**• TOP RATINGS •**

Skydiving: "What, Me Worry?" ...... 45　　The Top 10 Places
Hang Gliding: The Basics .... 47　　to Fly a Kite 49

Chapter 10: FISHING

• HOT TIPS •　　**• TOP RATINGS •**

Fly-Fishing .... 53　　The Top 5 Places to Fly-Fish 54
　　　　　　　　　　　　　　　　　　　　The Top 9 Places to Fish
　　　　　　　　　　　　　　　　　　　　　from a Pier..................................55
　　　　　　　　　　　　　　　　　　　　The Top 20 Lakes 58

Chapter 11: HUNTING

• HOT TIPS •

Where and What
to Hunt 67

Chapter 12: HORSEBACK RIDING

• TOP RATINGS •

The Top 32 Places
to Rent Horses 69

Chapter 13: WILDLIFE WATCHING

• TOP RATINGS •

The Top 11 Places to
  Bird-Watch 71
The Top 9 Places
  to Go Tidepooling 78
The Top 7 Wildflower Walks 81

• HOT TIPS •

Whale Watching Excursions 75
Watching Whales
  from Land 78
Wildlife Sanctuaries and
  Nature Preserves 83

Chapter 14: SUNSET WATCHING

• TOP RATINGS •

The Top 10 Places to
  Watch the Sun Go Down 85

Chapter 15: TOURING

• HOT TIPS •

Where to See Fall Colors 89

• TOP RATINGS •

The Top 14 Roads and
  Backroads to the Outdoors 91
The Top 11 Hot Springs
  and Mineral Baths 95

Part 2—Southern California Counties

Chapter 16: SAN LUIS OBISPO COUNTY

San Luis Obispo County Map 100

• FEATURED TRIPS •

Lake San Antonio 101
Morro Bay 103

Montana de Oro
  State Park 105
Pismo State Beach
  and Company 107
Lopez Lake 110

Chapter 17: INYO AND MONO COUNTIES

Mono County Map 114
Inyo County Map 115

• FEATURED TRIPS •

Skiing Mammoth Mountain
  and Vicinity 116

Mammoth Lakes 119
Rock Creek Canyon 126
Bishop Creek Canyon 128
Death Valley National
  Park 131

Chapter 18: TULARE AND KERN COUNTIES

Tulare County Map 138
Kern County Map 139

• **FEATURED TRIPS** •

Kings Canyon National Park 140
Sequoia National Park 145
Golden Trout Wilderness 151
Upper Kern Plateau and the
   Dome Land Wilderness 156
Mountain Home State
   Forest 158
Southwestern Sierra Nevada 160
Rafting the Kern River 164
Lake Isabella and
   Kern River Fishing 167
Red Rock Canyon State Park 170
Space Shuttle Landings 171

Chapter 19: SANTA BARBARA COUNTY

Santa Barbara County Map 174

• **FEATURED TRIPS** •

Jalama Beach............................... 175
San Rafael Wilderness 176
Figueroa Mountain 178
Biking the Wine Country 180
Lake Cachuma 182
The Santa Ynez River
   Valley 184
Hiking Gaviota Peak 186

Chapter 20: VENTURA COUNTY

Ventura County Map 190

• **FEATURED TRIPS** •

Mount Pinos 191
Ojai Valley Trail 192
Sespe Wilderness 194
Anacapa Island 196
Santa Cruz Island 198
San Miguel, Santa Barbara,
   and Santa Rosa Islands 200
Point Mugu State Park 202

Chapter 21: LOS ANGELES COUNTY

Los Angeles County Maps
   South 206
   North 207

• **FEATURED TRIPS** •

Angeles National Forest 208
Wildlife Waystation 214
Skiing and Snowboarding
   the San Gabriel Mountains 215
Malibu Creek State Park 218
Paramount Ranch 221
Red Rock Canyon Park and
   the Stunt High Trail 222
Topanga State Park......................223
Griffith Park's Horse Trails 226
Griffith Park Observatory
   and Telescope Night 227
Los Angeles County Beaches 229
Palos Verdes Peninsula.................231
South Bay Bike Trail.....................234
Backbone Trail 236
Catalina Island.............................237
Stoney Point 239

Chapter 22: SAN BERNARDINO AND RIVERSIDE COUNTIES

San Bernardino County Map 242
Riverside County Map 243

• **FEATURED TRIPS** •

Big Bear Lake 244
San Bernardino
  Mountains 245
Skiing and Snowboarding the San
  Bernardino Mountains 248
Joshua Tree National Park 251
Mojave National Preserve 254
Snowshoeing in the San
  Jacinto Mountains 258
San Mateo Canyon 260

Chapter 23: ORANGE, SAN DIEGO, AND IMPERIAL COUNTIES

Orange and Imperial
  County Maps 264
San Diego County Map 265

• **FEATURED TRIPS** •

Caspers Wilderness Park 266
Crystal Cove State Park 268
Sailing Orange County.................. 269
San Juan Trail 270
Palomar Mountain State Park/
  Palomar Observatory 271
Cuyamaca Rancho State Park 273
Anza-Borrego Desert State Park .. 275
San Diego Deep-Sea Fishing 278
San Diego Hot Air
  Balloons 280
Torrey Pines State Reserve........... 282
Sailboarding Mission Bay 283
Bates Nuts Farm's
  Great Pumpkins 285
Imperial Sand Dunes 286

Chapter 24: RESOURCES

• **HOT TIPS** •

Getting Home in One Piece 288
Photographing the
  Outdoors.................................... 295
Outdoor Gift Ideas 297

• **TOP RATINGS** •

Wilderness and
  Adventure Training.................... 299
Parks, Preserves, and Forests 303
Protecting the Wilderness 306

**APPENDIX: Other Bests and Worsts
  of Southern California** 308

INDEX 309

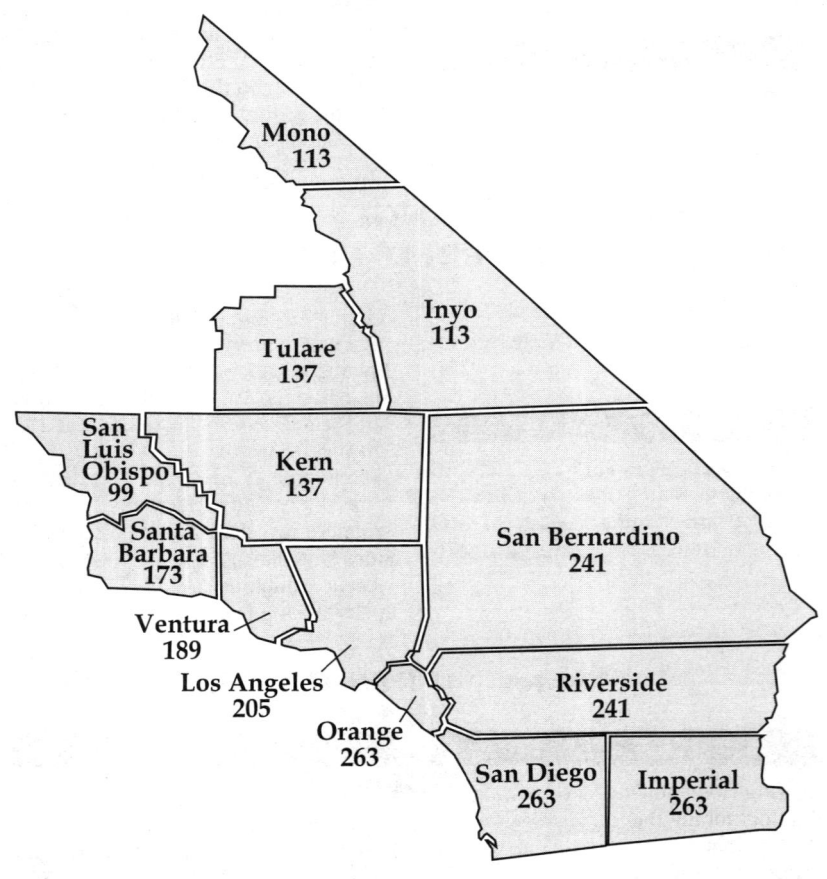

SOUTHERN CALIFORNIA

Part I:
ADVENTURES and ACTIVITIES

1
BACKPACKING

• **HOT TIPS** •

BACKPACKING READINESS

Ever wear a backpack that didn't fit or was packed incorrectly?

The pain usually begins three feet into your camping trip. Generally, the aching sensation starts in the shoulders. It feels like there are tiny men chipping away at your shoulder blades with little rusty hatchets. Then the pain spreads to your neck. The tiny men have put down their hatchets and have picked up crowbars. They are trying to separate your vertebrae—and they're doing it by hanging on to the nerve endings in your spinal cord. Ouch! That hurts!

And that's just the beginning. Soon, the headache kicks in. You begin to bend forward at a gravity-defying angle. Those brand-new lightweight boots—you picked them to help lighten the load—are rubbing your feet raw. As if this isn't bad enough, it's hot out and the air is thin—that's what happens at 10,000 feet.

You sit down on a rock. You lose your balance. Now you are lying in the middle of the John Muir Trail, floundering about like an upside-down turtle drunk on two bottles of tequila. You are a pitiful, pathetic, unsightly thing who should be stuck in a cage in the visitor center under the label: WHAT NOT TO DO.

When backpacking goes bad, it goes really bad. A dream vacation becomes a death march. There is only one way to get it right: spend a couple of days obsessively packing and repacking your backpack while testing it by marching up and down hills in your neighborhood. There is no other way.

Here are some other tips:

1. The backpack should never be more than one-third your weight. We encourage hikers to shoot for one-fourth of their weight, which is much more realistic. If a 150-pound man needs a 50-pound pack for a weekend backpacking trip, he has done something wrong. Pack light. Fight the urge to bring everything.

2. Pack the backpack with the heaviest items at the bottom. The idea is to keep the weight close to your center of gravity—which happens to be your hips. If the shoulders try to carry all the weight, well, forget about it. One hint: Don't bring heavy guidebooks, which add unnecessary weight to the pack. Instead, photocopy the pages you need.

3. Not everyone needs to bring everything. Split up items like food and utensils.

4. Weigh every item before you go. Bring the lightest possible version of any items you need.

We'll quickly address some of your major equipment needs. Most of the large sporting good stores, such as REI, Adventure 16, and Sport Chalet, rent camping equipment. We highly recommend renting before buying—renting is cheap, buying is often expensive.

SLEEPING BAGS

Unless you're planning to do some winter camping, a 20-degree bag is adequate for summer car camping in the Sierra. Those who tend to get cold while sleeping should get a zero-degree bag. Always sleep on a pad to avoid losing body heat to the cold ground. Bags filled with down are considered the warmest, but down is useless when wet. There are many good bags made of synthetic materials—try renting both synthetic and down.

Tents

Choosing one can be like buying a car. A good tent should be easy to put up and light to carry. It should also remain dry during rain (make sure you get a rain fly). In addition, the tent should be suitable for your destination. For example, a tent with stakes may be useless in a place where stakes can't be driven into the ground. You may want a freestanding tent instead. Do your homework. Learn as much as you possibly can before going. Don't be surprised—most often the surprise is unpleasant.

Stoves

Fires aren't permitted in many parts of the Southern California wilderness and, besides, cooking over a fire isn't always very easy in the backcountry. There are several types of stoves on the market, and each has its advantages and disadvantages. We have a Gaz brand butane stove, which costs about $30. We love it. It's very light and small, and the butane cartridges are reliable—although they cannot be refilled. A white gas stove is typically the model of choice for many backpackers. Its fuel containers can be refilled, it burns more efficiently, and it performs better than butane at low temperatures. Just be careful when lighting the stove—a fireball can sometimes result from carelessness.

Water Purification

Like stoves, there are many different models and they come in every shape and size imaginable. Those going on shorter trips should probably bring something small and light—even if it takes a few more minutes to pump a few gallons. Most importantly, get a filter that has a pore size of 0.2 or 0.1 microns, which is what removes things like giardia and other nasty parasites not to be messed with. In case the pump fails, have iodine tablets on hand—they're not ideal, but will work in an emergency.

Food

There are many, many books devoted to backcountry food, and we advise the inexperienced backpacker to check one out, even if it means sitting on the floor of the bookstore for a couple of hours. Our favorite is *The Well Fed Backpacker* (Vintage Books) by June Fleming. She quickly assesses the pros and cons of various equipment and provides a list of practical recipes. The easiest source of food, besides fresh fish (the chance of catching a fish while camping is in direct opposition to how badly you need the fish), is freeze-dried meals, which can be purchased at most large sporting goods stores or from catalogs such as Campmor. Other easy meals include rice with some kind of meat thrown in, macaroni and cheese, or, for the first night in the field, frozen meat that has thawed over the course of the day.

The Checklist

Every outfitter has its own backpacking checklist. Most are basically the same, though some are longer than others. Here's Steve's list, which he has cobbled together over the last few years:

1. comfortable backpack
2. maps and compass waterproofed in a sandwich bag
3. reliable tent with rain fly
4. ground cloth
5. sleeping bag and pad
6. waterproof matches, tube of fire starter, long-burning candles
7. water purifier
8. canteen/water bottles
9. single-burner stove
10. one pot and one pan with biodegradable soap
11. one small bowl, spork, and cup per person
12. first-aid kit with aspirin
13. food separated into zip-lock bags according to meal
14. appropriate clothes for the conditions, including a rain suit (Remember, it's best to dress in layers.)
15. pocket knife
16. AA battery powered flashlight with two extra batteries and bulbs
17. extra nylon cord
18. garbage bags
19. sunscreen
20. hat
21. toilet paper
22. garden spade for digging a latrine
23. camera

• TOP RATINGS •

THE TOP 4 EASY BACKPACKING TRIPS
In the Eastern Sierra

There's a lot of beauty in Southern California, for sure, but there's no place more beautiful than the Eastern Sierra.

The following trips are all relatively easy, although that doesn't mean you won't have to work—lugging a backpack uphill is rarely a picnic, especially at high elevations. One way to beat the altitude: Camp out at the trailhead for a day to help acclimate to the elevation and thin air.

All overnight users must have a permit issued by the U.S. Forest Service. Obtain permits either by phoning the Inyo National Forest Wilderness Reservation Service at (888) 374-3773 or by visiting one of the following Forest Service visitor centers: Mammoth Lakes (located at the intersection of Highway 203 and Old Mammoth Road); Bishop (at 798 U.S. 395, which is also called Main Street); Lone Pine Interagency Visitor Center (located along U.S. 395, just south of town); or the Blackrock Ranger Station (located on the Upper Kern Plateau at the intersection of Forest Service Roads 22S05 and 21S03). Quotas are in effect on many trailheads throughout the Sierra—get a permit in advance to prevent being shut out!

1. SKELTON LAKE, JOHN MUIR WILDERNESS

This beautiful lake sits in a basin above popular Lake Mary, near Mammoth Lakes. Looming high above the lake is a tall unnamed crag and Duck Pass, one of the easier passes across the Sierra Crest.

Skelton Lake (elevation 9,900 feet) is two miles up the Duck Pass Trail from the trailhead (elevation 9,100) at the end of Coldwater Campground. The first mile of the trail is initially steep, although there is plenty of shade. The trail also gets its share of day-users, many of whom are headed toward Skelton Lake.

There are a dozen good campsites to be found on the point at the northern end of the lake. There is good fishing in the lake for brook trout; also try the stream flowing from the lake at its southern end.

Trailhead camping is available at Coldwater Campground, which has 77 sites. Facilities include fire rings, picnic tables, flush toilets, and piped water. Fees are currently $12 per night. **Directions:** From Mammoth Lakes take Lake Mary Road west for three miles. At Lake Mary Loop Road, turn left. Follow the road halfway around the lake and turn into Coldwater Campground. Trailhead parking is at the end of the campground. **Fees:** Access is free. **Maps:** The USGS topographical map for Bloody Mountain is available at high-end sporting goods stores. The Tom Harrison Mammoth High Country trail map is also good. **Pets:** Dogs are permitted. **Contact:** Inyo National Forest, Mammoth Lakes Ranger District, (760) 924-5500. **Locator:** MAMMOTH LAKES. **See map on page:** 114.

2. CHICKENFOOT LAKE, JOHN MUIR WILDERNESS

The three-mile hike to Chickenfoot Lake might be the prettiest hike in the Eastern Sierra. As you hike through the Little Lakes Valley, you're staring straight ahead at four jagged 13,000-plus peaks: Mount Mills, Mount Abbot, Mount Dade, and the Bear Creek Spire. Meanwhile, the trail is cutting through meadow after meadow, often filled with wildflowers, while passing the little lakes for which the valley is named. Chickenfoot Lake, like all of its neighbors, is as pretty as they come—it's also filled with fish.

The trail begins at the Mosquito Flat Trailhead, located at the end of Rock Creek Canyon Road. Trailhead elevation is 10,200 feet, the highest trailhead in the Sierra. In order to get acclimated to the elevation, we highly recommend spending a night at the small trailhead campground, located across the small bridge that spans Rock Creek.

From the trailhead, the trail rises 561 feet to Chickenfoot Lake (elevation 10,761). With the exception of a steep hill at the beginning of the hike, most of the elevation gain is gradual, making this a relatively easy hike.

Directions: From Bishop take U.S. 395 north for 23 miles and turn left at Rock Creek Canyon Road (the exit is marked for Tom's Place). Go nine miles to the end of the road, where there is trailhead parking. **Fees:** Access is free. **Maps:** The USGS topographical map for Mount Morgan is available at high-end sporting goods stores. The Tom Harrison Mono Divide trail map is also good. **Pets:** Dogs are permitted. **Contact:** Inyo National Forest, White Mountain Ranger District, (760) 873-2500. **Locator:** ROCK CREEK CANYON. **See map on page:** 114

3. LITTLE POTHOLE LAKE, JOHN MUIR WILDERNESS

If you don't have a heart attack driving to the trailhead in Onion Valley, you'll have a great backpacking experience.

The road to Onion Valley begins in Independence, elevation 3,900 feet. In 15 miles, the road climbs 5,300 feet, literally switchbacking up the side of the Eastern Sierra. Views are incredible, although those squeamish about heights will want to crawl into the backseat and suck their thumb while whimpering like a baby.

Little Pothole Lake is located just off the Keorsage Pass Trail, in a natural basin that looks like . . . well, a pothole. The lake is tiny and sits beneath a large bluff, from which a waterfall spills over to the lake. Looming high above is the magnificent spire of 13,600-foot University Peak. Climb the boulders above the lake and have a look over 6,500 feet down to Independence and the Owens Valley. Do not forget film or a fishing rod; the lake is loaded with small brook trout.

The Keorsage Pass Trailhead begins at the end of the road, next to the parking lot. The trail is 1.5 miles long, gaining 800 feet. The ascent is mostly gradual, although there is little shade from the sun.

Bears have been very problematic at Onion Valley over the years. The Forest Service is now requiring that anyone camping between the trailhead and Keorsage Pass must use bear-proof canisters, available for rent from the Forest Service or some Adventure 16 stores. Hanging food from a tree does not work in this area, and we highly recommend you don't try it; letting a bear get your food creates "problem bears," which often have to be destroyed with a bullet to the head. Where are dead bears taken? The garbage dump.

The Onion Valley car campground is located at the trailhead. Facilities include fire rings, picnic tables, chemical toilets, piped water, and bear boxes. Fees are currently $12 per night.

Directions: From Independence take Onion Valley Road for 15 miles to the end of the road. **Fees:** Access is free. **Maps:** The USGS topographical map for Keorsage Peak is available at most high-end sporting goods stores. **Pets:** Dogs are permitted. **Contact:** Inyo National Forest, Mount Whitney Ranger District, (760) 876-6200. **Locator:** ONION VALLEY. **See map on page:** 115.

4. CASA VIEJA MEADOWS, GOLDEN TROUT WILDERNESS

This is an upside-down hike. The trail begins at the Blackrock Trailhead, elevation 9,500 feet, and then drops 800 feet in two miles before arriving at Casa Vieja Meadows. That means the hike out will require more work, although the elevation gain shouldn't be too taxing.

This large public pasture is ringed by forest and bisected by a small stream, Ninemile Creek, where you'll find native golden trout. It's a gorgeous area, far enough off the beaten path to avoid the crowds. The stargazing can't be beat—we highly recommend bringing along binoculars or a small tripod and telescope. Day hikes can be taken to either Jordan Hot Springs, the site of a former resort, or Monache Meadows, another public grazing area along the South Fork of the Kern River.

There is a small campground at the trailhead that is used mostly by equestrians preparing to enter the Golden Trout. Facilities include fire rings, picnic tables, chemical toilets, and piped water. There is no camping fee, although a free overnight wilderness permit is required.

Directions: From Los Angeles to the Blackrock Trailhead, take Interstate 5 north to Highway 14 (Antelope Valley Freeway). Take Highway 14 north to U.S. 395 north. Just three miles past the town of Pearsonville (comprised of a Shell station and a junkyard), turn left onto Ninemile Canyon Road; look for the sign indicating it is 25 miles to Kennedy Meadows. At Kennedy Meadows, the road changes names to Forest Service Road 22S05 and continues toward Sherman Pass. At the Blackrock Ranger Station (where you can get a wilderness permit), turn right onto Forest Service Road 21S03 and drive eight miles to the trailhead. From Kernville to the Blackrock Trailhead, take Mountain Road 99 north for 19 miles to Sherman Pass Road. Make a hard right turn and drive 36 miles, then turn left onto Blackrock Road and continue for eight miles. **Fees:** Access is free. **Maps:** The USGS topographical map for Casa Vieja Meadows and the U.S. Forest Service Golden Trout Wilderness map are both available at most high-end sporting goods stores. **Pets:** Dogs are permitted. **Contact:** Sequoia National Forest, Cannell Meadow Ranger District, (760) 376-3781. **Locator:** GOLDEN TROUT WILDERNESS. **See featured trip page:** 151.

2
HIKING

• TOP RATINGS •

THE TOP 4 PEAKS TO HIKE

We love statistics, having both worked as sportswriters. So here's one for your friends back east in Hiccup, Arkansas: Of the 25 states east of the Mississippi River, only five—Maine, New Hampshire, New York, Tennessee, and Virginia—have mountains with elevations over 5,000 feet.

In Southern California, 5,000 feet in some places is called a foothill. The tallest peak in Los Angeles County is double that: Mount Baldy (also known as Mount San Antonio), which reaches 10,064 feet. While Mount Baldy is impressive, it's nothing compared to the peaks of the Eastern Sierra, where there are dozens of peaks over 10,000 feet.

This section accounts for just four of the better known peaks in Southern California—Whitney (14,495 feet), San Gorgonio (11,499 feet), Telescope (11,049 feet), and San Jacinto (10,804 feet). Any serious hiker should have them in his or her portfolio.

However, these are also the kind of long hikes that must be approached with some caution. The trails are steep. It's extremely doubtful that anyone not in good shape will enjoy these hikes. Altitude sickness can be a problem for even those who are very fit. Take a day to acclimate to the elevation before you start hiking. Stay hydrated—do so by drinking a lot of water for a week before going on the hike. These mountains often create their own weather, so bring the essentials listed on page 288.

More than anything, plan ahead for the trip. Get in shape, and get the right maps and permits. These hikes can be immensely rewarding—if approached with the respect and preparation they deserve.

1. MOUNT WHITNEY, INYO COUNTY

After Mount Whitney, the next tallest mountain in the United States is in Alaska. This is it, folks, the tallest mountain in the continental United States.

Whitney poses a number of problems to hikers. The first is weather. The peak gets pounded with snow in the winter, and much of the trail is still covered with snow and ice until July. This leaves a very short two- to four-month window to make the climb. And since it's a climb everyone wants to make, the trail to the top gets very crowded, especially in July and August.

In recent years, the trail has suffered from overuse and experienced some ugly sanitation problems as a result of the lack of outhouses along the trail. As one ranger in Lone Pine explained, "It's not a wilderness experience anymore—or not a good one because of all the people on the trail."

The current U.S. Forest Service policy allows 150 permits for day hikes and 50 for backpackers to be issued each day between May 22 and October 15. Reservations can be made six months ahead of time—which means you should make a reservation exactly six months ahead of time. For example, by noon PST on March 10, 1998, all available permits for overnight trips had been reserved through September 10, 1998. If there are any permits left over for any particular day, you can obtain them through the Forest Service visitor center in Lone Pine.

The summit can be reached from both the east and the west. The Heroic Backpacker will make a weeklong odyssey through Sequoia and Kings Canyon National Parks and the John Muir Wilderness to reach Whitney. Obviously, that's not very practical. Therefore, the majority of people access the trail through the campground at Whitney Portal, which is 11 miles west of Lone Pine in the Owens Valley.

Whitney Portal is at an elevation of 8,700 feet. It's an 11-mile hike from Whitney Portal to the summit with an elevation gain of almost 6,000 feet. Most hikers arrive at Whitney Portal Campground a day before hitting the trail. The idea is to kick back and acclimate to the elevation.

Some people do Whitney as a day hike, while others spend a couple of nights on the trail. There are two backcountry campgrounds where hikers can spend the night on the trail—Outpost Camp, 3.5 miles from Whitney Portal, and Trail Camp, 6.5 miles in. Both campgrounds can get crowded. The only amenity at each is a solar toilet. The last certain water on the trail is from the ponds at trail camp. Bear precautions need to be taken from Whitney Portal to Outpost Camp, and marmot precautions need to be taken at both campsites. Wind and cold can be a problem—prepare for subfreezing temperatures at night.

After Outpost Camp, hikers rise above the tree line at about 10,500 feet. From that point on, much of the trail is solid rock. Finally, at the summit at 14,495 feet, hikers are suitably rewarded with the grandest view in Southern California.

"Off of Whitney you look down at the backside of the Sierra Nevada, and there are these incredible canyons to the west because Whitney is the headwaters of the Kern River and the Kaweah is nearby," says Wynne Benti, a Sierra Club member and the co-writer of *Climbing Mount Whitney*. "Then you can look to the east and look across the Owens Valley and see the White Mountains. There's just such a contrast between the desert and the great basin to the east and the entire Sierra range to the west—remember Mount Whitney is at the eastern end of the range. It's true that on a clear day you can see forever."

Directions: From Lone Pine drive west on Whitney Portal Road for 11 miles. **Permits:** Phone, write, or fax (we recommend phoning, not writing) the Inyo National Forest Wilderness Reservation Service, P.O. Box 430, Big Pine, CA 93513; (760) 938-1136, (888) 374-3773 toll-free, or fax (760) 938-3773. You must provide the following information: 1) Entry trail name; 2) entry date; 3) entry date alternative(s); 4) number of people in your party; 5) exit trail; 6) exit date; 7) exit date alternative(s); 8) any plans to spend the night in Sequoia, Kings Canyon, or Yosemite National Parks and, if so, where and when; 9) number of stock, if applicable, and; 10) name, address, and daytime phone number. Reservations are accepted six months in advance. Permits are free. There is a nominal fee for reservations and camping at Whitney Portal. **Maps:** USGS 7.5 minute topographic map of Mount Whitney, CA and Mount Langley, CA. **Camping:** Whitney Portal has 43 sites for tents or RVs. Only half

HIKING

of the sites are held for reservations; phone (800) 876-6200. Camping is $10 per night. **Fees:** $3 per person for an overnight permit, plus $1 per person if you are entering the Mount Whitney Zone past Timber Lake (if you're going to the summit, you are). Day hikers pay $2 per person. **Contact:** Inyo National Forest, Mount Whitney Ranger District, (619) 876-6200. The Inyo National Forest Wilderness Reservation Service also has a Web site: www.sierrawilderness.com. **Locator:** MOUNT WHITNEY. **See map on page:** 115.

2. SAN GORGONIO PEAK, SAN BERNARDINO COUNTY

There are two primary trails to the summit, which lies within the San Gorgonio Wilderness of San Bernardino National Forest: the South Fork Trail and the Vivian Creek Trail. We're going to tell you about Vivian Creek, the shorter but steeper of the two.

The trail is seven miles long, beginning at an elevation of 5,600 feet, just east of the tiny village of Forest Falls. There are three trail camps on the way to the summit—Vivian Creek, Halfway, and High Creek. High Creek, which is creekside, is the most popular because the push to the summit is easier.

If the weather is good and the smog isn't bad (and San Bernardino has the worst smog in the country), it's possible to see 100 miles in every direction, from the blue of the Pacific to the desert and to the Sierra in the north. That includes Mount Whitney, which may very well be your next destination.

Directions: To San Gorgonio Mill Creek Ranger Station from downtown Los Angeles, take Interstate 10 east to Highway 30/38 north. Follow Highway 38 to Mentone and then to Forest Falls. **Permits:** Wilderness permits are required to hike and camp on Mount San Gorgonio. There are quotas on the permits, so plan ahead. No more than 90 days before your trip and no less than 10, you can obtain a permit by mailing a request to: Wilderness Permits, San Gorgonio Mill Creek Ranger Station, 34701 Mill Creek Road, Mentone, CA 92359. You must provide the following information: 1) Entry trail name; 2) entry date; 3) number of people in your party; 4) backcountry campground requested; 5) exit trail (if different from entry trail); 6) exit date; and 7) name, address, and daytime phone number. **Fees:** Permits and camping are free. **Maps:** USGS 7.5 minute topographic map of Forest Falls and San Gorgonio. **Contact:** San Bernardino National Forest, San Gorgonio Ranger District, (909) 794-1123. **Locator:** MOUNT SAN GORGONIO. **See featured trip page:** 247.

3. TELESCOPE PEAK, INYO COUNTY

The Panamint Valley gets little ink in California. That's because there's nothing there. But the valley, wedged between the Eastern Sierra to the west and the Panamint Range to the east, is a long, dry, eerily beautiful piece of land.

Telescope Peak is the tallest peak in the Panamint Range, at 11,049 feet. Just below the peak, to the east, lie the dry environs of Death Valley. Telescope Peak is one reason that the valley receives so little rain; the Panamints catch any moisture that manage to get past the Sierra Nevada and the White Mountains. In fact, Telescope Peak is usually covered with ice and snow well into springtime.

The hike is a long one. It's seven miles from the trailhead to the summit with an elevation gain of 2,800 feet. The last section of trail in particular is brutally steep. But it's well worth it. At the summit hikers can look straight down into Badwater Basin, the lowest point in the United States. Then turn around and look to the west. Hey! There's the Eastern Sierra! Not bad.

There are two drive-in campgrounds near the Telescope Peak trailhead, Thorndike and Mahogany Flat. Both are small with no piped water but can serve as decent base camps. The hike can be completed in a day with an early start—the seven-mile descent will go by fairly quickly—but the truly adventuresome may want to consider a moonlight ascent to see the sunrise over the valley. Check the calendar to see when and where the moon will be—and only do this if you are an experienced mountaineer.

Do not forget to bring all the essentials (see page 288), along with plenty of water—this is Death Valley, after all. No permits are needed, but we recommend driving to the ranger station in Stovepipe Wells to leave a detailed itinerary. Leave another clearly marked itinerary in your car and tent at the campground. There's no such thing as being too cautious.

Directions: From Ridgecrest take U.S. 395 north to Lone Pine, turn right onto Highway 190, and drive 49 miles. At Panamint Valley Road, turn right and go 15 miles. At Wildrose Canyon Road, turn left and drive nine miles to Wildrose Campground, then continue another five miles to Mahogany Flat Campground, where the trailhead to Telescope is located. Note: The road between Panamint Valley Road and Wildrose Campground is unpaved for a stretch and very bumpy. Be careful of rocks and go slow. **Permits:** No permits are necessary to hike Telescope Peak. **Fees:** Access is free. **Maps:** USGS 7.5 minute topographic map of Jail Canyon and Telescope Peak, available at the visitor center at Furnace Creek and Stovepipe Wells. **Camping:** The Thorndike and Mahogany Flat Campgrounds are both free and available on a first-come, first-served basis. Of the two, Mahogany Flat has the better views. **Contact:** Death Valley National Park, (619) 786-2331. **Locator:** TELESCOPE PEAK. See map on page: 115.

4. MOUNT SAN JACINTO, RIVERSIDE COUNTY

If Whitney and San Gorgonio sound a bit imposing, Mount San Jacinto may be a bit more manageable. Reaching the summit of San Jacinto can be done in a day trip—if you don't mind hoofing it for six to eight hours.

San Jacinto, at 10,804 feet, is the second tallest mountain in the L.A. metropolitan area after San Gorgonio. The good news is that the Palm Springs Aerial Tram does a lot of the work, whisking hikers to an elevation of 8,516 feet. That leaves a hike of six miles with an elevation gain of 2,208 feet to reach the summit.

If day hiking to the summit, stop at the Long Valley Ranger Station just downhill from the tram's Mountain Station and get a day-use permit, which is free. The trail begins at the ranger station. Follow the trails and the signs to Little Round Valley Campground (1.8 miles). From the camp, turn right and follow the signs to the summit.

We defy you to find a guidebook anywhere that doesn't quote John Muir's famous quote about the view from the summit of San Jacinto. We'll

HIKING

continue this fine tradition. Muir's opinion of the view: "The most sublime spectacle to be found anywhere on this earth!"

Sounds like a thumbs-up.

Directions: To the Palm Springs Aerial Tram from downtown Los Angeles, take Interstate 10 east to Highway 111 south to Palm Springs. Go nine miles and turn right on Tramway Road, which leads to the tram. From San Diego take Interstate 15 north to Highway 60 east. Take Highway 60 to Interstate 10 east. Exit at Highway 111 south to Palm Springs. Go nine miles and turn right on Tramway Road. **Permits:** Day-use permits are free at the Long Valley Ranger Station near the top of the tram. To camp within the park, you'll also need a permit, which you should obtain ahead of time for trips mid-May through Labor Day. Write to Wilderness Permits, Mount San Jacinto State Park, P.O. Box 308, Idyllwild, CA 93549. You must provide the following information: 1) Entry trail name; 2) entry date; 3) number of people in your party; 4) backcountry campground requested; 5) exit trail (if different from entry trail); 6) exit date; and 7) name, address, and daytime phone number. **Fees:** Tram tickets (round-trip) are currently $16.95 for adults and $10.95 for children ages 5 to 12. Discounts for AAA members are available. **Maps:** USGS 7.5 minute topographic map of San Jacinto Peak, available at most large sporting goods stores. **Contact:** Mount San Jacinto State Park, (909) 659-2607. Palm Springs Aerial Tram, (619) 325-1391. **Locator:** MOUNT SAN JACINTO. **See featured trip page:** 258.

• TOP RATINGS •

THE PACIFIC CREST TRAIL

As wild as many adventures might be, few hold a candle to the grandeur and allure of the Pacific Crest Trail.

Beginning in Campo, California, on the Mexican border, the trail stretches 2,638 miles through California, Oregon, and Washington before reaching the Canadian border in the Pasayten Wilderness. During its journey, the trail passes through 24 national forests, seven national parks, 33 federal wilderness areas, six state parks, and four Bureau of Land Management areas.

Without a doubt, it is the premiere hiking and equestrian trail in the country—even more grand than the older and better known Appalachian Trail. After rising from the deserts of Southern California, the Pacific Crest Trail (those in the know call it "the PCT") climbs into the San Bernardino Mountains to the San Gabriel Mountains before descending into the Mojave Desert. The trail then climbs into the Sierra, where it quickly gains elevation, rising to 13,180 feet at Foster's Pass near Mount Whitney.

After crossing through four of California's national parks—Sequoia, Kings Canyon, Yosemite, and Lassen—the trail crosses into Oregon, following the crest of the Cascades. At the Oregon-Washington border, the trail reaches its low point of 140 feet above sea level, where it crosses the Columbia River. The trail then heads back into the Cascades, passing Mount St. Helens and Mount Rainier before reaching British Columbia.

The PCT was designed to straddle the ridges of the mountains, and it provides scene after scene of high country beauty: year-round streams, unblemished meadows, mountain peaks, remote lakes, and daily glimpses of what can fairly be termed God's Country.

Hiking the length of the trail is, as you would expect, the ultimate adventure. To make this hike is to surrender to the forces of nature, to be at the mercy of the elements, and, to a degree, to step back in time. Very few hikers can make the whole journey. Not only is it physically demanding, but few people can leave work for the four to six months the journey requires.

Most people hike bits and pieces of the PCT, hoping to cover the entire trail over a lifetime.

Okay. Maybe you don't want to hike the entire PCT anyway. But you could sure have fun hiking bits of the trail, a little of the time. The great thing about the PCT is that it's so big it always feels as if the adventure is just beginning.

Where to catch the trail?

The trail doesn't have many road crossings, but there are a few easy access points, the best of which is Devils Postpile and Agnew Meadows, both located in the San Joaquin River Valley, just below Mammoth Mountain. Other places to access the trail include: Angeles National Forest, near Blue Ridge Campground; San Bernardino National Forest, from the Cougar Crest Trail; and Cleveland National Forest's Burnt Rancheria Campground on Mount Laguna.

Contact: Incredibly helpful in planning a trip on the PCT is a free brochure that can be obtained by contacting the Pacific Crest Trail Association, 1350 Castle Rock Road, Walnut Creek, CA, 94598; (800) 817-2243. The PCT brochure includes a catalog of maps, which is very helpful. You can find the Pacific Crest Trail Association on the Internet at www.gorp.com/pcta. **Locator:** Entry points to the PACIFIC CREST TRAIL **(PCT)** are on maps on pages: 138, 139, 207, 242, 243, and 265.

• TOP RATINGS •

THE TOP 8 GEOLOGY HIKES

If you could gain access to a seismograph (go to www.usgs.gov on the Internet), you'd see that, even as you read this, somewhere in California the ground is shaking—if ever so slightly. California, like it or not, is a work in progress.

If California's geology interests you, there's no better place to start than John McPhee's book *Assembling California* (Noonday, 1994). McPhee, in an extremely entertaining manner, explores California's geology while explaining how the land got to be the way it is.

Let's face it, geology is everywhere in Southern California. What follows are a few places, both interesting and odd, that provide a glimpse into the forces that made the state and—here's a happy thought—could destroy it, too.

1. CARRIZO PLAIN, SAN LUIS OBISPO COUNTY

Want to see the San Andreas Fault in all its cracked, kinky glory? The vast, dusty, six-mile-wide Carrizo Plain, located in the western San Joaquin Valley, is one of the best places in California to examine the fault and all the topographic havoc it has wreaked for the past 20 million years.

The terrain is dry and sparse. That's good. The vegetation doesn't block the view of the fault. There are places where you can stand on one side of the fault and see where the landscape on the other side has shifted. The violent Fort Tejon quake of 1857 caused a 30-foot displacement of the land here. Late afternoon's long shadows provide the best viewing of quake-related scarps (cliffs) and sag ponds. Some streams here are believed to have been diverted as much as 400 feet from their usual sources due to quakes on the San Andreas.

Winter is the best time to visit to avoid the heat. At the plain, the Nature Conservancy runs the Goodwin Education Center, which is open from November through June.

Directions: From Bakersfield take Highway 99 south to Highway 166 west. Continue on Highway 166 to where it joins Highway 33 and keep going south to Soda Lake Road, turning right. Drive west on Soda Lake Road through the Carrizo Plain to the education center. From San Luis Obispo, take Highway 58 east to Soda Lake Road (near California Valley) and turn right. Drive southeast to the education center. **Fees:** Access is free. **Contact:** The Nature Conservancy's Goodwin Education Center, (805) 475-2131. Get a free "Geologic Auto Tour" guide of the plain by calling the Bureau of Land Management at (805) 391-6177. **Locator:** CARRIZO PLAIN. **See map on page:** 100.

2. BOYDEN CAVERN, TULARE COUNTY

Located just outside the Kings Canyon National Park boundary in Sequoia National Forest, Boyden Cavern highlights all of the area's geological wonders. The marble cave has stalactites, stalagmites, crystalline formations, and the usual oddities that can be found in caves. Boyden Cavern can be visited only with a guided tour, which lasts about an hour.

Directions: From Fresno take Highway 180 east and then north toward Kings Canyon. Parking for the cavern is at the bridge that crosses the South Fork of the Kings River. **Fees:** Cavern tours are $5.50 for adults, $3.25 for children. **Contact:** Sierra Nevada Recreation Corporation, (209) 736-2708. **Locator:** GRANT GROVE VILLAGE. **See map on page:** 138.

3. DEVIL'S PUNCHBOWL, LOS ANGELES COUNTY

Three earthquake faults converge at Devil's Punchbowl, located just south of Palmdale. Eroded rocks here are believed to match the tilted slabs of Mormon Rocks, located 25 miles to the southeast. That means some pretty good shakers probably caused the Punchbowl's rocks to slide 25 miles north along the Pacific tectonic plate—further proof that San Franciscans and Angelenos will someday be neighbors. The implications of such a shift are terrifying—if the 49ers move to L.A., we're out of here.

The park is basically a punchbowl-shaped canyon. There are several hiking trails in the 1,310-acre park. The one-mile Loop Nature Trail offers good fault-viewing through a unique high-desert wildlife habitat along Punchbowl Creek. A 3.7-mile hike leads to Devil's Chair, a narrow, white pillar of rock rising above the canyon floor. The Wilderness Institute offers guided geology hikes in the park; phone (818) 991-7327 for more information.

Directions: From San Bernardino take Interstate 15 northeast, exiting to Highway 138 west. At County Road N6, turn left. Drive seven miles to the park. **Fees:** Parking is $3. **Contact:**

Devil's Punchbowl County Park, (805) 944-2743. **Locator:** PEARBLOSSOM. **See map on page:** 207.

4. VASQUEZ ROCKS, LOS ANGELES COUNTY

Does this terrain look familiar? The *Flintstones* movie and numerous westerns have been filmed here. It's not hard to see why Hollywood likes this lunarlike landscape with its massive, tilted slabs of sandstone and caves. Highway 14 runs right through the middle of the rocks—way to go Caltrans! Spring and fall are the best times to visit because summers here are hotter than a camel's armpit. There is a short (one-third mile) interpretive hiking trail, which points out the area's geology and history. Your best bet is to go off-trail and climb up and over the boulders.

Directions: From Los Angeles take Interstate 5 north to Highway 14 north. Exit at Agua Dulce Canyon Road, turn left, and continue a short distance to the park. **Fees:** Parking is $3 per vehicle. **Contact:** Vasquez Rocks County Park, (805) 268-0840. **Locator:** SANTA CLARITA. **See map on page:** 207.

5. AMBOY CRATER, SAN BERNARDINO COUNTY

There must have been quite a show when this volcano blew 6,000 years ago in the area just outside the northeast portion of the Twentynine Palms Marine Corps Base. You can hike to the top of the 285-foot crater on the cone's north side for outstanding views of the lava field and surrounding area. The hiking trail is steep—allow two to three hours round-trip. If you schedule your hike between January and March, it'll be cooler and, as spring approaches, you're more likely to see wildflowers.

Directions: From Barstow drive 49 miles east on Interstate 40 to Ludlow and take the Ludlow exit. Turn right toward town and then make a left (east) on National Trails Highway. Drive 24 miles to the crater. Warning: Phone first for road and weather conditions. This place is way beyond the middle of nowhere. Bring plenty of extra water, a survival kit, and a cell phone. **Fees:** Access is free. **Contact:** California Desert Information Center in Barstow, (760) 252-6060. **Locator:** LUDLOW. **See map on page:** 242.

6. RAINBOW BASIN NATIONAL LANDMARK, SAN BERNARDINO COUNTY

Fascinated by fossils? You can catch a glimpse way back into Southern California's past by checking out the fossilized bones in sedimentary rock here, which include those of the North American mastodon, pronghorn antelope, camel, three-toed horse, and rhinoceros. One slight drawback: it's in the middle of nowhere.

Directions: From San Bernardino take Interstate 15 north. Exit at Highway 247 north and drive to the Rainbow Basin turnoff. **Fees:** Access is free. **Contact:** Bureau of Land Management, (760) 326-3896. **Locator:** BARSTOW. **See map on page:** 242.

7. TRONA PINNACLES, SAN BERNARDINO COUNTY

The pinnacles are a collection of tufa spires, similar to the strangely shaped rocks that emerge from Mono Lake. *Star Trek V: The Final Frontier* was filmed here, so you know that Trona Pinnacles is an otherworldly kind of place. In good light this is a super photography spot. It's a long side trip if going to Mammoth but isn't far from the road if heading up to Death Valley on the back route. Wear solid hiking boots because the tufa can cut up lightweight shoes.

Directions: From Ridgecrest drive east on Highway 178 for 15 miles. Turn right at the sign for the pinnacles parking area. **Fees:** Access is free. **Contact:** Bureau of Land Management, (760) 384-5400. **Locator:** RIDGECREST. **See map on page:** 139.

8. ANZA-BORREGO DESERT STATE PARK, SAN DIEGO COUNTY

The park has a variety of excellent sites. In the rocks of the Fish Creek Mountains a 20-million-year span of time can be traced from desert to marine estuary to delta and back to desert. At Split Mountain explore the canyon formed by an ancient stream that divided the Vallecito Mountains from the Fish Creek Mountains. You'll reach an area called the Windcaves by taking a two-mile round-trip hike from a trailhead just west of Split Mountain. In the Borrego Badlands area, Font's Point provides a view 400 feet down into gorges, hills, and massive buttes split by faulting. This area is considered by some to be the best place in the country to view sediments of the Pliocene and Pleistocene epochs. It's best to visit this desert park from fall through spring since summer temperatures fry the egg, then melt the sidewalk.

Directions: From Julian go east on Highway 78 through the state park to Split Mountain Road, then head south to the Fish Creek Ranger Station. To Font's Point from Julian, take Highway 78 east to Yaqui Pass Road north as it turns into Borrego Valley Road; continue north to County Road S22, turn east, and continue to the turnoff to Font's Point. **Fees:** Access is free.

Contact: Anza-Borrego Desert State Park, (760) 767-5311. **Locator:** ANZA-BORREGO DESERT STATE PARK. **See featured trip page:** 275.

• TOP RATINGS •

THE TOP 10 SCENIC HIKES

1. **BLUE LAKE,**
   INYO NATIONAL FOREST

   Locator: ONION VALLEY. **See map on page:** 115.

2. **REDWOOD CROSSING,**
   GOLDEN TROUT WILDERNESS

   Locator: GOLDEN TROUT WILDERNESS. **See featured trip page:** 151.

3. **MARBLE CANYON,**
   DEATH VALLEY NATIONAL PARK

   Locator: STOVEPIPE WELLS. **See featured trip page:** 131.

4. **CRESCENT MEADOW,**
   SEQUOIA NATIONAL PARK

   Locator: GIANT FOREST. **See featured trip page:** 145.

5. **BUCKHORN CAMPGROUND TO COOPER CANYON,**
   ANGELES NATIONAL FOREST

   Locator: WRIGHTWOOD. **See featured trip page:** 208.

6. **SESPE CREEK,**
   SESPE WILDERNESS

   Locator: SESPE WILDERNESS. **See featured trip page:** 194.

7. **HIKING THE SAND SPIT,**
   MONTANA DE ORO STATE PARK

   Locator: MONTANA DE ORO STATE PARK. **See featured trip page:** 105.

8. **MOUNT SAN JACINTO,**
   MOUNT SAN JACINTO STATE PARK

   Locator: MOUNT SAN JACINTO. **See featured trip page:** 258.

HIKING

9. SYCAMORE CANYON, POINT MUGU STATE PARK

Locator: POINT MUGU STATE PARK. **See featured trip page:** 202.

10. VIVIAN CREEK TRAIL, SAN GORGONIO WILDERNESS

Locator: SAN GORGONIO WILDERNESS. **See featured trip page:** 247.

3
ROCK CLIMBING

INTRODUCTION

We were hiking in Malibu State Park. In the distance, someone screamed a terrible scream—the kind of scream that starts at the toes and works its way up through the body. A primordial scream. A scream for the ages.

The trail rounded a corner and we soon saw the source of the scream: a young woman, clinging to the midpoint of a 100-foot-tall cliff. Her route was obviously a long, vertical crack in the rock. She was in a harness, attached to a rope anchored at the top of the cliff—so there was no danger of falling.

But she couldn't quite manage to pull herself up to the next minuscule toehold. She was exhausted. But she tried anyway. Once. Twice. Three times. Each time screaming. She couldn't make it. Her instructor stood below, shouting encouragement. For now, it was no use.

We watched for 10 minutes and then left. We returned to the same spot 30 minutes later. She was still there. In the same place. Still screaming.

In a nutshell, that's the best way to describe rock climbing: slow, tedious, and excruciating. A sport that requires prowess, strength, and abundant amounts of determination. Although the sport has been glamorized by magazines and Hollywood, consider the glamour to be fiction. In reality, rock climbing is as hard as it gets.

Southern California—surprise, surprise, surprise—also happens to be one of the rock climbing capitals of the world. Look around. There's the sheer granite of Yosemite's Half Dome; Tahquitz Peak in the San Jacinto range; Bishop Peak in San Luis Obispo; Mount Williamson in the San Gabes; and Joshua Tree National Park, a place rock climbers flock to from around the globe.

For those interested in getting involved, we highly recommend taking a lesson. Why?

"You have to take a lesson because you'll learn anchoring and rope tying skills that will basically save your life," says Eric Trevore, a Los Angeles–based climbing guide.

Many climbing outfitters offer classes ranging from one- or two-day seminars to weeklong affairs. Most classes emphasize three skills: 1) basic climbing moves; 2) learning how to tie climbing knots and how to use basic climbing equipment; and 3) belaying—how to set and use a safety rope.

Amateur climbing works like this: Two climbers find a rock or boulder worth climbing. At the top, a rope (called the "top rope") is anchored and thrown down to the bottom of the rock. The person on top of the rock is the belayer; the person on the bottom is the climber. The climber puts on a harness and threads the top rope through a device on the harness called a "blade of ice."

Now the climber starts to climb the rock—without using the top rope as an aid. The top rope is simply there in case the climber slips or falls. Should that happen, the blade of ice—which is essentially a braking device—catches the top rope. Coupled with the belayer properly holding the top rope, the climber is prevented from falling. "I've seen a hundred-pound woman [the belayer] easily catch a 200-pound man," says Trevore.

At its higher levels, climbers ascend rocks without the aid of a top rope. Instead, as they climb, these experts use anchors to install a safety rope in the rock face. At the most extreme levels of the sport, climbers sometimes require more than one day to scale a rock. Using advanced equipment, they can actually attach a small climbing tent to the side of a sheer-faced rock. The climber then sleeps in the tent, hanging hundreds, maybe thousands, of feet above the ground.

Needless to say, it's an interesting way to avoid car camping.

• **Hot Tips** •

Where to Rock Climb

There is no shortage of rocks to climb for climbers of all levels in Southern California.

Easy

Beginners should stick to the places where there are easily climbable boulders.

Stoney Point, in the northwest San Fernando Valley, just happens to be where Yvon Chouinard, the founder of Patagonia (the Ventura-based outdoor gear company), got his start. (See page 239 for more information on Stoney Point.)

Another excellent place is the Vasquez Rocks, located about 10 miles east of Santa Clarita, just off Highway 14 (the Antelope Valley freeway).

Intermediate

Intermediates will find popular climbing spots in Malibu Creek State Park near the visitor center and the cliffs in back of Point Dume State Beach, also in Malibu. Up the coast, Santa Barbara County has plenty of good locations, including Sespe Gorge, Gibraltar Rock, and Painted Cave. In San Luis Obispo, Bishop Peak is very popular with local climbers—the peak towers above the town and is already bolted.

Expert

Experts can find nirvana at a number of places. The Tahquitz and Suicide Peaks in San Bernardino National Forest near Idyllwild are well known in the climbing community (see page 260), as is Mount Williamson, which is located near Kratka Ridge in Angeles National Forest. The Taylor Dome, near the mountain village of Ponderosa in the Southern Sierra Nevada, is a miniaturized version of rock climbing's mecca, Yosemite National Park's El Capitan. Just south of Yosemite is Mammoth Lakes, where there are numerous climbing opportunities in both the nearby John Muir Wilderness and the Owens River Gorge, located to the southeast of town.

Joshua Tree National Park in Riverside County is considered one of the premiere rock climbing destinations in the country; climbers there have charted more than 3,700 different routes up the sides of the park's rocks, such as "Tiers for Fiers" and "Stick to What?" (See page 251 for more information on Joshua Tree National Park.)

Instruction

Adventure 16: West Los Angeles, (310) 473-4574. Tarzana, (818) 345-4266. Costa Mesa, (714) 650-

ROCK CLIMBING

3301. San Diego, (619) 283-2374 and (619) 234-1751. Solana Beach, (619) 755-7662.

First Ascent Climbing Services, Inc., (800) 325-5462.

Granite Staircase, San Luis Obispo, (805) 541-1533.

Joshua Tree Rock Climbing School, Joshua Tree National Park, (800) 890-4745.

Mammoth Mountaineering School, Mammoth Lakes, (760) 924-9100 or (800) 239-7642.

REI: Carson, (310) 538-2429; Northridge, (818) 831-5555; San Dimas, (909) 592-2095; Santa Ana, (714) 543-4142; Mission Viejo, (714) 348-1400.

Vertical Adventures, (714) 8554-6250.

Rock Climbing Gyms

Alpine Experience, Anaheim Hills, (714) 777-4884.

Crux, San Luis Obispo, (805) 544-CRUX.

Rockreation, Costa Mesa, (714) 556-ROCK.

Solid Rock Gym, San Diego, (619) 299-1124.

Vertical Hold, San Diego, (619) 582-7572.

4
CROSS-COUNTRY SKIING

• **INRODUCTION** •

The question most downhill skiers ask about cross-country skiing is perfectly reasonable: Why?

Exercise is a big part of it. But we suspect the real reason people are willing to strap their feet to elongated toothpicks, shovel-step uphill, and regularly do a faceplant at the bottom of most hills is to escape.

Go a little ways from the trailhead and, most often, the rest of the world is nowhere to be found. Just trees, snow, a breeze, and you.

There are two types of cross-country skiing trails: ungroomed and groomed. Beginners are well advised to cough up a few extra bucks and learn on a groomed trail. Imagine railroad tracks cut into the snow. Put the skis into the tracks and go. It beats hacking your way through crud.

Ski rentals are often available at or near most trailheads. Just like downhill skiing, a better bargain can be found at a local sporting goods store, such as Sport Chalet. Always phone first to check road conditions. Bring tire chains. We'll say it again: The place to learn how to install chains is not some mudhole on the side of the road—unless you enjoy providing giggles for the Highway Patrol guys.

• **TOP RATINGS** •

THE TOP 3
UNGROOMED TRAILS

1. MOUNT PINOS, VENTURA COUNTY
At 8,831 feet, Mount Pinos is the tallest mountain in Ventura County, and it usually snags enough storms to keep it covered under snow for most of the winter. A network of marked ungroomed trails can be found around the Chula Vista parking area at the top of the mountain. The most popular is the intermediate-rated Condor Summit Road Trail, which begins at the locked gate behind the outhouses. Arrive early—traffic is often congested at the bottom of the mountain. Trail maps (but not ski rentals) are available at the ski patrol cabin at the rear of the parking lot.

Directions: From downtown Los Angeles take Interstate 5 north for 70 miles to the Frazier Park Road exit and turn left. Continue on Frazier Park Road seven miles and turn right onto Cuddy Valley Road. Drive five miles and turn left on Mt. Pinos Road. Continue 10 miles up the road to the Chula Vista parking lot. **Fees:** Purchase a Forest Service Adventure Pass ($5 per day or $30 annually) at ranger stations or most large sporting goods stores. **Maps:** Obtain a trail map at the Chula Vista parking lot. **Contact:** Los Padres National Forest, Mount Pinos Ranger District, (805) 245-3731. **Locator:** MOUNT PINOS. **See featured trip page:** 191.

2. MOUNT SAN JACINTO, RIVERSIDE COUNTY
It takes just 10 minutes for the Palm Springs Aerial Tram to make the remarkable journey from the desert to the alpine environment of Mount San Jacinto State Park. The trail network begins at the ski and snowshoe rental shop just down the hill from the tram's mountaintop station. The going

isn't always easy, but it's possible to be back at poolside in Palm Springs by sunset.

Directions: From downtown Los Angeles take Interstate 10 east for 95 miles. Take Highway 111 south toward Palm Springs for nine miles and turn right on Tramway Road. Continue four miles to the tramway station. From San Diego take Interstate 15 north to Interstate 215 north to Interstate 10 east. Exit at Highway 111 to Palm Springs. Drive nine miles and turn right on Tramway Road. Continue four miles to the tramway station. **Fees:** Palm Springs Aerial Tram tickets are $16.95 for adults and $10.95 for children ages 5 to 12. There is a discount for AAA members. Use of Mount San Jacinto State Park is free. Snowshoes can be rented both by the hour and the day. **Note:** To avoid a wait at the tram, get there early in the day. **Pets:** Dogs are not allowed on the tramway, nor are they permitted in the state park. **Contact:** Palm Springs Aerial Tram, (619) 325-1391. Snow conditions, (619) 327-6002. Mount San Jacinto State Park, (909) 659-2607. **Locator:** MOUNT SAN JACINTO. **See featured trip page:** 258.

3. SEQUOIA AND KINGS CANYON NATIONAL PARKS, TULARE COUNTY

Giant sequoia trees are impressive any time of the year, but they're especially poetic in the winter when not surrounded by 18 plaid-adorned geeks determined to shoot more footage than Coppola did for *Apocalypse Now*. In Sequoia the trails are best accessed at the Wolverton winter use area, where ski rentals and maps are available. A popular route for expert skiers is the six-mile journey to the Pear Lake ski hut in the backcountry.

Phone (209) 565-3782 for more information. In Kings Canyon, the trails can be accessed from Grant Grove Village. Maps and ski rentals are available at the gas station. Two intermediate trails do a loop within the impressive Grant Grove of sequoias.

Directions: To Sequoia National Park from Highway 99, exit at Highway 198 and drive 37 miles to the park entrance. Continue up the General's Highway for 21 miles to the Wolverton Ski Area. To Kings Canyon National Park from Highway 99, exit at Highway 198 east. Drive five miles and exit to Highway 63 north. Drive 30 miles and turn right onto Highway 180 east. Follow Highway 180 into Grant Grove Village. **Fees:** Entrance is $10 per vehicle or $5 per person, good for seven days. **Contact:** Sequoia and Kings Canyon National Parks, (209) 565-3134. Daily weather and road conditions, (209) 565-3341. Web site: www.nps.gov/seki/. **Locator:** THREE RIVERS. **See featured trip pages:** 140 and 145.

• TOP RATINGS •

THE TOP 5 GROOMED TRAILS

1. RIM NORDIC, SAN BERNARDINO COUNTY

Located in the San Bernardino Mountains, just across the road from the Snow Valley ski resort, Rim Nordic has attracted quite a little following. It's a relatively new area, having begun operation in 1991. There are seven miles of groomed trails, with half rated as beginner. Country Road is a nice trail, taking skiers into a rolling meadow. Ski rentals and lessons are available.

Directions: From Los Angeles take Interstate 10 east to San Bernardino and Highway 30. Head north on Highway 30 and exit to Highway 330 north to Running Springs. In Running Springs, turn right on Highway 18 east. Drive five miles to Rim Nordic, which will be on the left. **Fees:** In 1997–98, trail passes were $8. **Contact:** Rim Nordic, (909) 867-2600. **Locator:** RUNNING SPRINGS. **See map on page:** 242.

2. MONTECITO-SEQUOIA NORDIC SKI RESORT, TULARE COUNTY

The lodge is on the General's Highway in the western Sierra, wedged between Sequoia and Kings Canyon National Parks. It's quite an operation with 45 kilometers of groomed trails and an additional 100 kilometers of ungroomed trails. This is a remote, heavily forested area in the winter that often sees some serious snowfall—people come here to ski, ski, and ski some more. Ski rentals, lessons, and lodging are available. This is a perfect place to get away from it all.

Directions: From Visalia take Highway 198 east for 37 miles to the entrance of Sequoia National Park. Continue 39 miles on the General's Highway to the lodge. **Fees:** In 1997–98, trail passes were $12 for a full day and $7 for the afternoon. **Contact:** Montecito-Sequoia Nordic Ski Resort, (800) 843-8677. **Locator:** THREE RIVERS. **See map on page:** 138.

3. TAMARACK CROSS-COUNTY SKI AREA, MONO COUNTY

Do not, under any circumstances, miss skiing at Tamarack, which is just 2.5 miles up the road from Mammoth Lakes, the Eastern Sierra capital of downhill skiing. The spine of the groomed trail system is Lake Mary Road, which is closed beyond Twin Lakes in the winter. This allows skiers access to loops around Lake Mary, Lake Mamie, Lake George, and Horseshoe Lake. The Lake Mary Loop is rated for beginners and should not be missed. Ski rentals, lessons, and lodging are available.

Directions: From Mammoth Lakes follow Lake Mary Road for 2.5 miles to the Tamarack Lodge. The ski center is located at the end of the parking lot. **Fees:** In 1997–98, trail passes were $15 for a full day, $10 for the afternoon, and $5 all day on Thursdays. **Contact:** Tamarack Lodge and Cross-Country Ski Center, (760) 934-2442 or (800) 237-6879. Web site: www.tamaracklodge.com. **Locator:** MAMMOTH LAKES. **See map on page:** 114.

4. YOSEMITE NATIONAL PARK, MARIPOSA COUNTY

Okay, okay. Yosemite is technically outside the area covered in this book. However, the crowds at the park have become so bad in the summer that winter is practically the only time the place can be visited without a hassle. And the skiing is good, too. The park has 24 miles of groomed trails and 90 miles of marked and ungroomed trails, all accessible from the Badger Pass Ski Area. The intermediate-rated Glacier Point Road travels 21 miles round-trip to Glacier Point, which offers a spectacular vista of Yosemite Valley. A favorite for experts is the trek to the Ostrander Ski Hut, located in the park's backcountry (reservations are required). Ski rentals and lessons are available.

Directions: From Fresno take Highway 41 north for 85 miles. Turn right on Glacier Point Road and drive to the Badger Pass Ski Area. **Fees:** Entry to the park is $20 per vehicle, good for seven days. **Contact:** Yosemite National Park, (209) 372-0200. Web site: www.nps.gov/yose. **Locator:** MARIPOSA COUNTY (no map).

5. ROYAL GORGE CROSS-COUNTRY SKI AREA, PLACER COUNTY

Here's the perfect place to spend a day off for those skiing in the North Lake Tahoe area. Located 45 miles west of Reno, on Interstate 80, Royal Gorge is the largest cross-country ski resort in North America. There are 88 groomed trails—80 percent of which are rated beginner or intermediate—totaling 328 kilometers in length. One of the most popular routes is the trek to Point Mariah, where skiers can gaze down into 4,417-foot-deep Royal Gorge. Ski rentals, lessons, and lodging are available.

Directions: From Reno drive west for 45 miles on Interstate 80. **Fees:** In 1997–98, trail passes were $16.50 midweek and $19.50 on weekends. **Contact:** Royal Gorge Cross-Country Ski Area, (800) 500-3871. **Locator:** PLACER COUNTY (no map).

5
BICYCLING

• TOP RATINGS •

THE TOP 11 BIKING AND ROLLERBLADING TRAILS

The trails listed below are all Class I biking trails. That means, in the language of California bureaucrats, these trails are "a separate right-of-way for bicycles, often fenced and found along flood-control channels and the beach." They're also free.

In other words, neither bikers nor 'bladers have to worry about eating the fender of some Hollywood producer who is too busy faxing a memo, placing a phone call, trying to change CDs, and making a cup of espresso to watch where his or her $100,000 Mercedes is going.

1. CABRILLO BIKE LANE, SANTA BARBARA COUNTY

The lane, a fancy word for trail (hey, it's Santa Barbara), covers three miles of the city, mostly along Santa Barbara's waterfront, passing the beach, harbor, and zoo. A tip for early risers: On weekends before 8 A.M., both the trail and Santa Barbara's downtown streets are all yours.

Maps: The Visitor Information Center will mail you a free map if you ask. **Contact:** Santa Barbara Visitor Information Center, (800) 927-4688. **Locator:** SANTA BARBARA. **See map on page:** 174.

2. COASTAL TRAIL, VENTURA COUNTY

This four-mile trail leaves San Buenaventura State Beach in Ventura, meandering north through the county fairgrounds and then briefly following the course of old Highway 1 before terminating near the town of Sea Cliff.

Maps: Phone the Ventura County Transportation Commission for a free map of bike trails in Ventura County. **Contact:** Ventura County Transportation Commission, (805) 654-2888. **Locator:** VENTURA. **See map on page:** 190.

3. SEPULVEDA BASIN BIKEWAY, LOS ANGELES COUNTY

There are two paved loops here in the San Fernando Valley; the western loop is 3.75 miles and the eastern loop is 5.25 miles. The basin is basically a big, flat park with some nice greenery. Insert your own Valley joke here.

Maps: A free map can be obtained by calling the Los Angeles County Bike Map Hotline, (213) 922-5622. **Contact:** Los Angeles Department of Parks and Recreation, (213) 485-5555. **Locator:** SHERMAN OAKS. **See map on page:** 206.

4. SOUTH BAY BIKE TRAIL, LOS ANGELES COUNTY

This 22-mile trail, stretching from the Pacific Palisades to Redondo Beach, is the jewel of the Los Angeles biking scene. Riders get to spend time in all of L.A.'s renowned beach communities, from Santa Monica to Venice to Manhattan Beach to Hermosa. There are dozens of snack bars along the way, as well as half a dozen piers. There is no shortage of bike racks for those who want to plop on the beach. Only one problem: It always seems as if you're peddling against the wind.

Directions: Access the trail anywhere along the L.A. coastline from Temescal Canyon Road in the Pacific Palisades to Redondo Beach. Parking is available in city lots for $5 to $9; there is also metered parking in some communities (good luck in the summer), and some free street parking. **Maps:** A free map of the trail can be obtained from the Metropolitan Transit Authority by calling the Los Angeles County Bike Map Hotline, (213) 922-5622. **Contact:** Los Angeles Department of Parks and Recreation, (213) 485-5555. **Locator:** VENICE. **See featured trip page:** 234.

5. SAN GABRIEL RIVER TRAIL, LOS ANGELES COUNTY

First, the good news: This 38-mile, mostly flat trail runs from the foothills of the San Gabriel Mountains in Azusa all the way to the Pacific Ocean in Seal Beach. Now the bad news: The trail follows the concrete San Gabriel River flood-control basin, and the L.A. County map warns riders that people have been robbed and assaulted here. Our advice is to ride during the day with friends and you'll be fine. Some of the views of L.A.'s historic industrial side of town are really quite interesting.

Maps: A free map can be obtained by calling the Los Angeles County Bike Map Hotline, (213) 922-5622. **Contact:** Los Angeles Department of Parks and Recreation, (213) 485-5555. **Locator:** GLENDORA. **See map on page:** 207.

6. BIG BEAR LAKE TRAIL, SAN BERNARDINO COUNTY

This six-mile trail covers much of the north shore of Big Bear Lake. Views, as would be expected, are pretty, especially at sunrise and sunset. Weekends are usually busy in Big Bear and the trail gets a lot of walkers, but early risers are rewarded with a chilly, scenic ride; keep an eye out for bald eagles in the winter. The trail begins (or ends) at Stanfield Cutoff just beyond the bridge.

Maps: The AAA map of the San Bernardino Mountains is available through AAA and at many bookstores. **Contact:** Big Bear Chamber of Commerce, (909) 866-4607 or 866-4608. **Locator:** BIG BEAR CITY. **See map on page:** 242.

7. LAKE PERRIS, RIVERSIDE COUNTY

Lake Perris is huge, and a nine-mile paved trail almost circles the lake, although there are a few portions that run through the parking lot. It's not worth going more than 30 minutes out of your way to use, but it is one of the few inland biking/skating trails of any length in this part of the state.

Maps: A free map of the area is available at the ranger's booth at the entrance to the lake. **Contact:** Lake Perris State Recreation Area, (909) 657-0676. **Locator:** MORENO VALLEY. **See map on page:** 243.

8. SANTA ANA RIVER TRAIL, ORANGE COUNTY

This is another one of those long, 20-mile-plus urban trails following a flood-control basin. Inland, the trail begins just outside of Featherly Regional Park, which is located near the Gypsum Canyon Road exit of the Costa Mesa Freeway (Highway 55). The trail then winds along the river to the sea at Huntington Beach State Park.

Maps: For a free map of bike trails in Orange County, phone (714) 834-3111. **Contact:** Orange County EMA/Transportation, (714) 834-3137. **Locator:** HUNTINGTON BEACH. **See map on page:** 264.

9. BEACH TRAILS, ORANGE COUNTY

Orange County has more than its share of Class I trails, many of which pop up along some streets out of the blue. The best-known trail is along the beach, of course, running from Sunset Beach in the north to the peninsula guarding Newport Harbor in the south. There is a one-mile stretch south of Huntington State Beach where the lane joins Seashore Avenue, so keep your guard up for cars. Also, the city of Huntington Beach enforces speed limits; keep an eye out for Buford T. Justice.

Maps: For a free map of bike trails in Orange County, phone (714) 834-3111. **Contact:** Orange County EMA/Transportation, (714) 834-3137. **Locator:** HUNTINGTON BEACH. **See map on page:** 264.

10. MISSION BAY PARK, SAN DIEGO COUNTY

There are five miles of Class I trail in the northwestern portion of Mission Bay Park, which is just north of downtown San Diego. Immediately north of where Mission Bay opens to the ocean, there is also a Class I bike trail that parallels Mission Beach and Pacific Beach. These are the most popular places to ride in San Diego.

Maps: Obtain a free map by phoning (619) 231-BIKE. **Contact:** San Diego Visitor Information Center, (619) 276-8200. **Locator:** MISSION BAY. **See map on page:** 265.

11. CORONADO ISLAND, SAN DIEGO COUNTY

As the knob that forms the northern part of Coronado Island thins out to an isthmus, this Class I trail begins at Glorietta Park in the north and runs alongside Highway 75 for seven miles to the south. There are views of downtown San Diego and occasional glimpses of the ocean, too.

Maps: Obtain a free map by phoning the number below. **Contact:** San Diego Regional Bikeway Information, (619) 231-BIKE. **Locator:** CORONADO. See map on page: 265.

• TOP RATINGS •

THE TOP 10 PLACES TO MOUNTAIN BIKE

In Southern California, mountain bikers seem to be as common as ocean waves, sunsets, and dumb bumper stickers. For example, Steve recently took a drug test and, with his urine sample hovering nearby, had a doctor graphically explain where there was some great single track in Moorpark.

The most important advice we can give mountain bikers is to wear a helmet, also known as a melon or bean protector. What goes up the mountain must come down the mountain—whether it be on the bike or off. Other good paraphernalia to have: padded biker shorts, a water bottle, a small patch kit for flat tires, and a detachable bike rack.

Finally, a word about fitness. No other sport in this book requires the aerobic stamina that mountain biking demands. No matter how cool a fully equipped mountain biker may appear, there is no substitute for having thighs of stone, lungs like a balloon, and great amounts of willpower.

The list below is designed to suggest one great ride in each county in Southern California. By no means do we mean to imply there aren't equally good, if not better, rides out there. You could write a very long book on mountain bike rides in Southern California—in fact, some people have.

We've also included our own rating system: Least Difficult, Difficult, and Most Difficult. The way we see it, mountain biking is never "easy." Least Difficult is for beginners, Difficult is for intermediates, and Most Difficult is for advanced riders. When the word "technical" is used in trail descriptions it generally means Most Difficult and requires the rider to have exceptional control of his or her bike.

The best way of finding good trails is word of mouth. Another great way is to join a local mountain biking club. There are dozens of clubs in Southern California, and the easiest way to find one that suits your needs is to go to your local bike shop and check out the bulletin board. If you have access to the Internet, do a search for Southern California mountain biking clubs. There's a ton of them.

1. CARRIZO PLAIN, SAN LUIS OBISPO COUNTY

Rating: Least Difficult

Got a thing for geology, eh? Or maybe you just want to go someplace where you won't run into too many people. If so, this long, gently rolling valley located on top of the San Andreas Fault is the place for you. Two unpaved roads, Soda Lake and Elkhorn Roads, connect the Reyes Ranger Station in the southeast end of the plain with the Nature Conservancy visitor center to the northwest—a distance of 30 miles. In between the two roads is the San Andreas Rift Zone. If you're on the trail when the Big One hits, you've got front-row seats. Hint: Stay away in the summer, when you'll melt. Another hint: Bring lots of your own water. To say there is nothing around is an understatement. We recommend leaving from the Nature Conservancy's Goodwin Education Center, which offers a good introduction to the area.

Directions: From Los Angeles take Interstate 5 north through the Tejon Pass, continuing for 37 miles to Buttonwillow and then exiting west onto Highway 58. Drive 45 miles to Soda Lake Road, turn left (south), and continue for another 14 miles to the entrance for the Painted Rock Visitors Center. **Contact:** Bureau of Land Management Caliente Resource Area, (805) 391-6000. The Nature Conservancy's Goodwin Education Center, (805) 475-2131. **Locator:** CARRIZO PLAIN. **See map on page:** 100.

2. MAMMOTH MOUNTAIN, MONO COUNTY

Rating: Least Difficult to Most Difficult

When the snow finally melts off this 11,000-foot behemoth, the ski resort ships mountain bikers to the top of the hill on both its gondola and its ski lifts. There are many ways down to the bottom, including some gentle hills and some that are insane. This is a big, big mountain, so elbow room will not be a problem.

Directions: From Mammoth Lakes take Highway 203 for five miles to the ski resort. **Contact:** Mammoth Mountain, (760) 934-0745. **Locator:** MAMMOTH MOUNTAIN. **See featured trip page:** 116.

3. UPPER KERN PLATEAU, TULARE AND KERN COUNTIES

Rating: Difficult to Most Difficult

The Forest Service rates 18 mountain biking trails in the Upper Kern Plateau as "most difficult" for good reason; they all require some moderate to steep ascents at elevations over 7,000 feet. Think you've got the lungs for it?

The Trout Creek Trail (Forest Service Trail 33E28) begins at Corral Meadow and follows Trout Creek upstream and then back down. The meadows, creek, mountains, and pines won't disappoint. Many people camping at Horse Meadow Campground bring bikes and tour the surrounding Forest Service roads, which are lightly trafficked, especially on weekdays. Hint: Get a Sequoia National Forest map as well as the Forest Service's "Kern Plateau Mountain Bike Trail Guide," both of which are available at the ranger station in Kernville. Another tip: Two Kernville outfitters operate mountain bike trips up here. Their numbers are listed below.

Directions: From Kernville take Mountain Road 99 north for 19 miles to the Johnsondale Bridge and turn right on Sherman Pass Road. Continue to the Blackrock Ranger Station, where the ranger will orient you to where the heck you are. **Contact:** Sequoia National Forest, Cannell Meadow Ranger District, (619) 376-3781. Mountain & River Adventures, (619) 376-6553. Sierra South Mountain Sports, (619) 376-3745. **Locator:** UPPER KERN PLATEAU. **See featured trip page:** 156.

4. EAST CAMINO CIELO AND JUNCAL CAMUESA ROADS, SANTA BARBARA COUNTY

Rating: Least Difficult to Difficult
East Camino Cielo Road begins at the San Marcos Pass and straddles the top of the Santa Ynez Mountains. To the south, there's Santa Barbara and the Pacific Ocean; to the north, the upper reaches of Los Padres National Forest and the Santa Ynez River Valley. One option is to park at the San Marcos Pass Ranger Station (located on East Camino Cielo Road, immediately after turning off Highway 154) and ride to the east, along the somewhat hilly road. Another option is to drive to the end of East Camino Cielo and turn left on Camuesa Road. Park near the Juncal Campground and ride west on Camuesa Road, which follows the Santa Ynez River downstream; remember, this means you will need to ride back uphill to return to the car.

Directions: From Santa Barbara take Highway 154 north for eight miles. At East Camino Cielo Road, turn right and drive a short distance to the San Marcos Pass Ranger Station, which will be on the left. To get to Juncal Camuesa Road, follow East Camino Cielo for 22 miles. Juncal Campground is at the intersection of East Camino Cielo and Juncal Camuesa Roads. **Contact:** Los Padres National Forest, Santa Barbara Ranger District, (805) 967-3481. **Locator:** SAN MARCOS PASS. **See map on page:** 174.

5. OJAI'S SHELF ROAD, VENTURA COUNTY

Rating: Least Difficult
Just behind downtown Ojai lies Shelf Road. It's easy to see why it has that name; the road appears to be a shelf sitting on the mountains that serve as the town's backdrop. The road is just 1.75 miles long and is closed to traffic. It's easy to reach from downtown Ojai, too: Just ride up either Signal Street or Gridley Street; both dead-end into Shelf Road, which runs between the two streets. There isn't much climbing, either, and the views are accessible to everyone. We recommend coupling this ride with a pedal on the paved Ojai Valley Trail, which begins in Ojai and runs for 8.8 miles along Highway 33.

Directions: From Ojai take either Gridley Street or Signal Street north until it ends at Shelf Road. **Contact:**

Ojai Valley Chamber of Commerce, (805) 646-8126. **Locator:** OJAI. **See featured trip page:** 192.

6. MOUNT WILSON TOLL ROAD, LOS ANGELES COUNTY

Rating: Most Difficult.

This ride up and into the San Gabriel Mountains is no secret to mountain biking enthusiasts; check out the crowd on any Saturday or Sunday morning. From the trailhead, it's a little over eight miles to scrumptious little Skyline Park, with an elevation gain of over 4,000 feet. Eek! If you can make it, great. Even if you can't, we certainly won't hold it against you—you're mortal! You'll have a goal to shoot for next time and there are plenty of beautiful views of the city all along the way.

Directions: From downtown Pasadena take Interstate 210 east, exiting at Sierra Madre Boulevard and turning left. Take Sierra Madre to Altadena Drive and turn left. At Crescent Drive turn right and then turn right again on Pinecrest Drive. Look for a gated fence on the right side of the road and park on the street. **Contact:** Angeles National Forest Supervisor's Office, (626) 574-5200. **Locator:** PASADENA. **See map on page:** 206.

7. SNOW SUMMIT SKI RESORT, SAN BERNARDINO COUNTY

Rating: Least Difficult

The ski resort is open to mountain bikers in the summer, when the resort needs to keep its cash flow flowing. Both you and your bike are hauled uphill on a ski lift and then it's up to you, Picabo Street on wheels, to find your favorite way down. There are great views of Big Bear Lake. Please try to avoid the agony of defeat.

Directions: From Los Angeles take Interstate 10 east to Highway 30 north. Exit north onto Highway 330, drive to Running Springs, then turn right on Highway 18 and continue all the way through the village of Big Bear Lake. At Summit Boulevard, turn right and drive to the resort. **Contact:** Snow Summit, (909) 866-5841. **Locator:** BIG BEAR CITY. **See map on page:** 242.

8. BLACK MOUNTAIN ROAD, RIVERSIDE COUNTY

Rating: Difficult to Most Difficult.

Not so far from the mountain village of Idyllwild, this sometimes paved, sometimes unpaved road climbs up Black Mountain, providing some nice views of Mount San Gorgonio, Mount San Jacinto, and Tahquitz Peak—not a bad triumvirate. If you make it to the top to the lookout, where the Pacific Crest Trail crosses the road, you've gone almost six miles with a 2,000-foot elevation gain. Not bad. Of course, you don't have to go all the way up either.

Directions: From Idyllwild drive north on Highway 243 for eight miles. Turn right on Black Mountain Road and park at the turnout. **Contact:** San Bernardino National Forest, San Jacinto Ranger District, (909) 659-2117. **Locator:** IDYLLWILD. **See map on page:** 243.

9. CRYSTAL COVE STATE PARK, ORANGE COUNTY

Rating: Least Difficult to Most Difficult.

The Moro Canyon Trail winds its way uphill through Moro Canyon, making a pleasant enough mountain bike ride for everyone. Advanced riders will appreciate some of the side trails, which take you up to Moro Ridge. Check out "Poles," which rises 400 feet in just one-quarter mile. We counted four sprawled bodies on Poles recently. Make the climb and you deserve the terror of trying to get down the thing without killing yourself.

Directions: From Laguna Beach, drive north on the Pacific Coast Highway (Highway 1) for four miles. At the stoplight in front of El Moro School, turn right and proceed to the visitor center. **Contact:** Crystal Cove State Park, (714) 494-3539. **Locator:** CRYSTAL COVE STATE PARK. **See featured trip page:** 268.

10. NOBLE CANYON, SAN DIEGO COUNTY

Rating: Difficult.

This is one of those rides that also pop up on mountain biking message boards on the World Wide Web. Here's why: It's about nine miles up the Pine Creek/Deer Creek fire road from the bottom to the top of the trail to the Sunrise Highway with a 2,600-foot elevation gain. And then it's another nine miles or so back down, all downhill. If you ask us, it's completely honorable to do only the downhill and have a car shuttle you back to the top so you can do it all over again.

Directions: From San Diego take Interstate 8 east, exiting at the Pine Valley turnoff heading north. Drive one-quarter mile to Old Highway 80 and turn left, continuing a little over one mile to Pine Creek Road, then turn right. Drive 1.5 miles and turn right at the trailhead turnoff. **Contact:** Cleveland National Forest, Descanso Ranger District, (619) 445-6235. **Locator:** MOUNT LAGUNA. **See map on page:** 265.

• HOT TIPS •

OTHER PLACES TO MOUNTAIN BIKE
The Best of the Rest

Up north in San Luis Obispo County, Montana de Oro State Park (see page 105) has a good reputation. Try Hazard Canyon, which will be on your left shortly after entering the park.

Los Robles Open Space is located in the midst of the Conejo Valley. There are 17 miles of trails here, most of which are single track. To get there, exit U.S. 101 at Moorpark Road south and turn right at Green Meadow. Phone: (805) 597-9192.

Nearby in Thousand Oaks is Wildwood Regional Park. There are numerous trails crisscrossing the rolling hills and grasslands, many of which are of the lung-busting variety. To reach the park, exit U.S. 101 at Lynn Road north and turn left at Avenida de las Arboles and proceed to the parking lot. Phone: (805) 495-6471.

Back in good ol' La-La Land, there's much to do in the Santa Monica Mountains. Cheeseboro Canyon in Agoura features the Sulphur Springs Trail, which travels straight into the canyon for six miles before ending. Exit U.S. 101 at Cheeseboro Road and head north for one mile, turning right onto a gravel road and parking in one of the two small lots. Phone: (818) 597-9192.

In nearby Topanga State Park (see page 223), leave the parking lot at park headquarters in Topanga Canyon and head to the split in the trail. Go uphill right or left and treat yourself to some fantastic ocean views ether way. Phone: (310) 455-2465.

At the end of Westridge Road in

the Pacific Palisades can be found a fire road that goes uphill for three miles to the old Nike missile site. Westridge Road is the first left off Mandeville Canyon, which is off Sunset Boulevard.

Moving south to Orange County, don't miss our favorite park in the area, Caspers Wilderness Park (see page 266); try the Bell Canyon Trail behind the locked gate from the Old Corral Picnic Area. Phone: (714) 728-0235 or (714) 728-3420.

Chino Hills State Park sits on the border of San Bernardino and Orange Counties and encompasses two canyons, Telegraph and Aliso, which make for rides rated "least difficult"—unless you head up the side trails for something a little more strenuous. The park entrance is located on Highway 71 in the suburb of Chino Hills. Phone: (909) 780-6222.

A pretty eucalyptus grove at the north end of the University of California San Diego campus has a 1.5-mile course that mountain bikers can use. The grove is located next to the new recreation building on campus.

Mission Trails Regional Park has several trails cutting through it, as the park's name implies. The park is bisected by Mission Gorge Road. The best place to park is on the Junipero Serra Trail, which can be accessed from Mission Gorge Road. Trails can be found on both sides of Junipero Serra. Phone: (619) 582-7800.

• HOT TIPS •

CALIFORNIA AIDS BIKE RIDE

The organizers of the California AIDS Ride call their event "the experience of a lifetime." Is it hyperbole or the truth?

"Absolutely it's the truth," says our friend David Colker, who participated in the ride last year. "By far, the best thing I've ever done."

The California AIDS Ride is this: In seven days, riders bicycle 525 miles from San Francisco to Los Angeles. Nights are spent in large tent cities that organizers erect at 60- to 80-mile intervals along the route. Money raised by the event—usually in the neighborhood of five million dollars per year—goes to the Los Angeles Gay and Lesbian Community Service Center and the San Francisco AIDS Foundation. Both agencies provide valuable services to those with HIV and AIDS-related diseases.

That, sadly, is no small number in California. Fortunately, when organizers first put the event together in 1994, bikers came out in droves even though the ride required each rider to solicit donations from the general public. In 1996 riders in California AIDS Ride III (which took place in early June) were required to raise $2,500 each in order to participate in the ride.

The fund-raising isn't easy, especially for people not accustomed to it. But for those who have the gumption to raise the cash (and the AIDS Ride helps with both ideas and support on how to do this), the reward is participating in a ride that would be extremely difficult to do without logistical support.

In 1996, the ride kicked off in San Francisco with the first leg ending over 80 miles away in Santa Cruz. The next five nights were spent at Greensfield, Paso Robles, Santa Maria, Lake Cachuma, and Ventura. On the seventh day, riders biked down the Pacific Coast Highway all the way through Malibu, before heading east at Santa Monica and finally reaching the end of the line in West Hollywood, where the closing ceremonies took place.

Ocean views, anyone? Along the way, riders were treated to vistas of the Pacific in between Paso Robles and Morro Bay, Shell Beach and Grover Beach, and off and on from the Gaviota Pass north of Santa Barbara all the way to Santa Monica.

Obviously, the logistics of the trip were out of this world. Preceding the riders to every overnight stop was a fleet of tractor trailers, which served as the support team. One truck housed a repair shop. Another had hot showers in it. Yet another truck served as a cafeteria. Bikers lined up and went through the buffet, enjoying their dinner out in the field. When it was time to crash for the night, tents hauled by yet another truck were supplied to the bikers. They needed it, too: In 1995 the first day of the ride was spent in a miserable rain.

Once out on the road, bikers also had support teams at the ready. Portable potties were available at planned intervals, as were snack stops (lots of granola and power bars) and medical attention. Any rider experiencing mechanical problems had a technical team at his or her disposal. "Before I signed up I thought it sounded organized, and then it actually turned out to be," says Colker.

Even with organization, riders are still faced with a daunting task: riding 525 miles in seven days. Two of our other friends, Geoff Mohan and Rebecca Bryant, also participated in 1995. Geoff's a big-time biker who was able to find the time to ride every day in preparation. Rebecca, his wife, didn't always have time to train, and she paid the price at day's end.

"They had this Vaseline-like stuff called 'butt wax,'" says Rebecca. "They would have it at the truck before you started every day. Everyone would line up and get a stick of it . . . ."

You get the idea.

Which brings us to the subject of training for the ride. Bikers should begin up to a year ahead of time, putting in as many miles as possible on a daily basis. One rider on the AIDS Ride Web page points out that training rides on steep hills isn't what's important—it's spending time in the saddle that is. In the weeks leading up to the AIDS Ride, bikers should routinely be taking 50-mile rides.

Don't worry. You don't have to train on your own. There are regular training rides for registered riders in both San Francisco and Los Angeles. The organizers will also gladly indulge riders with all kinds of training tips and information. As anyone who has done the ride will tell you, the AIDS Ride is a chance to both change your life and your community—for the better.

Contact: For a free brochure on the California AIDS Ride or to register, phone (213) 874-7474. Web site: www.aidsride.org.

6
BEACH CAMPING

• TOP RATINGS •

THE TOP 12 PLACES TO CAMP ON THE BEACH

Unlike the days of old, it's no longer possible to park the jalopy alongside the road and pitch a tent on a beach—a beach which these days probably belongs to a celebrity with a pit bull. Nevertheless, many still manage to sleep on the beach by the simple act of passing out. Problem is, the place they wake up in isn't so nice.

There are some—just not enough—pleasant beach campgrounds up and down the Southern California coast. Sometimes the Pacific Coast Highway is a little too close, but the surf usually drowns out the sound of the cars.

A couple of tips: Many of the beaches experience very cool evenings, with temperatures in the 50s, sometimes lower. Bring a pad for your sleeping bag to keep the cold ground from sucking away your body heat. It also helps to have a freestanding tent—stakes are not effective in the sand. The tent should seal with a zipper to keep sand from being blown inside.

The last item is the most important: Have a reservation. Beach camping is hugely popular, especially during the summer. Reservations are available through the PARK.NET phone system: (800) 444-7275. Currently, PARK.NET allows reservations for family or group camping to be made seven months in advance. Those who want to camp the weekend of the Fourth of July should phone five months in advance.

From north to south, here are the best Southern California beach camping spots:

1. PISMO STATE BEACH, PISMO BEACH

There is camping at two areas on the beach, but we recommend sticking with North Beach, with 103 sites for tents or RVs. The other camping area has 500 primitive sites within the Oceano Dunes State Vehicular Recreation Area, and there's nothing like camping next to someone performing a carburetor flush. Anyhow, the attraction of North Beach is that six miles of beachcombing, bird-watching, kite flying, and horseback riding are at your doorstep. Facilities include fire rings, picnic tables, piped water, and flush toilets. Note: If planning on visiting between Memorial Day and Labor Day, have a reservation!

Directions: From Santa Barbara take U.S. 101 north for 87 miles. Exit at Arroyo Grande Boulevard and turn left. Follow the road until it ends at the entrance gate to the beach. **Fees:** Camping at the recreation area's primitive sites costs $6 per night. **Pets:** Dogs are permitted on leashes; they are also allowed on the beach! **Contact:** Pismo State Beach, (805) 489-2684. PARK.NET, (800) 444-7275. **Locator:** PISMO STATE BEACH. **See featured trip page:** 107.

2. JALAMA BEACH

We give Jalama Beach our number one ranking. The beach is remote—14 miles from the Pacific Coast Highway, between Santa Maria and Santa Barbara—and very pretty, sitting under some pretty bluffs. The campground doesn't quite live up to the beach, but so what? Everything else about this place is great, including the highly recommended Jalama Burger, available at the snack bar. There's a small grocery, too. Activities? Surfing, swimming (watch the riptides), tidepooling, paragliding, sailboarding, and surf casting. There are 110 sites for tents or RVs. Facilities include flush toilets, showers, picnic tables, fire grills, and a small grocery store. Reservations are not accepted.

> **Directions:** From Santa Barbara take U.S. 101 north for 35 miles to Gaviota, exiting north onto Highway 1. Take Highway 1 for 13 miles and turn left on Jalama Beach Road. Stay on Jalama Beach Road for 14 gorgeous miles until the road ends at the beach. **Fees:** Sites are $14 to $18 per night. **Pets:** Dogs are allowed but must be leashed. **Contact:** Jalama Beach County Park, (805) 736-3504. Weather and surf conditions, (805) 736-6316. **Locator:** JALAMA BEACH. **See featured trip page:** 175.

3. REFUGIO AND EL CAPITAN STATE BEACHES

These popular beach campgrounds are 20 miles northwest of Santa Barbara on a beautiful part of the coastline, featuring cliffs falling into the ocean and tidepools. The campgrounds are wildly popular—we recommend a weekday trip during the summer. El Capitan has 140 sites and Refugio has 85 sites for tents or RVs. Facilities include grills, picnic tables, piped water, flush toilets, and showers.

> **Directions:** From Santa Barbara take U.S. 101 north 23 miles. Exit at Refugio State Beach. **Fees:** Sites are $14 to $18 per night, plus $1 for pets. **Pets:** Dogs are permitted on leashes in the campground but are not allowed on the beach. **Contact:** California State Parks, (805) 968-1033. **Locator:** GAVIOTA STATE PARK. **See map on page:** 174.

4. CARPINTERIA STATE BEACH, CARPINTERIA

You'll find lots to do at this wide and sandy beach, including tidepooling and beachcombing. According to locals, the gentle surf makes this the world's safest beach. Carpinteria is a popular stopping point between Los Angeles and Santa Barbara, which means reservations are advised in the summer. There are 262 sites for tents or RVs. Facilities include fire grills, picnic tables, flush toilets, and showers.

> **Directions:** From Ventura take U.S. 101 north for 15 miles, exit at Casitas Pass, turn left (west), and drive one mile to the campground. **Fees:** Sites are $14 to $25 per night in the winter, $17 to $28 in the summer. **Pets:** Dogs are permitted on leashes in the campground but are not allowed on the beach. **Contact:** Carpinteria State Beach, (805) 684-2811. PARK.NET, (800) 444-7275. **Locator:** CARPINTERIA STATE BEACH. **See map on page:** 174.

5. MCGRATH STATE BEACH, NEAR PORT HUENEME

There's plenty here—dunes, fishing, and two miles of beach—but McGrath is best known for its beach camping. Campsites on the dunes have nice ocean views, which sometimes include the Channel Islands. There's also a nature trail to the Santa Clara Estuary Natural Preserve, which is at the north end of the beach. There are 174 sites for tents and RVs. Facilities include fire grills, picnic tables, flush toilets, and showers.

> **Directions:** From Ventura take U.S. 101 south and exit at Seaward Avenue/Harbor Boulevard. Take Harbor Boulevard for four miles to the beach. **Fees:** Sites

are $14 to $18 per night. **Pets:** Dogs are permitted on leashes only in camping areas. **Contact:** McGrath State Beach and Santa Clara Estuary Natural Preserve, (805) 654-4744. PARK.NET, (800) 444-7275. **Locator:** PORT HUENEME. **See map on page:** 190.

6. THORNHILL BROOME STATE BEACH, POINT MUGU

The beach and campgrounds are located at the westernmost point of the Santa Monica Mountains, which collide with the sea at Point Mugu State Park. The beach is part of the park, where there's plenty of hiking and mountain biking—the park's La Jolla Canyon is just across the PCH from the campgrounds. There are 84 primitive tent sites or spots for RVs up to 31 feet long. Facilities include picnic tables, piped water, and pit toilets.

Directions: From Santa Monica take the Pacific Coast Highway north for 32 miles to the beach entrance. **Fees:** Sites are $10 to $11 per night, plus $1 for pets. **Pets:** Dogs are permitted on leashes in the campgrounds, but are not allowed on the beach or on trails in the state park. **Contact:** California State Parks, Point Mugu Ranger Office, (805) 986-8591. PARK.NET, (800) 444-7275. **Locator:** POINT MUGU STATE PARK. **See featured trip page:** 202.

7. SYCAMORE CANYON, POINT MUGU

Pretty little Sycamore Canyon Beach is fantastic, the perfect place to rest after a hike or bike ride in Point Mugu State Park. Unfortunately, the campground is NOT on the ocean side of the Pacific Coast Highway. At least you can still smell the salt water and hear the surf, which is just a short walk away. Facilities include grills, picnic tables, flush toilets, and showers.

Directions: From Santa Monica take the Pacific Coast Highway north for 30 miles to the beach entrance. **Fees:** Sites are $14 to $16 per night, plus $1 for pets. **Pets:** Dogs are permitted on leashes in the campgrounds but are not allowed on the beach or on trails in the state park. **Contact:** California State Parks, Point Mugu Ranger Office, (805) 986-8591. PARK.NET, (800) 444-7275. **Locator:** POINT MUGU STATE PARK. **See featured trip page:** 202.

8. LEO CARRILLO STATE BEACH, MALIBU

This is the closest beach camping destination to Los Angeles and, hence, the most popular, filling up most weekends of the year. Reservations are a must. There are two camping areas, one along the beach and the other in a canyon, for a total of 126 campsites for tents and RVs. Facilities include fire grills, picnic tables, piped water, flush toilets, and showers. For more on Leo Carrillo State Beach see page 80.

Directions: From Santa Monica take the Pacific Coast Highway north for 26 miles to the beach entrance. **Fees:** Sites are $14 to $18 per night, plus $1 for pets. **Pets:** Leashed dogs are permitted. **Contact:** California State Parks, (818) 880-0350. PARK.NET, (800) 444-7275. **Locator:** LEO CARRILLO STATE BEACH. **See map on page:** 206.

9. NEWPORT DUNES PARK, NEWPORT BEACH

Not actually on Newport Beach's sand, this spot is in Upper Newport Bay, right next to an ecological reserve. It's a private park with its own beach, and there's plenty to do; the park has a swimming pool, a saltwater lagoon with a water slide, boat rentals, and a playground. There are

406 sites for tents or RVs. Facilities include picnic tables, flush toilets, showers, laundry, and a recreation room. Fire grills are located nearby on the beach.

Directions: From Interstate 405 north or south, exit west at Jamboree Road. Drive toward the bay and turn right on Back Bay Road, which takes you to the park. **Fees:** Sites are $23 to $75 per night. **Pets:** Two dogs per site are permitted. However, no rottweilers or pit bulls are allowed in the campground. Period. **Contact:** Newport Dunes Park, (714) 729-3863. Camping reservations, (800) 288-0770. **Locator:** NEWPORT BEACH. See map on page: 264.

10. SAN CLEMENTE STATE BEACH, SAN CLEMENTE

The campground is located on a bluff above the beach, which is just a short walk away. All the usual beachcombing activities are here, along with something special for the physically challenged: San Clemente and nearby Doheny State Beach are the only two beaches in the area that have sand chairs. These special plastic wheelchairs can be easily pushed along the sand and right to the water. There are 160 sites for tents or RVs. Facilities include fire grills, picnic tables, piped water, flush toilets, and showers.

Directions: From Interstate 405 north or south, take the Avenida Califa exit and go west to the beach. **Fees:** Sites are $14 to $20 per night in the winter, $17 to $24 in the summer. **Pets:** Dogs are permitted on leashes in the campground but are not allowed on the beach. **Contact:** San Clemente State Park, (714) 492-3156. PARK.NET, (800) 444-7275. **Locator:** SAN CLEMENTE STATE BEACH. See map on page: 264.

11. SAN ONOFRE STATE BEACH, SAN ONOFRE

Like San Clemente State Beach, San Onofre has bluff-top camping with a short walk down to the sand. The downside is that Amtrak tracks are nearby, as is the San Onofre Nuclear Power Plant, where we pray Homer Simpson isn't working ("Doh!"). There are 220 campsites for tents and RVs. Facilities include fire grills, picnic tables, chemical toilets, and showers (with cold water only). Geiger counters are not provided. Heh, heh, heh.

Directions: From San Clemente take Interstate 5 south for three miles. Exit at Basilone Road and turn right to the beach. **Fees:** Sites are $17 to $18 per night. **Pets:** Dogs are allowed on leashes in the campground, but are not permitted on the beach. **Contact:** San Onofre State Beach, (714) 492-4872. PARK.NET, (800) 444-7275. **Locator:** SAN ONOFRE STATE BEACH. See map on page: 265.

12. SAN ELIJO STATE BEACH, CARDIFF-BY-THE-SEA

Located in San Diego County near Cardiff-by-the-Sea, this is the southernmost beach campground in the state park system and, according to some folks, the prettiest. There are 171 sites for tents and RVs on a bluff overlooking the beach. Facilities include fire grills, picnic tables, flush toilets, and showers.

Directions: From San Diego take Interstate 5 north about 20 miles. Exit at County Road S10, turn left, and drive two miles to the beach. **Fees:** Sites are $16 to $21 per night, plus $1 for pets. **Pets:** Leashed dogs are permitted in the campground but are not allowed on the beach. **Contact:** San Elijo State Beach, (760) 753-5091. PARK.NET, (800) 444-7275. **Locator:** SOLANA BEACH. See map on page: 265.

7
SURFING

• TOP RATINGS •

THE TOP 12 PLACES TO SURF

The statistics in this case do the talking: California has approximately 1.25 million surfers, more than any other nation in the world.

Without a doubt, many of those surfers fit the Spicoli prototype—Spicoli was the Sean Penn character in the classic (seriously) *Fast Times at Ridgemont High*. Words like "dude" and "heinous" are still very much part of their vocabulary. Although much of Southern California has been molded in the form of Middle America (some would argue it's the other way around), surfing remains parochial—it's something the natives do. Surfers have their own language and protocol. They are fiercely protective of their favorite waves. A friend of ours once wrote a story for the *Los Angeles Times* listing several good surfing sites. His friends didn't speak to him for weeks.

That's why the best way to learn how to surf is to glom onto an established surfer like an apprentice sucks up to a master. If worse comes to worst, check out the bulletin board at a local surf shop—as a last resort to actually getting a job, some surfers earn extra cash by giving lessons. Many surf shops also rent wet suits and boards.

A note about wet suits: When El Niño isn't around, water temperatures in much of Southern California are cool, only topping out in the high 60s during the summer and mid-50s in the winter. In the summer, a shorty suit (which covers only the upper legs and arms) will probably work.

Beginners should stick to two-foot waves. It's better to surf at high tide, when the waves break farthest from the shore. It's also good to find a beach without a rocky shore—what would you rather have cushion your fall—sand or rocks? Most importantly, don't surf at a beach where there is no one else surfing.

In the 1950s and 1960s, surfboards were much longer than they are today. These surfboards were easier to use although they lack the maneuverability and speed of today's lighter and quicker models. In recent years, longboards have made somewhat of a comeback thanks to the sport's older generation, which is still out there surfing. If you're learning to surf, we recommend using a longboard, about nine feet long. You'll lack the zip of a champ like Kelly Slater, but at least you might actually surf.

There is an unspoken etiquette among the surf crowd that should be observed. Generally, try to stay 50 yards away from other surfers—especially if you're a beginner. Surf code also dictates that it's a rookie's obligation to yield the right-of-way to more experienced surfers. When this protocol is broken, apologize profusely to whoever will listen.

It's hard to imagine well-established surfers needing a list of the great beaches in our region—those places are already firmly Rolodexed in their minds. For those new to the sport, however, here are a few tips:

SURFING

BEGINNER

1. Will Rogers State Beach, Los Angeles County

The surf crowd regards this lengthy beach in Santa Monica as the perfect place for the beginner. The waves break long, giving everyone plenty of room, and the surf is gentle.

Contact: Los Angeles County Beaches and Harbors, (310) 305-9546. **Locator:** WILL ROGERS STATE BEACH. **See featured trip page:** 230.

2. Countyline State Beach, Los Angeles County

The waves at Countyline, in northern Malibu, are slow and ridable thanks to the geography. Right across the street is Neptune's Net, a local roadhouse where tales of bravado can be told afterward.

Contact: Los Angeles County Beaches and Harbors, (310) 305-9546. **Locator:** LEO CARRILLO STATE BEACH. **See map on page:** 206.

3. Seal Beach, Orange County

This is the northern gateway to Orange County but without the glitz and party scene of the county's southern beaches. The northern half of the beach is perfect for families and novice surfers.

Contact: Seal Beach Lifeguard Station, (310) 430-2613. **Locator:** SEAL BEACH. **See map on page:** 264.

INTERMEDIATE

4. Pismo State Beach, San Luis Obispo County

There's often some mellow, albeit cold, water on both sides of the pier. Throw in the fact that Pismo is a major Central Coast beach hub.

Contact: Pismo State Beach, (805) 549-3312. **Locator:** PISMO STATE BEACH. **See featured trip page:** 107.

5. Rincon Beach County Park, Santa Barbara County

Rincon is the Spanish word for "corner" and the beach sits at the end of a point, making for some nice wave action. South of Carpinteria, follow Highway 150 to the beach from U.S. 101 to find it.

Contact: Santa Barbara County Department of Parks and Recreation, (805) 568-2460. **Locator:** CARPINTERIA. **See map on page:** 174.

6. Surfer's Point, Ventura County

This spot is particularly good for longboards—our pal Frank Manning first stood up on his board here, for those of you keeping score at home.

Contact: Ventura City Department of Parks and Recreation, (805) 652-4594. **Locator:** VENTURA. **See map on page:** 190.

7. Malibu Lagoon State Beach/ Surfrider Beach, Los Angeles County

Just north of the Malibu Pier, Surfrider is the most popular location for surfing in Malibu and has been the site of many competitions over the years. Three- to five-foot swells are the norm here.

Contact: California Department of Parks and Recreation, (818) 880-0350. **Locator:** MALIBU LAGOON STATE BEACH. **See featured trip page:** 230.

8. Huntington State Beach, Orange County

This is THE place to surf, a longtime home to surfing competitions. The big competitions and waves can often be found near the pier. This famous surfing capital, affectionately known as "Surf City," owes its big waves to an offshore reef built in the 1950s. Currents caused by Huntington Pier add to the action.

Contact: Huntington State Beach, (714) 536-1455. **Locator:** HUNTINGTON STATE BEACH. **See map on page:** 264.

9. SAN ONOFRE STATE BEACH, SAN DIEGO COUNTY

Surf right beneath the San Onofre Nuclear Power Plant! If the place melts down, you've got a front-row seat. Dude—check out that glow!

Contact: San Onofre State Beach, (714) 492-4872. **Locator:** SAN ONOFRE STATE BEACH. **See map on page:** 265.

ADVANCED

10. ZUMA BEACH, LOS ANGELES COUNTY

Zuma, near Malibu, draws equally well from both the north and south. The waves here can be tricky. This is not a place for the uninitiated.

Contact: Los Angeles County Beaches and Harbors, (310) 305-9546. **Locator:** ZUMA BEACH COUNTY PARK. **See map on page:** 206.

11. SWAMI'S BEACH, SAN DIEGO COUNTY

Located beneath a bluff in Encinitas, the beach isn't very sandy, but the waves can be huge. Swami's is hardly a secret in the surfing community.

Contact: Encinitas Community Services, (760) 633-2880. **Locator:** ENCINITAS. **See map on page:** 265.

12. TRESTLES BEACH, SAN DIEGO COUNTY

Named for the Santa Fe Railroad train trestles located at the south end of the beach at San Mateo Point, Trestles Beach isn't exactly easy to get to, making it all the more appealing to surfers—it's a 1.5-mile hike from San Onofre State Beach. This secluded beach just inside the San Diego County line is rocky with few swimmers. Be careful near the train tracks because trains still run this route.

Contact: San Onofre State Beach, (714) 492-4872. **Locator:** SAN ONOFRE STATE BEACH. **See map on page:** 265.

BOOGEYBOARDING

Surfboards, for sure, are intimidating and difficult to master. That's where the boogeyboard comes into play as the greatest beach invention since glow-in-the-dark Nerf balls.

The boogeyboard is a short (about three feet long), wide board usually made of hard foam. All you do is lie on it and paddle out to sea far enough to catch a decent wave. Then it's just a matter of riding the wave in and landing face first in the sand in front of a crowd of jeering teenagers. Fun, huh?

Boogeyboards are relatively easy to obtain. Most major sporting goods stores carry them, as do most major discount retail chains in Southern California. A boogeyboard can cost anywhere from $15 for the basic foam version to over $100 for a high performance board. Some surf shops rent boogeyboards—typically they cost $10 a day.

The key to fun boogeyboarding is to find nice, harnessable waves. You don't want six- or eight-foot monsters—leave those for experienced surfers. Instead, three- and four-foot swells will do the job. Second, it also helps to find a beach with good sandy bottoms to cushion you when you reach shore either on (hopefully) or off (probably) your board.

Don't boogeyboard at a beach where a lot of people are surfing. As our friend Trevor the Canuck says, "That way you don't have to worry about having Biff hang 10 into the back of your head."

Many amateur boogeyboarders use swim fins, which makes it easier to paddle out farther to catch the waves. Wet suits are a must in the winter, and many boogeyboarders wear T-shirts because foam boards and human skin aren't always compatible over long stretches of time.

BODYSURFING

Bodysurfing is exactly what it sounds like: Your body is the board. The most famous spot for bodyboarding is "The Wedge," located in Balboa at the very end of Balboa Boulevard. Waves, pushed together by two opposite pieces of land, often reach 10 feet in height and can punish, even kill, the uninitiated.

8
PICNICKING & PAINTBALLING

• TOP RATINGS •

THE TOP 10 PLACES TO PICNIC

1. **SILVER CREST PICNIC AREA, PALOMAR MOUNTAIN STATE PARK**

   Locator: PALOMAR MOUNTAIN STATE PARK. See featured trip page: 271.

2. **GREEN VALLEY PICNIC AREA, CUYAMACA RANCHO STATE PARK**

   Locator: CUYAMACA RANCHO STATE PARK. See featured trip page: 273.

3. **PARAMOUNT RANCH, PARAMOUNT RANCH PARK**

   Locator: PARAMOUNT RANCH PARK. See featured trip page: 221.

4. **RED ROCK ON THE LOWER SANTA YNEZ RIVER, LOS PADRES NATIONAL FOREST**

   Locator: SANTA YNEZ RIVER. See featured trip page: 184.

5. **WONDERLAND OF ROCKS, JOSHUA TREE NATIONAL PARK**

   Locator: JOSHUA TREE NATIONAL PARK. See featured trip page: 251.

6. **SPOONER'S COVE, MONTANA DE ORO STATE PARK**

   Locator: MONTANA DE ORO STATE PARK. See featured trip page: 105.

7. **THE BEACH, TORREY PINES STATE RESERVE**

   Locator: TORREY PINES STATE RESERVE. See featured trip page: 282.

8. **SAN MATEO CANYON, CLEVELAND NATIONAL FOREST**

   Locator: SAN MATEO CANYON. See featured trip page: 260.

9. **OLD CORRAL AREA, CASPERS WILDERNESS PARK**

   Locator: CASPERS WILDERNESS PARK. See featured trip page: 266.

10. **MOUNT LOWE SUMMIT, ANGELES NATIONAL FOREST**

    Locator: PASADENA. See featured trip page: 208.

• HOT TIPS •

PAINTBALLING: THE BASICS

Our friend Ed the Corporate Executive could barely speak, he was so flushed with excitement. His $300 Armani cufflinks were shaking, and he bounced up and down in his Bruno Maglis.

Ed was trying to tell us about this great new game he had discovered: paintball. As part of a corporate outing to promote teamwork, as well as cutthroat ruthlessness in the workplace, Ed's company had booked an outing at one of Southern California's premiere paintball fields. "I wiped out the whole accounting department," he boasted. "They deserved it, too, after what they did to my expense report."

What exactly is paintball? Basically, it's like a game of capture the flag, which you may recall from your childhood. If not, it goes like this: Each team is given half the playing field and a flag. The object of the game is to run like a madman onto the other team's side of the field, capture their flag, and return it to your team's home turf without being tagged by a member of the other team and taken prisoner. Adults, being adults, have replaced tagging by hand with tagging by paintball gun.

The paintball gun shoots paintballs—small paint-filled pellets that explode when they hit a person and leave a paint stain. Those hit by a paintball during the game are considered dead. When the game ends—games typically last 20 minutes or so—the dead are "resurrected" and are permitted to play in the next game.

Paintball guns use small CO_2 cartridges to propel the paintballs at a set velocity of 285 feet per second—the reason the paintballs sting a little when they hit. For those who must have their own paintball gun, you can spend anywhere from $80 to $1,500 on guns in different sizes, fashions, and barrel lengths. There are even high-tech sights available for purchase to make clocking an opponent from long ranges easier. It is against the rules to shoot someone either in the head or at close range.

There's little doubt that there are many paintballers who take the whole military aspect of the game way too far. One popular paintball field in Southern California even advertises the fact it has playing fields to simulate Bosnia and Vietnam. That's sick.

Many of paintball's faithful hate the extremist label they're tagged with because of the guns and the camouflage clothes (more on that in a second). Instead, many see the game as a graceful combination of many skills—namely running like hell and shooting simultaneously. Another helpful talent is to be able to shoot with both your right and left hands—in case you're pinned down behind a bunker by enemy fire.

Most paintball fields are open on weekends, reserving weekdays for corporate outings. Typically, they have a field for walk-ons, where it costs $20 to $30 to play all day. Even if you are alone or just with a friend, the referees will place you on a team and then let you all go at it. Another option is to get a group of friends together and rent a field for your own personal use. Prices vary, depending on the size of the group.

Most paintball fields rent equipment to those who don't have their own paintball arsenals. The equipment you'll need to play: a camouflage outfit (unless you want paint splattered all over your own clothes), a face mask and goggles, a paintball gun with CO_2 cartridges, and, of course, paintballs.

Everyone at Ed's company had so much fun the company scheduled another day playing paintball. Ed being Ed went looking for a superior weapon in a paintball catalog, where he found a paintball grenade. "It splatters everything with paint within 50 feet," he said. "Imagine what I'll be able to do to the secretary pool."

Actually, it's nothing ruder than anything Ed's done before.

PAINTBALL FIELDS

Close Encounters, Newhall, (213) 656-9179 or (805) 255-5332.

Fields of Honor, Sylmar, (805) 522-3939.

Mr. Paintball, Escondido, (619) 737-8870.

SC Village, Corona, (714) 489-9000.

9
SKYDIVING, HANG GLIDING, AND KITE FLYING

• HOT TIPS •

SKYDIVING: "WHAT, ME WORRY?"

The story idea was this: A reporter (Steve) for the local rag would drive out to Lake Elsinore one fine, sunny morning in April and bear witness to the way rookie skydivers dealt with fear. Would they crack? Cry? Pray?

This sounded like a reasonable enough idea—except for one problem. No one who showed up at the Jim Wallace Skydiving School that morning was scared. In fact, quite the opposite happened. Three people from all walks of life gladly made the leap of faith of a lifetime.

Here's how it works: The student goes through a training session that lasts about an hour. Then it's showtime. In the airplane the student is strapped to the instructor. At an elevation of 13,000 feet or so, they tandem jump out of the plane and free-fall until they reach an altitude of 5,000 feet—which takes about 45 seconds. The tandem then open the parachute and float gently back down to Mother Earth.

On this particular day, an interesting trio had signed up to participate in the exercise.

Heather, from San Diego, was celebrating her 18th birthday. She had wanted to jump for the last two years and now she was legal—skydiving was a gift from her mother, who said that "Heather has always had an interest in death-defying things."

Like many teens, Heather had a bit of the Gothic look going that morning—black fingernail polish and an Alice Cooper-type approach to the eyeliner. It suited the occasion well.

Was she scared? Not in the least, according to Heather. She did not appear to be lying.

Kevin, 32, was a manufacturing supervisor of electronics who lived in Escondido. He wore a Dallas Cowboys T-shirt with plaid shorts. He's a friend of Heather's mom. Skydiving sounded like fun—that's why he was here.

Was he scared—even just a bit? Nope. In fact, as Kevin and his instructor wiggled across the floor of the plane to the door, Kevin wore the beatific expression of a young man doomed to spend his life as, say, a *Playboy* photographer or beer taster.

Finally, there was Ransom. A professor of flute at Yale University who was visiting L.A. for work, he has played and recorded with symphonies all over the world. If you saw him walking down the street, "adrenaline junkie" would not be the first thought to come to mind.

Maybe he was at least worried.

Nope. Ransom equated jumping out of the plane to walking out on stage and playing a solo. Yes, there may be some apprehension backstage, but the rewards awaiting you on stage are too great to pass up.

This, of course, threw something of a cramp into the story Steve was supposed to write. In fact, the words that appeared in the newspaper were "Skydiving and these other extreme sports are, of course, escapes. Escape from what? Nonstop comfort. Information overload. Pressure. Whatever the reason, the advent of these extreme sports suggest that some people need these escapes so badly that fear becomes a nonissue."

But would it be a nonissue for the writer?

After Steve finished up his reporting, Jim Wallace kindly offered him a tandem free fall—on the house. Steve took about two seconds to ponder the ethical implications of this and then said "yes."

Steve had jumped out of a plane eight years before. But his jump was of the static line variety—meaning there's virtually no free fall. Instead, a static line, attached to the plane at one end and the skydiver on the other, opens the parachute after two or three seconds. The obvious drawback: no free fall.

The other problem with static line is the matter of exiting from the plane. You don't just leap out with a big goofy grin on your face. Instead, you climb out of the plane and hang from the strut supporting the wing until the jumpmaster signals it's time to let go. Some skydiving outfits still do it this way (usually the ones that use small planes), while others have systems that aren't quite so nerve-racking.

In the years since Steve made that jump, skydiving changed considerably. The biggest development was the tandem free fall, which allows pretty much anyone aged 18 to 100 to experience skydiving in its full glory.

So, one hour later, Steve found himself sitting in the lap of one Jim Wallace, who was securing the four straps that hold student to teacher.

When you're about to exit an airplane in flight, being in Wallace's lap is not a bad place to be. Wallace is in his early 50s but looks about 35. He looks like a man who has had a good life doing exactly what it is he loves doing.

Wallace, in fact, has made almost 15,000 jumps—the third most of anyone in the nation. He has also done extensive stunt work for the movies; his credits include *Point Break, Terminal Velocity,* and *Air Force One*, to name just a few. Once, for fun, he jumped out of a biplane at 18,000 feet and then free-fell 9,000 feet. At that point, he slowed himself down enough to climb back into a different biplane. "It was cosmic" is how Wallace describes it.

Steve wasn't on Wallace's lap for long. Soon they were wiggling across the floor of the plane. As the videotape shows (a videotape all guests to our home are required to watch), Wallace whispered something in Steve's ear as they knelt at the open door. Steve then turned to the guy holding the video camera and managed his best "What, me worry?" smile. And then they were out the door.

One piece of advice based on what happens next: Take a deep breath before exiting all aircraft in flight. On television and film, skydivers look like they're floating. Well, here's the news: They're not. They are, in fact, falling like a wet bag of cement.

That's how you feel for the first five to 10 seconds of a free fall. And then some sense of equilibrium returns. You are still falling at 120 miles per hour, but it's a controlled fall. Is it like flying? Well, it's pretty darn close.

Once the parachute opens—with a violent yank of the crotch, thank you—everything becomes very different. Now you're upright, with nothing but air under your feet. There's no noise. You're floating. There's also a pretty good view. On this particular day, it was easy to see Lake Elsinore, Lake Perris, Lake Skinner, and Lake Matthews. The Santa Anas, still springtime green, rose steeply to the west. In the distance were the snow-covered peaks of San Jacinto, San Gorgonio, and Baldy.

Was it scary? Well, yes—Steve was a little more nervous than the trio he was writing about. But, at the same time, it really wasn't that scary—it's fair to say skydiving is substantially more empowering than frightening.

Is it life altering? Several days after jumping, Steve received an e-mail from Ransom, the flutist, who was now sitting in London's Gatwick Airport, awaiting a flight for Florence.

Here's what Ransom wrote:

"Oddly enough, although I was Mr. Cool during the actual jump, my exhilaration and excitement over the experience are far more keen in retrospect. I do find myself thinking about it constantly and am longing to do it again. Life altering? Well, yes, in a certain way . . . for me it alters my perceptions of my world and its boundaries—as well as of who I am and what I am and am not capable of."

Skydiving, like all outdoor activities, has its risks. But, all things considered, the sport is basically safe.

SKYDIVING SCHOOLS

When picking a skydiving school, don't be shy about asking the following questions: What is your school's safety record? Have there been any accidents in the last 10 years? What was the cause of the accident (if the reason is faulty equipment, go elsewhere)? Who will my instructors be? What is their experience? Are they in good standing with the United States Parachute Association?

Most schools will mail you a brochure and videotape that shows you what to expect from your jump. If the school can't manage to mail you these materials, go elsewhere.

Tandem free falls for rookies typically cost between $150 and $200—please remember that this is not necessarily the time to go for the pure bargain. Static line jumps range between $120 and $180.

Most schools offer group discounts. Skydiving is certainly a way to loosen up the stiffs at work. It also makes for a terrific bachelor or bachelorette party. Anyone can ogle over a stripper. Not everyone can exit a moving airplane.

Air Adventures Skydiving, Inc., San Diego, (619) 661-6671.

Air Adventures West Skydiving Center, Taft, (805) 765-5550 or (800) 423-8908.

California City Skydive Center, California City, (760) 373-2733 or (800) 258-6744.

Jim Wallace Skydiving, Lake Elsinore, (800) 795-DIVE.

Parachutes Over San Diego, Chula Vista, (619) 421-0968.

Perris Valley Skydiving, Perris, (909) 657-3904.

Skydive Elsinore, Elsinore, (909) 245-9939.

• **HOT TIPS** •

HANG GLIDING: THE BASICS

Not so long ago two friends of ours decided their lives were incomplete without the ability to hang glide. So they called up a local hang gliding instructor and arranged to take lessons.

For days leading up to the lessons, they quietly told everyone of their plans. And, predictably, everyone's response pretty much ran along the lines of "Are you completely #&$!*% nuts?". Our friends took this as a compliment, since being nuts is generally accepted as being cool—at least that's what those soft drink commercials say.

Anyway, on the big day of their first lesson, our friends drove to Van Nuys, where Joe Greblo, owner of WindSports Soaring Center, guided them through a hang gliding video, an explanation of the theory behind hang gliding, and a discussion of hang gliding safety. With all this new information rattling around inside their still intact heads, our friends joined a class on top of a small hill in Simi Valley. "At this point, we were glad to learn that we wouldn't be taking 20-minute solo flights the first day," recalls one friend.

What our heroes learned at this point was how to put together and take apart a hang glider. They practiced mock launches—minus the hang glider. Finally, they were each assigned a hang glider with which they tried practice launches with an instructor running alongside.

This was easier said than done. With the heavy hang gliders on their backs, they ran straight down a hill until they "launched." The instructor held on to their harness to ensure that neither of them flew more than 10 feet off the ground.

"The problem is there are a lot of variables, like the wind, that you can't control," said one friend, who never quite took flight. "For everything that happens you have to counter it with a move to keep the glider going in a straight line. Some people got it. Others didn't. I was one of the ones who didn't, so I spent the day crashing a lot and eating dirt."

Our other friend did slightly better. Asked how the lesson went, he said, "It was great, but I think I'm going to concentrate on doing something else."

Uh-huh.

Money was a factor. Our heroes were surprised to learn how expensive hang gliding can be. At least 12 lessons are required to log the 72 hours of flying time that's needed to hang glide solo. Equipment costs can run anywhere between $3,000 and $8,000—no one buys a "cheap" hang glider.

There is little doubt that hang gliding has its rewards. At its highest levels, hang gliders can routinely reach altitudes of 10,000 to 15,000 feet—and sometimes higher. While it's not the norm, some advanced hang gliders in Southern California have even made the journey from Los Angeles to Las Vegas without once touching the ground.

Recreational hang gliding became popular after World War II, although the sport's safety record wasn't exactly spotless. Early hang gliders were difficult to handle in changing conditions, and the learning curve for newcomers to the sport was small. Accidents, many of them serious, happened frequently.

Hang gliding benefited from the same revolution that has helped numerous sports—lighter, more durable materials. This made it easier for hang gliders to get airborne and, more important, stay aloft. The hang gliding community has also done a commendable job of regulating itself, realizing it has to be at least moderately safe in order to stay legal.

Here's how it works: The pilot, harnessed and holding on to the crossbar, runs off the side of a hill or cliff and catches an updraft. The pilot then manipulates the hang glider using an aluminum crossbar, trying to find wind.

Once in the air, the hang glider searches for good air just like a surfer looking for a good wave. What the hang glider really wants to find are updrafts or "thermal lifts"—winds that literally lift the hang glider up and away to higher altitudes or to a "street" where there is continual upward moving air. Updrafts are usually found around mountains and cliffs.

If the winds die down, the hang glider gently descends to the ground. Like glider planes, hang gliders work on the principle that for every meter they descend, they go forward many more meters, thus the term gliding. Problem is, sometimes the winds die down when the hang glider is way off in the middle of nowhere. That's why every experienced hang glider has a story about the time they had to land somewhere in the desert, thus requiring a 15-mile walk to the nearest phone.

How to pick an instructor? Interview several of them, preferably in person. Make certain they have no obvious personality flaws; generally speaking, you are looking for someone who doesn't have suicidal tendencies. Only take lessons from instructors who are certified members of the U.S. Hang Gliding Association.

Of course, there are some folks who simply want to go for a hang gliding ride and then never do it again. Many instructors will teach students just enough so that they can go up for a tandem flight with an instructor in a two-person hang glider. In the summer of 1995, New Mexico Governor Gary Johnson did just that in what was either one heck of a publicity stunt or a sign that New Mexico's politicians are more interesting than most.

The best place to see hang gliders in action is the Torrey Pines Gliderport, located just north of San Diego on a huge bluff above the Pacific Ocean. From downtown San Diego, take Interstate 5 north, exit at Genesee Avenue, and turn left. Turn left at North Torrey Pines Road and proceed to Torrey Pines Scenic Drive, then turn right. Continue to the end of the road and the gliderport. Phone the number below for information.

Shops and Lessons

Adventures Unlimited, San Juan Capistrano, (714) 496-8000.

The Hang Gliding Center, San Diego, (619) 461-1441.

High Adventure, San Bernardino, (909) 883-8488.

Lake Elsinore Sports, Lake Elsinore, (909) 674-2453.

Torrey Pines Gliderport, La Jolla, (619) 452-9858.

WindSports Soaring Center, Van Nuys, (818) 988-0111.

• TOP RATINGS •

THE TOP 10 PLACES TO FLY A KITE

Let's just get it out of the way before the issue even comes up: Kite flying is not an activity for which only geeks need apply. In fact, kite flying has entered a new age in recent years and, as should be expected, Southern Californians have put an interesting spin on it.

Specifically, we're referring to kite buggies, which can best be described as a chariot pulled by a kite instead of a horse. The buggies were invented in Australia but have caught on in Southern California in a big-time way because: 1. People here are nuts, and 2. Southern California gives great wind.

How do these things work? The kite itself is up to 17 feet wide and resembles a huge air mattress on a couple of strings. The kite flier sits in a three-wheeled buggy, steering with his or her feet as the wind pulls the kite, which pulls the buggy. It may sound implausible, but one buggy reached a speed of 66 miles per hour in the California desert.

Obviously, riding a kite buggy isn't for everyone. It's a little on the expensive side, too. There are, however, plenty of cheaper and more traditional ways to fly a kite in Southern California, which just happens to have some of the best kite flying conditions in the country.

Of course, it depends on your flying needs. Do you simply want something easy to fly that's also affordable? Better get a traditional single-line kite made of nylon (which will run you between $10 and $20). Are you more interested in looks? Box kites are very pretty, although a tad more expensive.

Or do you want a kite that catches the wind so fiercely that it can actually pull you across the sand, depositing you like a total doofus in front of that hunk or hunkette you've been trying to impress? If so, maybe you should consider stunt kites, which begin at $20 and can cost as much as $1,200—that is, if you feel the need to own a kite bigger than your living room.

1. MORRO STRAND STATE BEACH, SAN LUIS OBISPO COUNTY

Morro Rock is to the south, the beach is wide open and endless, and the Central Coast feels like it's your personal playground. There's also a kite shop, Kites Galore, nearby on the Morro Bay waterfront.

Locator: MORRO BAY. **See map on page:** 100.

2. PISMO STATE BEACH, SAN LUIS OBISPO COUNTY

Pismo, like Morro, is a monster of a beach (eight miles long) with the largest dune preserve in the state. Late-afternoon thermals usually kick up about an hour before sunset, providing ideal conditions. Tip: Launch from the dunes above the beach.

Locator: PISMO STATE BEACH. **See featured trip page:** 107.

3. OXNARD STATE BEACH, VENTURA COUNTY

Oxnard is just south of Ventura, which is considered the perfect kite flying place in California. The winds here are just as steady and the beach has a good reputation among kite fliers.

Locator: OXNARD STATE BEACH. **See map on page:** 190.

4. VENTURA STATE BEACH, VENTURA COUNTY

According to the folks at Ventura's Village Kite & Toy Store, kite fliers from all over the world head for Ventura Beach. "There's almost always a wind here," says store employee Michelle Lewellyn. "And even if the wind is only two or three miles per hour, we have kites that can fly in those conditions." The constant wind is also the reason kite flying festivals are held here on Memorial Day and Labor Day weekends.

Locator: Ventura State Beach. **See map on page:** 190.

5. El Mirage Dry Lake Bed, Los Angeles County

This is strictly for the serious kite flier. The lake bed, situated south of Edwards Air Force Base near Palmdale, is located on a big, flat piece of desert, where there is nothing to stop the wind. One kite buggy reached speeds of 66 miles per hour here. Another dry lake, Ivanpah, is also popular with the buggy crowd, despite being in the middle of nowhere on the California-Nevada border.

Locator: Palmdale. **See map on page:** 207.

6. Malibu Bluffs Park, Los Angeles County

This nice, well-kept park (hey, it's Malibu) is right across the Pacific Coast Highway from the well-kept grassy lawns of Pepperdine University (hey, it's Pepperdine). Kite enthusiasts sometimes gather on the school's lawn, but university officials discourage it. So go across the street to Malibu Bluffs. The park sits on a bluff overlooking the ocean.

Locator: Malibu. **See map on page:** 206.

7. Lake Perris State Recreation Area, Riverside County

Steer clear in the summer, when temperatures are ungodly and signs are needed to remind the huge crowds to use the rest rooms instead of the lake. But in the winter the place is often empty and there's usually a nice breeze coming off the lake. The gravelly beaches on the lake's south shore are good places to launch, as are the huge picnic lawns behind the beaches.

Locator: Moreno Valley. **See map on page:** 243.

8. Balboa Park, Orange County

The park isn't very big, but it's near the Balboa Pier and receives those afternoon winds all kite fliers love. Look for "Big Mo," a 550-square-foot parafoil kite that is sometimes tied to a palm tree in the park by the owner of a nearby shop. The Newport SeaFest Kite Festival is held here every September.

Locator: Balboa Island. **See map on page:** 264.

9. Mission Bay, San Diego County

As the inland valleys heat up during the day, they begin to suck in cooler air from over the ocean. Thus, the picnic and play lawn on the eastern side of Mission Bay on East Mission Bay Boulevard between Sea World Drive and the San Diego Hilton hotel, enjoys nice breezes as the day progresses. We've driven by this lawn on numerous occasions and there's always been someone there flying a kite.

Locator: Mission Bay. **See map on page:** 265.

10. Torrey Pines State Reserve, San Diego County

The Torrey Pines–Del Mar area is huge with hang gliders and hot air balloonists because there always seems to be a breeze. The state beach lies at the foot of some wetlands with hills on both sides. It's a beautiful beach to begin with and one that always attracts kite enthusiasts.

Locator: Torrey Pines State Reserve. **See featured trip page:** 282.

Kite Shops

San Luis Obispo County

Kites Galore, Morro Bay, (805) 772-8322.

SKYDIVING, HANG GLIDING, AND KITE FLYING

SANTA BARBARA COUNTY
Come Fly a Kite, Santa Barbara, (805) 966-2694.

VENTURA COUNTY
Village Kite & Toy Store, Ventura, (805) 654-0900.

LOS ANGELES AREA
Kite Man, San Fernando Valley, (818) 892-6474.

Kites, Etc., Balboa, (714) 673-0450.

10
FISHING

• **HOT TIPS** •

FLY-FISHING

When it comes to fishing in Southern California, the deep-sea crowd gets most of the ink. For good reason. There is considerably more salt water than fresh in Southern California.

Fly-fishing gets some press, but the impression most have is that it's a novelty—the real stuff is in Montana or Alaska. They are right and wrong. Among Southern California anglers, fly fishers are a minority. However, this part of the state has some excellent, even world-class, fly-fishing.

Not surprisingly, the best fly-fishing is found in the Eastern Sierra—the Owens River and Crowley Lake, to mention two spots—as well as the numerous backcountry lakes in the mountains. Not only is the fishing productive, it's also scenic. When fishing the Owens River, with views of the Sierra to the west and the White Mountains to the east, getting skunked doesn't feel so bad. How could it when you're standing in the middle of a picture-perfect landscape?

What's the difference between fly-fishing and spin tackle?

The basic premise of fly-fishing is that it offers the fish a more natural presentation of the bait—the flies. The flies are designed to look like insects fish eat, such as stone flies, mayflies, and caddis. The casting, from an aesthetic point of view, certainly looks good. But it's not about looking good. It's about dropping that fly on the water in the same way an insect may land on or swim in the water. Fly-fishing, when it all comes together, will catch the fish that won't go anywhere near salmon eggs or Power Bait, two favorite baits of spin tacklers in the Sierra Nevada.

Fly-fishing can be quite technical—it's important to get the casting just right and there are several other variables, from choosing the correct fly to knowing how to quickly tie a variety of knots. The equipment isn't cheap. Flies are usually a dollar or two each, a bit expensive when you lose a half dozen in an afternoon. Fly rods come as cheap as $50 and as expensive as $1,000.

The best way to learn the sport is to take a class. Angelenos are lucky because one of the better classes is right in their backyard: The Sport and Science of Fly Fishing, taught by world-famous fly fisherman Neal Taylor, through UCLA's Extension program. Taylor is a former world casting champion who has fished around the globe, from high country lakes to backcountry rivers to the ocean. He has also coached three U.S. presidents.

We both took the class and give it our highest recommendation. Neal, as as befits any fisherman, is an incredible storyteller. The class loosely follows Neal's textbook but is often interrupted as he goes off on a tangent. And then a tangent of the tangent. This is not annoying. Quite the opposite, actually. Neal even has a sidekick, Cliff, who has been fishing with Neal for 20 years. The class meets for six night sessions at UCLA's main campus in Westwood. There are also two field trips, one a casting clinic (often held at Lake Cachuma, where Neal is a naturalist) and the other a weekend trip to the Eastern Sierra. You may not catch anything, but you'll learn plenty about fish behavior and insect identification.

Another good way to learn is to join a fly-fishing club. There are several clubs around Southern California, many of which offer seminars or lessons for newcomers, as well as field trips. Look for club listings in newspapers or at tackle stores.

Many fly fishers, especially those who are inexperienced and just want to catch something, hire guides. There are numerous guides working throughout the Eastern Sierra (they generally operate through the many tackle shops in Bishop or Mammoth Lakes), often to the tune of $100 to $200 per day. That's a lot of money. If you can afford it, great.

But we recommend extensively interviewing a guide beforehand. If you hire a guide who brings his own rod and begins fishing, you have been ripped off. Ask the guide to put his rod away or give you a refund. You are not paying all that money for someone else to fish. You are paying for someone to help you fish, whether it be choosing the right fly, working on your casting, or scouting the water for fish.

Fly-fishing, like all angling, rewards patience. Anyone who likes to fish should at least give it a try. Some find it too technical, others enjoy the challenge. Just make sure you like it before submitting your credit card to the many temptations of the Orvis catalog.

Contact: UCLA Extension, (310) 825-9971 or (818) 784-7006. Web site: www.unex.ucla.edu.

• TOP RATINGS •

THE TOP 5 PLACES TO FLY-FISH

Where to fly-fish? The easy answer is wherever there's water in the Eastern Sierra.

1. OWENS RIVER AND SAN JOAQUIN RIVER

The Owens River and the San Joaquin River are the two most popular streams.

On the Owens River, we recommend the popular stretch of water upstream and downstream from Benton Crossing. Another pretty stretch is the river's wild trout area, located north of Bishop, just downstream from the Pleasant Valley Campground. Only catch-and-release and barbless hooks are allowed in this area, which has some sizable, wily, and spook-prone brown trout. Good luck—you'll need it.

Locator: MAMMOTH LAKES. **See featured trip page:** 119.

2. LAKE CROWLEY

As far as lakes go, Lake Crowley seems to manufacture fish—it helps that the lake gets numerous plants throughout the year. Float tubing is the way for fly fishers to go at the lake, particularly in the north end, near the inlet of the Owens River. Float tubing can also be productive at a number of lakes in and around Mammoth. Try Lake Mary, Lake George, Twin Lakes, Lake Mamie, and Convict Lake.

Locator: LAKE CROWLEY. **See map on page:** 114.

3. KERN RIVER

In Southern California there are some interesting, and unlikely, places to fish. The Kern River is the most obvious. It's best late in the summer when flows are down. A stretch of river north of Kernville—north of the Johnsondale Bridge—is good for golden trout. It is catch-and-release, with barbless hooks only. The DFG patrols the area and will give anyone not complying with the rules a big, fat ticket.

Locator: KERNVILLE. **See featured trip pages:** 156, 164, and 167.

4. SESPE RIVER, MATILIJA CREEK, AND SANTA PAULA CREEK

Farther south there are a number of streams in Ventura County which have trout. Don't expect anything big—these are eight-inch fish. Some are wild, some are planters. Streams include the Sespe River, Matilija Creek (upstream from Matilija Dam), and Santa Paula Creek, just north of Santa Paula.

Locators: OJAI, SANTA PAULA. **See map on page:** 190.

5. PIRU CREEK

Moving over to Los Angeles County, there's always Piru Creek. Where's Piru Creek? Just 50 miles from downtown L.A., running for 15 miles between Pyramid Lake south to Lake Piru in Ventura County. The creek is in a gorge just west of Interstate 5. It's very pretty and even has a wild trout area with some small rainbows plying its water. The best access is from the Templin Highway exit off Interstate 5. Follow the highway north for four miles to the Frenchman's Flat parking area. In the summer, the creek is largely dependent on water releases from Lake Pyramid—phone the Los Padres National Forest Ojai Ranger District to check water levels; (805) 646-4348.

Locator: PYRAMID LAKE. **See map on page:** 207.

FLY-FISHING CLUBS

Conejo Valley Flyfishers, (805) 496-7332.

Sespe Flyfishers, (805) 6646-0593.

Sierra Pacific Flyfishers, (818) 998-1542.

Wilderness Fly Fishers, (310) 280-3459.

FLY-FISHING RESORTS

There are two well-known private ranches along the Owens River, just north of Mammoth Lakes: the Arcularius Ranch and Alper's Ranch. Both manage the river for conservation as well as fishing—thus, the fishing is terrific. They also limit the number of people fishing on any given day. Of course, it's not free—generally, the river is only open by appointment or for guests staying at the ranches. You've probably heard of Alper's trout—it's a huge trout that is planted throughout the Eastern Sierra.

Contact: Arcularius Ranch, (760) 648-7807 in the summer and (702) 782-7428 in the winter. Alper's Ranch, (760) 648-7334 in the summer, and (760) 873-3465 or (760) 647-6652 in the winter. **Locator:** MAMMOTH LAKES. **See map on page:** 114.

• TOP RATINGS •

THE TOP 9 PLACES TO FISH FROM A PIER

What can you catch from a pier? Well, almost anything—typical fish caught in California are halibut, mackerel, croaker, bonito, sea trout, smelt, bass, surf perch, and, occasionally, shark. Other interesting catches include beer cans, swimsuits, Frisbees, and assorted plastic objects, most of which are too disgusting to even mention.

We've seen people fish with pretty much anything from a pier, including the old bamboo stick with a string tied to it. Don't have saltwater tackle? No problem. There are bait and tackle stores on most piers or very close by.

As for bait, anything goes. Always inquire at the pier's tackle shop as to what's working (not that they'll necessarily tell you) and watch and see what the regulars are using. Of course, if all else fails, clean out the refrigerator. Generally, live bait always works best—small mackerel are a favorite pier fishing standby. But we've also seen people hook fish using Kentucky Fried Chicken (original recipe) and, of course, cheese.

In California, it is NOT necessary to have a fishing license to fish from a public coastal pier, although you must still follow California Department of Fish and Game regulations.

1. Cayucos Beach Pier, San Luis Obispo County

The Central Coast has some of the better fishing in the state and Cayucos, which is near San Luis Obispo, seems to get more fish than most piers. There are several bait and tackle shops next to the pier in the town of Cayucos.

Directions: From San Luis Obispo take Highway 1 north for 14 miles to Cayucos Beach. **Contact:** No contact number is available. **Locator:** Cayucos. **See map on page:** 100.

2. Morro Bay City T-Pier, San Luis Obispo County

Here's another Central Coast pier where fish, mostly perch, are landed on a consistent basis. There are several bait and tackle shops on the waterfront in the town of Morro Bay.

Directions: From San Luis Obispo take Highway 1 north for 13 miles to Morrow Bay, exiting at Main Street and turning right. At Beach Street, turn right. When you reach the Embarcadero, the main drag along the waterfront, turn right and go to the pier. **Contact:** Morro Bay Harbor Master's Office, (805) 772-6254. **Locator:** Morro Bay. **See featured trip page:** 103.

3. San Luis Pier, San Luis Obispo County

Miles of sand and surf at Avila Beach are adjacent to the pier, where more halibut (very tasty) are caught than at any other pier in Southern California. The pier has a bait and tackle shop.

Directions: From San Luis Obispo take U.S. 101 south for six miles, exiting at San Luis Drive and turning right (west). At Avila Drive turn right and continue to the parking area at the end of the street. **Contact:** Port San Luis Harbor, (805) 595-5400. **Locator:** Avila Beach. **See featured trip page:** 109.

4. Ventura Pier, Ventura County

The Ventura Pier was formerly 1,958 feet long, making it the longest wooden pier in Southern California. But the pier is consistently hammered by winter storms—one storm alone in 1994–95 removed 400 feet of pier. The state park system subsequently sold the pier to the city of Ventura, which hopes to raise enough money to restore the structure. In the meantime, the pier is open and has average fishing for perch in the winter and, in the summer, mackerel, bonito, and halibut. If you get really lucky, there will be a salmon run like there was in the winter of '94–95, which produced phenomenal fishing. A couple of liquor stores near the pier sell bait; Eric's Tackle shop is about 1.5 miles from the pier on Thompson Boulevard.

Directions: From the Los Angeles area take U.S. 101 north to Ventura. Exit at California Street and turn left. At Harbor Boulevard turn left and follow the road to the pier. **Contact:** Ventura City Parks, (805) 654-7838. **Locator:** VENTURA. **See map on page:** 190.

5. REDONDO BEACH PIER, LOS ANGELES COUNTY

The pier isn't as attractive as it once was, thanks to a devastating storm and fire in early 1988. But fishing survives here; the bonito catch can be pretty good throughout the summer. Try anchovies as bait. A bait and tackle store is on the pier.

Directions: From downtown Los Angeles take Interstate 110 south to the 190th Street exit. Turn right (west) and follow the street until it ends at Harbor Boulevard. Turn left on Harbor and proceed to the pier. **Contact:** Redondo Sportsfishing, (310) 372-2111. **Locator:** REDONDO BEACH. **See map on page:** 206.

6. SANTA MONICA PIER, LOS ANGELES COUNTY

It's more a carnival than anything else at this famous pier—watch out for bitter screenwriters throwing either their screenplays or themselves (or both) out to sea. A recent renovation expanded the rides area to include a small roller coaster; we suggest checking out the view from the large Ferris wheel. Fishing survives toward the end of the pier, where there is also an interesting exhibit of photographs detailing the pier's history. The Santa Monica Bait and Tackle store is on the pier.

Directions: From Los Angeles take Interstate 10 west. Exit at Fifth Street in Santa Monica. Turn left onto Broadway. The entrance to the pier is at the intersection of Broadway and Ocean Avenue. There is a $6 fee for parking, or you can park on the meter-lined streets in Santa Monica. **Contact:** Santa Monica Municipal Pier, (310) 458-8689. **Locator:** SANTA MONICA. **See featured trip page:** 231.

7. HUNTINGTON PIER, ORANGE COUNTY

Huntington Beach is a surfer's paradise, providing something to look for other than an empty hook when the fishies aren't biting. The pier has a bait shop.

Directions: From all points, exit Interstate 405 at Highway 39 south (also called Beach Boulevard). Turn right on the Pacific Coast Highway. The pier will be on the left, opposite where Main Street intersects with the PCH. **Contact:** Huntington Beach Visitors Bureau, (714) 536-5511. **Locator:** HUNTINGTON STATE BEACH. **See map on page:** 264.

8. CRYSTAL PIER, SAN DIEGO COUNTY

There is actually a hotel, the Dana Inn, on this San Diego pier (hey, they keep it clean). The pier has a bait and tackle shop.

Directions: From downtown San Diego take Interstate 5 north, exiting at Balboa and turning left. At Garnet Avenue, turn right. The pier is at the end of Garney at Mission Boulevard. **Contact:** Dana Inn and Marina, (619) 222-6440. **Locator:** SAN DIEGO. **See map on page:** 265.

9. Shelter Island Pier, San Diego County

The catch at this pier in San Diego Harbor is that all kinds of fish have to swim by the pier if they are coming or going into the harbor; your job is to make their journey a one-way trip to your dining room table. Heh, heh, heh. There's a bait and tackle shop on the pier.

Directions: From downtown San Diego take Interstate 5 north, exiting at Rosecrans and turning left. At Shelter Island Drive, turn left. The pier will be on your left. **Contact:** No contact number is available. **Locator:** SAN DIEGO. **See map on page:** 265.

• TOP RATINGS •

THE TOP 20 LAKES

"You can look at it, swim in it, put a boat in it, and fish in it. But there's one thing you can't do. And that's drink it."

—from the movie *Chinatown*

Thus, the reason Southern California has so many lakes. In the early part of the 20th century, Los Angeles' population was growing. To give water to this thirsty megalopolis and to prevent flooding, engineers dammed up stream after stream. Aqueducts from the Sierra Nevada, as well as the Colorado River, were built to deliver water to reservoirs. Today there is only one river remaining in Southern California that has yet to be dammed: the Sespe River in Los Padres National Forest.

Our lakes come big and small, scenic and drab. Most have ample "recreational opportunities," as the state likes to say. Fishing, of course, is huge. But so is canoeing, sailing, jet skiing, and waterskiing. There are even some lakes with decent beaches and swimming.

Below are our 20 favorite lakes in Southern California, listed from north to south. Several other favorites are covered separately in the other half of the book and are not on this list. They include Big Bear Lake (see San Bernardino County, page 244), Lake San Antonio and Lopez Lake (see San Luis Obispo County, pages 101 and 110), and Lake Cachuma (see Santa Barbara County, page 182).

1. Lake Crowley, Mono County

Anyone who has driven to Mammoth Lakes has seen Crowley sitting smack dab in the middle of the Owens Valley. The lake itself is just a huge holding tub of drinking water for the city of Los Angeles—and it literally resembles a tub. But, gosh, fish love the place. The big thing here is trout and perch. Opening day of the trout season—the last Saturday of April—is a mob scene. It's one long parade of boats and anglers up U.S. 395 north, often producing a banner day of speeding tickets, courtesy of the California Highway Patrol. Anyone who is serious about fishing must make the pilgrimage here because the catches can be great. The lake is just a 15-minute drive from Mammoth Lakes or 30 minutes from Bishop. Having a boat certainly helps; they can be rented from the marina if you don't have your own. Float tubers usually stick to the north end of the lake near the inlet of the Owens River.

Directions: From Bishop take U.S. 395 north for 29 miles to the lake. **Fees:** A day-use fee is charged. **Boat rentals:** Sixteen-foot aluminum fishing boats are available to rent at the marina. **Contact:** Lake Crowley Fish Camp,

(760) 935-4301. **Locator:** Lake Crowley. **See map on page:** 114.

2. Convict Lake, Mono County

Two miles west of the Mammoth Lakes airport is Convict Lake, nestled beneath some gargantuan peaks—it's worth going just for the view of Mount Morrison, a 12,268-foot slab of granite that towers over the water. The lake is stocked with trout and there is rarely a shortage of anglers on hand to test its waters. The shore fishing is perfectly okay, but you may want to rent a boat to cover more ground—the lake is huge. Be careful because winds can really pick up at the lake in the afternoon. The lake also has some small no-frills cabins, which are great if you're a hard-core fisher, not so great if you're trying to impress your honey bunny. There is a large U.S. Forest Service campground along Convict Creek (88 sites for tents or RVs, no reservations), just a short walk from the lakeshore. A grocery and tackle store is located next to the cabins. So is The Restaurant at Convict Lake Resort, which is absolutely the finest restaurant in the Mammoth Lakes area. Phone: (760) 934-3803. Meals are expensive—expect to spend $20 to $30 for an entrée—but it's worth it. Try the beef Wellington. While you're digging in, watch deer graze on the restaurant's front lawn.

Directions: From Mammoth Lakes take U.S. 395 south for three miles. Turn left on Convict Lake Road and drive three miles to the campground, cabins, and lake. **Fees:** Day use of the lake is free. **Boat rentals:** Small motorboats and canoes are available for rental. **Contact:** Convict Lake Resort, (760) 934-3800 or (800) 992-2260. Inyo National Forest, Mammoth Lakes Ranger Station, (760) 934-2505. **Locator:** Mammoth Lakes. **See map on page:** 114.

3. Lake Nacimiento, San Luis Obispo County

Absolutely beautiful, this large lake is located amid remote ranching country just north of Paso Robles. Just to seal the deal, Nacimiento also has a good reputation for bass fishing around the state. Lake San Antonio is five miles up the road, too, so a trip to one is more or less a trip to the other. If you're looking for bass, keep an eye on the fishing reports in the newspapers from February on, because when the fish start biting here, fishermen descend on the place.

Directions: From San Luis Obispo take U.S. 101 north for 25 miles to Paso Robles. Exit at County Road G14 and follow it west for 15 miles to the lake entrance. **Fees:** $10 per person on weekends, $6 per family on weekdays, or $8 per person on weekdays. **Boat rentals:** Bass boats, water-ski boats, canoes, and pontoon boats are available on a half-day and daily basis from $15 to $275. **Contact:** Lake Nacimiento, (805) 238-3256. **Locator:** Lake Nacimiento. **See map on page:** 100.

4. Santa Margarita Lake, San Luis Obispo County

Ah, we love these Central Coast lakes. And why not? The scenery always seems to be great (rolling hills and oaks), as are the nearby towns (San Luis Obispo is our favorite city south of San Francisco; see page 106). Santa Margarita isn't an overnight destination lake because there's no camping, but there is some decent fishing here, thanks to trout and bass plants from the Department of Fish and Game—in addition to the crappie, bluegill, and catfish already in the lake. If you're in the area and want to spend a day doing some freshwater fishing, this long, narrow lake is the closest. One note: You'll bake here in the heat of summer.

Directions: From San Luis Obispo take U.S. 101 north for nine miles, exiting east at Highway 58. Drive 3.3 miles, turn right onto Pozo Road, and continue seven more miles. At Santa Margarita Lake Road, turn left and proceed to the lake entrance. **Fees:** $5 day-use fee, plus $1.50 for dogs. **Boat rentals:** Boats with and without motors are available for half-day and full-day rentals from $18 to $65 depending on the season. **Contact:** Santa Margarita Lake, (805) 438-5485. Marina, (805) 438-3886. **Locator:** SANTA MARGARITA LAKE. **See map on page:** 100.

5. OSO FLACO LAKES, SAN LUIS OBISPO COUNTY

These twin lakes are located at the southern end of Pismo Beach, where they quietly escape all the attention, from both people and vehicles, given to the beach's northern end. The lakes are set among the Pismo Dunes, only a few hundred yards from the ocean. The fishing is so-so, but we've been here three times and there's always someone taking a shot at the freshwater bass in the two lakes. If you're hiking the dunes, the lakes are a nice, quiet destination. This is the place to stretch out and start the book you've been meaning to read for the last six months.

Directions: From downtown Pismo Beach take Highway 1 south to Oso Flaco Road. Turn right and continue to the parking area. **Fees:** Access is free. **Contact:** Pismo State Beach, (805) 549-3312. **Locator:** PISMO STATE BEACH. **See map on page:** 100.

6. SEQUOIA AND KINGS CANYON NATIONAL PARKS, TULARE COUNTY

Don't mind a little hike to a High Sierra lake from your car, eh? Well, this is just the place for you. The backcountry in Sequoia National Park is dotted with small alpine lakes, many of which are above the tree line at 11,000 feet. There is no stocking of the lakes in either park, as per national park rules, although there are some small trout to be found in many of the lakes. The rule of thumb in both parks is that if you catch something, you've done well. If you come up empty, well, the scenery is as good as it gets. The closest backcountry lakes for day hikers are Pear Lake in Sequoia National Park (6.2 miles from the Wolverton parking area) and the Pothole Lakes in Kings Canyon (5.5 miles from Onion Valley on the Eastern Sierra side of the park).

Directions: From Los Angeles take Interstate 5 north through the Grapevine to Highway 99. Take Highway 99 north for 95 miles and exit east at Highway 198. It is about 50 miles to the entrance of Sequoia and another 68 to the entrance of Kings Canyon. **Fees:** The $10 entrance fee per vehicle is good for seven days. **Contact:** Sequoia and Kings Canyon National Parks, (209) 565-3134. **Locator:** KINGS CANYON and SEQUOIA NATIONAL PARKS. **See featured trip pages:** 140 and 145.

7. LAKE CASITAS, VENTURA COUNTY

Outside of the Sierra, Casitas is often considered the prettiest lake in Southern California. Located in the foothills of the Santa Ynez Mountains between Ventura and Ojai, the lake is sur-

10 FISHING

rounded by rolling hills dotted with oaks. It is huge—2,500 surface acres—and has a small island in the middle that you can boat to.

Casitas, along with Castaic, is considered one of the best bass lakes in the state; a 21-pound, three-ounce largemouth was caught here recently, and bass from five to 10 pounds can be common. Could a world-record fish be next? Some people think so. There is plenty of shore fishing, too, and the campgrounds are nice enough to recommend. Waterskiing and swimming aren't allowed; if you're visiting, bring the fishing rod.

Directions: From downtown Los Angeles take U.S. 101 north for 75 miles to Ventura, exiting north at Highway 33. Continue for 12 miles and turn left (west) onto Highway 150. Go another four miles to the lake. **Fees:** The day-use fee is $5. **Boat rentals:** Rentals are available from $21 to $64 per day, depending on size. For information, phone (805) 649-2043. **Camping:** Almost 500 sites for tents and RVs, many with full hookups, are available for $12 to $37 per night. Reservations are suggested; phone: (805) 649-1122. **Contact:** Lake Casitas Recreation Area, (805) 649-2233. **Locator:** LAKE CASITAS. **See map on page:** 190.

8. LAKE PIRU, VENTURA COUNTY

Sitting around all winter, stewing, stir crazy, and ready to strap on those water skis? Well, it's no secret that Piru is one of the closest big waterskiing and jet skiing lakes to Los Angeles. The lake is located along the border of Los Padres National Forest. Folks in the San Fernando and Simi Valleys, as well as in Santa Clarita, can get their boats out of the yard and into the water in 90 minutes or less, easy.

The fishing runs from average to very good—we landed a big ol' sunfish in one of the coves on the lake's eastern shore.

Directions: From downtown Los Angeles take Interstate 5 north for 35 miles and exit west at Highway 126. Drive 12 miles and exit at Piru Canyon Road heading north. The entrance to the park is in six miles. **Fees:** Day-use parking is $6. **Boat rentals:** Small motorboats can be rented from the lake's marina. **Contact:** Lake Piru, (805) 521-1231. **Locator:** LAKE PIRU. **See map on page:** 190.

9. LAKE CASTAIC, LOS ANGELES COUNTY

On June 2, 1932, a gentleman named George Perry caught a 22-pound, four-ounce largemouth bass in Georgia, which is still an all-tackle world record. But 59 years later, Venice's Mike Arujo caught a 21.74-pound largemouth at Castaic. Our landlord, Tony O'Connell, who netted the beast, says, "It looked like a bowling ball with eyes." Get the picture? Castaic is the domain of the bass fisherman, any of whom would be glad to break Perry's record, which could easily result in over a million dollars in product endorsements. There's fishing in both the upper and lower lake—many people think the lower is the better of the two.

Directions: From downtown Los Angeles take Interstate 5 north for 40 miles, exiting at Hughes Road, which will take you to the lake entrance. **Fees:** The day-use fee is $6 per vehicle on weekends, free on weekdays. **Boat rentals:** Boats can be rented from $24 per hour and up. **Contact:** Lake Castaic, (805) 257-4050. Marina, (805) 257-2049. **Locator:** LAKE CASTAIC. **See map on page:** 207.

10 FISHING

10. PYRAMID LAKE, LOS ANGELES COUNTY

If you've ever driven through the Grapevine on Interstate 5, you've seen this beautiful lake with steep mountains rising from the water. On cloudy or rainy winter days, this place looks almost otherworldly. But Pyramid, despite appearing natural, is actually a storage center for the State Water Project, which moves water from the Sierra through the San Joaquin Valley to Los Angeles. The fishing can be good because bass are moved downstate by the project—weird, huh? There is relatively little shore fishing because of the steep slopes bordering the lake. Your best bet is to rent a small motorboat to explore the five arms of the lake.

Directions: From downtown Los Angeles take Interstate 5 north for 60 miles, exiting west at Hungry Valley Road, which takes you to the lake entrance. **Fees:** The day-use fee is $6 per vehicle. **Boat rentals:** Motorboats can be rented for $25 to $40 per day. **Contact:** Pyramid Lake Concession, (805) 295-1245. **Locator:** PYRAMID LAKE. See map on page: 207.

11. SILVERWOOD LAKE, SAN BERNARDINO COUNTY

Just east of the Cajon Pass and Interstate 15 are the San Bernardino Mountains and a chain of lakes: From east to west, they're Silverwood, Gregory, Arrowhead, Green Valley, and the big pooh-bah, Big Bear. Silverwood's location is a bit unusual because it's at the northern rim of the mountains with the Mojave Desert 3,500 feet below. The lake has it all: waterskiing, jet skiing, sailing, fishing (lots of trout plants), swimming, picnicking, camping, and hiking (13 miles of trails are within the recreation area). And it's in quite a scenic area to boot. In the winter of 1996–97, the lake was partially drained for repairs. The low water levels revealed remains of the town of Cedar Springs, which was bought out by the state and then flooded with the lake in 1971.

Directions: From San Bernardino take Interstate 15 north through the Cajon Pass, exiting east at Highway 138. Continue about 10 miles to the lake entrance. **Fees:** There's a $6 parking fee. **Boat rentals:** Half-day and full-day fishing boat and pontoon boat rentals range from $23 to $49. **Contact:** Silverwood Lake, (760) 389-2281. Marina, (760) 389-2320. **Locator:** CRESTLINE. See map on page: 242.

12. LAKE GREGORY, SAN BERNARDINO COUNTY

If we were fishing with a child, we'd come to Lake Gregory before going to any other lake. Gregory is small at just 120 acres, but it's located at 4,500 feet in the San Bernardino Mountains, just a few miles from the Rim of the World Highway. This is an alpine setting—aaah—and, appropriately, the lake is stocked with rainbow trout. Rowboats can be rented, with the additional option of bringing your own electric trolling motor; no gasoline-powered motors are allowed on the lake. There are plenty of shore fishing, too, as well as numerous picnic spots and two 300-foot water slides to come to the rescue of parents with The Bored Child.

Directions: From San Bernardino take Highway 18 straight up into the mountains and then turn left onto Highway 138. At Lake Drive, turn right and continue to the lake. **Fees:** Entrance to the park is free. There are fees for the water slides. **Boat rentals:**

Rowboats can be rented for $8 for two hours. **Contact:** Lake Gregory Regional Park, (909) 338-2233. **Locator:** CRESTLINE. **See map on page:** 242.

13. LAKE HEMET, RIVERSIDE COUNTY

Lake Hemet is located in the San Bernardino National Forest at an elevation of 4,334 feet, just nine miles south of the village of Idyllwild. That means the lake, which is also surrounded by the pine-covered San Jacinto Mountains, has a quasi-alpine feel to it. Another nice thing about Lake Hemet is it's small, at only 434 acres, making it about two-tenths the size of Lake Perris, the behemoth of Riverside County lakes. Nor is there any waterskiing or jet skiing at the lake. That means fishing is the main attraction, especially for rainbow trout. There is also a large campground with more than 500 sites for tents and RVs. Phone Lake Hemet Campground for camping and general information, (909) 659-2680.

> **Directions:** From downtown Los Angeles take Highway 60 east for 60 miles to Highway 74 south. Lake Hemet is on Highway 74, nine miles past the village of Idyllwild. **Fees:** The day-use fee is $7. **Boat rentals:** Small aluminum boats with motors can be rented for either a half-day or full day. **Camping:** The 500-plus sites for tents and RVs come with fire rings, picnic tables, and piped water. Flush toilets and showers are available. **Contact:** Lake Hemet Municipal Water District, (909) 658-3241. **Locator:** IDYLLWILD. **See map on page:** 243.

14. LAKE PERRIS, RIVERSIDE COUNTY

What a weird location for a lake. Everything around Lake Perris is dry and rocky. This is a place where water seemingly has no business. Yet there's plenty of water here—the lake covers 2,370 surface acres and is a haven for water-skiers and jet skiers. There are times, especially in the summer, when the lake can be every bit as loud as the jets taking off and landing at nearby March Air Force Base.

However, Lake Perris can be an outstanding spot for fishing. It certainly has a good reputation among the hard-core anglers of the area, who are mostly after the elusive and large spotted bass; several world records have been set here. As for the rest of us, the main players include largemouth bass, crappie, and bluegills. A three-pound, 15-ounce bluegill was once caught here—which is to bluegills what Moby Dick is to whales. The key at Perris is to rent a small motorboat from the marina; the shore fishing is lousy and you'll just end up losing lures to the rocky lakeside.

As for the lake as a recreation area, it's okay. Not great. Not bad. Just okay. Summertime can produce meltdown-inducing temperatures at Perris, making the lake a respite for the masses. There are even huge signs on the beach to remind people to "please use the bathrooms"—which says all that needs to be said about the lake's summer clientele. Take our advice, visit here from fall through spring, when the hordes are at home.

> **Directions:** From downtown Los Angeles take Highway 60 east for 50 miles to Interstate 215 south. Exit at the Ramona Expressway east and turn left onto the marked access road for the lake. **Fees:** There's a $6 day-use fee per car. **Pets:** Dogs are allowed in the recreation area but must be leashed. They are not allowed on the

beach or in the water. **Boat rentals:** Fifteen-foot, six-passenger boats with a six-horsepower motor can be rented for $24 for two hours or $33 per day. **Contact:** Lake Perris State Recreation Area, (909) 657-0676. Marina, (909) 657-2179. **Locator:** MORENO VALLEY. **See map on page:** 243.

15. LAKE SKINNER, RIVERSIDE COUNTY

Unlike Lake Perris, Skinner doesn't allow water-skiers or jet skiers, meaning your ears can relax here. The fishing isn't bad either. Catfish are the big thing in the summer, but the lake also receives trout plants and has an ample population of largemouth bass. How to catch a big catfish? Get some mackerel at the marina and cut it up. Use a sliding sinker and fish the bottom of the lake. Get out those deep-fat thermometers and fry that bad boy. Keep in mind, though, that in the summer you'll be the one getting fried here. It gets hot. The lake also has a campground for tents and RVs.

Directions: From downtown Los Angeles take Highway 60 east to Interstate 15 south. Exit at Rancho California and turn left, heading east. Follow the road (past the wineries) for nine miles to the lake. From San Diego take Interstate 15 north. Exit at Rancho California and turn right, following the road for nine miles to the lake. **Fees:** Day use is $2 for adults, $1 for children. This doesn't include fishing fees, which are $5 for adults and $4 for youths under 15 years of age. **Pets:** Dogs are allowed for a $2 entrance fee. You may be asked to present their vaccination papers. Dogs are not permitted within 50 feet of the lake. **Boat rentals:** Four-passenger motorized fishing boats or 10-passenger pontoon boats can be rented for three hours, six hours, or all day, with fees ranging from $27 to $145. **Camping:** There are 257 sites for tents or RVs. Reservations are recommended during the summer. **Contact:** Lake Skinner County Park, (909) 926-1541. Marina, (909) 926-1505. **Locator:** TEMECULA. **See map on page:** 243.

16. IRVINE LAKE, ORANGE COUNTY

If you fish at this privately run lake, you'd better know how to skin a catfish because Irvine is loaded with blues and channels that break lines, rods, and reels. A blue cat weighing 59 pounds, four ounces was caught here in 1987, which at press time was still the state record. Mackerel is a popular bait for the channel cats, which are dumped into the lake by the truckload. If you have a good day (or night—a good time to fish for cats), here's how to skin that sucker: 1) With knife or scissors, cut off the fins; 2) make a cut in the skin around the head; 3) use a towel or gloves to pull the skin back toward the tail and away from the fish; 4) chop off the head; 5) don't forget to remove the guts!; 6) dip it in your favorite breading and fry. Yummy.

Directions: From Los Angeles take Interstate 5 south to Highway 91 east. At Highway 55, turn right (south) and drive four miles to Chapman Avenue. Turn right, continuing for nine more miles to the lake. Chapman turns into Santiago Canyon Road. **Fees:** Entrance costs $12 per adult, $5 for children ages 4 to 12. **Boat rentals:** Boats with and without motors can be rented for a half-day or full day, with prices ranging from $30 to $40. **Pets:** Dogs are not permitted. **Contact:** Irvine Lake, (714) 460-4940. **Locator:** Orange. **See map on page:** 264.

17. Lake Cuyamaca, San Diego County

Cuyamaca, at an elevation of just over 4,600 feet, is on the boundary of Cuyamaca Rancho State Park, not far from the granddaddy of all state parks, Anza-Borrego. The pretty lake sits amid alpine-like surroundings and has a good reputation for its trout fishing, since the water stays cooler longer than the many San Diego County lakes at lower elevations. The combo of decent fishing, good hiking, and better-than-average campgrounds within the state park make Cuyamaca a good weekend destination.

Directions: From downtown San Diego take Interstate 15 north to Interstate 8 west. Exit north at Highway 79 and continue through Cuyamaca Rancho State Park to the turnoff for the lake on the right. **Fees:** The fishing fee is $4.75 a day for adults, $2.50 for kids. **Boat rentals:** Rowboats and fishing boats with motors can be rented. **Contact:** Lake Cuyamaca, (760) 765-0515. **Locator:** Cuyamaca Rancho State Park. **See featured trip page:** 273.

18. Lake Jennings, San Diego County

This is a good "family" lake. By that we mean it's on the smaller side, it's a good area for picnics, and it doesn't receive the fishing pressure that some of the other, more renowned San Diego lakes do. Jennings gets both trout and catfish plants and has sunfish, which are the perfect fish for kids to aim for. (Hint: Try little poppers and jigs.)

Directions: From downtown San Diego take Interstate 15 north to Interstate 8 east. Continue 16 miles and exit at Lake Jennings Road, turn right, and drive one mile to the lake entrance. **Fees:** The day-use fee is $4.25. **Boat rentals:** Fees range from $10 to $20 per day. **Contact:** San Diego County Parks Department, (619) 565-3600. **Locator:** Santee. **See map on page:** 265.

19. El Capitan Lake, San Diego County

Sometimes you can judge a book by its cover. El Capitan translates loosely to "the mother of all bass fishing lakes," a tag that El Capitan wears well. Again, keep your eye on the weather as winter turns to spring. As the water grows warmer and gets in the high 50s and low 60s, the bass start hitting. If that doesn't excite you into an uncontrollable tizzy, you may be interested to know that water-skiers and jet skiers are permitted in the roughly 1,500-acre reservoir.

Directions: From San Diego take Interstate 8 east, exiting north at Highway 67. At El Monte Road, turn right and drive to the lake entrance. **Fees:** The fishing fee is $4 for adults, $2 for ages 15 and under. **Boat rentals:** Boats with and without motors are available for half-day and full-day rentals, with fees ranging from $6 to $25. **Contact:** El Capitan Lake, (619) 668-2050. **Locator:** El Capitan Lake. **See map on page:** 265.

20. Lake Morena, San Diego County

Good fishing near the Mexican border? "Hah!" is probably your answer. But Morena is one of those oddities that somehow has one of the better spring bass seasons in Southern California. Elevation has something to do with it: the lake is at 3,500 feet in the very southern end of Cleveland National Forest. Although the lake's water levels have sometimes slipped in recent years, the bass hit strong in the spring. Check the fishing reports in the local papers.

Directions: From San Diego take Interstate 8 east for 53 miles. Exit at County Road S1 and turn right. Drive five miles to Oak Drive and turn right again. Continue to the lake entrance.

Fees: The day-use parking fee is $2; there's a $3.50 fishing fee for adults, $2 for ages 15 and under. **Boat rentals:** Boats with and without motors are available for half-day and full-day rentals, with fees ranging from $6 to $25. **Contact:** Lake Morena County Park, (619) 478-5473. San Diego County Parks Department, (619) 565-3600. **Locator:** LAKE MORENA VILLAGE. **See map on page:** 265.

11
HUNTING

• HOT TIPS •

WHERE AND WHAT TO HUNT

Until recently, the number of people hunting nationwide had been in a steady decline. Why?

A country with roots in the rural heartland now has most of its people living in cities. Hunting is a sport that gets handed down from one generation to the next. But nowadays there are few people to hand it down to.

And then there's the Bambi factor. Few other sports have become as politically incorrect as hunting—despite the fact that hunting is the oldest sport of them all. Wildlife, once abundant, is just a fraction of what it once was.

Hunters to some degree have themselves to blame for the black eye given to their sport. Unsportsmanlike conduct and reckless disregard for gun safety are still relatively uncommon. Yet they occur often enough to make headlines—all of which hurt the sport.

In the last few years, there has been somewhat of a pro-hunting backlash. Perhaps the best book on the subject out there is 1997's *Heart and Blood: Living with Deer in America* by Richard Nelson (Knopf). Nelson thoughtfully provides an overview of deer populations nationwide, as well as the conflicts that inevitably arise when deer management programs are established. He also explores his own passion for deer hunting, writing in great detail about the cycle of life and death on this planet. Hunters, non-hunters, and, particularly, those who loathe hunting should read it.

The following information is designed to help newcomers to the sport find a place to begin.

I'M LOCKED AND LOADED AND READY TO HUNT—WHERE DO I GO?

Hold your horses, pardner. First things first: No one goes hunting in California until they purchase a hunting license. And no one is permitted to purchase a license until they have attended a California Department of Fish and Game hunter safety training class.

The 10-hour class is covered in one day. It's free and open to all members of the public. At the end of class, participants must pass a quiz. For more information on class times and locations, phone the DFG Long Beach office at (562) 590-5670.

WHAT CRITTERS ARE OUT THERE?

Big game species include deer, wild pigs, black bear, elk, antelope, and bighorn sheep. Resident game birds frequently hunted are pheasant, quail, chukar, grouse, wild turkeys, and doves. Popular waterfowl are ducks, geese, brants, and coots.

Generally speaking, the hunting is considered much better in Northern California—there's more water and fewer people and, thus, more animals.

EXCUSE ME, BUT DID YOU SAY WILD PIGS? AS IN LORD OF THE FLIES?

Well, not quite. Most of the pigs have escaped from farms. Others are descendants of European wild pigs released into the wilds of Monterey County in 1925. Most of the pigs are hairy and reproduce prolifically: in a single year, a sow can have three litters of eight to 10 pigs each. Some pigs weigh up to 300 pounds.

Wild pigs are found in 18 of California's 58 counties, including Santa Barbara and San Luis Obispo. Be warned. Bagging one is very difficult, especially on public lands. It's doubtful you'll even see one unless you're an expert.

Your best bet? Shell out a few hundred dollars to a private guide who has access to hunting on private land. To obtain a list of guides, phone the DFG Monterey office at (408) 649-2870.

WHERE ARE THE BEST PLACES TO GO HUNTING?

We recommend hunting at a club, such as the 1,250-acre Antelope Valley Sportsmen's Club, located in Lancaster (phone 805-724-1291). The obvious advantage is that there is definitely game on the club's land—meaning it's likely that most hunters will at least get a shot at something.

For example, pheasant hunting is popular at the club. Here's how it works: The club releases several pheasant into the field and then sends the hunter into the vicinity of the release. It's up to the hunter to flush and shoot the pheasant—field dogs can be rented to help with this. The recovery rate on the birds is generally just over 80 percent.

In the L.A. area there is also hunting for deer, antelope, elk, black bear, wild turkey, and other small game at the 270,000-acre Tejon Ranch, located in the San Gabriel Mountains. For more information on hunting memberships at the ranch, phone (805) 248-6774.

Hunters may also try waterfowl hunting on wildlife refuges. For example, the Kern National Wildlife Refuge, near Delano in the San Joaquin Valley, opens some land for duck hunting each season (in the fall and winter). Most of the hunting is free roam and reservations are needed. For more information, phone the refuge at (805) 725-2767.

ANY SPECIAL RULES TO BE AWARE OF?

You bet. The DFG has voluminous rules governing method (type of weapon and ammunition), bag limits, shooting hours, and season.

In addition to hunting licenses, hunters must purchase tags to hunt most big game or stamps to hunt migratory waterfowl. Tags are often sold by lottery and often must be applied for months ahead of time. State bird stamps can be purchased at many sporting goods stores. Federal bird stamps, required at national wildlife refuges, can be purchased at a post office.

I'VE ALWAYS THOUGHT IT WOULD BE MANLY TO BAG MY OWN THANKSGIVING DINNER . . .

Okay, grab a bag and head down to the supermarket. That's your best chance.

Actually, the wild turkey populations on the Central Coast are fairly healthy. Too bad it's so damn hard. Turkeys tend to be shy, especially in the fall when they are on everyone's most-wanted list.

The standard technique is for hunters to conceal themselves and try to lure the turkey with a call simulating either a hen or a challenging gobbler. Sometimes the calls do nothing. Sometimes they attract other wildlife—like coyotes. Sometimes they actually work.

On public land, turkeys can be found in Los Padres National Forest and Monterey County's Fort Hunter Liggett, which opens its grounds to hunters. For more information, phone Fort Hunter Liggett at (408) 386-3310.

12
HORSEBACK RIDING

• TOP RATINGS •

THE TOP 32 PLACES TO RENT HORSES

California is horse country—as much so as any other western state. Although there isn't a superabundance of places to rent horses, there's not exactly a shortage either.

The Sierra Nevada has a tremendous number of pack stations on both the western and eastern sides of the range. Some people just take a guided day trip to a backcountry lake, while others take a multiday trip into the backcountry. The obvious advantage: It's easier than backpacking.

Some people go a different direction. They ride into a backcountry campsite where they are dropped off. A few days later, depending on prior arrangement, the horses or mules return to the campsite to pick up campers and their equipment.

Of course, renting a horse isn't exactly like renting a car. Some stables require customers to be accompanied by a guide—particularly stables in mountain areas. Other stables will allow customers to ride alone but do not permit riders to take the horses to a trot or gallop.

A few words of advice:

Wear hiking boots or, preferably, cowboy boots. You'll be more comfortable. Wear jeans, not shorts. Be smart. Watch out for branches. In the extremely rare event you should ever be thrown from a horse, try to relax your body before hitting the ground. Stiffening up and sticking out arms and legs is a good way to break a bone.

EASTERN SIERRA

1. **BERNER'S PACK OUTFIT, ONION VALLEY**
   Contact: (760) 387-2797.

2. **BISHOP PACK OUTFITTERS, BISHOP CANYON (NORTH LAKE)**
   Contact: (760) 873-4785.

3. **COTTONWOOD PACK STATION, HORSESHOE MEADOWS**
   Contact: (760) 878-2015.

4. **MCGEE CREEK PACK STATION, MCGEE CREEK CANYON**
   Contact: (760) 935-4324.

5. **PINE CREEK PACK STATION, PINE CREEK CANYON**
   Contact: (760) 387-2797.

6. **RAINBOW PACK STATION, BISHOP CANYON (SOUTH LAKE)**
   Contact: (760) 873-8877.

7. **REDS MEADOW AND AGNEW MEADOWS, MAMMOTH LAKES**
   Contact: (760) 934-2345.

8. **ROCK CREEK PACK STATION, ROCK CREEK CANYON**
   Contact: (760) 935-4493.

SAN LUIS OBISPO COUNTY

9. **HORSEBACK ADVENTURES, PASO ROBLES**
   Contact: (805) 238-5483.

10. **THE LIVERY STABLE, OCEANO**
    Contact: (805) 489-8100.

KERN AND TULARE COUNTIES

11. **KINGS CANYON NATIONAL PARK, CEDAR GROVE PACK STATION, CEDAR GROVE VILLAGE**
    Note: Cedar Grove Pack Station is closed in winter. **Contact:** (209) 565-3464.

HORSEBACK RIDING

12. **KINGS CANYON NATIONAL PARK, GRANT GROVE STABLES, GRANT GROVE VILLAGE**
    Note: Grant Grove Village is closed in winter. **Contact:** (209) 565-3464.

13. **SEQUOIA NATIONAL PARK, MINERAL KING PACK STATION, MINERAL KING**
    Note: Mineral King Pack Station is closed in winter. **Contact:** (209) 561-3039.

14. **SEQUOIA NATIONAL PARK, WOLVERTON PACK STATION, WOLVERTON MEADOW**
    Contact: (209) 565-3039.

SANTA BARBARA COUNTY

15. **CIRCLE B RANCH STABLES, GOLETA**
    Contact: (805) 968-3901.

16. **SAN YSIDRO STABLES, MONTECITO**
    Contact: (805) 969-5046.

VENTURA COUNTY

17. **TONY ALVIS' LOS PADRES WILDERNESS OUTFITTERS, LOS PADRES**
    Contact: (805) 648-2113.

LOS ANGELES COUNTY

18. **BAR "S" STABLES, GLENDALE**
    Contact: (818) 547-0203.

19. **CIRCLE "K" STABLES, BURBANK**
    Contact: (818) 843-9890.

20. **GRIFFITH PARK HORSE RENTALS, BURBANK**
    Contact: (818) 840-8401.

21. **SUNSET RANCH, 3400 NORTH BEACHWOOD DRIVE, HOLLYWOOD**
    Contact: (213) 469-5450.

SAN BERNARDINO COUNTY

22. **BALDWIN LAKE STABLES, EAST BIG BEAR CITY**
    Contact: (909) 585-6482.

23. **ROCKING K STABLES, BIG BEAR LAKE**
    Contact: (909) 878-4677.

RIVERSIDE COUNTY

24. **GUIDED MULE RIDES, PALM SPRINGS**
    Note: Mule rides are at the top of the Palm Springs Aerial Tram. **Contact:** (760) 327-6699.

25. **RANCH OF THE 7TH RANGE, LA QUINTA**
    Contact: (760) 777-7777.

26. **SMOKE TREE STABLES, PALM SPRINGS**
    Contact: (760) 327-1372.

SAN DIEGO COUNTY

27. **BEACHFRONT HORSE RENTALS, SAN DIEGO**
    Contact: (619) 428-4330.

28. **BRIGHT VALLEY FARM, INC., SPRING VALLEY**
    Contact: (619) 670-1861.

29. **HILLTOP HORSE RENTAL, SAN DIEGO**
    Contact: (619) 424-3662.

30. **HOLIDAYS ON HORSEBACK, DESCANSO**
    Contact: (619) 445-3997.

31. **PINE VALLEY STABLES, PINE VALLEY**
    Contact: (619) 473-8151.

32. **SANDI'S RENTAL STABLES, SAN DIEGO**
    Contact: (619) 424-3124.

13
WILDLIFE WATCHING

TOP RATINGS

THE TOP 11 PLACES TO BIRD-WATCH

Mr. Purple Martin: I think I see one.
Ms. Yellow-Rumped Warbler: Does he have all the markings?
Mr. Purple Martin: Let's see. Long, greasy hair. Fuzz around the lower lip. A blank, droll expression of the face. Droopy apparel and a board with four wheels where the feet would ordinarily be.
Ms. Yellow-Rumped Warbler: Ah, yes. I believe it's a Grungius smellius skateboarderius.
Mr. Purple Martin: A most loathsome species, isn't it?
Ms. Yellow-Rumped Warbler: I've lost my appetite. You can have my worm.

In actuality, California probably has better bird-watching than people-watching—even though our fair state does boast an endless variety of freaks.

For example, consider the bird population of Santa Barbara County. In recent years there have been approximately 450 or so species of birds spotted in the county. In the United States and Canada alone, experts believe there are between 650 and 700 species of birds. The conclusion: Two-thirds of the bird species seen in the United States and Canada can be found in Santa Barbara County, including about 175 species that do not occur on the East Coast.

"Every New Year's Day I get up before it's light out and head out to start my birding for the year," says Los Angeles Audubon Society field guide Karen Johnson. "I go to a few areas around the city and always see at least a hundred different birds."

Southern California is one of the premier bird-watching spots in the country for two reasons. First, the state has an incredible mix of ecosystems, thanks to its varied geography. Second, California lies below the Pacific Flyway, which serves migrating birds as a kind of a north-south freeway over the western coast of North America. Many species of birds, such as Canada geese, take the flyway south for the winter and end up in places such as the Encino Reservoir in the San Fernando Valley. What that says about the intelligence of the Canada goose, well, we're not sure.

If you are already a bird-watcher or have considered becoming one (it is a lifestyle choice after all), check out one of the National Audubon Society's local chapters—they're an incredible resource. There are dozens of such chapters in Southern California. Throughout the year each chapter offers fields trips and hikes to some of the better birding locations, as well as invaluable assistance into learning how to identify birds. The Los Angeles chapter has an especially good bookstore in Plummer Park in West Hollywood, where birders will find guides for virtually any region in the world.

What does it take to become a full-fledged bird-watcher? The primary requisite is curiosity, but it doesn't hurt to have a birding field guide with lots of pretty pictures in it. No one publishes a better one than National Geographic's *Field Guide to the Birds of North America*, which is sold at most bookstores for about $20.

Most birders keep lists of how many types of birds they see in any given year. Really serious birders also keep lifetime lists of birds seen, the idea generally being that whoever dies having seen the most birds, wins.

Two indispensable aids to any birder are a hat and binoculars. Some birders take it a step further and get a telescope, which they mount on tripods for long-range bird viewing.

For those who would like to take one long step beyond that, there are many audiotapes and a few CD-ROM software packages to help identify birds by listening to their calls and songs. In theory it sounds like a great skill to have and, besides, it's essential for those hoping to get a glimpse of one of the rarer species. The risk, of course, is that sitting around and practicing birdcalls is a great way of convincing 99.9 percent of the population that you've gone certifiably loony-tunes.

Birding can be very seasonal—about 150 species of birds seen in California are visitors. The best time of the year is in the spring when winter and spring migration patterns overlap.

Below is just a sampling of some of the better birding locations in Southern California. If you begin reading birding guides, you'll find that some recommend going to such places as sewage dumps, cemeteries, or a specific tree on a mountain to find certain species. We can understand cemeteries, maybe, but sewage dumps?

How To Learn More

The Los Angeles chapter of the Audubon Society has quite a good bookstore, with a wide variety of guides from all over the world. The bookstore is located at 7377 Santa Monica Boulevard, West Hollywood, CA 90046-6694; (213) 876-0202.

The Audubon Society is world-renowned for its conservation and research programs. There are dozens of chapters throughout Southern California. To find a local chapter and learn more about the society and birds, try the society's Web site: www.audubon.org.

UCLA's Extension Program frequently offers bird-watching classes, such as its spring 1998 class, Field Studies of California Birds II. This class and others like it are intended as an introduction to the ecology, natural history, and observation of birds. For more information or to get a catalog, phone UCLA Extension, (310) 825-9971 or (818) 784-7006. Or visit their Web site: www.unex.ucla.edu.

1. Lake Cachuma, Santa Barbara County

Cachuma is one big lake, but the A-1 time of year there is December and January, when bald eagles arrive from up north for a two-month stay. Two-hour boat tours to see the bald eagles and other migratory birds are offered from December until the end of February. Cachuma also attracts numerous other birds year-round. Renting a boat and cruising along the shore while looking in trees is your best bet.

Directions: From Santa Barbara take Highway 154 up and through the San Marcos Pass. The entrance to the lake will be on your left, 17 miles after leaving Santa Barbara. **Fees:** There's a $5 day-use fee for the lake. **Contact:** Cachuma Lake Recreation Area, (805) 688-4658. **Locator:** Lake Cachuma. **See featured trip page:** 182.

2. Mount Pinos, Ventura County

Both the smallest and largest birds in North America could once be seen here:

The Calliope hummingbird is just three inches long, while the California condor has a wingspan of 10 feet. The last California condor in the wild was captured in 1987, and recent efforts to release condors on Pinos failed partly because the large birds kept running into high-tension wires. Nevertheless, the hummers survive (look for red feathers under the chin), as do the hairy woodpecker, pygmy nuthatch, and brown creeper. Who thinks of these names?

Directions: From Los Angeles take Interstate 5 to the Frazier Park Road exit and turn left. Drive on Frazier Park Road for 14 miles to the parking lot at the base of Mount Pinos. Continue nine miles up the road to the Chula Vista parking lot and the trailhead to the summit. There are numerous other trailheads along the way. **Fees:** A Forest Service Adventure Pass is required. A day pass is $5 or an annual pass is $30, good within the Los Padres, Angeles, San Bernardino, and Cleveland National Forests. Purchase passes at ranger stations or at most large sporting goods stores. **Contact:** Los Padres National Forest, Mount Pinos Ranger District, (805) 245-3731 or (805) 245-3462. **Locator:** MOUNT PINOS. **See featured trip page:** 191.

3. CHANNEL ISLANDS, VENTURA COUNTY

Do you know the meaning of the word "pelagic?" According to our dictionary it's "of the open sea or ocean," and pelagic birds are exactly what you're going to see in great numbers on all of the Channel Islands. Brown pelicans are one of the most majestic of all birds and there are plenty of them around Anacapa's famous Arch Rock. Anacapa is the easiest island to reach—it's just a 90-minute boat ride from the mainland—but the other islands offer all kinds of unique birding opportunities. Island Packers is the park's designated concessionaire for taking people to the islands.

Directions: To reach Island Packers in Ventura Harbor from all points north or south, exit U.S. 101 at Victoria. Take Victoria south and turn right onto Channel Islands Boulevard. Go over the bridge and turn left at Harbor Boulevard. Island Packers is on the left in the Marine Emporium, next to Tug's restaurant. **Fees:** Island Packers offers a variety of packages to Anacapa, Santa Cruz, Santa Rosa, and Santa Barbara Islands. **Contact:** Channel Islands National Park, (805) 644-8262. Island Packers, (805) 642-7688 for information and (805) 642-1393 for reservations between 9 A.M. and 5 P.M., seven days a week. Island Packers Web site: www.isle.net/~ipco. **Locator:** CHANNEL ISLANDS NATIONAL PARK. **See featured trip pages:** 196, 198, and 200.

4. MALIBU LAGOON, LOS ANGELES COUNTY

On the human side of things, many species of surfer can be found here. On the bird side, hit the lagoon in back of the beach for seabirds and then try hiking up the creek a bit to spot hummingbirds. If you're one of those people who make a list of how many species of birds they can see in a day, 100 is an attainable number here.

Directions: From Santa Monica take the Pacific Coast Highway north for 12 miles, following the signs to the parking area. There is limited free parking on the Pacific Coast Highway. **Fees:** Day parking is $6. **Contact:** California State Parks, (818) 880-0350. **Locator:** MALIBU LAGOON STATE BEACH. **See map on page:** 230.

5. Tucker Wildlife Sanctuary, Orange County

The main attraction here is in July and August when large numbers of migrating hummingbirds arrive. The 12-acre sanctuary has a small cabin where bird feeders are set up year-round and the hummers know a good thing when they see it. In the old days—birds have been fed here since 1926—the hummers used to arrive in droves. Their numbers are now reduced (thanks to development), but you'll still probably see more hummers here than anywhere else. There are also two nature trails and two bird-observation points. The sanctuary, run by a non-profit foundation, is open seven days a week from 9 A.M. to 4 P.M.

Directions: From Irvine, take Interstate 5 south, exit at El Toro Road, and turn left (east). Drive eight miles, not fretting over El Toro becoming Santiago Canyon Road. At Modjeskta Grade Road, turn right and continue to the sanctuary parking lot. **Fees:** A $1.50 donation per person is suggested. **Contact:** Tucker Wildlife Sanctuary, (714) 649-2760. **Locator:** IRVINE. See map on page: 264.

6. Upper Newport Bay Ecological Reserve and Regional Park, Orange County

It's easy to see why the locals love this place, which has some very nice hiking and biking trails as well as great bird viewing. As many as 30,000 to 50,000 birds representing about 200 species have been counted here during the migratory season, which runs from October through March. Two endangered species can also be found in the reserve: the tiny California gnatcatcher and the light-footed clapper rail, which ties its floating nest to cordgrass so that it doesn't float away with the changing tides. In fact, the reserve has a higher population of clapper rails than any other place in the nation. The park is open seven days a week from sunrise to sunset.

Directions: From Interstate 405 north or south, exit west at Jamboree Road. Drive toward the bay and turn right on Back Bay Road, which takes you to the park. **Fees:** Access is free. **Contact:** Orange County Regional Parks, (714) 640-1751. **Locator:** NEWPORT BEACH. See map on page: 264.

7. Silverwood Wildlife Sanctuary, San Diego County

Silverwood Sanctuary, near the town of Lakeside, is owned by the San Diego Audubon Society. The focus of the sanctuary is birds of the chaparral, with 145 species of birds having been seen here. There are 10 miles of hiking trails across the 700-acre sanctuary, as well as an observation point. The sanctuary is open to the public every Sunday from 9 A.M. to 4 P.M. for hiking and there are guided walks at 10 A.M. and 1:30 P.M. geared toward understanding geology and plant life. Please note there are no hikes offered in July, and the sanctuary is closed in August.

Directions: From downtown San Diego, take Interstate 8 east for 16 miles, exiting north onto Highway 67. Exit at Mapleview Street, turn right, and drive to Ashwood Road and turn left. Ashwood Road turns into Wildcat Canyon Road. The sanctuary is 4.8 miles from the intersection of Mapleview and Ashwood, located at 13003 Wildcat Canyon Road. **Fees:** Access is free. **Contact:** Silverwood Wildlife Society, (619) 443-2998. **Locator:** SANTEE. **See map on page:** 265.

8. TIJUANA SLOUGH NATIONAL WILDLIFE RESERVE, SAN DIEGO COUNTY

The slough is where the Tijuana River meets the sea. And where environments change, there's usually wildlife. In this case, look for a variety of herons and terns. The reserve covers 2,500 acres and literally abuts the Mexican border. There's a visitor center open Wednesday through Sunday, hiking trails open every day, and bird hikes offered every Saturday morning—phone for reservations and times.

Directions: From downtown San Diego, take Interstate 5 south, exiting at Coronado Avenue and turning right (west). At Third Avenue, turn left and drive to Caspian Way, then turn left again. Drive 100 yards. The visitor center is on the right. **Fees:** Access is free. **Contact:** Tijuana Slough State Park, (619) 575-3613. **Locator:** IMPERIAL BEACH. **See map on page:** 265.

9. SALTON SEA NATIONAL WILDLIFE REFUGE, RIVERSIDE AND IMPERIAL COUNTIES

This 35-mile-long, shallow lake is to birds what O'Hare International Airport is to humans. More than 400 species abound here because the Salton Sea is at the bottom of the Pacific Flyway and it's a large body of water. Many migrant birds are also blown to the lake by either windstorms in the desert or storms out to sea. The refuge includes a visitor center, observation tower, and short hiking trail.

Directions: From San Diego, take Interstate 8 east for 107 miles, exiting at Forrester Road and turning left (north). Drive 20 miles to Westmoreland and then continue straight through the stop sign on County Road S30. Drive seven miles to the intersection with Gentry Road. Continue north on Gentry; the visitor center is at the intersection of Gentry and Sinclair Roads. **Fees:** Access is free. **Contact:** United States Fish and Wildlife Service, (760) 348-5278. **Locator:** SALTON SEA. **See maps on pages:** 243 and 264.

10. LAKE SAN ANTONIO, SAN LUIS OBISPO COUNTY

Contact: Lake San Antonio, (805) 472-2311. For Eagle Watch Tour reservations, phone Monterey County Parks, (408) 755-4899. **Locator:** LAKE SAN ANTONIO. **See featured trip page:** 101.

11. MORRO BAY, SAN LUIS OBISPO COUNTY

Contact: Morro Bay State Park, (805) 772-7434; Morro Bay Chamber of Commerce, (805) 772-4467 in California and (800) 231-0592 outside California. **Locator:** MORRO BAY. **See featured trip page:** 103.

• HOT TIPS •

WHALE WATCHING EXCURSIONS

Of all the unbelievable things about Southern California, seeing a real whale up close and personal might be the most amazing. Not only are whales beautiful, they are big. Really big.

A compact car is 10 feet long or so and weighs about 2,000 pounds. A mature Pacific gray whale is often between 30 and 45 feet long and weighs 75,000 to 100,000 pounds. To make another comparison, the next largest mammal, the African elephant, is about 25 feet long and weighs approximately 16,000 pounds.

Estimates vary, but it's generally believed that 18,000 to 25,000 gray whales migrate from their summer feeding area in the Arctic's Chukchi Sea to the warm lagoons of Baja Mexico. In Baja, the whales either mate or give birth to the baby whales conceived in Mexico the year before. Generally the whales are southbound from November through February and then northbound from February through April.

For those willing to invest a little time, the whales aren't very difficult to see. The best way to see a whale is to shell out $20 or so and take a whale watching excursion on a boat—many of which get to within 10 feet of the behemoths. Whale watching boats leave from Morro Bay, Santa Barbara, Ventura, Redondo Beach, San Pedro, Long Beach, and San Diego.

While there's no guarantee you will see a whale, it's fairly rare for a whale watching boat to get shut out. Because the whales migrate year after year, their routes are fairly well known to the boat captains. So if the boats troll the right waters long enough, chances are a whale will happen by. Captains also hire pilots, who spot the whales from the air and then radio locations of whales to the boats.

Whales, for some inexplicable reason, seem to be intrigued by the boats. For example, on Steve's first whale watching trip from Redondo Beach, things were quiet for an hour or so, providing just enough time for a whole boatload of elementary school kids to suffer chain reaction seasickness.

Suddenly a whale spout was seen a few hundred yards away. The boat circled around and—boom!—the whale surfaced 10 yards from the boat. For the next 20 minutes, the whale continued to swim alongside the boat, allowing everyone to view the barnacles covering much of its skin. On several occasions it dove, splashing the water with its tail hard enough to get a few people wet.

How cool was it? For 20 minutes, the school kids stopped puking.

WHALE BEHAVIOR

Whales are infinitely complex mammals—scientists are still struggling to understand why it is they behave as they do. However, there are several types of whale behavior that are well chronicled, including:

Spouting—When the whale surfaces to exhale through its blowhole. The whale is exhaling air, not water. But the air hits the water so hard it creates the misty spray often associated with spouting.

Sounding—When the whale dives below the surface, which often throws the tail clear out of the water momentarily.

Spyhopping—When the whale sticks its head out of the water as if looking around. Some scientists believe the whales are looking for markings on land that help them navigate.

Breaching—When the whale jumps three-quarters of the way out of the water and then falls over backward, as if playing dead or pretending to be a drunken frat boy at UCLA.

DIFFERENT KINDS OF WHALES

There are two basic types of whales: toothed and baleen.

Many species of toothed whales exist. Willy, from the film *Free Willy*, was an orca, and Moby Dick was a sperm whale. Although these whales do have teeth and do eat fish, they aren't quite as nice or as mean, respectively, as fiction has made them out to be.

Instead of teeth, baleen whales use plates of whalebone called baleen to strain their favorite food, plankton. Gray whales, which are commonly seen off the California coast, are baleen whales. So are blue whales, which have grown to be 100 feet long on occasion, and are the largest of the whale species.

SAVING THE WHALES

Until 25 years ago, whales were heading toward extinction after being hunted ruthlessly for the previous 200 years. Hunters sought whales for their meat and oil, which was used in lamps, perfume, and soap.

Beginning in the 1930s, an organization called the International Whaling Commission (IWC) tried to stop the overhunting of whales. Most countries responded by thumbing their noses at the IWC, and the slaughter continued: about 30,000 whales were being killed each year.

It wasn't until the late 1960s and early 1970s that people became interested in saving the whales. What got people interested? At first, it was recordings of the strange and beautiful sounds made by humpback whales. "Save the Whales" became part of the hyper-holistic culture of the early 1970s—it's safe to say some inhaling accompanied the whale sounds spinning on the turntable.

Finally, in 1972, the United States made it illegal to hunt whales in U.S. waters. In 1975, the IWC, now with the U.S.'s backing, again set quotas on the number of whales allowed to be killed each year.

Whale hunting decreased, but not enough. So in 1985 the IWC declared that all further whale hunting would be illegal. Most of the world's countries agreed to go along with the ban. As a result, many species of whales have bounced back from near extinction.

But both gray whales and blue whales are still endangered. Before hunting there were approximately 400,000 blues. Today there are an estimated 12,000.

A SAD WHALE STORY

In the middle of September 1996, several people on boats saw something strange floating in Long Beach Harbor. It was a 48-foot-long fin whale, which had apparently been hit by a boat and killed.

Fin whales are rare. Most of them were killed in whale hunts in the 1800s and the early part of the 1900s. The ones that remain, according to scientists, rarely come close to the shore.

By the end of the week, the whale washed up on Bolsa Chica State Beach, where it was found by surfers. (We saw it the next day. The smell was almost unbearable, but the size was impressive.)

Workers and scientists from the Los Angeles County Museum of Natural History studied the whale and prepared to bury it. But before they could do so, vandals cut off the whale's tail and stole its jawbone. This is a crime—it's illegal to harm an endangered species, whether the animal is dead or alive.

SEASICKNESS

Don't be ashamed. Many people puke at sea. Here are a few tips. One, inquire about ocean conditions before planning your trip—the days preceding a storm are often rough. Two, put aside your morbid curiosity and never watch someone else get sick. Three, if you're fairly certain your sea legs aren't going to hold up, go to your local pharmacy and try one of the several anti-motion sickness medications on the market. Remember, most of the medications have to be taken well ahead of the boat ride.

EXCURSION COMPANIES

Virg's Fish'n, Morro Bay, (805) 772-1222.
Santa Barbara Museum of Natural History, Santa Barbara, (805) 682-4711.
Sea Landing Sportfishing, Santa Barbara, (805) 963-3564.
Cisco Sportfishing, Ventura Harbor, (805) 985-8511.
Island Packers, Ventura Harbor, (805) 642-1393 or (805) 642-7688.
Cabrillo Marine Aquarium, San Pedro, (310) 832-2676.
L.A. Harbor Cruises, San Pedro, (310) 831-0996.
L.A. Harbor Sportfishing, San Pedro, (310) 547-9216.
Spirit Cruises, San Pedro, (310) 548-8080.
22nd St. Landing, San Pedro, (310) 832-8304.
Islandia Sportfishing, Mission Bay, (619) 222-1165.
Seaforth Sportfishing, Mission Bay, (619) 224-3383.
Fisherman's Landing, Point Loma, (619) 222-0391.
H&M Landing, Mission Bay, (619) 222-1144.
Point Loma Sportsfishing, Mission Bay, (619) 223-1627.

• **HOT TIPS** •

WATCHING WHALES FROM LAND

The best places from land are generally high ground on a peninsula. A small whale watching park at Point Vicente on the Palos Verdes Peninsula, between L.A. and Orange County, is one of the best locations (see page 232). Point Vicente is also home to one of the American Cetacean Society's two whale census centers in Southern California. Phone: (310) 377-5370.

Volunteers at the census center sit outside pretty much all day, every day, during the winter looking for whales. The data they record—and they record everything—are combined with information from three other census centers on the West Coast. The volunteers, when not too busy, are usually quite willing to help visitors spot whales, which are typically seen five to 10 miles offshore.

There is also the added bonus that you never know what might show up. On January 29, 1996, a "super pod" of 60 killer whales surfaced between Point Vicente and Catalina. No one is sure where they came from or why the whales (also known as orcas) were traveling in unusually large numbers. But there they were.

Other good places to try? Point Loma in San Diego is considered as good as Point Vicente. As for beaches, try the following: Carpinteria, El Capitan, Refugio, Gaviota, Goleta, Leo Carrillo, Sycamore Canyon (Point Mugu), Point Dume, Zuma Beach, Dana Point, Cabrillo, and Torrey Pines.

• **TOP RATINGS** •

THE TOP 9 PLACES TO GO TIDEPOOLING

Fact: More than half of all life forms in the world are found within one mile of the ocean's edge.
Fact: It may well be that our distant ancestors slogged their way out of a tidepool.
Fact: Tidepooling is not something just for dorks or kids.

Tidepools are the rocky puddles near shore that are covered with water during high tide but exposed during low tide. The pools are home to a community of sea life that includes anemones, sea stars, sand crabs, jellyfish, mussels, and, sometimes, octopuses.

There are four tidepool zones. The low zone is mostly underwater, only exposed during extreme low tides. Mid-zone tidepools are usually exposed every day for a short time during low tides. High-zone tidepools are exposed twice every day during high tides. Splash-zone tidepools, which are the closest to land, are only splashed by waves.

The sea life in tidepools varies according to the tidepool zone. Sea stars and octopuses are considered more fragile and make their homes in the mid-zone and sometimes high-zone tidepools. Sea anemones are common in the mid and lower zones. Hard-shelled animals such as limpets, chitons, and snails tend to make their homes in the high zone tidepools. Periwinkles and barnacles can usually be found in the splash zone.

Tides come in and go out in 12-hour cycles. There are usually two high tides and two low tides every day. Check local newspapers or fishing supply stores for tide tables. Tidepools are best to visit within an hour of low tide. Fall and winter are prime seasons for tidepooling because tides are at their lowest. Tides are most extreme during new and full moons.

The best place to learn about tidepools is at aquariums and museums. The Cabrillo Marine Aquariumin San Pedro [Phone: (310) 548-7562] and the Sea Center at Stearns Wharf in Santa Barbara [Phone: (805) 962-0885] both have touch pools, which are basically petting zoos for water creatures. The Santa Barbara Museum of Natural History conducts tidepool outings. Phone: (805) 682-4711. The Channel Islands National Park Visitor Center at Ventura Harbor has a man-made indoor tidepool and rangers give talks about the animals living there. Phone: (805) 658-5730. Farther south, the Orange County Marine Institute holds cruises and has a tidepool exploration program. Phone: (714) 496-2274.

Yes, there is such a thing as tidepool etiquette. Never ever remove anything from a tidepool—often it's illegal to do so. Before exploring a tidepool, stand at the pool's edge for a few minutes so the creatures don't get spooked.

Here is a list of some of the best places to find tidepools in Southern California:

1. MONTANA DE ORO STATE PARK, SAN LUIS OBISPO COUNTY

Spooner's Cove, once used by smugglers, is the park's favorite tidepooling and picnicking spot. Look for sea urchins, hermit crabs, and sea cucumbers in the tidepools, which are formed by steeply tilted rock layers jutting seaward. Tide tables can be obtained at park headquarters.

Contact: Montana de Oro State Park, (805) 528-0513 or (805) 772-7434 between 9 A.M. and 3 P.M. **Locator:** MONTANA DE ORO STATE PARK. See **featured trip page:** 105.

2. CARPINTERIA STATE BEACH, SANTA BARBARA COUNTY

Carpinteria has gentle surf and a gradual drop-off, which makes it perfect for small children. Along with a tidepool, there are a campground and sand sculpting contests on Saturdays during the summer. Anyone can com-

WILDLIFE WATCHING

pete in the free contests, which draw as many as 200 competitors.

Contact: Carpinteria State Beach, (805) 684-2811. **Locator:** CARPINTERIA STATE BEACH. **See map on page:** 174.

3. FRENCHY'S COVE, VENTURA COUNTY

You'll need to take a boat to this spot on Anacapa Island in Channel Islands National Park. Frenchy, a hermit, liked it here so much he lived here for more than 30 years. Look for octopus in the lower pools out by Cat Rock. Red and black striped shore crabs dart around the higher pools.

Contact: Channel Islands National Park, (805) 658-5730. **Locator:** ANACAPA ISLAND. **See featured trip page:** 196.

4. LEO CARRILLO STATE BEACH, LOS ANGELES COUNTY

This beach, located in northern Malibu, is popular with families because of the tidepooling, sea caves, and camping. These tidepools are a bit unusual because they consist of cobblestone, which can fill with sand after a storm. Tidepool observers can easily see the change in habitat from splash zone to high tide zone.

Contact: California Department of Parks and Recreation, (818) 880-0350. **Locator:** LEO CARRILLO STATE BEACH. **See map on page:** 206.

5. MALIBU LAGOON STATE BEACH, LOS ANGELES COUNTY

Best known to surfers as Surfrider Beach, this place is classic Malibu. A 10-acre lagoon formed by the beach is home to a rare salt-marsh habitat of birds and fish. Low tide exposes rocks on the ocean side of the lagoon, forming tidepools with crabs, urchins, anemones, and other creatures.

Contact: California Department of Parks and Recreation, (818) 880-0367. **Locator:** MALIBU LAGOON STATE BEACH. **See featured trip page:** 230.

6. PALOS VERDES PENINSULA, LOS ANGELES COUNTY

The beaches surrounding the peninsula are some of the best places in the Los Angeles area to explore tidepools. You can learn about seashore life at the Cabrillo Marine Aquarium in San Pedro and then experience it for yourself at the nearby tidepools. Point Fermin and Whites Point in San Pedro and Abalone Cove in Rancho Palos Verdes are the area's tidepool hot spots, featuring bat stars and sponges. Just after a full or new moon from March through August, come to the beaches here to see the tiny, silver grunion, which come ashore at night to spawn.

Contact: Cabrillo Marine Aquarium, (310) 548-7562. **Locator:** PALOS VERDES PENINSULA. **See featured trip page:** 231.

7. CRYSTAL COVE STATE PARK, ORANGE COUNTY

This state park's 3.25 miles of undeveloped coastline sits between Corona del Mar and Laguna Beach. The shoreline holds some of Orange County's best tidepools. The pools are located at Pelican Point, near the Crystal Cove Historic District, and at Reef Point, which is just a little bit south of the district.

Contact: Crystal Cove State Park, (714) 494-3539. **Locator:** CRYSTAL COVE STATE PARK. **See featured trip page:** 268.

8. DANA POINT MARINE LIFE REFUGE, ORANGE COUNTY

Tidepoolers at this Orange County spot should keep their eyes peeled for crabs, sea stars, anemones, sea urchins, and other tiny sea beasts. Naturalists from the Orange County Marine Institute teach classes on marine life and lead occasional tours to the tidepools. There is also a free, self-guided tour. The tidepools are located at the end of Dana Point Marina near the Marine Institute. Nearby Doheny State Beach has an interpretive center with a 500-gallon tidepool tank.

> **Contact:** Orange County Marine Institute, (714) 496-2274. Doheny State Beach, (714) 496-6172. **Locator:** DANA POINT. **See map on page:** 264.

9. LA JOLLA, SAN DIEGO COUNTY

Marine creatures thrive in this warm San Diego–area water. The Steven Birch Aquarium, part of the Scripps Institution of Oceanography at University of California San Diego, is just south of the tidepools and a great place to start. The aquarium has a tidepool exhibit and offers guided trips in fall and winter, the prime tidepooling seasons—at press time, the Birch Aquarium tidepool trip was $11 for adults and $7 for children. Some of the spots that the guided trips visit (or you can explore on your own) include La Jolla Shores, near the Scripps campus; the southern portion of Cardiff State Beach; Hospital Point south of La Jolla Cove; and Swami's Beach in Encinitas.

> **Contact:** Steven Birch Aquarium, (619) 534-7336. **Locator:** LA JOLLA. **See map on page:** 265.

• TOP RATINGS •

THE TOP 7 WILDFLOWER WALKS

One of the most tried and true cycles of nature in Southern California is the spring bloom of wildflowers. One day it can be gloomy and cold with no end to the rain in sight. And then—boom!—the next morning it looks like elves took to the landscape with a box of crayons.

Perhaps John Muir, in his "My First Summer in the Sierra," said it best: "In the Great Central Valley of California, there are only two seasons—spring and summer. The spring begins with the first rainstorm, which usually falls in November. In a few months the wonderful flowery vegetation is in full bloom, and by the end of May it is dead and dry and crisp as if every plant had been roasted in an oven."

As California natives know, there is a very small window in which to see native plants in full bloom—late winter and early spring. As one Forest Service ranger told us in late March, "This is the time of year when everyone starts calling about the wildflowers."

The California poppy, the state flower, is to wildflowers what Jayne Mansfield was to brassieres: Big. The poppies, which are orange with four petals, bloom on open slopes from Oregon to California for only a few weeks each spring. If you are not sure what they are, you have probably seen them anyway. Interestingly, the poppy does best in the high deserts, especially the western edge of the Mojave.

But the poppy can be fickle. The flower's seeds, which drop to the ground in May, lie dormant until ideal winter conditions prevail—the poppy needs a winter with average to above-average rainfall. Even more importantly, the poppy needs cold weather to kill off the weeds and other nonnative plants that compete with the poppy for water and sunlight.

There are numerous places to see poppies. Although the poppy reserve

WILDLIFE WATCHING

in Lancaster is best known, many people think the slopes around Gorman are better. Our friend Stephanie Stassel Bluestein went to Gorman in 1991, the best poppy season in recent years. Photos were taken of Stephanie standing in the poppy fields, and it's fair to say it looks like she's standing on the set of *The Wizard of Oz*.

But the poppy is not the only star to shine in the springtime in Southern California. In the deserts, especially Anza-Borrego Desert State Park in San Diego County, cactuses flower along with dandelions and sunflowers, to name but a few. On the Channel Islands coreopsis blooms in the spring; Oxnard and Ventura residents can see Anacapa Island's golden fields from 11 miles away. In the meadows of the Southern Sierra in Kern County, 175 different wildflowers bloom, including California poppies, baby blue-eyes, lupines, and monkey flower.

There are thousands of places in Southern California to see wildflowers. Some are immensely popular, others are rarely visited. Here are a few tips:

1. CALIFORNIA POPPY RESERVE, LOS ANGELES COUNTY

The poppy reserve is like a home run hitter. It has spectacular years and it has off years when it just can't connect. The reserve has slumped a bit the last few years, and there's no telling when it will return to its glory days. The reserve is located near Lancaster, on Avenue I, 15 miles west of Highway 14.

Contact: California Poppy Reserve, (805) 724-1180. **Locator:** LANCASTER. **See map on page:** 207.

2. SEQUOIA NATIONAL FOREST, KERN COUNTY

The Upper Kern Plateau, the Dome Land Wilderness, and the Golden Trout Wilderness are all known for having high country meadows that are reliable sources of wildflowers. These are beautiful places to hike and camp, and make a great side trip if you're in Kernville for a little springtime whitewater rafting.

Contact: For the Upper Kern Plateau and the Dome Land Wilderness, phone the Sequoia National Forest, Cannell Meadow Ranger District, (760) 376-3781. For the Golden Trout Wilderness, phone the Inyo National Forest, Mount Whitney Ranger District, (760) 876-6200. **Locator:** GOLDEN TROUT WILDERNESS, UPPER KERN PLATEAU, AND DOME LAND WILDERNESS. **See featured trip pages:** 151 and 156.

3. FIGUEROA MOUNTAIN, SANTA BARBARA COUNTY

Figueroa is hardly a secret to wildflower enthusiasts. The Davy Brown Trail, particularly on the lower part of the mountain, is the best way to see fiddleneck, shooting stars, lupine, and cream cups.

Contact: Los Padres National Forest, Santa Lucia Ranger District, (805) 925-9538. **Locator:** FIGUEROA MOUNTAIN. **See featured trip page:** 178.

4. CHANNEL ISLANDS NATIONAL PARK, VENTURA COUNTY

Anacapa is the easiest island to reach, but Santa Cruz is the best for wildflowers because the island has a freshwater supply feeding more than 600 species of plants. Santa Rosa, a former ranch, has rolling grasslands that light up with wildflowers, also. And, of course, Anacapa has its sensational display of coreopsis.

WILDLIFE WATCHING

Contact: Channel Islands National Park, (805) 658-5730. **Locator:** CHANNEL ISLANDS NATIONAL PARK. **See featured trip pages:** 196, 198, and 200.

5. HUNGRY VALLEY STATE VEHICULAR RECREATION AREA, LOS ANGELES COUNTY

The California poppy displays can be just as good here, if not better, than at the California Poppy Reserve in Lancaster. From Santa Clarita, take Interstate 5 north for 22 miles, past the Six Flags Magic Mountain amusement park, exit at Hungry Valley Road, and turn left. Cross under the freeway to the recreation area.

Contact: California State Parks, (805) 248-7007. **Locator:** GORMAN. **See map on page:** 207.

6. SANTA MONICA MOUNTAINS, LOS ANGELES COUNTY

The wildfires of 1993 resulted in some very good wildflower displays in northern Malibu in 1994 and '95, and the big wildfire of September 1996 should provide good results for the next few years. There are several good spots: the Sycamore Canyon Trail in Point Mugu State Park, the Mishe Mokwa Trail in Circle X Ranch, and the Nicholas Flat Trail, which is located across the Pacific Coast Highway from Leo Carrillo State Beach.

Contact: Santa Monica Mountains National Recreation Area, (818) 597-9192. **Locator:** SANTA MONICA MOUNTAINS. **See maps on pages:** 190 and 206.

7. ANZA-BORREGO DESERT STATE PARK, SAN DIEGO COUNTY

Anza-Borrego has some of the best springtime flora displays you'll find anywhere. Unfortunately, a lot of the cactus flora can also be unpredictable. We saw the ocotillo bloom recently at Anza-Borrego, which actually threw a reddish haze over the desert floor. When the park has a good year, the rainbow of colors includes yellow dandelions, white primrose and lily, purple sand verbena, red monkey flower and ocotillo. Typically, the bloom begins at the lower elevations anywhere from late February through April.

The park has a wildflower hotline that visitors can call to check on the status of the bloom: (760) 767-4684. You can also send a self-addressed, stamped postcard to the park. About two weeks before peak bloom hits, you'll get the card in the mail. The address: WILDFLOWERS, Anza-Borrego Desert State Park, Box 299, Borrego Springs, CA 92004-0299.

Contact: Anza-Borrego Desert State Park, (760) 767-4205. **Locator:** ANZA-BORREGO DESERT STATE PARK. **See featured trip page:** 275.

• **HOT TIPS** •

WILDLIFE SANCTUARIES AND NATURE PRESERVES

Sprinkled throughout Southern California are nature and wildlife preserves managed by various government agencies or privately funded groups. Generally, the public is invited to explore these reserves and preserves, although sometimes it is necessary to make an appointment with the appropriate agency.

1. BOLSA CHICA ECOLOGICAL RESERVE, ORANGE COUNTY

Across from Bolsa Chica State Beach is this 1,000-acre reserve, a damaged tidal marsh that the California Department of Fish and Game has been restoring since 1973. There's a 1.5-mile trail through the reserve, which begins as a wooden walkway crossing the estuary from the parking lot.

Contact: California Department of Fish and Game, (562) 590-5670. Bolsa Chica State Beach, (714) 846-3460. Amigos de Bolsa Chica, (714) 897-7003. **Locator:** HUNTINGTON BEACH. See map on page: 264.

2. COACHELLA VALLEY PRESERVE, RIVERSIDE COUNTY

This preserve is a joint effort by the Nature Conservancy and the Bureau of Land Management to protect the endangered Coachella Valley fringe-toed lizard. A 1.5-mile nature trail, which passes through a palm oasis, is very nice.

Contact: Bureau of Land Management Palm Springs–South Central Office, (760) 251-4800. **Locator:** INDIO. See map on page: 243.

3. DESERT TORTOISE RESEARCH NATURAL AREA, KERN COUNTY

This BLM-managed area near California City in the Mojave Desert is set aside for the study of the desert tortoise, an endangered species. Visit in the early spring and you may see one—although it's hardly a sure bet. Don't go after May 1, when the heat out here is too extreme.

Contact: Bureau of Land Management, Ridgecrest Office, (760) 384-5400. **Locator:** CALIFORNIA CITY. See map on page: 139.

4. KERN NATIONAL WILDLIFE REFUGE, KERN COUNTY

This would be a duck hunter's paradise if it wasn't a wildlife refuge. The salty marshes near the Central Valley town of Delano feature bird-viewing with an emphasis on the many duck species.

Contact: U.S. Fish and Wildlife Service, (805) 725-2767. **Locator:** DELANO. See map on page: 139.

5. THE LIVING DESERT, RIVERSIDE COUNTY

This 1,200-acre preserve near Palm Desert has six miles of trails and attracts a whole host of species. An interesting visitor center will help you understand what it is you're seeing.

Contact: The Living Desert, (760) 346-5694. **Locator:** RANCHO MIRAGE. See map on page: 243.

6. SANTA ROSA PLATEAU ECOLOGICAL RESERVE, RIVERSIDE COUNTY

This 15,000-acre preserve in Riverside County is comanaged by the Nature Conservancy and four other agencies. You'll find rolling hills with sycamores, oaks, small creeks, and native grasses.

Contact: The Nature Conservancy, (909) 677-6951. **Locator:** SANTA ROSA PLATEAU. See map on page: 243.

7. TUPMAN TULE ELK STATE RESERVE, KERN COUNTY

Tule elk were once abundant in Southern California. Now they're not. But the elk can commonly be seen year-round at this preserve near the happening burg of Buttonwillow in the Central Valley, either on your own or on a guided tour.

Contact: California Department of Parks and Recreation, (805) 765-5004. **Locator:** BUTTONWILLOW. See map on page: 139.

8. WHITTIER NARROWS NATURE CENTER, LOS ANGELES COUNTY

Although smallish at 277 acres, this preserve near El Monte attracts well over 200 species of birds, making it a good place for beginning birders to rack up some numbers.

Contact: Los Angeles County Parks, (626) 444-1872. **Locator:** EL MONTE. See map on page: 207.

14
SUNSET WATCHING

• TOP RATINGS •

THE TOP 10 PLACES TO WATCH THE SUN GO DOWN

With sunsets so accessible to pretty much everyone in Southern California—they are the most democratic thing about our state—you have to look just a little harder for a sunset that truly inspires life-changing, contemplative deep thoughts, as sunsets are supposed to do.

As everyone knows, great sunsets almost always involve water. After all, the sun sinking into the sea is a cottage industry of its own, as any visit to a souvenir shop will prove. On the other hand, some of the better sunsets are viewed from up high, where the changing light gives perspective to the valleys below. Desert sunsets shouldn't be ignored, either. Low angle sunlight on a previously drab desert landscape seems to bring a crayon box full of colors out of hibernation. Not to mention the deep blues and reds evident in the desert's high, wide-open skies.

Here, starting with our personal favorite, are the 10 best sunsets worth riding off into:

1. SANDSTONE PEAK, LOS ANGELES COUNTY

If you're willing to hike for 1.5 miles uphill on the Backbone Trail (it's a strenuous hike), you'll get a real treat because Sandstone Peak is the tallest mountain in the Santa Monicas at 3,111 feet. When it's clear out, two of the Channel Islands are visible—Anacapa to the northwest and Catalina to the southwest. There are also views of Point Mugu to the west and parts of the western San Fernando Valley to the north, as well as the South Bay all the way to the Palos Verdes Peninsula. A journal is kept underneath a monument and compass built into the rock. Bring a pen and record your deep thoughts as the sun sets on this incredible panorama.

Directions: From Santa Monica take the Pacific Coast Highway north for 28 miles. At Countyline State Beach, turn right onto Yerba Buena Road. Follow the road uphill for about six miles to Circle X Ranch. The ranger station will be on the right. Continue on Yerba Buena another mile or so to an unsigned gravel parking lot on the left side of the road. The trail begins just past the locked gate. When the trail levels out at its highest point, look for the sign with a hiker on it pointing to the left (it doesn't say anything about the peak on the sign). Follow the short trail to Sandstone Peak. **Fees:** Access is free. **Contact:** Santa Monica Mountains National Recreation Area, (818) 597-9192. Circle X Ranch Ranger Station, (310) 457-6408. **Locator:** LEO CARRILLO STATE BEACH. **See map on page:** 206.

2. TELESCOPE PEAK, DEATH VALLEY NATIONAL PARK

There is a very simple reason why this is one of the best sunsets you'll find anywhere: The lowest point on the continent is 11,000 feet beneath you, and Mount Whitney, the highest point in the lower 48, at 14,495 feet, is visible 100 miles to the west. The sun sets behind Whitney and the Sierra, shutting out lights on the beautifully stark Death Valley. It's a long, arduous climb to the top of Telescope, which requires special preparation. (For more information on Telescope Peak, see page 9.)

Directions: From Ridgecrest take U.S. 395 north to Lone Pine, turn right onto Highway 190, and drive 49 miles. At Panamint Valley Road, turn right and go 15 miles. At Wildrose Canyon Road, turn left and drive nine miles to Wildrose Campground, then continue another five miles to Mahogany Flat Campground, where the trailhead to Telescope is located. Note: The road between Panamint Valley Road and Wildrose Campground is unpaved for a stretch and very bumpy. Be careful of rocks and go slow. **Permits:** No permits are necessary to hike Telescope Peak. **Fees:** Access is free. **Contact:** Death Valley National Park, (619) 786-2331. **Locator:** TELESCOPE PEAK. **See featured trip page:** 131.

3. KEYS VIEW, JOSHUA TREE NATIONAL PARK

On a clear day here you can see over 100 miles south to the Salton Sea and, beyond that, Mexico. To the east is 10,000-foot-plus Mount San Jacinto and below that, Palm Springs and the Coachella Valley. In between there is the desert and mountains and even a freeway far below, a minuscule streak of light on a gargantuan landscape.

Directions: From downtown Los Angeles take Interstate 10 east for 99 miles to the Highway 62 exit, about 45 miles past San Bernardino. Take Highway 62 north for 26 miles to the town of Joshua Tree or go 15 miles farther to the town of Twentynine Palms. Each town has a well-marked entrance to the park. From San Diego take Interstate 15 north to Highway 60 east. Take Highway 60 to Interstate 10 east. Exit at Highway 62 north. Take Highway 62 north for 26 miles to the town of Joshua Tree or go 15 miles farther to the town of Twentynine Palms. **Fees:** A $5 entrance fee admits you to the park for seven days. **Contact:** Joshua Tree National Park, (760) 367-7511. **Locator:** JOSHUA TREE NATIONAL PARK. **See featured trip page:** 251.

4. RETURN VOYAGE FROM CHANNEL ISLANDS NATIONAL PARK

If you visit one of the Channel Islands for the winter, especially November through January, your boat should be returning to Ventura about 4 p.m. Chances are the sun will be setting right in the wake of the boat, forcing you to choose between watching the sun or the pod of dolphins performing their acrobatics just a few yards away.

Directions to Island Packers in Ventura Harbor: From all points north or south take U.S. 101 to Ventura and exit at Victoria. Take Victoria south and turn right onto Channel Islands Boulevard. Drive over the bridge and turn left at Harbor Boulevard. Drive one-quarter mile. Island Packers is on the left in the Marine Emporium, next to Tug's restaurant. **Directions to the Channel Islands National Park Visitor Center:** Exit U.S. 101 at Victoria and turn left. At Olivas Park Drive, turn right. After Harbor Boulevard, Olivas Park runs straight into Spinnaker Drive. The visitor center is located at the end of the road, alongside the harbor. **Fees:** Round-trip transportation by boat to Santa Cruz by Island Packers is $47. Prices for kayak tours vary. **Contact:** Channel Islands National Park, (805) 658-5730. Island Packers, (805) 642-7688 for information and (805) 642-1393 for reservations between 9 A.M. and 5 P.M., seven days

SUNSET WATCHING

a week. Island Packers Web site: www.isle.net/~ipco. Paddlesports, (805) 899-4925. Kayak tours are also offered by Aqua Sports (in Goleta), (805) 968-7231, and Adventours Outdoor Excursions (in Santa Barbara), (805) 963-2248. **Locator:** CHANNEL ISLANDS NATIONAL PARK. **See also featured trip pages:** 196, 198, and 200.

5. DEL CERRO PARK, PALOS VERDES

The actual park itself is tiny, but it sits atop the Palos Verdes Peninsula, allowing for views of the peninsula falling into the sea below, Catalina Island to the west, and northern portions of the South Bay and Malibu—which are over 20 miles away.

Directions: From Los Angeles Airport take Interstate 405 south to the exit for Hawthorne Boulevard south. Follow Hawthorne south for 10 miles until it dead-ends into Palos Verdes Drive South. Turn left and drive one mile. The entrance to the park will be on your right. **Fees:** Entrance to the park is free. Admission to the whale interpretive center is $2 for adults, $1 for children. **Contact:** Point Vicente Park, (310) 377-5370. **Locator:** RANCHO PALOS VERDES. **See featured trip on page:** 231.

6. BLUE RIDGE CAMPGROUND, ANGELES NATIONAL FOREST

The campground is just across a road from one of the lifts at Mountain High. But check out the valley views of the Sheep Wilderness just south of the lift. The sun sets behind the wilderness area, and sunsets in the San Gabriel Mountains rarely are anything less than spectacular..

Locator: WRIGHTWOOD. **See featured trip page:** 208.

7. SILVER CREST PICNIC AREA, PALOMAR MOUNTAIN STATE PARK

The picnic area sits at an elevation of just over 5,000 feet and looks out at the beautiful Pauma Valley more than 3,000 feet below. Everywhere you look there are hills and mountains and greenery and it's all far away from city smog and freeways. As the fat guy and bald guy say, "two big thumbs-up."

Directions: From Temecula take Interstate 15 south for 11 miles, exit at Highway 76, and turn left (east). Drive on Highway 76 for 21 miles and then turn left onto County Road S6. Follow County Road S6 for seven miles, twisting and winding up the side of the mountain, and turn left onto County Road S7. Follow the signs for two miles to the entrance to Palomar Mountain State Park. **Fees:** Day-use parking is $5. Pets are $1 extra. **Contact:** Palomar Mountain State Park, (760) 742-3462. **Locator:** PALOMAR MOUNTAIN STATE PARK. **See featured trip page:** 271.

8. CHAIR NUMBER 8, SNOW SUMMIT, SAN BERNARDINO NATIONAL FOREST

As you ride to the top of the mountain on Chair 8, you may notice the sky is turning all sorts of funny colors. Glance behind you for a look at Big Bear Lake. When you get to the top, enjoy the view of the sun setting behind the San Bernardino Mountains for a few moments before skiing your way down to the lodge.

Directions: From Los Angeles take Interstate 10 east for 60 miles to Redlands, exiting to Highway 30 north. Take Highway 30 to Highway 330 north and then continue 15 miles up and into the mountains to Running

Springs. In Running Springs, follow Highway 18 east for 12.5 miles to Big Bear Lake. Drive through Big Bear Village and turn right on Summit Boulevard. **Contact:** Snow Summit, (909) 866-5766. Snow reports: L.A. County, (310) 390-1498; Orange County, (714) 972-0601; Inland Empire, (909) 866-4621; San Diego County, (619) 294-8786; San Fernando Valley, (818) 242-0032. Web site: www.snowsummit.com. **Locator:** BIG BEAR CITY. **See featured trip page:** 248.

9. GRIFFITH PARK OBSERVATORY, LOS ANGELES COUNTY

This refuge from the city allows for views of much of the L.A. basin all the way from downtown to the ocean—if it's clear. If not, chances are still good the Southland will turn various shades of crimson.

Directions: From downtown Los Angeles, exit U.S. 101 at Hollywood Boulevard and turn right. At Western Avenue, turn left. Follow Western uphill and around a sharp right turn—the road is now called Los Feliz Boulevard. At Fern Dell Road, turn left into Griffith Park. Fern Dell turns into Western Canyon Road. Continue uphill, following signs to the Griffith Park Observatory. **Fees:** Telescope night is free, as is parking at the observatory. Admission to the observatory's Hall of Sciences is also free. **Contact:** Los Angeles Astronomical Society, (213) 673-7355. Griffith Park Observatory, (213) 664-1181. Sky reports, (213) 663-8171. Web site: www.griffithobservatory.org. **Locator:** GRIFFITH PARK. **See featured trip page:** 227.

10. PISMO STATE BEACH, CENTRAL COAST

The beach here is wide and long—the state-regulated portion of the beach is eight miles long. There are also some fantastic dunes throughout the beach (avoid the ones in the state vehicle recreation area), the perfect place to sit and watch the sun plop into the sea. For more information, see Pismo State Beach on page 107.

Directions: To reach Pismo State Beach from Santa Barbara, take U.S. 101 north for 87 miles. Exit at Grand Avenue and turn left. Follow the road until it ends at the entrance gate to the beach. Use the Highway 1 exit for the town of Pismo Beach. **Fees:** The day-use fee for the beach is $6. **Contact:** Pismo State Beach, (805) 549-3312. **Locator:** PISMO STATE BEACH. **See featured trip page:** 107.

15
TOURING

• TOP RATINGS •

WHERE TO SEE FALL COLORS

Autumn in Southern California seems to whiz by in one afternoon. One October day it's 90 degrees and you're at the beach. The next day it rains one-tenth of an inch and the TV news jugheads are trotting out their new "Storm Command" theme song. And, thus, it's the start of winter.

Although it goes against the popular belief, there are fall colors in Southern California—it just takes them a little time to warm up and appear. Mixed in with the endless hills of chaparral are the occasional deciduous trees—those whose leaves turn colors, die, and then fall off. In Southern California, these color producers are oaks, maples, sycamores, and, at higher elevations, aspen. It's not quite New England, but then again, New England pays the price with six months of Arctic-like conditions.

One tip: Treat fall colors as if they're wildflowers. Phone first to make sure the colors are turning.

SAN LUIS OBISPO COUNTY

Lopez Lake is a good place to visit; you won't have to go far past the visitor center, where you can often find wild turkeys wandering around under a canopy of oaks. Other good spots can be found in the wineries around Paso Robles and County Road G14 between Paso Robles and Lake Nacimiento. If you like to do the boat thing, try the shores of Lake San Antonio or a drive up County Road N16.

Contact: Lopez Lake Recreation Area, (805) 489-1122. Paso Robles Chamber of Commerce, Lake San Antonio, (805) 472-2311. **Locator:** ARROYO GRANDE. **See featured trip pages:** 101, 103, and 110.

KERN AND TULARE COUNTIES

Our tour, ladies and gents, begins near the tiny village of Mineral King, which is 25 miles deep into the southern portion of Sequoia National Park. In the surrounding forest, there are stands of both cottonwood and aspens, both of which are excellent color producers. Keep in mind this is far from the folks who are merely off the beaten path. We recommend camping or renting a cabin in the private community of Silver City (which is actually within the park) for a cozy weekend. Highway 155 between the San Joaquin Valley in the west and the village of Alta Sierra in the east has rolling ranchlands of oak, too, which you'll enjoy if the drive doesn't frighten you to death. Note: Don't wait until it snows and the road to Mineral King closes, which often occurs by the end of October.

Contact: Sequoia and Kings Canyon National Parks, (209) 565-3341. For cabin rentals in Silver City, phone (209) 561-3223. **Locator:** THREE RIVERS. **See featured trip pages:** 140 and 145.

SANTA BARBARA COUNTY

You may have noticed that the words "Jalama Beach" keep popping up throughout this book. Here we go again: In the hunt for fall colors, try the drive from Highway 1 to Jalama Beach on Jalama Beach Road. It's 14 miles of glorious, rolling ranchland with creeks and oaks and color. Although it's in the middle of nowhere, the beach is an excellent destination—our favorite beach in Southern California. Wild cards in the county include Figueroa Mountain and the banks of the Santa Ynez River and Manzanita Creek, all within Los Padres National Forest.

Contact: Jalama Beach County Park, (805) 736-6316. Los Padres National Forest, Santa Lucia Ranger District, (805) 925-9538. **Locator:** JALAMA BEACH, FIGUEROA MOUNTAIN and SANTA YNEZ RIVER. **See featured trip pages:** 175, 178, and 184.

VENTURA COUNTY

One of our favorite drive-in campgrounds is Wheeler Gorge, located on Highway 33 about two miles north of Wheeler Hot Springs. The campground sits right next to Matilija Creek underneath oaks and sycamores within Los Padres National Forest. The fall and winter light in this canyon is already beautiful, and the fall colors only add to the splendor. Speaking of brilliant, try a picnic in Libbey Park in downtown Ojai, the Ojai Valley Trail, or a walk to Bart's, the eclectic little bookstore in the neighborhood behind downtown Ojai.

Contact: Ojai Valley Chamber of Commerce, (805) 646-8126. Los Padres National Forest, Ojai Ranger District, (805) 646-4348. **Locator:** OJAI. **See featured trip page:** 192.

LOS ANGELES COUNTY

Some of the best shots of fall color can be found in the San Gabriel Mountains and the Santa Monica Mountains. In the San Gabes, shoot for any of the canyons on the front range—places like Millard Canyon, Big Santa Anita Canyon, or Iceberg Canyon near Mount Baldy. Also in the Angeles National Forest, near the village of Wrightwood, is the Blue Ridge Trail. From Wrightwood take the Angeles Crest Highway west for two miles and park at the Forest Service ranger station, located on the right side of the road. The trailhead is on the other side of the highway near the rest rooms. The trail climbs the ridge, where it passes through the Blue Ridge Campground and then terminates at the bottom of a ski lift belonging to the Mountain High ski resort. Near the bottom of the lift there are outstanding views to the south of the San Gabriel Mountains.

In the Santa Monicas try Solstice Canyon (administered by the Santa Monica Mountains Conservancy); it has big leaf maples that turn bright orange. Another nice, if unexpected, place is the area surrounding the Los Angeles Equestrian Center in Burbank, as well as the foothills of Griffith Park.

Contact: Angeles National Forest, (818) 574-5200. Santa Monica Mountains National Recreation Area, (818) 597-9192. Santa Monica Mountains Conservancy, (310) 456-5046. **Locator:** MALIBU, WRIGHTWOOD, MOUNT BALDY. **See featured trip page:** 208.

SAN BERNARDINO COUNTY

A drive on Highway 38 from Angelus Oaks to Onyx Summit is good for a display of California black oak, as is the drive on Highway 18 in the San Bernardino Mountains from Running Springs to the Snow Valley ski resort. Within the San Gorgonio Wilderness, the Aspen Grove Trail is a good way to see one of only two aspen groves in this part of the state. Get a free permit at the Mill Creek Ranger Station in Mentone and then continue on Highway 38 for 25 miles, turning right on Forest Service Road 1N02. Go another 1.5 miles, turn right at the fork, and then drive another 1.5 miles to the parking area for the trailhead.

Contact: San Bernardino National Forest, San Gorgonio Ranger District, (909) 794-1123. **Locator:** REDLANDS. **See featured trip page:** 245.

ORANGE COUNTY

Talk about great picnic spots. It's hard to beat Ronald W. Caspers Wilderness Park. We suggest setting up your spread near the windmill, where you'll find some good fall color, and then taking a hike on the 0.7-mile Nature Loop, which passes through a forest of oaks and sycamores that looks like something you would find in Ohio (minus the cactus).

Contact: Caspers Wilderness Park, (714) 728-0235 or (714) 728-3420. **Locator:** CASPERS WILDERNESS PARK. **See featured trip page:** 266.

SAN DIEGO COUNTY

San Diego County's best shot at fall colors is in Palomar Mountain State Park. At an altitude over 5,000 feet, there are distinctive seasons up on the mountain and some beautiful forests, too. We suggest taking the drive down to Doane Pond from the park entrance and then choosing a place to hike. There are also some good color opportunities on Highway 76 in the Pauma Valley between Interstate 15 and the top of Palomar Mountain. Other wild cards in the county are the area around Julian, Balboa Park in San Diego, and Cuyamaca Rancho State Park east of San Diego.

Contact: Palomar Mountain State Park, (619) 742-3462. Cuyamaca Rancho State Park, (619) 765-0755. **Locator:** PALOMAR MOUNTAIN STATE PARK. **See featured trip page:** 271.

• **TOP RATINGS** •

THE TOP 14 ROADS AND BACKROADS TO THE OUTDOORS

Time for a quiz:

1. When a pedestrian steps into a crosswalk:
   a. Motorists should stop.
   b. The car behind you must stop.
   c. The pedestrian has it coming.

2. The steering wheel is:
   a. A vital component of an automobile.
   b. For use in emergencies.
   c. An excellent bookrest.

3. If you have an accident with a celebrity you should:
   a. Act as you would normally.
   b. Make sure your camcorder batteries are charged.
   c. Use a 9-iron.

4. A sudden, illegal lane change is okay if:
   a. A truck is about to run you over.
   b. That lane just didn't feel right.
   c. Your travel coffee cup lid comes loose.

As you may have guessed, the correct answer to all of the above questions is "c." If you passed, thus proving you are a capable motorist, here are a few drives a wee bit on the scenic side. Important safety tip: Keep your eyes on the road.

1. HIGHWAY 1, SAN LUIS OBISPO COUNTY

People come from all over the world to drive this stretch of the Pacific Coast Highway between San Luis Obispo and the Monterey Peninsula. In short,

TOURING

you will straddle seaside cliffs for over a hundred miles in some of the absolutely most gorgeous, untamed scenery to be viewed on planet Earth. Drive carefully; a 500-foot plummet off a cliff into the sea will erode your car's lifespan.

Directions: From San Luis Obispo head north on Highway 1. **Locator:** SAN LUIS OBISPO. **See map on page:** 100.

2. COUNTY ROADS G-14 AND G-19, SAN LUIS OBISPO AND MONTEREY COUNTIES

Get out the AAA map for this one. From Paso Robles, take G-14 through some of the prettiest ranching country you'll ever see: mountains, hills so green it doesn't seem possible (in the winter and spring), wildflowers, creeks, and the occasional small waterfall. If it's winter, count how many cars you see on G-19. If you make it to 10, you'll have seen twice as many cars as we did.

Directions: From San Luis Obispo take U.S. 101 north for 29 miles to Paso Robles, exiting to County Road G-14 north. G-14 and G-19 intersect just south of Lake San Antonio. **Locator:** PASO ROBLES. **See map on page:** 100.

3. U.S. 395, INYO COUNTY

From its junction with Highway 14, driving northbound on U.S. 395 is synonymous with going someplace special. On the left side of the car: the Sierra Nevada. On the right side of the car: the White Mountains. Popular destinations from 395 include the Golden Trout Wilderness, Mount Whitney, Onion Valley, Death Valley, the Ancient Bristlecone Pine Forest, Bishop Canyon, Rock Creek Canyon, the Owens River, Hot Creek, Lake Crowley, Mammoth Lakes, June Lake, Mono Lake, Yosemite National Park, and, most importantly, Schatz Bakery in Bishop—get the jalapeño cheese bread. Mmmm.

Directions: From Los Angeles take Highway 14 north to its junction with U.S. 395. **Locator:** LONE PINE, INDEPENDENCE, BISHOP. **See map on page:** 115.

4. GENERAL'S HIGHWAY, TULARE COUNTY

The road begins at the southern entrance to Sequoia National Park. About five miles after entering the park, the real fun begins—the highway gains 4,700 feet in a little over 16 miles in a series of hair-raising switchbacks. At the top is the main attraction, the giant sequoia trees. Great hiking and photography opportunities abound. Tire chains are often required in the winter. During and immediately after a storm, the road is likely to close.

Directions: From Highway 99, exit at Highway 198 east. Go 48 miles to the entrance of Sequoia National Park. **Special note:** Motor homes over 22 feet long are "discouraged" by the park from using the stretch of highway between Buckeye Flat Campground and the Giant Forest. **Locator:** THREE RIVERS. **See map on page:** 138.

5. HIGHWAY 155, KERN COUNTY

It was late on a Sunday night. We were driving from Kings Canyon National Park, looking for a shortcut to Kernville. On the map, Highway 155 looked like a reasonable choice. Sixty-four miles and thousands of turns later, we descended an 11 percent grade to arrive at Kernville. At that point, we soothed our nerves with a six-pack—which calmed us down enough to the point we could go get a real drink. The next day we told a ranger about our drive. "That's too bad you did it at night," she said. "You missed all the oaks and ranches. The forest around Alta Sierra is some of the prettiest land around here." Only later did we learn how right she was.

Directions: From Bakersfield take Highway 99 north for 25 miles to Delano, exiting to Highway 155 east. The first 10 miles are a straight shot through Central Valley farmland. The next 44 miles are Howdy Doody time. **Locator:** DELANO. **See map on page:** 139.

6. JALAMA BEACH ROAD, SANTA BARBARA COUNTY

The beach is great, but the road is better. Twisting and winding through pretty ranchland for 14 miles, the road connects Highway 1 to Jalama Beach, the farthest beach from the Pacific Coast Highway in the state. Go in the springtime, when everything is green except the cows. The road is narrow, so be careful.

Directions: From Santa Barbara take U.S. 101 north for 35 miles to Gaviota, exiting north onto Highway 1. Take Highway 1 for 13 miles and turn left on Jalama Beach Road. **Locator:** JALAMA BEACH. **See map on page:** 174.

7. HIGHWAY 33, VENTURA COUNTY

Recently designated a state scenic byway, Highway 33 provides a taste of rural California reminiscent of Ventura County's agricultural heritage. After Ojai, development is sparse, except for some fruit stands, citrus groves, and small businesses, as the road twists uphill into the Sierra Madres. Here, you are surrounded by Los Padres National Forest, where there are a number of campgrounds and hiking/backpacking trails to both the Sespe and Matilija Wilderness Areas. After 56 miles, 33 eventually spits you out in the remote southwestern corner of the Great Central Valley.

Directions: From Ventura take U.S. 101 north, exiting east onto Highway 33. **Locator:** OJAI. **See map on page:** 190.

8. HIGHWAY 127, INYO AND SAN BERNARDINO COUNTIES

The 88-mile stretch of Highway 127 between Death Valley Junction in the north and Interstate 15 in the south is some of the loneliest road you'll ever find. Steve drove this road on a Saturday afternoon and saw two cars in the first 27 miles. This is serious desert; it's beautiful in the golden light of winter. This is a great backdoor entrance to Death Valley National Park, especially for those living east of Los Angeles and San Diego. Gas it up before you go. Call boxes are basically nonexistent.

Directions: From the Southland take Interstate 15 east to Baker and exit north onto Highway 127. **Locator:** BAKER. **See maps on pages:** 115 and 242.

9. RIM OF THE WORLD SCENIC BYWAY, SAN BERNARDINO COUNTY

"Ladies and gentlemen, we are making our final approach into Los Angeles . . . ." It only seems like you're flying when driving Highway 18 between San Bernardino and Big Bear Lake at night. The lights of San Bernardino and the Inland Empire are far,

far below and it very much feels like you really are peering off the rim of the world.

Directions: From Los Angeles take Interstate 10 east, exiting at Interstate 215 north. Take Interstate 215 to Highway 30 east; soon thereafter, exit north at Highway 18. **Locator:** RUNNING SPRINGS. **See map on page:** 242.

10. MULHOLLAND DRIVE, LOS ANGELES COUNTY

"Fifty-five miles of scenic splendor" is how Mulholland Drive was billed when construction of this twisting road was completed in 1924. Stretching from Hollywood through the Santa Monica Mountains to the ocean, this famed thoroughfare boasts equally mesmerizing views of the city and the mountains. The road can also be used to access three state parks in the Santa Monicas—Stunt Ranch, Paramount Ranch, and Peter Strauss Ranch—as well as the Arroyo Sequit before ending at Leo Carrillo State Beach in Malibu. One small problem: Between Encino and Woodland Hills, Mulholland is a dirt road closed to through traffic. Detour around it on Ventura Boulevard, one of the ugliest stretches of road in America.

Directions: In Los Angeles, Mulholland Drive can be accessed from Laurel Canyon Road, Coldwater Canyon Road, Beverly Glen Drive, Interstate 405, and Topanga Canyon Boulevard. **Locator:** BEVERLY HILLS and SANTA MONICA MOUNTAINS. **See map on page:** 206.

11. ANGELES CREST HIGHWAY, LOS ANGELES COUNTY

It took workers 27 years to complete the Angeles Crest Highway (Highway 2), the winding mountain byway through the San Gabriel Mountains. In fact, a companion road east of the highway was washed out and abandoned after the great flood of 1938. Upon completion in 1956, the Angeles Crest finally gave firefighters access to difficult-to-reach forest fires. The road passes more than a dozen trailheads, including the Pacific Crest Trail.

Directions: From Interstate 215, exit north onto Highway 2. **Locator:** LA CANADA. **See map on page:** 206.

12. ORTEGA HIGHWAY, ORANGE COUNTY

This road begins innocently enough in San Juan Capistrano before rising into the Santa Ana Mountains and Cleveland National Forest. The road is narrow and there are voluminous twists and turns—speeding fines are doubled, so be careful. This is also a very popular ride for motorcyclists, most of whom seem to believe they are racing for the Kawasaki factory team. After 25 miles, the road finally descends to Lake Elsinore.

Directions: Take Interstate 5 to San Juan Capistrano and exit east onto Highway 74. **Locator:** SAN JUAN CAPISTRANO. **See map on page:** 264.

13. HIGHWAY 76, SAN DIEGO COUNTY

Welcome to the Pauma Valley, one of the prettiest agricultural valleys in Southern California. Stop and buy a bag of tangerines at a fruit stand at the junction of Highway 76 and Interstate 15 and then enjoy the ride through the valley before turning left on County Road S7 and going straight up Palomar Mountain. Breathtaking views abound.

Directions: From Corona take Interstate 15 south for 48 miles, then exit east onto Highway 76. **Locator:** PALO-

MAR MOUNTAIN STATE PARK. **See map on page:** 265.

14. HIGHWAY 78, SAN DIEGO COUNTY

The road begins at Interstate 15 in Escondido and then travels 75 miles through subalpine mountains and valleys before descending into Anza-Borrego Desert State Park and finally ending at the seemingly lifeless Salton City. At the far end of the road, pick your way down to the smelly Salton Sea, once slated for development as a resort destination until common sense intervened. A lovely shortcut: Leave Highway 78 at the village of Wynola and take Wynola Road for 3.5 miles, where it rejoins Highway 78.

Directions: Take Interstate 15 to Escondido and exit east onto Highway 78. **Locator:** ESCONDIDO. **See map on page:** 265.

• TOP RATINGS •

THE TOP 11 HOT SPRINGS AND MINERAL BATHS

There's no shortage of geothermal activity in Southern California, meaning there's no shortage of naturally occurring hot springs.

In layman's terms, hot springs occur when groundwater comes into contact with lava or magma which has worked its way upward through the earth's crust. The heated groundwater then circulates back to the earth's surface (heat rises!) and collects in pools, flows out of rock surfaces, or finds its way into an existing creek. If the water is more than 15 degrees warmer than the annual air temperature at a given location, the spring is officially designated a hot spring.

On its way to the surface the hot water dissolves rocks—thus the term "mineral water." For centuries, people have believed that this mineral water (which often includes stinky sulfur) had healing powers. No one really knows if that's scientific fact. However, anecdotal evidence points to the truth that a long soak often doesn't suck.

Most of Southern California's best-known hot springs are on private property and are run as private resorts. You'll have to pay for a soak at these places, which usually charge by the hour.

There are still many more hot springs that lie on public lands and can be used for free. Always—not sometimes—test the water before getting in. The water temperature can vary. For example, the water in the Sespe Hot Springs hovers near 200 degrees, which is way too hot for a soak. But if you go just a little farther downstream, the water is very comfortable. Also watch out for broken glass around hot springs; studies have shown previous users of hot springs are often slobs and idiots.

PRIVATE RESORTS

1. AVILA HOT SPRINGS AND RV PARK, SAN LUIS OBISPO COUNTY

Hot springs and Winnebagos? It's actually weirder than it sounds, but you can soak by the hour at this private resort, which dates back to 1897.

Directions: From Santa Barbara take U.S. 101 north for 95 miles, exiting at Avila Beach Road and turning left. The park is at 250 Avila Beach Road. **Contact:** Avila Hot Springs and RV Park, (805) 595-7302. **Locator:** AVILA BEACH. **See featured trip page:** 109.

2. Sycamore Mineral Springs, San Luis Obispo County

Sycamore Mineral Springs offers motel rooms with private tubs that tap into the springs' hot sulfur water. There are tubs located outside in a forest of sycamore and live oaks. The resort is near U.S. 101 just south of San Luis Obispo.

Directions: From Santa Barbara take U.S. 101 north for 95 miles, exiting at Avila Beach Road and turning left. Sycamore Mineral Springs will be on the left. **Contact:** Sycamore Mineral Springs, (805) 595-7302 or (800) 234-5831. **Locator:** AVILA BEACH. **See map on page:** 100.

3. California Hot Springs, Tulare County

Every day 350,000 gallons of 125-degree water come out of the springs, which are located beneath a series of rock cliffs. The resort is really an RV park, the latest incarnation on this land to have captured the water for recreational purposes. Sequoia National Forest surrounds the resort on three sides. The springs are available to RV guests or walk-ons.

Directions: From Los Angeles take Interstate 5 north to Grapevine and exit north onto Highway 99. At County Road J22, turn right and continue to the RV park. **Contact:** California Hot Springs, (805) 548-6582. **Locator:** CALIFORNIA HOT SPRINGS. **See map on page:** 138.

4. Glen Ivy Hot Springs, Riverside County

This is the mother of all hot springs resorts and it gets the mother of all crowds, too. "Big and obnoxious," says one of our friends, who coincidentally is also big and obnoxious. The main attraction is an Olympic-sized pool with piped-in mineral water from the hot springs. There are also whirlpools, clay baths, champagne baths (don't ask), and massage therapists who will turn your muscles into pizza dough.

Directions: From Anaheim take Highway 91 east for 15 miles to Interstate 15 south. Drive eight miles and exit at Temescal Canyon Road, turning right. Drive one mile; the road ends at Glen Ivy. **Contact:** Glen Ivy Hot Springs, (909) 277-3529. **Locator:** CORONA. **See map on page:** 243.

HOT SPRINGS ON PUBLIC LAND

5. Kern Hot Spring, Tulare County

The upside: This hot spring is in a beautiful, remote place deep within Sequoia National Park. The downside: It's at least a three-day backpacking trip from the nearest road. But it's always nice to have something to dream about, right?

Directions: If you are really serious about hiking the High Sierra Trail, you have already been studying your topos for months. Hint: Kern Hot Spring is just north of Chagooba Falls, alongside the mighty Kern River. **Contact:** Sequoia National Park, (209) 565-3134. **Locator:** SEQUOIA NATIONAL PARK. **See featured trip page:** 145.

6. Miracle Hot Springs, Kern County

Like many of the hot springs on public lands, this site once contained a hotel, but it burned down in 1975. All that remains are the rock tubs built around the hot springs, which can be found by taking a short trail from Hobo Campground on the south side of Highway 178.

Directions: From the town of Lake Isabella take Highway 178 south into the

Kern River Canyon. After five miles, turn left into the parking area for Hobo Campground. The trail to the hot springs begins at the south end of the campground. **Contact:** Sequoia National Forest, Greenhorn Ranger District, (805) 871-2223. **Locator:** LAKE ISABELLA. **See map on page:** 139.

7. TECOPA HOT SPRINGS COUNTY PARK, INYO COUNTY

If there wasn't a hot spring on this land, it's doubtful the place would ever have been touched by man. The hot springs, which are the main attraction of this campground, are free to the public. Bathhouses have been constructed around the springs, and there are separate facilities for men and women because bathers have to be naked (they also have to shower first) to prevent any diseases from getting into the pools via someone's swimsuit. Don't make this a destination, but it's an interesting stopping point between Death Valley National Park and Baker on Highway 127. The springs are closed Tuesdays, Sundays, and Fridays from 7 A.M. to noon.

Directions: From Baker take Highway 127 north for 53 miles to the park entrance on your right. From Furnace Creek in Death Valley, take Highway 190 east for 27 miles to Highway 127, turning right at Death Valley Junction. Drive 35 miles south to the park entrance on your left. **Contact:** Inyo County Parks, (760) 852-4264. **Locator:** TECOPA. **See map on page:** 115.

8. AGUA CALIENTE HOT SPRING, SANTA BARBARA COUNTY

This popular hot spring makes for a perfect day trip from Santa Barbara. A resort was once here, but it burned to the ground long ago. The tubs are lined with concrete and there are changing rooms. Before soaking take a hike upstream along Big Agua Caliente Creek—an especially nice hike in the spring or fall.

Directions: From Santa Barbara take Highway 154 north for eight miles. At East Camino Cielo, turn right and drive 22 miles—this will turn into a maintained dirt road. At Juncal Camuesa Road (also known as Pendola Road), turn left and drive nine miles to Middle Santa Ynez Campground. Turn right and follow the road to the Caliente picnic area and hot spring. **Contact:** Los Padres National Forest, Santa Barbara Ranger District, (805) 967-3481. **Locator:** SAN MARCOS PASS. **See map on page:** 174.

9. LAS CRUCES HOT SPRING, SANTA BARBARA COUNTY

This isn't the nicest or hottest spring you'll find—it's a little on the stinky side—but it's a short hike in Gaviota State Park from U.S. 101 if you're headed to or from the Central Coast.

Directions: From Santa Barbara to the Gaviota Peak trailhead, take U.S. 101 north for 35 miles and exit at Highway 1 north. At the top of the exit ramp, make a hairpin turn to the right onto a small road paralleling the exit ramp. Continue about 200 hundred yards until the road ends at the parking area. Self-register and pay the $2 day-use fee at the gate. Follow the fire road uphill to a marked footpath leading to the hot spring. **Contact:** Gaviota State Park, (805) 968-1711. **Locator:** GAVIOTA STATE PARK. **See map on page:** 174.

10. SESPE HOT SPRINGS, VENTURA COUNTY

Only those planning on camping in the Sespe Wilderness in Los Padres

National Forest will visit the Sespe Hot Springs. Why? It's a hard 17.5-mile hike to the hot springs from the trailhead at Lion's Campground. Be very, very careful of the water here, which can reach 200 degrees and put you in the hospital. Soak downstream!

Directions: From Ojai take Highway 33 north for nine miles to Rose Valley Road and turn right. The trail begins at the locked gate at the end of the road. **Contact:** Los Padres National Forest, Ojai Ranger District, (805) 646-4348. **Locator:** SESPE WILDERNESS. **See featured trip page:** 194.

11. DEEP CREEK HOT SPRINGS, SAN BERNARDINO COUNTY

This destination in San Bernardino National Forest requires a 12-mile round-trip hike on the Pacific Crest Trail. Nonetheless, the hot springs are very popular on most weekends and often attract small crowds. Keep in mind that bathing suits are required, although many hikers seem to "forget"; stay away if you're afraid of Naked People.

Directions: From Interstate 15, exit to Highway 138 and head east. At Highway 173, turn left and follow the road for eight miles until it becomes a dirt road; look for the trailhead and parking area for the Pacific Crest Trail. Start on the trail, cross the Mojave Flood Control Dam, and then pick up the trail on the other side of the dam. Hike up the creek, following occasional signs to Deep Creek Hot Springs. **Contact:** San Bernardino National Forest, Arrowhead Ranger District, (909) 337-2444. **Locator:** HESPERIA. **See map on page:** 242.

Part 2:
SOUTHERN CALIFORNIA COUNTIES

16
SAN LUIS OBISPO COUNTY

• Featured Trips •

Lake San Antonio 101
Morro Bay 103
Montana de Oro
    State Park 105
Pismo State Beach
    and Company 107
Lopez Lake 110

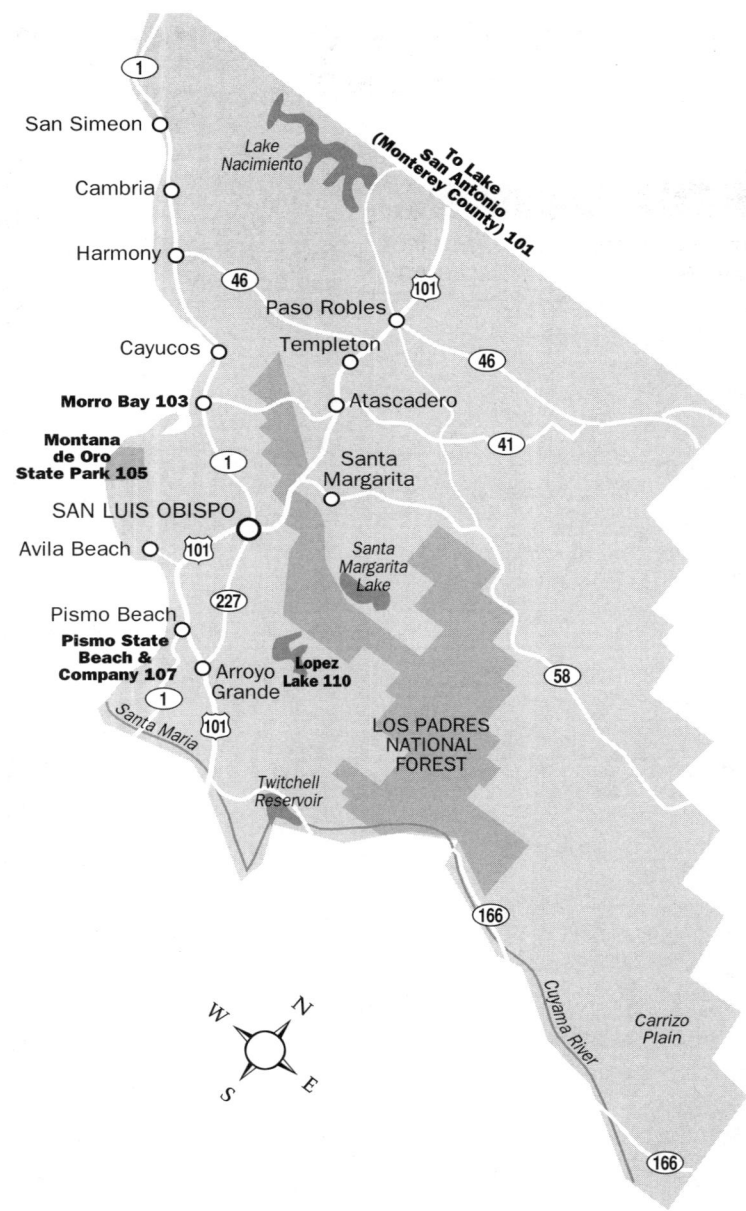

SAN LUIS OBISPO COUNTY

• FEATURED TRIP •

LAKE SAN ANTONIO
North of Paso Robles, near the Monterey County line

It was the first weekend in March and about a dozen birders were gathered in a boat on Lake San Antonio to hopefully see one of the dozen or so bald eagles wintering at the lake. We figured that even if the great birds pulled a no-show, being on a lake for three hours with a bunch of birdwatchers would probably pass as entertainment.

The roofless platform pulled away from the dock at 1 P.M. Just minutes later, we were up to our eyeballs in wildlife. On the shore, a dozen deer grazed on deep, green grass. A few hundred yards away, a turkey vulture stood on a tree stump with its wings sticking straight out—its way of drying its feathers. A great blue heron flew by. On the shore, watusi cattle grazed—a local rancher had imported them from Africa. On the starboard side of the boat, two grebes performed their mating ritual, literally running on the water.

At this point our trip was 15 minutes old.

And then we saw the bald eagle. Perched on a tree about 200 yards away was a big brown clump. Through binoculars the eagle looked like one you'd see imprinted on a quarter. The brilliant white head was just the same as on the cover of all those birding books we always see in bookstores. Its huge yellow talons wrapped around the branch.

The eagle looked down a few times, noticing us. And then it took flight, showing off its seven-foot wingspan. Across the lake it soared before diving down and grabbing something out of the water. Ranger Steve, our guide on the tour, mentioned that an eagle can see a fish in the water from a mile away; in other words, eagles can see with the naked eye what we have to use ordinary field binoculars to see. Thus, the term "eagle eyed."

The eagle immediately went to a tree on the north side of the lake, and we followed. There, the boat was able to pull within 100 yards of the eagle—the tours try to never get any closer for fear of bothering the birds. Through our binoculars we could see the eagle skinning a fish; twice it picked up the fish by the tail and waved it around. Maybe he was proud of his catch.

Before the two-hour eagle tour was over, we saw five more bald eagles, along with a whole range of waterfowl including Canada geese, white pelicans, red-tailed hawks, cormorants, and a woodpecker, among others. According to Ranger Steve, it's fairly rare that the eagle tours are shut out, although it has happened (Mother Nature doesn't believe in "or your money back" guarantees).

Lake San Antonio offers eagle tours in January and February every winter, although the bald eagles generally begin to arrive from the Pacific Northwest in November and December before departing sometime in March or April. Tours leave twice a day on weekends (at 9:30 A.M. and 12:30 P.M.) and, generally speaking, the afternoon tour is usually the more comfortable of the two weather-wise. The tours last about two to two and a half hours.

Lake San Antonio, like most lakes

in California, is a reservoir, formed by the construction of a dam in 1965. Surrounded mostly by rolling hills of grass and dotted with clusters of oaks, the lake sits amid some of the Central Coast's prettiest ranchland—a reminder of how California must have looked a century ago.

The lake can be ungodly hot in the summer—100-degree days are not unusual—when it hosts a regular army of water-skiers and "partiers," according to Ranger Steve. If the weather pulls through for you, January and February temperatures can be pleasantly mild; we had 65 degrees and sunny on the first Saturday in March. On the other hand, winter weather can also be cold, rainy, foggy, and possibly snowy.

The lake makes a convenient side trip from Paso Robles or the great town of San Luis Obispo—there is plenty of hiking and fishing available, too. If the weather holds, you may want to consider camping along the lake's north shore. San Antonio is one of the very few lakes in the state that allow campers to pitch a tent or park RVs at lakeside.

At one point on our eagle tour, we passed some motor home people sunning themselves, totally unaware that a bald eagle was perched in a tree next to their campsite. Even when our boat stopped and a dozen people with binoculars began staring at their campsite, these folks still didn't catch on—they must have thought we were admiring their portable satellite dish.

Why do eagles like Lake San Antonio? Bald eagles, like many other waterfowl, fly south on the Pacific Flyway when it comes time to migrate for the winter. The flyway is basically a bird's version of a freeway that stretches over the west coast of North America. The eagles, looking for fresh water with lots of fish and insects, often choose to winter at remote lakes where there is little contact with humans. Over the years, San Antonio has proven to be one of the most consistent habitats for the eagles; 72 were spotted here in 1984, although numbers have declined somewhat in recent years.

Directions: From San Luis Obispo take U.S. 101 north for 25 miles to the exit for County Road G14 in the town of Paso Robles. Continue on scenic G14 for 26 miles to the Lake San Antonio South Shore entrance. At the entry gate, have the ranger point the way to the marina. **Fees:** Day-use entrance to Lake San Antonio is $6 per vehicle. Eagle Watch Tours are $8 per person, $6 for senior citizens on Fridays, and $17 for the Sunday brunch tour, which includes food and champagne. There's also a $3 fee for those wanting to make a reservation. **Maps:** A small map of the lake is given to you upon entry to the park. **Pets:** Dogs are allowed, on leash, on the park's trails. Dogs are not allowed on the eagle watch boats. **Camping and cabins:** The lake's south shore has three campgrounds with 458 tent and RV sites, including some with full or partial hookups. The south shore also has a marina, grocery store, boat rentals, and a service station. The lake's north shore has four miles of shoreline available to campers. For reservations or information, phone (805) 472-2311. One- to three-bedroom cabins are available for rental on the lake's south shore. For rates and reservations, phone (805) 472-2313. **Rental boats:** The marina rents everything under the sun, including fishing boats, ski boats, jet skis, and patio boats. For more information, phone the marina, (805) 472-2818. **Contact:** Lake San Antonio, (805) 472-2311. For Eagle Watch Tour reservations, phone Monterey County Parks, (408) 755-4899. **Locator:** LAKE SAN ANTONIO.

PASO ROBLES

Paso Robles is kind of like a miniature, rural San Luis Obispo. The land surrounding the town is covered with several vineyards (many of which are open for wine tasting) and ranches. The area offers one of the better fall color displays in this part of the state. The town is about 20 miles from both Lake Nacimiento and Lake San Antonio and has several inns and motels, including the always reliable Best Western [Phone: (805) 246-4740], and Travelodge [Phone: (805) 238-0078].

• FEATURED TRIP •

MORRO BAY
West of San Luis Obispo

Morro Bay is to birds what O'Hare Airport is to weary holiday travelers. The bay's estuary is a place where weary birds, migrating south for the winter on the Pacific Flyway, can take a break and rest their poor little wings.

However, there is one notable difference between the bay and the airport: Morro Bay is certainly more fit for human habitation than O'Hare.

The best way to see Morro Bay and the thousands of birds it hosts is in a kayak or canoe. The bay covers 2,100 acres and its waters are smooth because a sand spit protects it from the Pacific Ocean. The sand spit is four miles long—it's part of Montana de Oro State Park—and makes a perfect destination for ambitious kayakers.

A large part of the bay is actually part of Morro Bay State Park. The park's marina rents kayaks and canoes, as does Kayaks of Morro Bay at 611 Embarcadero in the town of Morro Bay. The state park also has a campground down the road from the marina; the town of Morro Bay has no shortage of motels.

Check the tide tables before heading out into the bay. Generally, it's preferable to be out at high tide because it lessens the chance of getting stuck in the mudflats; someone at the marina will surely remind you that if you get stuck, they'll still charge you for the time for someone to come and rescue you. High tide also makes it easier to land on the sand spit and navigate the many small streams that cut through the mud, allowing you to get closer to the birds.

If you're into wildlife, bring along a laminated bird guide or field book. There's a good chance that you will see several species of birds in just a few hours.

The sand spit is totally uninhabited (other than by mule deer) and undeveloped. The whole narrow piece of land is comprised entirely of sand dunes. It's a wild place to picnic because you have the Pacific Ocean on one side, the bay and the estuary on the other, and 578-foot-tall Morro Rock looming overhead—smack next to three tall smokestacks, courtesy of a Pacific Gas and Electric Company power plant. Needless to say, it's an interesting juxtaposition.

The kayaking can be great throughout the year if the weather cooperates. But there's something in the air—literally—during the winter months when tens of thousands of birds descend upon the estuary. Our

SAN LUIS OBISPO COUNTY

advice: Enjoy the spectacle, cover your head, and wear white clothing.

Directions: To reach the Morro Bay State Park marina from San Luis Obispo, take Highway 1 north for 11 miles, exiting at South Bay Boulevard. At State Park Road, turn right and follow the road into Morro Bay State Park. Just as the road begins turning sharply to the right, the entrance to the marina will be on the left. **Fees:** There is no day-use fee. **Maps:** A free map of the park is available at the park's Museum of Natural History on State Park Road. Museum hours are 10 A.M. to 5 P.M. daily except for Christmas, Thanksgiving, and New Year's Day. We also recommend the "Enviromap Guide to Seashore Life," which is published by Etech and can be purchased at the visitor center. **Pets:** Dogs are permitted in the campground only, where they must be leashed. **Kayak and canoe rentals:** Both kayaks and canoes can be rented at the Morro Bay State Park marina; kayaks are $6 an hour for a single and $10 an hour for a double. For more information, phone the marina at (805) 772-8796. Kayaks can also be rented in the town of Morro Bay, at Kayaks of Morro Bay (805-772-1119) or Kayak Horizons (805-772-6444). **Camping:** Morro Bay State Park has 134 sites for tents and RVs in a nice, shady camp. Only 20 sites have hookups. Facilities include flush toilets, showers, picnic tables, and fire grills. Camping fees range from $14 to $16 per night. For reservations, which are recommended during the summer, phone PARK.NET, (800) 444-7275. **Contact:** Morro Bay State Park, (805) 772-7434; Morro Bay Chamber of Commerce, (805) 772-4467 in CA and (800) 231-0592 outside CA. **Locator:** MORRO BAY.

A MORRO BAY WEEKEND GETAWAY

Morro Bay's kind of a funny looking town, seemingly built more for the needs of tourists than residents. On the charm scale, we'd rate Morro Bay below Santa Barbara, but above Ventura. There are plenty of fairly cheap motels near the water—we stayed at the perfectly adequate Best Western El Rancho. Phone: (805) 772-2212.

The downtown area is more schmaltz than substance. A walk down the town's embarcadero takes you past restaurants with names like The Finicky Fish, Fish Shanty, The Great American Fish Company, The Whale's Tail, The Fish Bowl, and, of course, The Galley.

Summer brings beachgoers, anglers, hikers, bikers, campers, and kayakers. Winter is very quiet, with boating and whale watching the primary activities. If cursing at a little white ball is your thing, there's a nice golf course over in the state park.

Our food favorite: Breakfast at Dorn's Original Breakers Cafe, 801 Market Street. Phone: (805) 772-4415.

WHAT'S AN ESTUARY?

According to the official Morro Boy Estuary guide, "Estuaries—where rivers and creeks meet the sea and fresh water mixes with salt—are among the earth's richest and most productive habitats."

In the case of Morro Bay, the estuary is formed by two creeks bringing runoff water from the Santa Lucia Mountains into the bay. The water also brings sand and silt, which results in the nutritious (to birds, that is) mudflats that cover two-thirds of the bay at low tide. Unfortunately, too much silt and sand are filling up Morro Bay too quickly—the result of erosion caused by overdevelopment.

More than 70 types of birds reside in the bay, including two dozen threatened species, such as peregrine falcons, Brandt's cormorants, brown pelicans, the Morro Bay kangaroo rat, and the black rail.

• FEATURED TRIP •

MONTANA DE ORO STATE PARK
West of San Luis Obispo, on the Central Coast

Once upon a time, the bluffs above the ocean in Montana de Oro State Park served as a replica for Normandy Beach. The U.S. military, in the process of training its troops for the June 1944 invasion of France, needed someplace that presented similar obstacles: a difficult beach landing for the infantry, followed by a challenging climb up the cliffs and bluffs while under heavy bombardment.

Today, Montana de Oro isn't quite as remote as it was then, nor is it as noisy—even though one piece of unexploded ordnance was found in the park in 1995. Often the only sounds are the wind and the surf pounding the rugged coast, as well as a few hoots and hollers from some of the 131 species of birds that have been spotted in the park. Along the coast, the windswept dunes tumble down to the immense, rugged bluffs, which offer beautiful vistas of the California coastline. On the clearest of days, it's possible to see 100 miles north to Big Sur.

The park is one of the largest—as well as the most beautiful—in the state system, covering nearly 8,000 acres. It has seven miles of coastline, with sandy trails that hug the tops of bluffs and lead down to coves and tidepools. In addition, the park includes a large backcountry with several trails following inland streams and others climbing peaks that are covered with poppies and wildflowers in the spring. Thus the Spanish name Montana de Oro, which translates to "Mountain of Gold."

A good starting point is the visitor center, which can be found along Los Osos Valley Road, three miles past the park entrance (we told you the park is big). The center sits on a hill overlooking the large beach at Spooner's Cove, a popular spot for picnicking, sunbathing, and general frolicking. To the north of the cove, the Dune Trail hugs the top of the bluffs, with several small trails descending to the rocky coastline.

At the far northern end of the park, there is a sand spit that extends four miles into Morro Bay before ending just shy of Morro Rock. Make no mistake about it: Visiting the sand spit is mandatory. Why? Because it's one of the most unusual landforms in the state. The thing most noticeable about the spit is that it's narrow, no more than a hundred yards wide in some places. It's really all sand and dunes, but check out these views while walking north: On the left, there's the Pacific Ocean; straight ahead, there's 578-foot-tall Morro Rock, commonly known as the Gibraltar of the Pacific; and to the right is the Morro Bay estuary, which tens of thousands of birds call home.

Another great way to access the sand spit is to take the Rim Trail down from Los Osos Valley Road—parking is on your right, immediately after entering the park. This trail cuts through a eucalyptus forest, planted by an early rancher who was hoping to make some money logging. In time, he learned that eucalyptus are ornamental trees, not logging trees. (As Homer Simpson says, "Doh!") The result, however, is a beautiful, if unlikely, forest.

Three other trails are worthy of mention:

The Bluff Trail extends south from Spooner's Cove all the way to the park's southern border. Corallina Cove and Quarry Cove are accessible from the trail; both are good places to go tidepooling. Likely finds in and around the tidepools here include sand crabs, sand dollars, gooseneck barnacles, sea stars, tidepool sculpin (small fish), anemones, and shield limpets.

Coon Creek Road and Isley Creek Road both follow creeks uphill into the park's higher reaches. Both are good—although strenuous—mountain biking trails, as are Hazard Canyon Road (just inside the park's border) and the Ridge Trail. Both trails are accessible from the park's main road.

If you only have a day, go for a walk under the bluffs or, better yet, get out on the sand spit. Sit down and have a picnic. Bring along a deep thought, a good book, or a warm companion. And, don't forget the camera. There's enough scenery here to fill a photo album.

If you find yourself looking up at the bluffs and wondering about all the diagonal stripes, the explanation for this can be found just off the coast of California, where two tectonic plates are rubbing against one another. The result of this high-level friction is that ancient, layered seafloors are gradually being pushed to the earth's surface.

Directions: From downtown Los Angeles take U.S. 101 north for 199 miles to San Luis Obispo. Exit at Los Osos Valley Road, turn left, and drive five miles. Los Osos will bear to the left and turn into Pecho Valley Road. Continue to the park entrance—there isn't any entrance gate, but there is a sign. **Fees:** Admission to the park is free. **Maps:** A small map of the park can be purchased at the visitor center for $1. **Pets:** Dogs are permitted in the park and campground, but they must be leashed and are not allowed on trails. **Camping:** There are 50 sites for tents and RVs in a pretty little campground behind the visitor center with plenty of oaks for shade. Facilities include pit toilets, piped water (bring your own drinking water), picnic tables, and fire grills. Several of the sites are called "environmental sites," meaning they require a short hike from the parking lot. Fees are $8 to $10 per night. For reservations, which are advised during the summer, phone PARK.NET at (800) 444-7275. **Contact:** Montana de Oro State Park, (805) 528-0513 or (805) 772-7434 between 9 A.M. and 3 P.M. **Locator:** MONTANA DE ORO STATE PARK.

SAN LUIS OBISPO: JEWEL OF THE CENTRAL COAST

For our money, San Luis Obispo is one of the nicest cities in all of Southern California. It's just a 15-minute drive from SLO to either Montana de Oro or Morro Bay. San Simeon is also only 40 miles north.

San Luis (pronounced Lewis) Obispo, with a population of just over 40,000 and a noticeable absence of strip malls, resembles a junior version of Santa Barbara—although SLO has the advantage of not being overrun by

Angelenos every weekend. In particular, the town has a beautiful downtown area centered around a historic mission and bisected by a creek. Many of the town's buildings are made of brick. The city has soul!

The accommodations are downright affordable—there are plenty of motel rooms in the $50 to $70 range. Most of the motels are located on Monterey Street, near U.S. 101—we like a no-frills motel called The Sands, which accepts dogs. Phone: (800) 441-4657. Downtown is about a one-mile walk from the motel or a two-minute drive. Because SLO is also a college town (California Polytechnic State University), food and drink are cheap.

The only downside to the city is the fact that some of the major retail chains have moved into its shopping district in the last few years, including an immense Victoria's Secret. Who exactly is wearing all that lingerie in such a small town is a mystery.

THE CHINA SYNDROME, PART II?

What's the story with all the air raid sirens in Montana de Oro State Park? Pacific Gas and Electric Company's Diablo Canyon nuclear power plant is just south of the park. Diablo Canyon also happens to be sitting near an earthquake fault, which didn't exactly make it a very popular project in the eyes of many area residents. Although PG&E has lost millions of dollars on the plant since building it, the company insists the place is there to stay—and it's safe. Probably the best that can be said is that so far they've been right.

• FEATURED TRIP •

PISMO STATE BEACH AND COMPANY
On the sandy Central Coast

One of the great stretches of beach coastline in Southern California just happens to be in a place where the weather sometimes fails to cooperate: the oft-foggy, oft-chilly Central Coast. When it's sunny and warm—bingo! When it's not—well, don't say we didn't warn you.

From south to north, the beaches (in order) are: Oceano Dunes State Vehicular Recreation Area, Pismo State Beach, Shell Beach, and, finally, Avila State Beach. All told, there are about 23 miles of almost-uninterrupted sand here. At the right time of the year—between Labor Day and Memorial Day—beachgoers will often have the beach to themselves.

What's there to do? Vegetating on the beach is our number one activity here—lessons are probably available through most community colleges for those unskilled in this fine art. Those needing greater stimulation should consider swimming, fishing, surfing, kite flying, camping, horseback riding, and/or repeated trips to the ice cream stand. Those with dogs will be pleased to hear that this is one of the few state beaches where dogs are welcome—as long as they are on leash.

1. OCEANO DUNES STATE VEHICULAR RECREATION AREA

This is actually the southern half of Pismo State Beach. The beach is four miles long—stretching from Oso Flaco in the south to Grover City in the north. As you probably guessed from the name, cars are permitted on the beach. It's a tradition dating back to earlier in the century, when the beaches offered the best roads to area residents.

Truth be told, it's an unsettling sight at first—then again, it beats parking four miles away. One ranger explained it to us this way: "There's not much cars can do to the sand." Indeed, more often the question is what can the sand do to the cars? Once in a while, it gets people stuck.

Behind the beach are a network of dunes where off-road vehicles are permitted. This is the downside of the beach. Although the ATVs probably aren't hurting the sand much either, they sure are loud. Plus, it's difficult to understand why anyone in Southern California would want to spend more time in a car.

At the southern end of the state beach is the Pismo Dunes Natural Preserve, the largest network of coastal sand dunes in the state—complete with small Oso Flaco Lake, which is crossed by a boardwalk. This part of the beach often receives scant attention even when the rest of the beach to the north is crowded.

Directions: See directions for Pismo State Beach below. **Locator:** PISMO STATE BEACH.

2. PISMO STATE BEACH AND SHELL BEACH

The remainder of Pismo State Beach—from the Grover City entrance to the Pismo Beach Pier and beyond to Shell Beach—is for pedestrians only. The beach is incredibly wide—much larger than even the largest of the Los Angeles County beaches. In back of the beach is a small network of dunes that provide an overview of the whole place.

Unfortunately, there are few places remaining in Southern California where horses can be ridden on the beach. Fortunately, Pismo State Beach is one of them. The Livery Stable, located in Oceano at 1205 Silver Spur Place, rents horses and provides boarding for people with their own horses. Phone the stables at (805) 489-8100 or e-mail them at: silspur@ix.netcom.com.

Pismo Beach is an old beach town—emphasis on old. It's more or less the capital of the "Five Cities" region of the Central Coast (from south to north, Arroyo Grande, Oceano, Grover City, Pismo Beach, Shell Beach, and the unofficial sixth city, Avila Beach) and the place where most tourists stay. Depending on the lighting and your frame of mind, Pismo Beach borders between seedy and charming in an Addams Family kind of way. A better description: If you think La Jolla is as good as it gets, you'll hate Pismo. If you find La Jolla snooty and pretentious, Pismo is your kind of place.

The town has a variety of motels and hotels, ranging from the almost-condemned to the very expensive. Two nice places to stay with great views are a pair of Best Westerns, both of which sit on bluffs above the ocean: the Shore Cliff Lodge [Phone: (805) 773-4671] and the Shelter Cove Lodge [Phone: (805) 773-3511].

Shell Beach is the large swath of sand north of the Pismo Beach Pier. At the northern end, the beach narrows and bluffs begin to rise behind the beach. The scenery becomes more "classic" Central Coast; there are small pocket beaches all the way up to Avila Beach.

The town center of Shell Beach is only three blocks long, and there are buildings on just one side of the street. The other side of the street is an embankment up to U.S. 101. We had a pleasant stay at the Spyglass Inn, which sits on a bluff that provides ocean views, as well as a southern vista of the "Five Cities" area. The motel often has deals going in the low season, and it permits dogs in some rooms. Phone: (805) 773-5298

If you go just a little north of the Spyglass on Shell Beach Road, there is a walkway next to the Cliffs at Shell Beach hotel; the path leads down to a beautiful beach.

Directions: To reach Pismo State Beach from Santa Barbara, take U.S. 101 north for 87 miles. Exit at Grand Avenue and turn left. Follow the road until it ends at the entrance gate to the beach. Use the Highway 1 exit for the town of Pismo Beach. **Fees:** The day-use fee for the beach is $6. **Maps:** The most adequate map of the area is the AAA map for San Luis Obispo County, available at many bookstores and at AAA offices. **Pets:** Dogs are allowed on Pismo State Beach and Shell Beach; they must be leashed. **Camping:** There are two campgrounds at Pismo State Beach: Pismo Coast Village and North Beach. The Coast Village is a cheesy stopover for motor homes. It even has a miniature golf course—need we say more? North Beach is much nicer, located near the dunes. It has 100 sites for tents and RVs. Facilities include flush toilets, picnic tables, and fire grills. Camping fees range from $17 to $24 per night. For reservations, which we recommend from spring through fall, phone PARK.NET, (800) 444-7275. For camping information, phone Pismo State Beach, (805) 489-2684. **Note:** Not every car is cut out for the beach. Certainly, four-wheel drives and many recreational vehicles will do just fine in the usually hard-packed sand. But some low-slung compacts may get stuck. Ask the ranger at the gate for her or his opinion. There is also some free parking on nearby streets (good luck!). **Contact:** Pismo State Beach, (805) 549-3312. **Locator:** PISMO STATE BEACH.

3. AVILA BEACH

Avila Beach is a tiny town tucked between a bluff and San Luis Bay. Avila Beach, the town, has a small business district half a dozen blocks long; right across the street is the state beach. This is, of course, terribly convenient for those bathers who feel the sudden need for a corn dog and a T-shirt. There's a pier that shoots right into the bay from downtown and is a splendid place to take in a sunset. The far northern end of the beach, called Olde Port Beach, narrows considerably and gets a little rocky. It's lightly used compared to the other beach, and we're glad to report this beach has welcomed our dog, Molly, on several occasions.

On the way to Avila Beach from U.S. 101, you'll pass a great farmer's market/petting zoo and then Sycamore Mineral Springs, a hotel that has mineral baths in the rooms, as well as a collection of tubs out back in a pretty, woodsy area. The hotel also has a famous restaurant called The Gardens of Avila. Phone the hotel at (805) 595-7302 or the restaurant at (805) 595-7365.

Directions: From Highway 1/U.S. 101, take the Avila Beach exit west. Once in town, continue west on Harford Drive. Olde Port Beach is located before the old wooden pier (Port San Luis, not the modern Union Oil pier).

Fees: Access is free. **Pets:** Leashed dogs are allowed at Avila State Beach, the first beach as you enter town. Olde Port Beach allows dogs off-leash (arf!). **Contact:** Port San Luis Harbor District, (805) 595-2381. **Locator:** AVILA BEACH.

WHERE'S THE CLAMS?

Pismo Beach was once famous for the Pismo clam. In the earlier part of this century, the large clams were plentiful and crowds delighted in digging up and taking home all the clams they could eat. Today, the clams still exist, but it is extremely difficult to find one that is $4^1/_2$ inches across, the legal size for harvest.

The general thinking is that the clams were so big in the past only because their natural predators suffered so greatly in the 1800s: sea otters were killed by Russian fur trappers and Native American populations fell drastically as a result of diseases brought to California by the Europeans and Russians. And, as you might expect, too many of the clams were taken throughout much of the twentieth century.

The clams have recovered—thanks to a ban on clam harvesting throughout much of the 1980s. But sea otters are back in huge numbers, too, and they often eat the clams before they can grow very large. Our loss, their gain.

If interested in clamming, contact a state park ranger to find out the current regulations—they change often. You'll need a fishing license and a clam fork, which can be purchased in the town of Pismo Beach. The fork should have a gauge on it to measure the clam (to make sure it's over $4^1/_2$ inches).

The best clamming is at low tide in about one foot of surf. Stick the fork in the ground and dig for the clam. If the clam isn't the right size, put it back where you found it with the open side of the clam facing out to sea.

CHEAP EATS

Clam chowder in a bread bowl is the "hamburger" of the central coast—every place seems to have it. Those not on a budget should check out the Olde Port Inn, on Avila Beach's Port San Luis Pier. It's a bit of a tourist spot, but the restaurant has hard-to-resist views of the sea—and not just out the picture windows. The tables are made of glass, allowing diners to look all the way down to the water beneath the pier. Port San Luis Pier is a working pier for commercial fishermen; there are vendors selling fresh seafood up and down the pier.

• **FEATURED TRIP** •

LOPEZ LAKE
East of San Luis Obispo, in the Santa Lucia foothills

The best time of year to go camping at Lopez Lake Recreation Area is, undoubtedly, early fall, just when the first hints of Thanksgiving are in the air.

During this time, the three-armed, deep blue lake located just a dozen miles from the ocean is bathed in the low, golden light of the approaching winter sun. The rolling hills surrounding the lake are golden. Autumn colors abound.

Roaming this terrain with utmost confidence are wild turkeys. We're not just talking about a few of these gobblers. There are hundreds of them, on the hills, near the campsites, waiting to greet you at the ranger station. If the sight of these huge birds doesn't make your mouth drool for a barbaric, carnivorous, down and dirty Thanksgiving Day feast, you're just not trying. Or you're a vegetarian.

As you probably guessed, there is no hunting at Lopez Lake—if there was, the place would resemble the OK Corral. However, there does happen to be some pretty nice family camping here—especially in the fall and spring before it gets too hot and the masses arrive.

In recent summers, the park's 354 campsites were fully booked 22 weekends of the year, meaning it's likely that a large, extended family reunion could end up in the camping spot next to you. Ask a park ranger about the crowds in the summer, as we did, and the ranger will likely pale and develop a nervous tic before mumbling, "Fall's a really nice time to camp here, too."

But is there anything to do in the fall?

You bet.

Obvious activity number one: Rent a boat. The lake covers 974 surface acres and has 22 miles of shoreline. The Lopez Lake Marina and Store rents a variety of boats, from small fishing boats to pontoon boats. The marina keeps long hours (6 A.M. to 9 P.M. in the summer and 7 A.M. to 5 P.M. in the winter).

The lake is regularly stocked and is teeming with trout, bass, catfish, crappie, and sunfish, so there are fish for both the skilled and unskilled angler. The best place for beginners is any of the alcoves. Try fishing in shallow water, especially where there's structure, such as rocks or logs. The setup for your rod is easy. Try a small- to medium-sized hook (a No. 8 will do fine) and a bobber. For bait, use night crawlers. You may not catch a fish resembling a trident submarine, but you'll probably catch something.

There are a dozen or so short hikes in the hills surrounding the lake—most of which are a good place to take in the sunset. In addition to the turkeys and deer (both of which will probably visit your campsite), there are also occasional sightings of mountain lions and black bears.

The more ambitious hiker might be interested in the 21,678-acre Santa Lucia Wilderness, one of 10 such areas in Los Padres National Forest. The designation of "wilderness" is the highest form of protection that can be bestowed upon the land by the U.S. Congress. No mechanized vehicles of any type are allowed within wilderness areas—not even bicycles.

The Santa Lucia Wilderness protects much of the Lopez Creek watershed, which feeds into the lake. The area is rugged, typically Southern Californian (lots of chaparral) and at relatively low elevation; there's nothing above 3,000 feet. The area is just to the north of the lake, but getting to it is a chore requiring an almost 15-mile drive on a twisty, narrow road. For those of you checking a road map while reading this, follow Lopez Canyon Drive to Hi Mountain Road to Upper Lopez Canyon Road. We highly recommend checking road conditions and directions with a Forest Service ranger before going; phone the Los Padres National Forest, Santa Lucia District office at (805) 925-9538.

There are three main trails in the wilderness: Lopez Canyon, which follows the creek, and Big Falls and Little Falls, which follow two of Lopez Creek's tributaries. Again, this is for the ambitious day hiker or backpacker who wants to use Lopez Lake as a base camp. Summers are blazing hot, often in excess of 100 degrees, and you can expect highs in the 90s during the day with lows in the 50s at night. Fall, winter, and spring temperatures range from very agreeable during the day—60s and 70s—to mild to freezing at night (20s to 50s).

No matter the time of year, Lopez Lake can make a nice day trip from colorful Pismo Beach, which is only 25 minutes away. Along the way, you'll pass through Arroyo Grande, the perfect place for an ice cream or antique fix.

Directions: From Santa Barbara take U.S. 101 north for 87 miles to the Grand Avenue exit. Turn right and follow Grand Avenue through the cute town of Arroyo Grande, where Grand Avenue becomes Lopez Drive. Follow Lopez Drive to the lake entrance.

Fees: The day-use fee is $4 per car. **Maps:** Maps of Lopez Lake, including hiking trails, are provided for free at the entrance station to the lake. **Pets:** Dogs are allowed in the campgrounds only and must be on leash. You may be asked to provide proof of their rabies vaccination. **Camping:** Lopez Lake has 354 sites for tents and RVs, many with full or partial hookups. Facilities include flush toilets, showers, and phones as well as a marina, Laundromat, and grocery. Reservations are taken up to six months in advance and are highly recommended between April and October. Fees are $13 to $21 per night. For reservations and information, phone (805) 489-8019 between 8 A.M. and 5 P.M. Monday through Friday. **Contact:** Lopez Lake Recreation Area, (805) 489-1122. **Locator:** LOPEZ LAKE.

17
INYO AND MONO COUNTIES

- **FEATURED TRIPS**

SKIING MAMMOTH MOUNTAIN
AND VICINITY 116

MAMMOTH LAKES 119
ROCK CREEK CANYON 126
BISHOP CREEK CANYON 128
DEATH VALLEY
    NATIONAL PARK 131

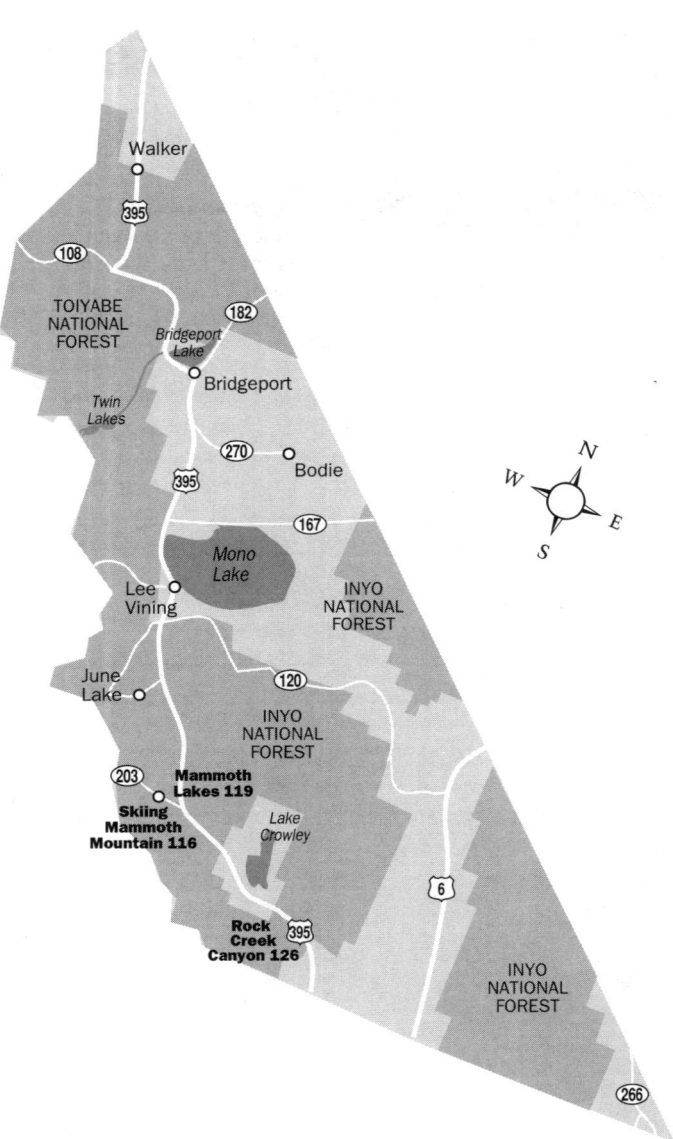

MONO COUNTY

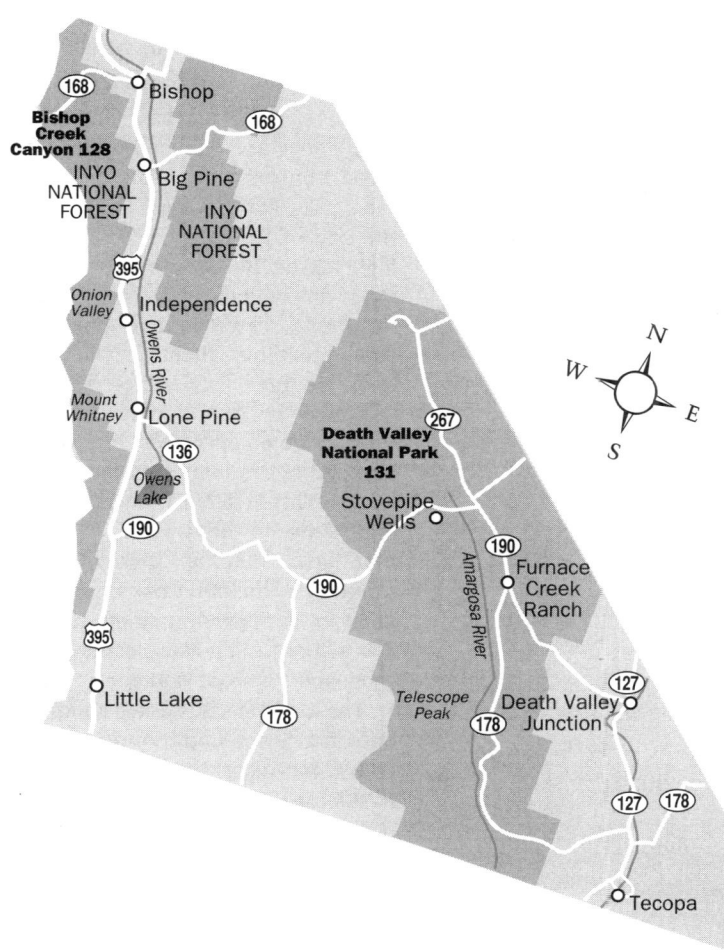

INYO COUNTY

• FEATURED TRIP •

SKIING MAMMOTH MOUNTAIN AND VICINITY
In the eastern Sierra

MAMMOTH MOUNTAIN

Where's the best view of the Sierra—that's also easiest to reach?

Try the top of Chair 23, which takes you to the summit of Mammoth Mountain. This perch, at 11,000 feet in elevation, gives you a 360-degree panorama of some of the best geography this side of the Himalayas.

To the east is the Owens Valley, the volcanic domes of the Long Valley Caldera, and the White Mountains. To the west: the heavily forested San Joaquin River watershed slicing through the Sierra Nevada on its way to the Great Central Valley. To the south: the high peaks of the Eastern Sierra. To the north: the jagged pinnacles of the Minarets, among the most photographed mountains in the world.

Mammoth Mountain may not be the absolute best ski resort in the United States, but we've skied all over the West and our feeling is that Mammoth is certainly in the top five. The mountain has everything: size (3,000 acres of terrain), versatility (there is plenty of terrain for experts and beginners), access (a scenic five-hour drive from Los Angeles), and affordability (plenty of cheap beds and eats).

The ski resort covers half of Mammoth Mountain, meaning the resort is actually wider than it is tall. There are 27 lifts, and herein lies the problem: The lifts were numbered in the order they were built, not according to geography. This makes it somewhat difficult for newcomers to find their way around—it's kind of like learning L.A.'s freeway system. For example, to get from the Chair 15 outpost back to the main lodge, a skier takes the 15 to the 16 to the 2, hopefully not turning down the wrong run on the way.

The resort has two base lodges, the Main Lodge and Canyon Lodge (with a third on the way in the next few years). The Main Lodge is located near the end of Highway 203. It is the higher of the two lodges, closer to the top of the mountain, and is open from early in the season through spring and summer skiing, when the lower part of the mountain is closed for the year.

Canyon Lodge is directly above the town of Mammoth Lakes, in a neighborhood of condominiums and town homes. There really isn't much difference between the two lodges—they both have cafeterias (there is also a cafeteria in the Mid Chalet, which is midway up the mountain at the gondola station), ski rentals, lockers, a ski shop, and a first aid station.

The town operates a free shuttle to both the Main Lodge and Canyon Lodge. Since parking can be a major hassle at either lodge, it is best to make sure your lodging is near one of the shuttle routes in town. The red line services the Main Lodge, the yellow and blue lines go to Canyon Lodge, and the green line goes to the Chair 15/24 outpost, where a third base lodge will be built in the next few years. Perhaps someday the multimillion-dollar people mover—you can't miss it on your drive up the mountain—will actually be put into service.

Where to ski? Get a map and let's go.

BEGINNER

Chairs 11 and 27 service four very easy, gentle runs next to the Main

Lodge. If these runs were any flatter, you'd need a lift to go down them. There is also good beginner terrain off Chair 7, just above Canyon Lodge. For beginners who are ready to start pushing themselves, we recommend Jill's Run, accessible from Chair 6, which begins at the Main Lodge.

INTERMEDIATE

With the exception of the double black diamond runs, a solid intermediate can ski almost anywhere at Mammoth. Broadway and Stump Alley are two huge, wide runs with a steady pitch—both are good places to warm up in the morning. If you are comfortable on these runs, proceed farther up the mountain on either Chair 3 for a run down Solitude or Chair 5 for a run down St. Anton to the Main Lodge; this is a real thigh-burner. The pitch from these chairs is a little greater, but the runs are wide. Just keep turning! Attack the mountain! Don't be afraid to fall!

The best intermediate terrain—as well as the least crowded—is found off Chair 9, all the way on the mountain's southern flank. From the top of 9, try the intermediate-rated Gold Hill run, which is one of the longer runs on the mountain. Don't do this late in the day when you're tired; that's when most ski injuries occur.

ADVANCED AND EXPERT

The truly expert runs at Mammoth all begin at the top of the mountain and drop down the treeless bowl below. Both the "drop out" and "wipe out" series of runs should gain your attention.

Cornice Bowl, just to the left of the top of Chair 23, is probably Mammoth's most well-known run. It begins very steep and then mellows somewhat before depositing skiers near the mountain's tree line.

Advanced skiers will love it. Intermediates will look at Cornice Bowl all day and decide it doesn't look that steep . . . until they get to the top and peer over the edge. That's when the knees start knocking.

Actually, it's really not that bad. The key to Cornice Bowl, for intermediates, is to make the first two turns. Yeah, we know. That's kind of like saying the key to flying an airplane is not crashing. But it's true. Make those first two turns and you'll be fine. If you don't make those first two turns, the result will be a buttslide halfway down the mountain. Steve performed such a feat a few years back. His ego eventually recovered.

Directions: From Los Angeles take Interstate 5 north to Highway 14, then continue north to U.S. 395. Drive 162 miles and exit at Highway 203, turning left. It's seven miles to the ski resort. From San Diego and San Bernardino, take Interstate 15 north to U.S. 395 north. Drive 262 miles on U.S. 395 and exit at Highway 203, turning left. It's seven miles to the ski resort. **Fees:** In 1997–98, an adult full-day lift ticket at Mammoth Mountain during the regular season was $47. **Contact:** Mammoth Mountain: (888) 4MAMMOTH. Mammoth Lakes Visitor Bureau: (800) 367-6572. Weather information: (760) 873-3213. Road conditions (CalTrans): (800) 427-ROAD. Web site: www.mammoth-mtn.com. **Locator:** MAMMOTH LAKES.

JUNE MOUNTAIN

When Mammoth gets crowded on the weekends or holidays, a fun alternative might be skiing or snowboarding at June Mountain, located 10 miles north of Mammoth Lakes. The resort is owned by Mammoth Mountain, although it is nowhere near the size of Mammoth. Still, June Mountain has 2,300 feet of vertical drop. (If it were located at Big Bear or in the San Gabes it would be Southern California's best ski resort.)

The terrain tends toward advanced and expert. From the road, the place looks absolutely foreboding—the bottom half of June Mountain is rated entirely single black or double black diamond. That's why the main lodge is located halfway up the mountain. Lifts from the main lodge take skiers to two summits, Rainbow and June, with Rainbow being the way to go for intermediates.

More than anything, June Mountain is a no-frills kind of place. We wouldn't recommend it for beginners, but intermediates will enjoy themselves. In 1997–98, the resort continued its Wednesday special, with a full-day lift ticket costing just $10. That's the best bargain in skiing anywhere, hands down.

Directions: From Mammoth Lakes, take U.S. 395 north for 20 miles. Exit at June Lake Loop and turn left. The ski resort will be on the right. **Contact:** June Mountain Ski Area, (760) 648-7733. **Locator:** JUNE LAKE.

SPRING SKIING

When winter storms slam into the Sierra Nevada, they find their way into every nook and cranny. Inevitably, storms follow the San Joaquin River Valley and then slam into Mammoth Mountain. Heavy snowfall is the result, averaging over 300 inches each winter.

The prodigious amounts of snow translate into a generous spring skiing season at Mammoth. In a good snow year, Mammoth will stay open to Memorial Day, often much later. After the severe winter of 1995–96, Mammoth kept part of the mountain open to skiers until mid-August!

The spring season generally begins after Easter. The price of lift tickets drops—usually by $10 or so—and most of the skiers disappear. As the days warm, the resort usually cuts back its hours, closing at 2 P.M.—by which time the snow is turning to slush.

The key to spring skiing is to not arrive first thing in the morning, when the slopes can be very icy. Your best bet is to go grab a hearty breakfast and then ski from 10 A.M. to 2 P.M. There will be no lift lines and it won't take long to work yourself into a suitable state of exhaustion.

One other note: The great thing about skiing during May is that you can spend the remainder of the day fishing; trout season opens the last weekend in April. Although area lakes will be crowded on the weekends, there are often few anglers around on the weekdays. Here's an idea: If Lake Mary Road is not yet open, try snowshoeing to Lake Mary for some late-afternoon casting.

CROSS-COUNTRY SKIING

The popularity of the downhill skiing at Mammoth often overshadows the high quality of cross-country skiing both in and just outside of town.

The Tamarack Lodge and Cross Country Ski Center is located in the Mammoth Lakes Basin, above town. The green-, blue-, and black-rated trails follow all of the summer roads in the basin, allowing skiers to pick routes around such gems as Lake

Mary, Lake Mamie, Lake George, and Horseshoe Lake.

The entire basin is heavily forested, with Sierra peaks looming above. It is extremely quiet back here and particularly beautiful when it's snowing. We especially recommend the three-mile round-trip around Lake Mary. Along the way, look for chickadees, which will swoop down from the trees and literally eat right out of your hands.

A trail pass—$15 for a full day in 1997-98—is required to ski the groomed trails of the Tamarack ski center. However, there are other options for those who want to ski for free in the Mammoth area. Inyo National Forest has a marked—make that loosely marked—series of ungroomed trails beginning at the Mammoth Visitor Center and Ranger Station, which is on Highway 203 just as you enter town. A word of caution: Some of these trails intersect with snowmobile trails. Look before you cross—chances are, the snowmobilers won't.

Directions: To reach the Tamarack Lodge and Cross Country Ski Center from Mammoth Lakes, take Highway 203 uphill to the intersection with Minaret Road. Continue straight to Lake Mary Road. Drive two miles to the closed gate. Turn right into Tamarack Lodge. The cross-county ski center is at the far end of the parking lot. **Fees:** In 1997-98, trail passes were $15 for a full day, $10 for an afternoon, and just $5 on Thursdays. **Contact:** Tamarack Lodge and Cross Country Ski Center, (760) 934-2442 or (800) 237-6879. Web site: www.tamaracklodge.com. **Locator:** MAMMOTH LAKES.

GREAT EATS

Mammoth Lakes rates high on the scale of quantity and quality gastronomic delights. Breakfast recommendations: The Stove (644 Old Mammoth Road) and The Breakfast Club (corner of Old Mammoth and Highway 203), two fine establishments whose owners believe a plate of food should resemble a mountain. Under no circumstance—except extreme vegetarianism—should anyone pass up the perfectly cooked, flavorful burger at Berger's (Minaret Road, in North Village). Complement it with a bowl of fries and a chocolate shake. Don't worry—you'll burn it off skiing. Maybe.

• **FEATURED TRIP** •

MAMMOTH LAKES
The gem of the Eastern Sierra

Hiking, camping, and fishing. These are not just activities. These are the loins from which life springs, the reason to endure another week of work, the reason to imprison oneself in a tin can of an automobile and drive 300-plus miles to Mammoth Lakes.

Located in a glacial-carved valley in the Eastern Sierra, Mammoth Lakes has enough hiking, camping, and fishing to fill many summers. The funny thing about Mammoth is that it gets most of its press during the ski season. Yes, the skiing at Mammoth Mountain is terrific. But ask any local and they'll tell you that summer is when Mammoth is at its best.

The town of Mammoth Lakes, elevation 7,600 feet, is surrounded by the best of the best. To the north and the west are the Ansel Adams Wilderness and Yosemite National Park. To the south, the John Muir Wilderness.

To the east, the beautiful Owens Valley and the White Mountains, a range altogether different in look than the Sierra. Get the picture? This is top-shelf scenery.

The town of Mammoth Lakes sits just above the high desert of the Owens Valley. The town is largely covered by trees, and high peaks surround it—including Mammoth Mountain, a dormant volcano that happens to be a wonderful ski resort. While the scenery surrounding the town is unbelievable, the town itself is so-so. The modern version of Mammoth Lakes was largely built in the 1970s by developers and real estate agents from Los Angeles and, as would be expected, they screwed up. Too many strip malls, not enough sidewalks, and cheaply built and maintained condos are Mammoth Lakes staples.

This will soon change. A huge corporation from Canada, called IntraWest, has bought a share of the ski resort and considerable property in town. IntraWest seems intent on overcorrecting the town's development problems by building 2,000-plus condominiums. IntraWest, invoking John Muir's name, says it will transform Mammoth into a four-season resort—despite the fact that anyone can go to Mammoth any season of the year, get a cheap room, and find plenty to do.

At least for now, Mammoth Lakes does retain a certain charm of being someplace the wealthy and powerful have not yet commandeered as their personal J. Crew catalog. Cheap motels and eats are the rule, not the exception. There are also plenty of cabins and campgrounds, many of which are quite nice.

It helps to understand the town's geography. The town sits within a valley carved by a glacier and, today, bisected by Mammoth Creek. Just above town is the Mammoth Lakes Basin. Twin Lakes, Lake Mary, Lake Mamie, Horseshoe Lake, and Lake George are the five lakes in the basin, and all can be reached by car—when the basin isn't snowed in between November and May (and sometimes later). A network of trails from the basin leads into the backcountry, where hundreds of other lakes can be reached by foot.

The backside of Mammoth Mountain falls steeply into the valley of the San Joaquin River, the area known as Reds Meadow. The river's headwaters are north of town, near Yosemite, just west of the Sierra Crest. The river flows south, then west, cutting its way across the Sierra Nevada, before spilling into the San Joaquin Valley and then out to sea.

A road from Mammoth down to Reds Meadow is open during the summer and early fall; opening day for the road depends on the snowmelt. There are several Inyo National Forest campgrounds along the river, as well as Devils Postpile National Monument, a peculiar formation of rock columns, compliments of some heavy-duty volcanic activity polished by a glacier. The road finally ends at Reds Meadow, a popular resort and an important rest stop on both the Pacific Crest and John Muir Trails. Just south of Reds Meadow is another big tourist attraction: Rainbow Falls, one of California's most spectacular waterfalls.

Hiking

A lifetime of hiking opportunities can be found in the Mammoth Lakes area. Here is our sampler—five beautiful hikes that provide a taste of what the area is about.

INYO AND MONO COUNTIES

1. Emerald Lake

This is a short hike of just 1.5 miles round-trip, gaining 500 feet in elevation. The trail begins at the day-use parking lot at the end of the Cold Creek Campground, near Lake Mary, and climbs to this small, beautiful alpine lake. The trail loosely follows Coldwater Creek and offers a stunning vista of the granite, snowcapped Mammoth Crest.

Directions: From Mammoth Lakes take Lake Mary Road uphill from town for 2.5 miles. Turn left at Lake Mary Loop Road. Turn left into Coldwater Campground and drive to the day-use parking lot at the end of the road. **Locator:** Mammoth Lakes.

2. Mammoth Pass

Here is a popular hike over one of the easier passes in the Eastern Sierra (this is also the pass between the Sierra Crest and Mammoth Mountain). The trailhead is located at the parking lot for Horseshoe Lake, amid the same area where numerous trees have died because of underground volcanic activity. The trail climbs steeply for one mile to Mammoth Pass and then descends to Reds Meadow, a distance of 4.6 miles. In the summer, a shuttle bus runs between Reds Meadow and Horseshoe Lake, making this a great one-way hike.

Directions: From Mammoth Lakes take Lake Mary Road uphill from town for three miles, until it dead-ends in the parking lot for Horseshoe Lake. The lake is on one side of the lot, the trailhead on the other. Look for the bulletin board. **Locator:** Mammoth Lakes.

3. Rainbow Falls

This is probably the most popular trail in the Mammoth Lakes area—for good reason. The trail begins at a parking lot near Reds Meadow Resort and loosely follows the San Joaquin River downstream for 1.5 miles before reaching the falls. You can also start the hike at the Devils Postpile Trailhead; follow the trail past the postpile for two miles to the falls. A long and steep staircase leads from the top of the falls to the bottom. Remember, what goes down, must come up.

Directions: From Mammoth Lakes take Highway 203 until it ends just past the ski resort. The road turns into a narrow, paved road, descending to the San Joaquin River Valley. Follow it for seven miles. The parking lot for the trailhead is located on the right side of the road, just before the entrance to Reds Meadow. **Note:** During the summer, all visitors to the San Joaquin River Valley must take a shuttle after 7:30 A.M. The shuttle leaves from the Mammoth Mountain Ski Resort on Highway 203 and costs $8. It is not inconvenient, runs often, and will stop anywhere requested. **Locator:** Mammoth Lakes.

4. Shadow Lake

The hike begins at Agnew Meadows and ends 3.5 miles later at Shadow Lake, located within the Ansel Adams Wilderness. The lake is set at an elevation of 8,736 feet and is surrounded by snowcapped peaks. This is one of the easier, less demanding hikes into the backcountry—but that's not saying it's easy.

The trail begins at the day-use parking area at Agnew Meadows. Do NOT take the "high" trail to Thousand Island Lake. Rather, follow the Pacific Crest Trail markers. The trail skirts around Agnew Meadow and then joins the PCT. Bear to the right.

You'll soon enter the Ansel Adams Wilderness and then drop into the San Joaquin River Valley.

The trail bottoms out and enters the forest, passing tiny Olaine Lake before coming to a fork. Go left and cross the river on a footbridge. Here comes the most difficult part of the trail: a series of switchbacks up an exposed ridge, totaling a 700-foot ascent.

The trail then follows a creek and some small waterfalls to Shadow Lake. It skirts the northern side of the lake—pick a boulder for sunbathing and fishing (there are some small brook trout in there). Shadow Lake was formerly a popular backpacking destination, but its shores began to look too much like a campground. Thus, backpackers need to soldier on—phone the Forest Service for current backcountry camping restrictions.

Directions: From Mammoth Lakes take Highway 203 until it ends just past the ski resort. The road turns into a narrow, paved road, descending to the San Joaquin River Valley. Follow it to the bottom of the hill and turn right into Agnew Meadows. The parking lot is just past the pack station. **Note:** During the summer, all visitors to the San Joaquin River Valley must take a shuttle after 7:30 A.M. The shuttle leaves from the Mammoth Mountain Ski Resort on Highway 203 and costs $8. It is not inconvenient, runs often, and will stop anywhere requested. **Locator:** MAMMOTH LAKES.

5. CRYSTAL LAKE

Here's a short but steep hike to another beautiful backcountry lake, a 1.5-miler with an elevation gain of 700 feet. Hikers are rewarded with numerous vistas of the Mammoth Lakes Basin, so bring plenty of film. The lake sits below enormous Crystal Crag, a 10,377-foot-tall tower of granite that looms over the entire basin.

The trail begins at the parking lot for Lake George. Look for the road from the parking lot uphill to Woods Lodge. The trailhead is just to the right of the road. The trail goes straight uphill, passing above the cabins of Woods Lodge (an excellent place to stay, by the way). Then, at one-half mile, it begins a series of switchbacks high above Lake George, heading around the lake's backside toward Crystal Crag.

The trail eventually crosses a creek and then arrives at the lake, elevation 10,000 feet. It's a beautiful windswept basin, with all sorts of interesting rock formations.

Directions: From Mammoth Lakes take Lake Mary Road uphill from town for 2.5 miles to the second left turn onto Lake Mary Loop Road. Drive over the small bridge over the lake's outlet and turn right onto the road to Lake George. Park in the Lake George day-use lot. **Locator:** MAMMOTH LAKES.

CAMPING

There are 15 car campgrounds in and around Mammoth Lakes. Fourteen are administered by Inyo National Forest and one—at Devils Postpile National Monument—is administered by the National Park Service.

Many of the campgrounds around town are not open until June, depending on the snowmelt. Always phone ahead to check road conditions. Don't be a Johnny Do-Do and "assume" there will be a campground with sites available. We all know what happens to people who assume.

1. San Joaquin River

The best campgrounds in the area can be found in the San Joaquin River Valley. In order, we like Upper Soda Springs (29 sites) the most, followed by Agnew Meadows (21 sites), Minaret Falls (28 sites), Pumice Flat (17 sites), Reds Meadow (56 sites), and Devils Postpile (21 sites). All campgrounds are open to tents and RVs.

Upper Soda Springs is right alongside the San Joaquin River and is a great choice for those who like to fish. The river receives regular plants near the campground, but we recommend following the Pacific Crest Trail north of camp, where it gets considerably less fishing pressure. Many of the sites are quite spacious, and the campground is relatively shady; bring a sleeping pad because the ground is rocky.

Agnew Meadows sits above the river—it's a 20- to 30-minute hike to the river in the Ansel Adams Wilderness—but the sites tend to be more spacious than at the other campgrounds. Minaret Falls is also right alongside the river and there's some awesome fishing south of the campground. Problem is, the sites are very cramped. When the campground is full, don't expect a lot of elbow room.

Pumice Flat is like Minaret Falls—great when it's not crowded, annoying when it is. Reds Meadow is nowhere near the river. Some of the sites are large, but the place has kind of a scattered feel. Devils Postpile is located along one of the most beautiful stretches of the San Joaquin River. But the entire area is overrun with tourists flocking to Devils Postpile National Monument. Besides, the campground resembles a gravel pit. It's perfectly fine for the RV crowd, not so great for tents. There are, however, flush toilets for those who can't go without.

Facilities at the Forest Service campgrounds include fire rings, picnic tables, piped water, and chemical toilets. Bring some firewood—don't denude the nearby forest. No reservations are accepted. Fees range from $8 to $12 per night. This is a very popular spot in the summer. To get a place, show up in the morning!

2. Mammoth Lakes Basin

There are five campgrounds within a stone's throw or short walk of a lake: Lake George (16 sites), Lake Mary (48 sites), Twin Lakes (23 sites), Coldwater (77 sites), and Pine City (11 sites). All of the campgrounds are shady, pleasant, and popular. Because the basin receives a ton of snow each winter (20 feet and counting by the end of February 1998), the campgrounds open at different times. Twin Lakes usually opens first, in May, followed by Pine City and then the rest. All campgrounds are open to tents and RVs except for Pine City, which is for tents only.

Lake George is our first choice. It's small and within easy walking distance of Lake George, Lake Mary, and Lake Mamie. Coldwater is the shape of a long cigar, divided by two roads. There are some very pretty sites—on one side of the campground the sites back up to Coldwater Creek; on the other side the sites are bordered by Mammoth Creek. But those two roads, so close to many sites, are kind of annoying.

All in all, each of the campgrounds in the Mammoth Lakes Basin is nice. Remember, the elevation is 8,700-plus feet, so expect some chilly nights.

3. Near Town

Three campgrounds are practically in town—New Shady Rest (95 sites), Old Shady Rest (51 sites), and Pine Glen (11 sites). All three are located behind the Mammoth Lakes Ranger Station, and all are open to tents and RVs.

Though nice enough, the camps are a little too close to Main Street (Highway 203). Just across Main Street from the campgrounds is a McDonald's. It can't be seen from any of the sites, but just knowing that a chocolate shake and large fries are a five-minute walk from the campground is a bit unsettling. You may find yourself waking up in the night, stumbling out of the tent, and screaming, "Isn't there anywhere left in the freaking United States where some freaking clown isn't trying to sell me a freaking hamburger?" If you do feel like venting, please do so before 10 P.M., when quiet time starts.

Facilities at the above campgrounds include fire rings, picnic tables, piped water, and flush toilets. No reservations are accepted—you want a site, get there early. A paved bike lane leads from the campgrounds to Shady Rest Park. There is also a multitude of trails in the forest behind the campgrounds—this is where the Forest Service does some small-scale logging. Yes, there are a couple of small, unfortunate clear-cuts, financed by your tax dollars.

An alternative to the above trio is Sherwin Creek Campground (87 sites for tents and RVs), located along Sherwin Creek Road just west of town. The campground is secluded and quite lovely, dotted with pine trees and huge boulders. Sherwin Creek runs right through the campground and offers decent fishing prospects. It's a five- to 10-minute drive from the campground to Von's and the rest of town. Sherwin Creek is a good alternative for early season camping trips when the Mammoth Lakes or San Joaquin River campgrounds may not yet be open.

Fishing

To put it bluntly, the trout fishing in and around Mammoth Lakes is terrific. There are streams, rivers, reservoirs, and backcountry lakes, some of which are considered world-class destinations. The fish include rainbow trout, brook trout, brown trout, and golden trout.

You'll need a valid California fishing license to fish anywhere in the Mammoth area. Both fly-fishing and spin tackle are popular. A number of sporting goods and fly-fishing stores in Mammoth sell tackle, bait, and licenses. Because the area receives significant fishing pressure, only kill fish that are going to be used—otherwise, be a good soldier and practice catch-and-release.

Crowley Lake, a reservoir for the city of Los Angeles, is 10 miles south of town on U.S. 395. On the opening day of trout season, it's an unbelievable scene, with thousands upon thousands of anglers descending upon the lake. It's not exactly beautiful, but it sure does produce fish. For best results, rent a boat. Convict Lake is just west of the airport. It's worth going just for the view of Mount Morrison, a 12,268-foot granite formation that towers over the water.

The Owens River is world famous for two reasons. The Owens is one of the primary water sources for Los Angeles. William Mulholland's famous Los Angeles Aqueduct carries water from the river 300 miles south, an endeavor fictionalized in the movie *Chi-*

natown. However, north of Bishop—before the water is sucked from the river—the Owens River offers outstanding fly-fishing. The best-known places are the three wild trout sections: Hot Creek, east of the Hot Creek Hatchery; a small section of the river south of Pleasant Valley Reservoir (catch-and-release with barbless hooks only); and another short stretch near Benton Crossing.

Hot Creek empties into the Owens River. The creek is best known among tourists for its geothermal activity. But a small stretch of the creek upstream from the geothermal area is a world-famous fishing spot. This is a place where the experts go, and a bad cast can get you some very dirty looks. Why? The fish are gigantic, thanks to this being catch-and-release, barbless hooks only. Most of this three-mile stretch is privately owned; there are public access points, but it's hard to figure out which is which. This is one of the few areas where we recommend having a guide.

Other good fisheries: Mammoth Creek, Sherwin Creek, Convict Creek, and McGee Creek (south of town on U.S. 395).

The Mammoth Lakes Basin is heavily fished, with the exception of Horseshoe Lake. All of the lakes get plants, and we've seen them stocking—some of the trout tossed in are huge. Boat rentals are available at each of the lakes, which are also popular with float-tubers. There is plenty of shore fishing at each lake; just be careful of branches, tree limbs, and, of course, human limbs.

The San Joaquin River is an excellent fishery, both in terms of productivity and scenery. There are several stretches where the river cuts through meadows so pretty it's hard to concentrate on tying a knot. The river gets plants near all of the campgrounds, but we recommend hiking to sections of the river between the camps. Fly fishers love it down here—later in the season, when the flow drops, this is a great river to wade around in. But it's a good river for spin tackle also. There are golden trout in the river, most often found upstream from Agnew Meadows, in the Ansel Adams Wilderness.

Finally, there are dozens of backcountry lakes that can be hiked or backpacked to from the Mammoth Lakes area. Here is just a short listing of the more popular lakes in which to fish: Duck Lake, Deer Lakes, Franklin Lakes, Thousand Island Lake (the headwaters of the San Joaquin River), Garnet Lake, Shadow Lake, Ediza Lake, and Lake Virginia.

Directions: Mammoth Lakes is 306 miles north of Los Angeles. From downtown Los Angeles, take Interstate 5 north, then head north and east on Highway 14 to U.S. 395. Take U.S. 395 to Highway 203 and drive west for three miles to town. **Visitor center:** The Inyo National Forest Mammoth Lakes Visitor Center is literally the first building you'll see on the left side of Highway 203 when driving into town. Rangers are on hand to answer every conceivable question. **Fees:** Use of the national forest is free, but there are fees for the campgrounds. **Maps:** A map of Inyo National Forest is available at the visitor center. **Pets:** Dogs are permitted in the national forest. They should be leashed in all campgrounds and under direct control on trails. **Contact:** Inyo National Forest, Mammoth

Ranger District, (760) 924-5500. **Locator:** MAMMOTH LAKES.

• FEATURED TRIP •

ROCK CREEK CANYON

Between Bishop and Mammoth, in the Eastern Sierra

One of the most fascinating things about the Eastern Sierra is how different each canyon is from the next. Bishop Canyon looks different from Mammoth Lakes, although they are just 45 miles apart. And Rock Creek Canyon, located between the two, has a very distinct, separate look.

It's a good look, too. As Rock Creek Road gains in elevation, the canyon becomes increasingly spectacular. In the distance, the jagged 13,000-foot-plus peaks of Bear Creek Spire, Mount Dade, Mount Abbott, and Mount Mills can be seen. The walls of the canyon become steeper, the trees more dense, the light more golden. The road goes past pretty (and natural) Rock Creek Lake before finally ending at the Mosquito Flat parking area. The elevation: 10,300 feet, making this the highest paved road in the state of California.

Like the other canyons and valleys of the Eastern Sierra, Rock Creek Canyon is a great destination for a weekend getaway. Everything you need is located there—campgrounds, trails to backcountry lakes, plenty of easy-to-access fishing in Rock Creek and Rock Creek Lake. There are even cabin rentals available at Rock Creek Lodge, which is right next to Rock Creek. The lodge is open year-round. In the summer, there's fishing and hiking. In the winter, cross-country skiing. The cabins are cozy and well maintained—not too rustic, not too lavish. Just right.

HIKING

There are four primary trails in Rock Creek Canyon. The Mosquito Flat parking area serves as the trailhead for two of them, the Mono Pass Trail and the highly recommended Morgan Pass Trail to the Little Lakes Valley.

The Morgan Pass Trail to the Little Lakes begins at Mosquito Flat and continues up and into a glacial basin that includes a bunch of little lakes—in order, it's Mack Lake, Marsh Lake, Heart Lake, Box Lake, Long Lake, Chickenfoot Lake, Upper Morgan Lake, and Lower Morgan Lake. Sitting rather comfortably over the valley are the aforementioned 13,000-foot-plus peaks. The valley is quite lush and the lakes are all very pretty. From the trailhead to Lower Morgan Lake is a distance of 4.5 miles. The trail isn't too steep, but remember that the elevation is over 10,000 feet.

Anyone who has read much about the Sierra has probably heard about Mono Pass. It's one of the more brutal ways to get over the Sierra Crest with an elevation of 12,643 feet. Problem is, the trailhead is 10,300 feet and the 2,300-foot difference is spread out over just three miles. Throw in a heavy backpack and a hot day, and phzzzz. The view makes up for it, however.

Two other trails worth mentioning: The Tamarack Lakes Trail begins at the Pine Grove Campground and goes 5.5 miles to Bucks Lake and Tamarack Lakes, which sit in a rocky basin. Not as overwhelmingly scenic as the Little Lakes Valley, but nonetheless, very interesting.

The Hilton Lakes Trail begins at Rock Creek Lake and goes to Lower and Upper Hilton Lakes—a distance of just over five miles. These are the total opposite of the Tamarack Lakes, with trees everywhere. The Hiltons have a formidable reputation among anglers; between the two lakes it's possible to catch rainbow, brook, brown, and golden trout. Do not leave the insect repellent back at camp. The skeeters up here are tough—don't give in! Fight back!

Camping

There are seven Forest Service campgrounds in Rock Creek Canyon: Palisade (5 sites), East Fork (133 sites), Pine Grove (11 sites), Upper Pine Grove (8 sites), Rock Creek Lake (28 sites), Iris Meadow (14 sites), and Big Meadow (11 sites). We wouldn't call any of them spectacular, but most of them will certainly do.

The best is Rock Creek Lake Campground, located right along, you guessed it, Rock Creek Lake. This is also the camp that's most sought after—if you're hoping for a spot on a summer weekend, get there early on Friday; no reservations are accepted. The forest up here is very pretty, as is Rock Creek. Take a hike and try wetting a line.

Of the other campgrounds, we recommend Palisade and Pine Grove. Palisade is tiny, with just five sites—only three of which can host a motor home—and it's right alongside Rock Creek. Pine Grove isn't as nice, but it works. There are just 11 sites here, five for tents only.

Immediately, disqualify two others, Iris Meadow and Big Meadow, neither of which is far enough into the canyon. Also scratch East Fork from the list, since it's too big, with 133 sites. Think of a motel without walls.

All Forest Service campgrounds in Rock Creek Canyon have fire rings, picnic tables, piped water, and flush or chemical toilets. No reservations are accepted. Fees range from $8 to $12 per night.

Fishing

Just past the lodge, Rock Creek broadens, cutting through a drop-dead gorgeous meadow A trail follows the creek, and it's one that any enthusiastic fisher must take. The water is beyond gin-clear. Small trout can be seen darting back and forth across the waters. Go ahead, try to catch them. We did, for an entire afternoon recently. We tried everything—Julie used her fly rod, Steve his spin tackle. Nothing. Then again, the photos turned out gorgeous. Note: The farther you go on the trail, the prettier it gets.

Fishing at the lake is easier. It receives a lot of plants, courtesy of the DFG, and the water isn't so clear; thus the fish don't spook as easily. But anyone staying in Rock Creek Canyon should try to hoof it on one of the trails to a backcountry lake. Most popular are the Tamarack Lakes, the Hilton Lakes, and the Little Lakes. We recommend the Little Lakes. No one, and we mean no one, has ever said the Little Lakes Basin is less than awesome. Maybe you'll catch a fish, too.

Directions: From Bishop take U.S. 395 north for 18 miles and turn left at the intersection for Tom's Place. Rock Creek Road begins here; follow it up and into the canyon. **Fees:** Day use of Rock Creek Lake, Rock Creek, and all hiking trails is free. **Maps:** Get a map of Inyo National Forest at ranger stations or most large sporting goods stores. Or purchase maps by mail, by sending $4 to the USDA-Forest Service, Attn: Map Room 807, 630 Sansome Street, San Francisco, CA 94111; request the Inyo National Forest map.

Pets: Dogs are permitted. **Contact:** Inyo National Forest, White Mountain Ranger District, (760) 873-2500. Rock Creek Lodge, (760) 935-4170. **Locator:** ROCK CREEK CANYON.

• FEATURED TRIP •

BISHOP CREEK CANYON
West of Bishop, in the Eastern Sierra

It's time for another driving quiz. Pencils up and go!

Someone just cut me off for no reason.
1. I should react by:
   a) Backing off and being thankful no one got hurt.
   b) Hanging up on my agent and phoning 9-1-1.
   c) Reaching into the glove compartment for my Glock.
2. When the light turns from yellow to red, it means:
   a) Absolutely nothing.
   b) All economy cars must stop.
   c) Speed up—you don't want to miss the next light, too.
3. When the road is wet, it's best to:
   a) Only read your friend's screenplay at stoplights.
   b) Think happy thoughts.
   c) Drive faster to lessen the time you spend on slick roads.

If you think the regular roads of Southern California are bad—like we do—you ain't see nothing yet. Just wait until you get a load of the road to North Lake Campground, at the far end of Bishop Creek Canyon.

The road is narrow, unpaved, and cut into the side of a vertical cliff. The view is wonderful—straight down to the tune of 1,000 feet. To help motorists pay attention, there's no guardrail. Traffic has a peculiar way of meeting at the exact point where the road is narrowest. Last, but certainly not least, there's a blind turn that forces uphill-bound cars to stick to an outside line.

Two bits of good news: 1) The more you drive on the road, the less frightening it gets, as you become used to constant fear; 2) At the end of the road lies one of the prettiest, as well as highest, little U.S. Forest Service campgrounds in Southern/Central California.

North Lake Campground has several fine attributes. First and foremost, RVs can't get to it because they can't navigate the aforementioned road. The campground sits at an elevation of 9,500 feet, making it one of the highest car campgrounds in the Eastern Sierra. It's also a small camp, with just 11 sites. One side of the campground is bordered by the gushing North Fork of Bishop Creek, while the other sits under 13,204-foot-tall Mount Emerson, an immense red slab of rock. Two important trails into the John Muir Wilderness begin at the campground: the trail to the Lamarck Lakes and the Piute Pass Trail, which leads over Piute Pass into Humphreys Basin.

And that's not all. The campground has four walk-in sites, numbered one through four. These are huge sites, located in a small meadow that is bordered by the creek. The farthest site is just over 100 yards from the parking lot. A short walk down the road is North Lake (good fishing) and Bishop Pack Outfitters, which offers horseback trips into the John Muir Wilderness, Inyo and Sierra National Forests, and Kings Canyon National Park. Phone: (760) 873-4785.

The campground has two slight drawbacks. Because of the elevation, it's typically only open from July through September, although the dates can vary due to the snowmelt. Also, during the backpacking season, a fair number of backpackers will be hiking through camp. They're a quiet bunch—after all, they are either already exhausted or about to be.

Hiking

The Piute Pass Trail begins at the campground and travels 4.8 miles to 11,423-foot Piute Pass (an elevation gain of almost 2,000 feet), making it one of the easier passes to climb in the Eastern Sierra. Of course, that's a relative statement.

The trail follows the North Fork of Bishop Creek all the way to the Sierra Crest. Along the way, there are many small waterfalls, as well as Loch Leven Lake and Piute Lake. The trail begins surrounded by aspens, but after two miles or so it is mostly above the tree line, meaning it's a fine way to see some serious granite. It is beautiful up here, but can be very hot on a sunny day. Remember, the sun's ultraviolet rays are much more powerful at high elevations.

The trail to the two Lamarck Lakes (lower and upper) also begins at the campground. It's 2.5 miles to the upper lake (10,918 feet), with an elevation gain of 1,700 feet. There are beautiful views of Mount Emerson and the surrounding Piute Crags—although Mammoth Lakes is just 40 miles away, the geology here is much different.

The two above hikes are certainly nothing to sneeze at. However, if you are going to be in the area, there is one day hike that absolutely cannot be missed: the trail to Blue Lake (elevation 10,400 feet). The lake is, as the name suggests, deep blue, and is surrounded by six peaks over 13,000 feet. As outdoors writer Tom Stienstra once wrote, it is almost impossible not to take the best photograph of your life here.

The trailhead is located on Highway 168 between the Sabrina Campground and Lake Sabrina. It's on the left side of the road—look for a bulletin board that may or may not have anything posted on it. There are a few day-use parking spaces near the trailhead. Parking can also be found up the road at Lake Sabrina or down the road in the parking lot located at the turnoff to North Lake.

The trail to Blue Lake is 3.1 miles long, with an elevation gain of approximately 1,200 feet. You start by skirting the eastern side of Lake Sabrina, then enter the forest and begin a series of switchbacks, crossing two small creeks. After leaving the forest, the trail climbs an exposed ridge that offers stunning views of the valley carved by the Middle Fork of Bishop Creek, the creek that is dammed downstream to form Lake Sabrina.

The final push to the lake is a series of switchbacks carved into an avalanche path. At the top, the trail skirts several house-sized boulders before finally spitting hikers out at the lake. Pick a rock and have a picnic. Or go fishing; it's not terribly hard to pull a small rainbow from the lake.

Because the trail is so exposed to sunlight, we recommend that day hikers get an early start. The lake is so beautiful most people want to spend an entire day there.

The Rest of Bishop Creek Canyon

In our humble opinion, North Lake Campground and the Blue Lake Trail are the best of Bishop Creek Canyon. But in all fairness, this is an immense area with a ton of camping, hiking, and fishing opportunities.

Bishop Creek Canyon is actually made up of two canyons. The main canyon follows the Middle Fork of Bishop Creek to Lake Sabrina, where the creek was dammed. The other canyon follows the South Fork of the creek all the way to South Lake, where the fork was dammed. Why all the dams? Hydroelectric power, courtesy of the local utility company.

CAMPING

There are nine Forest Service campgrounds in the canyon, including North Lake Campground. Most of them are just okay, with crowded sites and too close to the road. Next to North Lake, Sabrina is probably the second best—half of the 18 sites back up to the Middle Fork of Bishop Creek, where there is some decent (but often crowded) fishing. The campground can accommodate tents or RVs.

Along Bishop Creek's south fork, the Table Mountain Group Campground is the best. It is located in a small meadow through which the creek meanders. This is a popular, pretty, and often quite productive place to fish. These are gin-clear waters, so be extra careful not to spook the fish.

The largest campground in the canyon is Four Jeffrey, which has 106 sites for tents and RVs. The South Fork of Bishop Creek runs past some of the sites, a plus, although this campground tends to get very crowded.

Facilities at all the Forest Service campgrounds in the canyon include piped water, flush or vault toilets, fire pits, and picnic tables. No reservations are taken—it's first come, first served. If you arrive on a Friday in July or August after 5 p.m., good luck. Fees are $12 per night. For more information, phone the Inyo National Forest, White Mountain Ranger District at (760) 873-2500.

LODGING

There are three popular lodges within Bishop Creek Canyon, all of which offer cabin rentals. It's not a bad way to go for those who don't like camping—there is plenty of day hiking and fishing in the canyon. Reservations are highly recommended during the summer months.

Cardinal Village Resort is in the small village of Aspendell, right along the Middle Fork of Bishop Creek. It's a very pretty site, located well below the main road, Highway 168. For information, phone (760) 873-4789.

Parchers Resort is located just below South Lake, along the South Fork of Bishop Creek. The creek is especially beautiful here, as it tumbles its way downhill over waterfalls and through canyons. The lodge has a small restaurant and operates a pack station for trips into the backcountry. For information, phone (760) 873-4177.

Bishop Creek Lodge is just across the road from the South Fork of Bishop Creek. The cabins are very cute and some are quite large; we stayed in a large two-bedroom that also had a nice kitchen and a bathroom the size of a small barn. The lodge has a small restaurant and bar. For information, phone (760) 873-4484.

FISHING

Bishop Creek Canyon is extremely popular with anglers, and for good reason: It produces a lot of fish, compliments of stocking by the DFG.

Lake Sabrina and South Lake are huge. You'll need a boat to fish them properly; small motorboats can be rented at both lakes. North Lake is very small and perfectly suited to fly-fishing. It can be fished from shore or float tube. The creek immediately below the lake is beautiful—the view of Mount Emerson easily compensates for getting zilched.

There are hundreds of places to fish along both the Middle and South Forks of Bishop Creek. Access is easiest near the campgrounds, but that's also where the crowds are. We recommend starting at a campground and then hiking upstream.

The South Fork has some particularly impressive stretches, where there are deep pools and wide-open spaces for fly fishers to cast. The best stretch is between the Willow Campground and tiny, crystal clear Weir Lake—there is a small parking lot at the lake. Another superb spot is the area immediately upstream and downstream from the Table Mountain Group Campground.

The best time of the year to fish this area is in the fall, in late September and early October. The fall colors are great, as is the fishing. The elevation and season make for some chilly camping, but there are always the three lodges in the canyon as well as hundreds of motel rooms 15 minutes down the road in Bishop.

Directions: From Bishop to North Lake Campground, take Highway 168 east for 17 miles. Turn right at the signed turnoff to North Lake (Forest Service Road 8S02). Drive two miles to the campground. **Fees:** Day use of Bishop Canyon is free. **Maps:** Get a map of Inyo National Forest at ranger stations or most large sporting goods stores. Or purchase a map by mail, by sending $4 to the USDA-Forest Service, Attn: Map Room 807, 630 Sansome Street, San Francisco, CA 94111; request the Inyo National Forest map. Tom Harrison Cartography publishes the "Trail Map of the Mono Divide High Country," a topographic map that's especially useful for day hikers. A better topographic map is the USGS map for Mount Thompson and Mount Darwin. **Pets:** Dogs are permitted in all campgrounds, but they must be leashed. **Contact:** Inyo National Forest, White Mountain Ranger District, (760) 373-2500. **Locator:** BISHOP CREEK CANYON.

• FEATURED TRIP •

DEATH VALLEY NATIONAL PARK

East of the Owens Valley, in the middle of nowhere

Ever see a sunset on a winter weekday in Death Valley National Park?

Quiet. Creepy. Desolate. Big. Beautiful. Unforgiving. Those are the kind of words—not to mention bad writing—that only begin to describe Death Valley. It's a wide expanse of land that humbles a person before he or she even steps out of the car, a place so remote and uninhabited that leaving the beaten path seems to be a life and death decision (and, in fact, it can be).

How big is this place? Death Valley is larger than the state of Delaware, one and a half times the size of Yellowstone National Park. Death Valley is over 100 miles long from north to south and at some points is 50 miles wide. At 3.3 million acres, it's America's largest national park. Permanent population: Less than 500 brave, crazy, weathered souls.

Death Valley is the hottest and driest place on Earth. Period. The record high was 134 degrees Fahrenheit in 1913, but it reached 127 degrees in both 1994 and 1995. In 1972, the ground at the visitor center on one brutally hot day was found to be 201 degrees. On any given day, the humidity in Death Valley is often less than 1 percent. Little wonder the park averages less than two inches of rain per year.

And yet people flock here during the summer. "We get a lot of French and German tourists in July and August," one ranger told us. "They've heard about the legend of the place, and they want to go back home and say they survived the Death Valley heat."

Those with their sanity intact should consider visiting between October and April, when daytime temperatures are mild—and often downright pleasant—ranging from the 60s to the 80s. Nights are chilly, with temperatures often in the 30s on the valley floor. What's fascinating about the valley is the power of the sun. Even on a 60-degree January day, the sun's intensity is noticeably stronger on exposed skin. Look around and a message left behind by the Bailey Geological Party in 1900 is easily understood: "20 Miles from Wood/20 Miles from Water/40 feet from Hell/God Bless Our Home."

Hiking

It was just before 8 A.M. on a cool January morning in Death Valley. After driving up the bumpy, unpaved road (a recurring theme in Death Valley) from Stovepipe Wells, we parked at the entrance to Mosaic Canyon. From Highway 190, the canyon wasn't even visible—all that could be seen was the solid rock of the Panamint Mountains, which form the western wall of Death Valley.

At first, Mosaic Canyon is like a narrow hallway through the rock. The canyon walls are vertical and look like polished marble. The canyon itself is a wash, formed by rainwater gushing through the rock for thousands and thousands of years.

After walking 15 minutes or so, the canyon opens to a wide, 50-yard expanse where the trail splits in several directions. We take the middle line, walk a few steps, and look up at three bighorn sheep dead ahead on the trail.

They look at us. We look at them. They look at one another. They defy gravity and scramble straight—and we mean straight—up a 20-foot-tall slab of vertical rock. At the top, they proceed to stand and watch us for the next 30 minutes. We sit on a rock and watch them. A standoff. Finally, they disappear behind the rock. Then we see them again, clambering up another ledge that would challenge even the best rock climber.

Mosaic Canyon is one of the easier to find hikes in a national park that has few established trails for day hikers or backcountry users. Because of this, most visitors to Death Valley tend to drive around to the park's signature attractions and fall into the dreaded drive-park-videotape-drive rhythm.

Listed below are a handful of good day hikes in Death Valley that are relatively easy to get to. Your best bet might be to pick out two or three hikes that are in relatively close proximity to one another in the park. For example, you can spend the morning exploring the valley floor (before it gets too hot), an afternoon in Mosaic Canyon, which has some shade, and then finish up the day on the sand dunes.

Remember to always bring plenty of water, a hat, and sunglasses. People melt here like Popsicles in a microwave.

The hikes:

Mosaic Canyon: The turnoff to Mosaic is just a few yards before the Stovepipe Wells Motel. The trail goes about 1.5 miles up the canyon before you reach a dry waterfall blocking your way. Advanced and experienced climbers can find their way around the waterfall. Hint: Try going to the left.

Sand Dunes: The dunes complex begins about two miles south of Stovepipe Wells on the east side of Highway 190. Your best bet is to park along the road and just walk into the dunes (there is also a very bumpy unpaved road that takes you around the dunes' backside), where you can easily spend a couple of hours exploring. Keep on the lookout for kit foxes, coyotes, lizards, and sidewinders. The dunes are a most excellent place to watch a Death Valley sunset, too.

Salt Creek: Seemingly out of nowhere, Salt Creek emerges from the earth for about a mile. The creek is often only a foot wide and even less deep, but a small oasis has popped up around it. A half-mile-long boardwalk has been constructed along the creek, which is interesting. When you get to the end, hop off the boardwalk and walk as far as you want into the borax fields on the valley floor. Feel that sun beating down.

Jayhawker Canyon: Begin at the 3,000-foot-elevation sign on Highway 190, 2.3 miles past Emigrant Junction (heading west). This is the route miners took in 1850. The trail continues for five miles to the base of Pinto Peak. Allow at least five hours for the entire hike.

Telescope Peak: The trail—only for extremely fit hikers or backpackers—begins at Mahogany Flat Campground at the end of Wildrose Canyon. From 11,049-foot-tall Telescope Peak—a mountain covered with juniper, pinyon, and bristlecone pines—you can see the lowest point on the continent to the east, Badwater Basin, and to the west the highest point in the lower 48, 14,494 foot-tall Mount Whitney. For more information on this hike please see page 7.

Wildrose Peak: A junior version of the Telescope Peak hike, Wildrose is 9,054 feet tall and offers equally stunning views of Death Valley, as well as the Eastern Sierra. Moderately strenuous with a 2,000-foot elevation gain, the hike is 8.4 miles round-trip; allow six to eight hours.

Fall Canyon and Titus Canyon: Here's more canyon hiking, similar to Mosaic Canyon. Drive north on Scotty's Castle Road from the junction with Highway 190 for about 15 miles. Turn right onto the unpaved road to Titus Canyon. Park in the Titus Canyon parking lot and either follow the road into Titus Canyon or walk one-half mile north (use your compass) to a wash that leads into Fall Canyon. In Fall Canyon, a dry waterfall will block your passage after three miles. Both of these are remote. Check with a ranger at the visitor center at Stovepipe Wells or Furnace Creek first.

Keane Wonder Mill: This short hike, about a two-mile round-trip, takes hikers to a big wooden mine building sticking out of the side of a mountain. The unpaved road to the trailhead is on the Beatty Cutoff midway between Highway 190 and Highway 374.

Skidoo Site: The sparse remains of this old mining town is 7.3 miles down the end of an unpaved road off Emigrant Canyon Road above the valley's western rim. Drive in, park, and take a short hike so you can say you went "exploring off on your own" in Death Valley.

CAMPING

Death Valley has nine campgrounds and all but two of them have one thing in common: They're butt ugly. These campgrounds have rocky surfaces, little shade, and, to the jaded eye, resemble a rock quarry. Air mattresses or foam pads are a must for tenters. Not surprisingly, these campgrounds are mostly the domain of RVers. The Reluctant Camper—and we all know one—will probably not enjoy the experience.

The campgrounds:

Furnace Creek: Open all year, 136 sites for tents and RVs. The campground is located behind the visitor center and is the only one on the valley floor with trees. Facilities include piped water, flush toilets, showers, picnic tables, and fire grills. Fees are $16 per night. Reserve through PARK.NET by phoning (800) 365-2267.

Texas Springs: Open October to April, 92 sites for tents and RVs. It's ugly, but the best of the uglies. Facilities include flush toilets, picnic tables, fire grills, and piped water. Fees are $10 per night. No reservations are accepted except for group sites; call PARK.NET, (800) 365-2267. RVers are not allowed to run their generators here at any time.

Sunset: Open October to April, 1,000 sites for tents and RVs. We're not sure if this is a campground or a prison work camp. Facilities include piped water and flush toilets. Fees are $10 per night. No reservations are needed.

Stovepipe Wells: Open October to April, 200 sites for tents and RVs. You'll be camping in a parking lot, but the village is at your disposal, with a grocery store, bar, and restaurant. Facilities include flush toilets and piped water. Fees are $10 per night. No reservations are needed.

Emigrant: Open April to October, 10 sites for tents or RVs. It's ugly, but free. Flush toilets and water are provided. No reservations are needed.

Mesquite Spring: Open year-round, 30 spaces for tents and RVs. It's near Scotty's Castle, but 30 to 40 miles from most of the park's day hiking and the visitor center. Still, it's better than most camps in the park. Facilities include flush toilets, picnic tables, fire grills, and water. Fees are $10 per night. No reservations are needed.

Wildrose: Open year-round, 30 sites for tents or RVs. This is camping in a gravel pit-type atmosphere in the Panamint Mountains. Water is available April through November. There's no fee, and no reservations are needed.

Thorndike: Open March to November, eight sites for tents only. Thorndike is at elevation 7,500 feet and makes a good base for the climb to Wildrose or Telescope Peaks. Pit toilets are provided. There is no water, so bring your own. No fee and no reservations needed.

Mahogany Flat: Open March to November, 10 sites for tents only. Mahogany Flat is at elevation 8,200 feet and makes a good base for the climb to Wildrose or Telescope Peaks. Pit toilets are provided, but there's no water. No reservations are needed.

INYO AND MONO COUNTIES

LODGING

Death Valley is one of the few places where we would recommend lodging over camping. Nights can be chilly in Death Valley from the fall through spring, and the campgrounds just aren't nice enough to justify sleeping outside, unless there are budgetary concerns (you're broke, for example).

There are three lodges in Death Valley:

Furnace Creek Inn: This is a high-class resort for Beverly Hills types or Europeans with too much money. Surprise!—we haven't stayed there. But it sure looks nice. Rates are $150 to $300 per night. For information, phone (619) 786-2345.

Furnace Creek Ranch: This one earns our recommendation. The rooms are in several one-story buildings spread around an oasis, and many have sliding glass doors leading to ground-level patios. The village of Furnace Creek is larger than Stovepipe Wells and there's a little more to do here—namely golf, tennis, and lounging by a pool. There are also a Laundromat, post office, restaurant, and bar, as well as the visitor center. In case you're wondering, the Devil's Golf Course is made possible by water piped in from a nearby spring. Rates are $80 to $100 per night. For information, phone (619) 786-2345.

Stovepipe Wells Inn: Here is a no-frills motel, meaning no phone and no TV. It serves its purpose, but the rooms down at Furnace Creek Ranch are better. Bring a good book or hunker down at the restaurant bar and see how much tequila you can drink. There's plenty of room outside to throw up and not hit anything. Rates are $40 to $75 per night. For information, phone (619) 786-2387.

SIGNATURE ATTRACTIONS

Like many of our national parks, Death Valley has its share of well-known vistas, turnouts, and things every video buff has to tape for inexplicable reasons:

Badwater Basin: The sign tells you that you're at 292 feet below sea level, the lowest point in the United States. A good place to go to say you've been there, we suppose. Also, a favorite place for the camcorder crowd, who must be hoping to bore to death friends and family upon their arrival back in Tokyo or Berlin.

Dante's View: The familiar panorama of the valley floor from the eastern side is terrific. It's a bit of a drive to get there (23 miles from Furnace Creek), but the view rarely disappoints, especially at sunset.

Harmony Borax Works: The old ruins from this mining facility are interesting enough. Not enough to make you want to move there, mind you, but it does give you some insight to the history of the place and the very brave, possibly crazy, people who first worked here. The works are just north of Furnace Creek on Highway 190.

Scotty's Castle: Scotty was basically an attention-seeking nut who poured most of his money into building a castle in the desert. At least William Randolph Hearst had the good sense to build his castle with an ocean view. Anyhow, Scotty's is 50 miles from Furnace Creek. We could take it or leave it, although the drive up Scotty's Castle Road is wonderfully remote.

BACKCOUNTRY HIKING

Death Valley isn't very well suited for backpackers. Only those who really know what they are doing should even think about it and, even then, they should stop at the main visitor center in Furnace Creek and consult with a park ranger about potential destinations and their associated dangers. Also, ask for the "National Park Service Backcountry Hikes" flyer, which details 10 backcountry destinations. Having a 4x4 helps, also, since most unpaved roads are very rough.

Note: If backpacking in the desert, never camp near a watering hole. An animal may think you are trying to take its supply and will fight you for it. Also, do not use water from springs, as much of it has been polluted by wild burros. This means you have to haul water with you—at least one gallon per person per day—which can be a very heavy proposition.

Biking

There isn't much room on the sides of Highway 190 for biking, but during winter weekdays there's so little traffic you'll often have the road to yourself. Wear bright colors so the folks sleeping at the wheel of their RVs will wake up before pancaking you. The scenery, obviously, makes this ride more interesting than most. Our advice: Bring along a geologist for a running commentary.

Directions: From Los Angeles take Interstate 5 north to Highway 14 north. Continue through Palmdale, Lancaster, and Mojave. From Mojave, drive 48 more miles on Highway 14 to U.S. 395 north. Follow U.S. 395 for 42 miles and turn right onto Highway 190. Drive 75 miles to the village of Stovepipe Wells or another 23 miles farther to Furnace Creek. **Note:** Telescope and Wildrose Peaks and the nearby campgrounds are NOT in the valley. From Highway 190, turn right onto Emigrant Canyon Road and follow the signs to the park. Have a map handy before entering Death Valley, as well as your AAA card (a cell phone can't hurt either). **Special note:** If traveling to Death Valley when it's hot, try to drive early in the morning or late in the day. Turn off the air-conditioning on all uphill grades. **Fees:** The $10 per automobile park entrance fee is good for seven days. **Maps:** A free National Park Service map of Death Valley is provided when you pay the entrance fee at either the Furnace Creek or Stovepipe Wells Visitor Centers. The AAA map of Death Valley is very good; it's available at many bookstores or AAA offices. For backpackers or backcountry hikers, specific USGS topographic maps of Death Valley can be purchased at the Furnace Creek Visitor Center or by phoning the Death Valley Natural History Association at (619) 786-3285. **Pets:** Dogs are allowed only in the campgrounds, but they must be leashed. Death Valley is a terrible, possibly deadly, place for dogs because of the heat and sun. **Contact:** Death Valley National Park, (619) 786-2331. **Locator:** DEATH VALLEY NATIONAL PARK.

18
TULARE AND KERN COUNTIES

• FEATURED TRIPS •

KINGS CANYON NATIONAL
    PARK 140
SEQUOIA NATIONAL PARK 145
GOLDEN TROUT WILDERNESS ... 151
UPPER KERN PLATEAU
    AND THE DOME LAND
    WILDERNESS 156
MOUNTAIN HOME
    STATE FOREST 158
SOUTHWESTERN SIERRA
    NEVADA 160
RAFTING THE KERN RIVER 164
LAKE ISABELLA AND KERN
    RIVER FISHING 167
RED ROCK CANYON
    STATE PARK 170
SPACE SHUTTLE LANDINGS 171

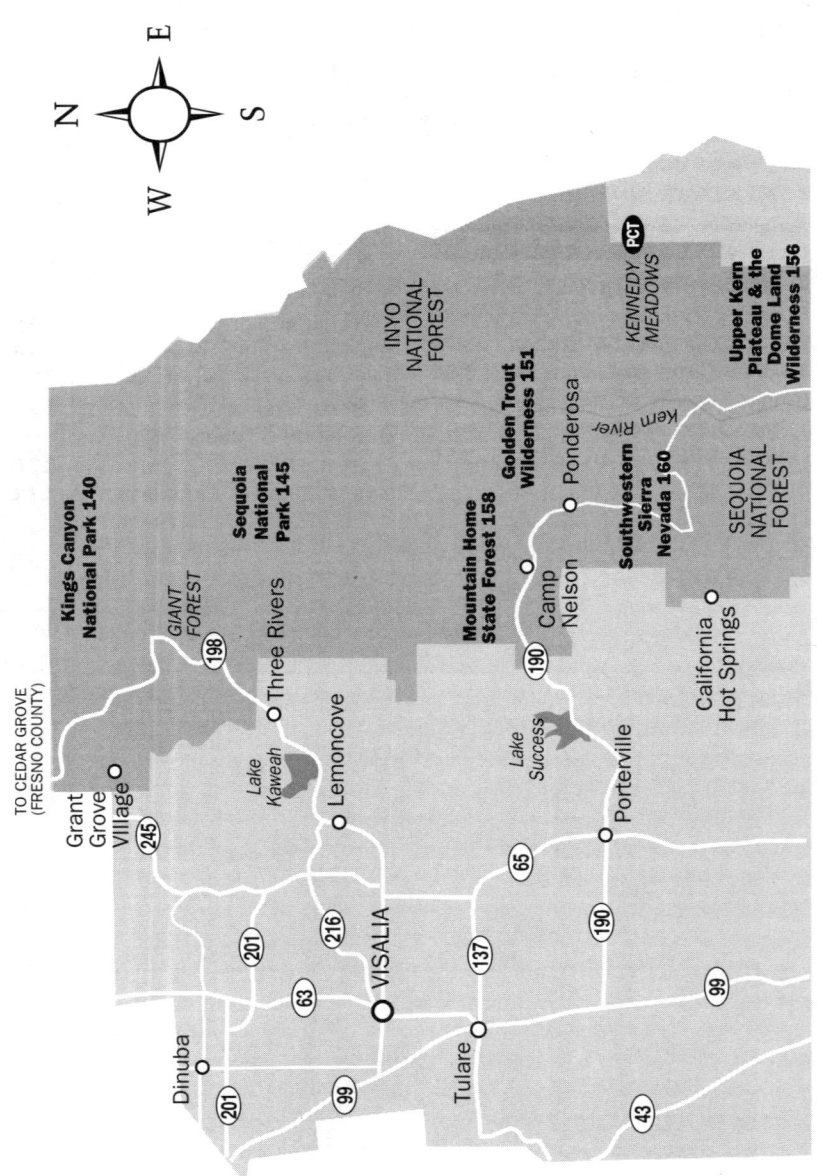

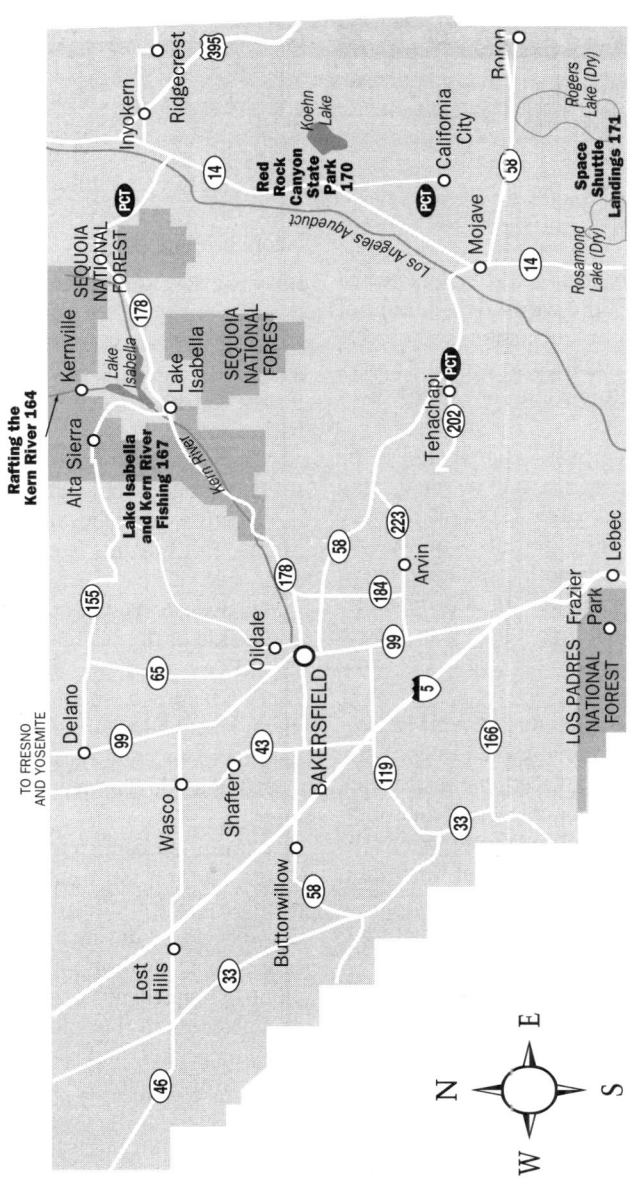

KERN COUNTY

• FEATURED TRIP •

KINGS CANYON NATIONAL PARK

East of Fresno, in the Sierra Nevada

It contains the second largest roadless section in the United States. It has some of the most dramatic, untouched scenery in the world. It is a land of 10,000-foot-tall peaks and 6,000-foot-deep valleys where wild rivers run. And it is a land few people ever see.

Kings Canyon National Park is the best of the best, a land so rugged and remote that to visit its backcountry just once in a lifetime is an accomplishment. It's both a sin and a blessing that of the hordes of people who visit Kings Canyon each year, only a small percentage make it to the backcountry.

Kings Canyon and Sequoia National Parks are administered as one park, although the adjacent parks are often referred to separately. From the southernmost boundary of Sequoia to the northernmost boundary of Kings Canyon is a distance of 75 miles, all of which is wilderness and all of which is within the Sierra Nevada.

Kings Canyon has two highly visited developed areas. Grant Grove is in a small sliver of the park, about an hour east of Fresno. The main draw here is the Grant Grove of giant sequoias. The village has a visitor center at Grant Grove, a restaurant (open daily from 7 A.M. to 7 P.M.), market, gift shop, post office, horse stable, and gas station, where cross-country skis and snowshoes can be rented. There are three large, popular campgrounds nearby.

Cedar Grove is the jumping-off point for those heading into the park's interior. The village and the four nearby campgrounds are located at the end of Highway 180, along the South Fork of the Kings River. There are also a motel and ranger station. Note: There is NOT a gas station, so fill the tank before heading in.

INTO THE BACKCOUNTRY

On a recent visit, we stopped by the Grant Grove Visitor Center and asked a couple of the park service's rangers if they had ever visited King Canyon's backcountry.

"Just got transferred here from Rocky Mountain National," said one.

"Heard it's unbelievable," said the other. "But haven't been there myself."

Then we asked the man who rented us skis at the village gas station. "Yep, I've been there," he answered. "Get up before dawn and drive down there. Then I hike in a couple of hours and fish. But I get out before it gets dark. I don't do that overnight stuff in there."

Planning a backcountry trip into Kings Canyon isn't easy. The first problem is that the road to Cedar Grove is closed during the winter because it's at the bottom of a canyon prone to frequent avalanches. The second problem is that planning a trip takes time, skill, and chutzpah. After Cedar Grove, there are no developed campgrounds.

How to plan such a trip? First, write the park to request a copy of "Backcountry Basics," an eight-page newsletter with information on things you must know to survive in the backcountry (altitude sickness, bears, drinking water, where to set up camp, etc.). Once a destination is determined, we recommend using USGS topographical maps, available at many high-end sporting goods stores. There are also several extremely detailed backpacking guides to the park; the "Backcountry Basics" newsletter lists several worthy titles.

There are over 1,000 miles of hiking trails in both parks. In Kings Canyon, some popular backcountry routes are the 34-mile loop around the Rae Lakes area, as well as the John Muir Trail, which passes through the eastern side of Kings Canyon in the south before cutting across the park in the north, going through the extremely remote, extraordinarily beautiful Evolution Valley. The valley is below the tree line, providing a seven-mile-long patch of green in the otherwise rocky land of granite above 10,000 feet. It's a world many hikers dream about, but relatively few enter.

Permits: Wilderness permits must be obtained to backpack in the park. To reserve a permit, write to Wilderness Permit Reservations, HCR 89, Box 60, Three Rivers, CA 93271; or fax your permit request to (209) 565-4239. Include the following information: name, dates of travel, method of travel (foot or horse), number of people in group, the trailhead and trails you plan to use, and where you plan to camp. Beginning in 1998, there is a $10 nonrefundable fee for making a reservation. For backcountry information, phone (209) 565-3708.

Hiking

Not everyone can or wants to backpack into the high country. There are plenty of great day hikes, both short and long, easy and strenuous:

Zumwalt Meadow: Just one mile long, the trail loops around a beautiful alpine meadow. The trail can be reached by driving through the village of Cedar Grove on Highway 180 for 4.5 miles to the trailhead parking area.

Mist Falls: This trail, also known as the Woods Creek Trail, leads to one of the largest waterfalls in Kings Canyon, 100-foot-tall Mist Falls. The trailhead is at Road's End six miles east of Cedar Grove Village on Highway 180. It's a four-mile hike to the falls with a strenuous 600-foot elevation gain in the final mile. Much of the hike is along the South Fork of the Kings River. Safety note: Keep off the rocks around the falls; they are slippery. Reckless hikers have fallen here and died.

North Grove Loop: The 1.5-mile trail begins at the parking area for the Grant Tree (near Grant Grove Village) and casually winds its way through the forest of giant sequoias. It's a good way to see the trees and stretch your legs for a bit.

Redwood Canyon: This 6.5-mile loop trail takes you to the largest grove of giant sequoias in the world—bigger than the Giant Forest and Grant Grove. It doesn't get the publicity because there is no road in (a good thing), although there is a wonderful hike. To reach the trailhead from Grant Grove Village, take Highway 180 south for six miles and turn right onto Redwood Saddle, which is unpaved. At the fork in the road, turn left and continue to the parking area for the trailhead. The trail splits shortly after the trailhead; head toward Hart Tree. The trail tunnels through a sequoia at one point, satisfying those disappointed to learn that the giant sequoia tunnel tree for cars was actually in Yosemite National Park, until it fell in 1969.

Camping

There are seven campgrounds in the park accessible by car. Three of the campgrounds are in the Grant Grove area and the other four are in the Cedar Grove area, which closes in the winter. Because the campgrounds are located near the villages, campers have markets and ranger stations nearby in both villages.

It is also important to note that none of the campgrounds in Kings Canyon, with the exception of the Canyon View Group Campground, accepts reservations. And, yes, the campgrounds fill up quickly on summer weekends, when the cool temperatures are a huge relief for those suffering in the heat of the San Joaquin Valley. Always phone the park first to check weather and road conditions and try to arrive at the campground as early as humanly possible, especially from Memorial Day to Labor Day.

Azalea: Open year-round, with 114 sites for tents and RVs. This is the only campground open year-round in the park. It's pretty, set near Grant Grove Village and within easy walking distance of the Grant Grove of giant sequoias. Facilities include fire rings, picnic tables, flush toilets, phones, a dump station, and pay showers. Fees are $12 per night.

Sunset: Open Memorial Day to mid-September, with 119 sites for tents and RVs. Sunset is located just south of Azalea in a pine forest. Facilities include flush toilets, phones, and pay showers. Fees are $12 per night.

Crystal Springs: Open mid-May to late September, with 66 sites for tents and RVs. A little farther up the road from the village, Crystal Springs is our pick as nicest campground in Grant Grove (hint: ask for spacious site 14). You're in a pine forest here, with unpaved roads in back of the camp for hiking purposes. Facilities include fire rings, picnic tables, flush toilets, phones, and pay showers. Fees are $12 per night.

Sentinel: Open early May to late October, depending on snowmelt/snowfall, with 83 sites for tents and RVs near Cedar Grove Village. The campground is set along the South Fork of the Kings River. Try to get a spot at the back of the campground near the river. Facilities include fire rings, picnic tables, flush toilets, a phone, and a dump station. Fees are $12 per night.

Sheep Creek: Open early May to late October, depending on snowmelt/snowfall, with 111 sites for tents and RVs near Cedar Grove Village. The campground is set along the South Fork of the Kings River. Try to get a spot at the back of the campground near the river. Facilities include fire rings, picnic tables, flush toilets, a phone, and a dump station. Fees are $12 per night.

Canyon View Camp: Open early May to late October, depending on snowmelt/snowfall, this is the smallest campground in the park with just 37 sites for tents or RVs. It's on the eastern side of Cedar Grove Village and it also backs up to the South Fork of the Kings River. Facilities include fire rings, picnic tables, flush toilets, a phone, and a dump station. Note: The Canyon View Group Camp has four sites for tents only; each site can accommodate 20 to 40 people. Fees are $12 per night.

Moraine: Open early May to late October, depending on snowmelt/snowfall, with 120 sites for tents or

RVs. Located on the eastern side of Cedar Grove Village, this is the final developed campground before entering the park's backcountry at Road's End. Facilities include fire rings, picnic tables, flush toilets, a phone, and a dump station. Fees are $12 per night.

Kings Canyon in the Winter

First things first. We were not lost. We just weren't entirely sure of our exact location. Or how much daylight was left. Or where our car was. Or which trail we were cross-country skiing on.

Other than that small matter, it sure was pretty in the snow-covered forest on this last weekend of February.

Our afternoon skiing had started innocently enough. After renting some dirt-cheap—and not terribly well-maintained—equipment, from the Chevron station in Grant Grove, we kicked off on an adjacent trail.

After crossing the road, we skied down into Grant Grove. The cross-country ski trails in Kings Canyon are marked with little green (intermediate) or blue (beginner) circles on the trees. We saw some green circles and started skiing, believing we were on the General Grant Tree Loop.

Soon, we were skiing past the magnificent giant sequoias. At one point, the trail even passed through a sequoia that had fallen and broken in two upon hitting the ground. Yet, even on its side, the tree was significantly taller than either of us.

A little later, the trail veered away from the road, descending deeper into the forest. Now there was little or no sound except for our skis gliding through the snow. Every now and then we would hear a woodpecker hard at work (what a great place to be a woodpecker).

Now, the map we had purchased indicated the loop was three miles around. We skied, skied, and skied some more. First, the basket broke on one of Steve's cheap rental poles, making it rather hard to turn.

Then, the basket broke on Steve's other cheap rental ski pole. In effect, Steve was now skiing with two sticks. Henceforth, a turn went something like this: Steve would plant one of the poles into the crusty snow. The stuck pole would then act kind of like a pole vault, sending Steve face-first into the snow. Fun, it was not.

Anyhow, after two hours of doing this—in significantly more than three miles—we began to wonder about our location. Like all couples must do, we blamed one another for incorrectly following the map, not being able to follow the trail, not putting laundry away, etc.

The story ends, of course, with our finding our way back to the main road and walking a few hundred yards to our car. In retrospect, the map did show the correct route of the trail, but we humbly suggest to the National Park Service that the trail is longer than three miles.

Ah well, live and learn. It was still a beautiful place to spend a Sunday in February and, at least for one afternoon, we had disappeared, almost literally, into the High Sierra.

Snowplay Information

Ski rentals: Skis, poles, and boots can be rented for a half day or full day from the ski rental shop inside the gas station in Grant Grove Village. Or, better yet, you can rent good equipment at many sporting good stores in Southern California for very reasonable prices. **Trails:** Purchase a much-needed map of the ski trails inside the Grant Grove Visitor Center. Study it very carefully. **Snowplay areas:** There are two snowplay areas suitable for sledding in the park; one is in the Azalea Campground near Grant Grove Village and the other is Big Stump, located just inside the entrance to the park on Highway 180. **Snowshoe hikes:** As in Sequoia National Park, ranger-led snowshoe hikes are conducted on weekends during winter for the princely sum of $1 per person (see Sequoia National Park, page 145, for more information). Reservations are needed; phone the Grant Grove Visitor Center at (209) 335-2856.

GENERAL INFORMATION

Directions: From San Diego or Los Angeles, take Interstate 5 north through the Grapevine. Exit at Highway 99 north and follow the freeway for 95 miles to Highway 198 east. Drive five miles and exit to Highway 63 north. Drive 30 miles and turn right onto Highway 180 east. Follow this road into Grant Grove Village. Or, continue another 30 miles to Cedar Grove Village. **Fees:** The park entrance fee of $10 per vehicle or $5 per person (hikers and cyclists) is good for seven days. **Maps:** A free map of the park is given to you upon admission. We recommend also purchasing the Tom Harrison Cartography Recreation Map of Sequoia and Kings Canyon National Parks, available at many bookstores and the park visitor centers. **Pets:** Dogs are only allowed in the park's campgrounds and developed areas, but must remain on leash. Dogs are not permitted on any trails. **Lodging:** There are cabins and rooms in lodges available for rent at both Grant Grove and Cedar Grove (prices range from $45 to $80), as well as a new 30-room lodge at Grant Grove scheduled to open in the fall of 1998. For more information, phone (209) 335-5500. **Pack trips:** Cedar Grove Pack Station is located east of Cedar Grove Village, offering one-hour to all-day rides, and backcountry pack trips. For more information, call (209) 561-4621. **Contact:** Kings Canyon National Park, (209) 565-3134; daily weather and road conditions, (209) 565-3341. Web site: www.nps.gov/seki/. **Locator:** KINGS CANYON NATIONAL PARK.

IF YOU CAN FIGURE IT OUT . . .

One of Kings Canyon's mysteries in the winter is the number of pickup trucks that can be seen carrying snow from the park down Highway 180 to Fresno. The explanation: People in the San Joaquin Valley are bringing back snow to cover their yards so their children can play. Why not bring the children to the snow? One man, while diligently shoveling snow into his Chevy at a heart attack pace, told us this was easier. We still haven't figured that one out.

BEAR HANGS

Making bear hangs is rarely easy, but it's the most important of all camp chores. Here are two popular bear-hang methods, each of which requires 25 feet of nylon rope:

1. Find two trees about 10 feet apart, each with a sturdy branch 15 feet above the ground. Throw the rope over one branch and tie it to that tree's trunk. Tie your sealed food bag (a nylon bag lined with a garbage bag is best) to the rope's middle. Throw the rope's other end over the second branch. Pull the rope so the food is suspended between the two trees, 10

feet off the ground and five feet from each branch.

2. Tie a throwable rock to one end of the rope. Tie the other end of the rope to your food bag. Throw the rock over a branch about 15 feet off the ground and at least 10 feet from the tree trunk. Pull the rope so the bag is 10 to 13 feet off the ground. Tie the rock end of the rope around another nearby tree or use a stick to counterbalance the rock in parks where bears have been known to chew through rope. Curse us when this takes three hours to accomplish. Important safety tip: Don't hit yourself or others in the noggin with the rock.

• FEATURED TRIP •

SEQUOIA NATIONAL PARK
Deep in the Sierra Nevada

It was midnight and we were arriving in just about the most beautiful place we couldn't see. Having left L.A. only three hours earlier, we were chugging our way up Highway 198, a twisty two-lane road that would end in the tiny town of Three Rivers.

The light of a full moon was trying to force its way through the clouds. The pancake-flat San Joaquin Valley had given way to the foothills of the Western Sierra. On our left we could hear the sound of angry running water. Up and over an arched two-lane bridge, we got a brief glimpse of the Middle Fork of the Kaweah River, tumbling downhill from Sequoia National Park.

It was late February, not exactly the best time of the year to camp in the High Sierra, which had been buried under a foot of snow the previous weekend. So we decided to stay the night in a cozy little motel called the Buckeye Tree Lodge, located just outside of Three Rivers, about half a mile from the park entrance. Our greeting: A posted note on the motel's bulletin board warned of bears invading the parking lot.

Entering the front door of the motel room, we immediately set our sights on the back door. About 20 yards outside that door was the Kaweah. We went to sleep to the tune of the rumbling river water.

The next morning, the woman at the front desk told a story: Once upon a time, a bear had hopped onboard a neighboring motel's dumpster. The dumpster broke loose from its mooring and started to roll down the road—with the bear riding it—before crashing into the guardrail. "That," said the woman, "I would have liked to see."

Only in the Sierra.

THE MAIN ATTRACTIONS
There are parts of Sequoia National that everyone wants to see—and they are well worth seeing.

Like anyone else who visits the park, there was no way we were going to miss the main attraction, the Giant Forest of sequoia trees, one of which is the gargantuan General Sherman Tree.

The Giant Forest is located at the top of the General's Highway, a twisty and narrow road that climbs right up the side of a mountain from the park's entrance. At the top of the mountain, the scenery becomes more high-altitude alpine and visitors begin to see the giant sequoia trees.

In and around the Giant Forest are several of the park's most popular campgrounds, the Lodgepole Visitor Center, Crescent and Round Meadows, popular hiking trails, and the park's lodge and cabins.

A word of warning: Most of the park's 800,000 or so annual visitors are headed for this stretch of the General's Highway. And about 400,000 of those people are headed here during June, July, or August (260,000 in August alone one recent year). "Like an assembly line of people," said a friend of ours following a summertime visit.

Walking smack in the middle of the aptly named Giant Forest, a young man came up to us, holding the hand of his shivering girlfriend. "Where's the big tree?" he asked in his best I-think-I'm-married-to-my-cousin voice. Feeling helpful, we pointed him in the direction of the chap from Los Angeles who had parked his Jaguar in the middle of the General's Highway and then decided to take a nap.

All of the trees in the Giant Forest are comically huge, but none more so than the General Sherman Tree, which resembles the side of a barn and brings new meaning to the word "girth."

The statistics do the talking: At press time, the Sherman Tree was 275 feet tall, had a circumference of 103 feet, and was believed to be 2,300 to 2,700 years old. The Sherman Tree is, in fact, the biggest single living thing by volume, outside of the underground fungus in Michigan discovered a few years ago. "Yes, we've heard all about the fungus," says park ranger Mary Anne Carlton, when asked about the comparative merits of the fungus. "But do you want to call some white gunky thing underground the greatest living thing, or this tree?" Good point.

In the face of such a grand statement as the Sherman Tree, there is really only one thing most visitors can do: Stand in front of the tree, spread their arms wide, and have their photo taken.

Day Hiking

Most of the more interesting trails for day hikes can be found in and around the Giant Forest area at the park's higher elevations. If driving into the park in the summer months, try to arrive as early as possible. Traffic is slow and parking is tough—think Vons on Super Bowl Sunday.

Congress Trail: The trail travels two miles through the heart of the Giant Forest. The trailhead can be found at the General Sherman Tree in the midst of the Giant Forest. There's a parking area for the forest along the General's Highway.

Crescent Meadow: You have to respect the word of John Muir, who called this meadow the "gem of the Sierra." Yes, it's that pretty, with great wildflower displays from spring through summer. The meadow can be accessed on a road from Giant Forest Village, but we suggest hiking there from the General Sherman Tree, a distance of about 1.5 miles. Head toward Thorp's Log, then to the Crescent Meadow Trail, which loops around the meadow.

High Sierra Trail: This 71-mile trail begins at Crescent Meadow and ends at Mount Whitney, on the other side of the park. Okay, 142 miles is a tough day hike, but the first four miles of the trail from Crescent Meadow leads hikers to the scenic 9,046-foot Panther Peak.

Crystal Cave: One of the many little-known facts about Sequoia National Park is that the place is littered with caves. Crystal Cave is the best known of them and the only one open for exploration by the public. Tickets have to be purchased at either the Lodgepole or Foothills Visitor Centers for the 50-minute tours of the cave. Bring a jacket; it's chilly inside, even during the summer.

Marble Fork Trail: The 3.75-mile trail begins at the back of the Potwisha Campground. The trail is initially level, following the Marble Fork of the Kaweah River. Then the fun starts as the trail climbs a hillside. High above the river now, you'll continue to Marble Falls, a pretty waterfall. Keep in mind, the scenery here is more typical of Southern California than of the alpine settings in the Giant Forest above.

BACKPACKING

Even when traffic on the General's Highway resembles the Hollywood Freeway, there is no shortage of room in the backcountry. However, planning a backpacking trip in Sequoia National Park takes some work. Do some reading, study maps, get in very good shape—the high country can be unforgiving to the unprepared.

Wilderness permits are required for those camping in the backcountry; there are quota systems in place from the end of April to the beginning of October. Reservations are accepted for the summer season beginning March 1. Beginning in 1998, there is a $10 nonrefundable fee for making a reservation; payment can be made by personal check, money order, or credit card.

To obtain a permit write to: Wilderness Permit Reservations, HCR 89, Box 60, Three Rivers, CA 93271; or fax your permit request after March 1 to (209) 565-4239. Include the following information: name, dates of travel (entry and exit dates), method of travel (foot or horse), number of people and stock in group (the maximum is 15 people and 20 horses), the trailhead and trails you plan to use, and where you plan to camp.

Be sure to mention if you're planning to hike from the national park into any of the surrounding wilderness areas, such as the John Muir Wilderness or Golden Trout Wilderness, which are administered by the U.S. Forest Service. The permit issued to you by the National Park Service will cover that travel. Conversely, if you're beginning on Forest Service land and traveling into the national park, the Forest Service permit is all that's required—as long as it says you're going into the national park.

Where to go? There are hundreds of possibilities. Keep in mind that the High Sierra Trail, the 71-mile link between Mount Whitney in the east and the Giant Forest in the west, is a sort of main highway for hikers across the park. On the eastern side of the park, the trail follows the Kern River through the spectacular Kern River Canyon, which is 4,000 to 6,000 feet deep in places. Many backpackers also head into the backcountry from the Mineral King section of the park—there are numerous trips to high-country lakes.

Contact: For backcountry information, phone (209) 565-3708.

CAMPING

Most of Sequoia National Park's drive-in camps are accessible from the General's Highway. If you're in a car, no problem. If you have a motor home over 22 feet long, the park "suggests" that you don't try to navigate the section of the General's Highway between Buckeye Flat Campground in the south and the Giant Forest in the north. Take that recommendation very seriously, both for your safety and the safety of others.

All of the campgrounds are available on a first-come, first-served basis with the exception of the Lodgepole Campground, which accepts reservations. Only Potwisha Campground, at the park's lower elevations, is open year-round. During the summer, all of the campgrounds fill up quickly. Arrive as early as possible.

Lodgepole: Open year-round, with 250 sites for tents and RVs. This is a full-service campground located at 6,700 feet in elevation at the northern end of the Giant Forest on the Marble Fork of the Kaweah River. It goes without saying that the scenery is great and there are excellent hikes nearby. Facilities include fire rings, picnic tables, flush toilets, a phone, pay showers, and a dump station. Fees are $12 in the spring and fall, $14 in the summer; there is no fee in the winter. Reservations can be made up to five months in advance by calling PARK.NET at (800) 365-2267.

Dorst: Open from Memorial Day to Labor Day, with 218 sites for tents and RVs. The campground is also located at 6,700 feet in elevation, but is in the northwestern corner of the park and necessitates a longish drive (30 minutes at least) to many of the trails heading into the backcountry. Facilities include fire rings, picnic tables, flush toilets, a phone, and a dump station. Fees are $12 per night.

Potwisha: Open year-round, with 44 sites for tents and RVs. Here's a pretty campground with plenty of trees and grass, just off the General's Highway, which is a little too close (although the road is little traveled at night). Since the camp is in the foothills of the park, the mountains around seem a bit more reminiscent of Southern California than of the high country. But the raging Kaweah River passes right by the campground; try to get sites 18 or 20, which are on grassy spots above the riverbank. Facilities include fire rings, picnic tables, flush toilets, a phone, and a dump station. Fees are $12 per night.

Buckeye Flat: Open from mid-April to mid-September, with 28 sites for tents; no RVs are allowed. A bit higher than Potwisha at 2,800 feet, the camp is located right off the General's Highway before the road starts its serious, steep climb to the park's higher elevations. Facilities include fire rings, picnic tables, and flush toilets. Fees are $12 per night.

South Fork: Open year-round, with 13 sites for tents; RVs are not recommended. South Fork is way off the beaten path in the far southern edge of the park. Facilities include fire rings, picnic tables, and pit toilets. There is no drinking water at this campground. Fees are $12 per night.

Atwell Mill: Open Memorial Day through September, weather permitting, with 21 sites for tents; trailers are not permitted and RVs are strongly discouraged. Located at 6,540 feet in the Mineral King section of the park, Atwell is a good jumping-off point to see the backcountry. Facilities include fire rings, picnic tables, pit toilets, and phones. The water is turned off after September. Fees are $6 per night through September and then free until the campground closes.

Cold Springs: Open Memorial Day through September, weather permitting, with 40 sites for tents; trailers are not permitted and RVs are not recommended. This spot is located at 7,500 feet in the Mineral King section of the park near numerous trails heading into the backcountry. If you're really ambitious and fit, try hiking to Franklin Pass at 11,680 feet. Facilities include fire rings, picnic tables, pit toilets, and phones. The water is turned off after September. Fees are $6 per night through September and then free until the campground closes.

SEQUOIA NATIONAL PARK IN THE WINTER

SNOWSHOEING

The park offers ranger-guided tours of the Giant Forest, snowshoe rentals included, for a fee of $1 per person.

On a recent visit, eight people had signed up to go on the hike, led by park ranger Mary Anne Carlton. None of us had ever snowshoed. Mary Anne looked around the group, as if trying to estimate the day's dork quotient, and said, "Well if you can walk, you can snowshoe." Her suspicions were justified when she observed Julie's attempt to attach snowshoes to her hiking boots, which just happened to both be both for the left foot, as well as two different sizes—the result of a quick pre-trip purchase in L.A. The lesson to be learned from this: Open the boot box before leaving the store, then leaving town.

The wooden snowshoes were about one foot wide and three feet long. A snowshoe works by spreading a person's weight across a greater area, thus preventing him or her from sinking or being swallowed alive by deep snow.

As Mary Anne predicted, the hardest part about snowshoeing was strapping the things on around our hiking boots (we recommend having waterproof boots, preferably one left and one right). Basically, it's true; if you can walk, you can snowshoe. It's hard to imagine anyone of any age not enjoying plopping around in the snow in these things.

For the next two hours we walked in the forests surrounding an open meadow, admiring more of the giant sequoias. The exercise was great, the quiet of the forest soothing. The information was both fascinating and alarming—one woman was a little disturbed to learn that the giant sequoias produce cones with male seeds that pollinate the female seeds of the same tree. "Isn't that incestuous?" she quietly asked, over and over again.

We saw sequoias of every shape and size. Most were easily over 200 feet tall, the lowest branch never more than 150 feet off the ground. We even passed a tiny sequoia, one that was only six feet tall. Someone asked Mary Anne how old it was.

"Hard to tell," she said. "Maybe around 50 years old or so."

Contact: To make a reservation for a winter snowshoe hike (only offered on weekends) with a park ranger, phone the Foothills (Ash Mountain) Visitor Center at (209) 565-3719.

CROSS-COUNTRY SKIING

Besides the snowshoe hike with a park ranger, Sequoia National Park offers some nice terrain for cross-country skiing. Skis and snowshoes can be rented at a ski shop located next to the Wolverton parking lot.

This isn't just a great way of seeing much of the park in the winter—it's the only way. Remember, Sequoia National typically gets over 100 inches of snow every winter. Yet, temperatures often remain mild. You can get out into the forest, ski or snowshoe, picnic on a large rock (of which there is no shortage), and then head back to the city or a motel room in Three Rivers. One other tip: Get a map of the ski and snowshoe trails at the ski rental shop.

What are the best trails? Well, it's hard to imagine anyone being disappointed in the Giant Forest. Check out the Congress Loop, Round Meadow, or Long Meadow. All are very pretty when covered with the white stuff.

ANOTHER CROSS-COUNTRY SKI OPTION

Just outside the park's boundary is the Montecito-Sequoia Lodge, which grooms its own 45 kilometers of cross-country trails during the winter. There's also access to another 100 kilometers of backcountry trails. The lodge has rooms, a meal plan, and offers easy access to both Sequoia National Park and the Grant Grove area of Kings Canyon. Summer activities include hiking, tennis, and boating on a small lake. For more information, phone the lodge, (209) 565-3388.

GENERAL INFORMATION

Directions: From San Diego or Los Angeles take Interstate 5 north through the Tejon Pass, exiting to Highway 99 north. Take Highway 99 for 99 miles, exiting onto Highway 198 east. Drive 37 miles to Three Rivers and the park entrance. The Giant Forest and the village are another 16 miles on the General's Highway. **Fees:** The park entrance fee of $10 per vehicle, $5 per person (hikers and cyclists) is good for seven days. **Maps:** A free map of the park is given to you upon admission. We recommend also purchasing the Tom Harrison Cartography Recreation Map of Sequoia and Kings Canyon National Parks, available at many bookstores and the park visitor center. **Pets:** Dogs are only allowed in campgrounds and developed areas and must be leashed. They are not permitted on the trails. **Lodging:** There are several motels located in Three Rivers, near the park's southern entrance. We recommend the Buckeye Tree Lodge (209-561-5900) or the Best Western Holiday Lodge (209-561-4119). The Giant Forest Lodge is near much of the park's good stuff and has rustic cabins and motel rooms, which will run you anywhere from $35 to $120 depending on the season and how comfy you choose to be. For more information, phone (209) 565-3134 and punch your way through the robot-voiced menu. **Horse rentals:** During the summer, horses can be rented at either the Wolverton Pack Station, which is near the Giant Forest, or at Mineral King, located in the far southern section of the park. A variety of trips are offered, including half-day, one- and two-day rides, as well as overnight pack trips (in the $120 range). For more information, phone Sequoia National Park at (209) 565-3134. **Visitor centers:** The park has two visitor centers: Foothills (Ash Mountain) and Lodgepole. Foothills is located at Ash Mountain, along the General's Highway, just a mile past the entrance to the park. Lodgepole is located on the General's Highway also, just beyond the Giant Forest. **Contact:** Sequoia National Park, (209) 565-3134; daily weather and road conditions (updated daily at 9:30 A.M.), (209) 565-3341. Web site: www.nps.gov/seki/. **Locator:** SEQUOIA NATIONAL PARK.

THE EMBATTLED TREES

For hundreds of years, the only real danger to the existence of the giant sequoia was lightning.

Not anymore. In the 1800s, loggers

descended on the giant sequoia forests in and around Sequoia National Park. By 1890, lumberjacks had succeeded in felling about one-third of all the giant sequoias before John Muir convinced Congress to protect large numbers of the trees in a national park.

Even with logging of the sequoias a thing of the past, both the trees and the park face other dangers. Winds carrying filthy air from Sacramento, Fresno, the Bay Area, and the pesticide-laden Central Valley blow straight through the park. Much of the pollution is ozone from cars. How bad is it? Although ozone cannot be seen or smelled, there are days when the ozone levels in Sequoia National Park exceed that of the perpetually smoggy Los Angeles area.

Scientists and rangers have begun to notice the deteriorating effects of the ozone on many of the park's conifers. The sequoias, for now, seem big enough and strong enough to withstand the assault. But no one knows how much longer they can tolerate it.

Mineral King

The Mineral King Valley is located in the southern section of the park at the end of an obscenely twisty 25-mile road that begins in Three Rivers. Along the way, the road passes through Silver City, a small private community completely surrounded by the park. The Silver City Store rents barebones cabins for about $60 a night. There are also two campgrounds, Atwell Mill and Cold Springs, in the area.

Mineral King has a pack station, which offers guided rides into the backcountry. There are also many hiking trails accessible from Mineral King; many high country lakes can be reached via day hikes.

There is no access to Silver City and Mineral King during the winter. They usually open again in the late spring. Phone the park for details.

Sorry—Wrong Park, Wrong Year

At the Lodgepole Visitor Center, we mentioned to a ranger that we were writing this book. "Better take this flyer," she said.

On the flyer was a photo of a car driving through the trunk of a giant sequoia—a scene that is legendary. "The most frequently asked question I get is where to find that tree," said the ranger with a slightly pained expression. "The thing is, the tree is in Yosemite. And it's not even there anymore. It fell over in '69."

Well, Sequoia National Park does have an auto log of its own, but its auto log was tunneled through after it had fallen over on its side. Yosemite's, at the time it was tunneled, was still standing.

• **Featured Trip** •

Golden Trout Wilderness
Into the beautiful southeastern Sierra Nevada

Gastronomes on the Trail

An acquaintance Randi of Reseda, was tired of men. For one gloriously free weekend, neither she nor three of her friends wanted to encounter any of the smelly, stinky, lyin', cheatin', slothlike subspecies of humankind commonly known as man.

So, Randi and her friends began planning a backpacking trip deep into the southeastern Sierra, specifically a beautiful place they kept hearing about called the Golden Trout Wilderness. Randi & Co. made a few phone calls that pretty much clinched the deal. They learned that the Golden Trout Wilderness, which is located in Sequoia and Inyo National Forests, is a mixture of alpine meadows, huge mountains, forests of pine and sequoias, boulders, and mountain streams where native—not planted—golden trout still lurk.

In short order, Randi & Co. found a couple of old backpacks, borrowed other supplies from coworkers, loaded up Randi's Pathfinder, and said, "Goodbye L.A., hello mountains."

Well, sort of. It was more like "Hello, Ridgecrest," the not-so-lovely Mojave Desert town where they roughed it in the local EconoLodge. But the adventure began the next morning, when they turned off U.S. 395 and drove up twisty Ninemile Canyon Road into the mountains. After an hour or so, they finally landed at a small Forest Service ranger station. There, they met the ranger who had for weeks helped them plan their odyssey over the phone, answering one question after another. We'll call her Ranger X.

Ranger X quickly confessed that she isn't much of a hiker and that, in fact, she had never been to the Golden Trout Wilderness. With that, Randi & Co.'s adventure had begun.

They started down the long, dusty, and sometimes steep Blackrock Trail. Soon, they were passing through meadows filled with wildflowers. Lupine was most prevalent, but there were also white, yellow, red, and orange wildflowers. In other words, a regular Rose Bowl parade, minus the crowds.

After hiking 2.5 miles, Randi & Co. passed through Casa Vieja Meadows, a broad swath lined by old grazing fences from the days before this was designated a federal wilderness area. The terrain became more rugged, too, as pines, ferns, and boulders replaced the meadows.

Finally, our intrepid group stumbled into the Jordan Hot Springs Campground after their rigorous 5.5-mile hike. Although a wilderness camp, the site had a few rough-hewn tables and a fire ring and was set in a nice little clearing. After setting up camp, Randi & Co. took a short hike to the Jordan Hot Springs, a former resort summarily removed after the U.S. Forest Service took over the land. There is still a small pool, pipe-fed with water from the hot spring. Here—close your eyes if you're under 21—our intrepid backpackers got stark naked and enjoyed a hot soak under the stars.

The finale to the evening was dinner: grilled chicken with pesto; rice pilaf cooked with bouillon, onions, and parmesan; salad with Dijon/lemon dressing; and "seven sin" bars. Over their meal, Randi & Co. tried to figure out why their packs were so damn heavy.

Breakfast the next day: scrambled eggs with tomato and onion, bagels, and turkey bacon. The main event of the day (besides dinner—we'll get to that in a moment) was a 10-mile jaunt on the Hells Hole Trail, which parallels swift-moving Ninemile Creek, to an 80-foot waterfall. Dead tired, Randi & Co. didn't make it to a second waterfall farther down the trail.

After another soak in the hot spring, the group enjoyed a dinner of tricolor pepper stir-fry with broccoli and rice. Chocolate chip cookies from Trader Joe's was dessert. Patting their filled tummies, the women traded conversation with a couple of other campers while, overhead, falling stars left streaks in a sky already lit by a full moon.

Night quickly turned into breakfast: pancakes studded with reconstituted dried blueberries, syrup boiled from brown sugar and water. Breakfast faded into another hot spring session sans bathing suits, interrupted by the arrival of 16 teenage members of a Los Angeles Boy Scout troop. The hot spring soak soon dissolved into lunch, which was an eclectic smorgasbord of soup with dumplings, tuna, carrots, and cheese.

Randi & Co. broke camp at this point, hiked back to Casa Vieja Meadows, set up camp for the night, and—you guessed it—enjoyed their last meal in the wild: linguine with clam sauce and cooked carrots. The group, however, was too weary to have dessert and thus decided to forgo the blueberry cobbler.

And that was that. Randi & Co. hoofed it back to their car in a couple of hours and drove back through Kernville, where they stopped for—what else?—lunch: hamburgers and beer.

It was a nice respite from all that nasty camp food.

General Information

Directions: The Golden Trout Wilderness covers 305,804 acres in both the Inyo and Sequoia National Forests. The three most popular access points for the Golden Trout are: the Blackrock Trailhead to the south, Horseshoe Meadows to the east, and Mountain Home State Forest to the west. **Permits:** Permits to enter the wilderness area are not necessary for day hikers, but they are mandatory for anyone planning on staying overnight within the wilderness. There are quotas on some trailheads. For current quota information, phone the Inyo National Forest, Mount Whitney Ranger District at (760) 876-6200. **Best time to visit:** Depending on the amount of snowfall the previous winter, the Golden Trout Wilderness usually opens by Memorial Day. We recommend going when the days are long, from June through mid-August. The wilderness area ranges in elevation from 4,600 feet at Forks of the Kern to 12,432 feet at Mount Florence, which is near Mineral King. It can snow as late as May and as early as September, but summer temperatures are often very hot—in the high 80s and 90s. Always, always bring sunscreen, bug spray, sunglasses, and a hat. All stream water absolutely must be filtered, as the Forest Service allows some cattle grazing within the wilderness area. **Fees:** Use of the wilderness area is free. **Maps:** The Forest Service map of the Golden Trout Wilderness can be purchased at most large outdoor recreation stores in California or at the Blackrock Ranger Station. Or purchase maps by writing to the USDA-Forest Service, Attn: Map Room 807, 630 Sansome Street, San Francisco, CA 94111; request both the Sequoia and Inyo National Forest maps and send $4 for each map. For backpackers, USGS topographic maps are recommended. Consult the Forest Service maps or phone the Forest Service to find out which USGS maps correspond to the area you're planning on visiting. **Pets:** Dogs are permitted. **Contact:** Inyo National Forest, Mount Whitney Ranger District, (760) 876-6200. Sequoia National Forest, Cannell Meadow Ranger District, (760) 376-3781. **Locator:** GOLDEN TROUT WILDERNESS.

BLACKROCK TRAIL

The Blackrock Trailhead is located about 90 minutes from Kernville or an hour from U.S. 395, in the east. The road to the trailhead is often closed until mid- to late spring because of snow. The trailhead also has a parking lot for backcountry visitors.

The trailhead best serves those wishing to visit the southern portion of the Golden Trout. Jordan Hot Springs and the Ninemile Creek drainage are the prominent geographical features—there are also dozens of small meadows. Keep in mind that the hike from the trailhead (elevation 9,000 feet) to Jordan Hot Springs (elevation 6,500 feet) is six miles, with an elevation loss of 2,500 feet. This means that it's a long and often exposed 2,500-foot climb from Jordan Hot Springs back to the trailhead.

Those interested in car camping and taking day hikes into the wilderness have three campgrounds to choose from along Forest Service Road 22S05: Kennedy Meadows (39 sites), Fish Creek (40 sites), and Troy Meadows (70 sites). All three campgrounds are free. Facilities include fire rings, picnic tables, and pit toilets. Phone first to see whether the piped water at the campgrounds is turned on or off. Fish Creek and Troy Meadows have no garbage cans; you must pack out your trash. RVs can access all three campgrounds.

Kennedy Meadows is located right along the South Fork of the Kern River at an elevation of 6,900 feet; the PCT passes through camp and the river offers good fly-fishing opportunities. Fish Creek and Troy Meadows are closer to the wilderness, at elevations of 7,400 and 7,600 feet, respectively. Fish Creek is adjacent to both campgrounds and is teeming with small golden trout. Both campgrounds have some especially roomy sites; if you can snag site 19 at Troy Meadows, congratulations! It's huge, with several large trees offering shade and a meadow right behind it.

The only drawback to all three campgrounds is that they are popular with Off Highway Vehicle owners since there are a number of trails nearby. For the most part, these folks aren't too noisy, but there's always one guy who absolutely has to fire up his dirt bike at 6:30 A.M.

Directions: From Los Angeles take Interstate 5 north to Highway 14 (Antelope Valley Freeway). Take Highway 14 north to U.S. 395 north. Just three miles past the town of Pearsonville (comprised of a Shell station and a junkyard), turn left onto Ninemile Canyon Road; look for the sign indicating it is 25 miles to Kennedy Meadows. At Kennedy Meadows, the road changes names to Forest Service Road 22S05 and continues toward Sherman Pass. This is the last chance for food and gas; there is a bar and restaurant called the Grumpy Bear, as well as the Kennedy Meadows General Store. At the Blackrock Ranger Station, turn right onto Forest Service Road 21S03 and drive eight miles to the trailhead. To reach the trailhead from Kernville, take Mountain Road 99 north for 19 miles to Sherman Pass Road. Turn right and drive 36 miles, then turn left onto Blackrock Road and continue for eight miles. **Safety note:** The first 10 miles of Ninemile Canyon Road from U.S. 395 are extremely steep, with the narrow road clinging to the side of a deep canyon; the drop-off is thousands of feet and there is no guardrail. Do not drive on this road in any kind of adverse weather. Do not drive on this road at night. If you are scared of heights, do not drive and do not look out the window. Curl up in the backseat and suck your thumb. We're serious. This road is a butt-clencher in every sense of the phrase. **Contact:** Inyo National Forest, Mount Whitney Ranger District, (760) 876-6200. Sequoia National Forest, Cannell Meadow Ranger District, (760) 376-3781. **Locator:** GOLDEN TROUT WILDERNESS.

HORSESHOE MEADOWS

There are three small walk-in campgrounds located around Horseshoe Meadows: Horseshoe Meadows Equestrian Camp (10 sites), Golden Trout (12 sites), and Cottonwood (12 sites). All three are for the use of backpackers heading into the backcountry and have a one-night stay limit. The elevation is 10,000 feet. Fees are currently $5 per night. Reservations are not accepted; all sites are available on a first-come, first-served basis. Facilities include fire rings, picnic tables, vault toilets, and piped water.

There are several good trails leading into the wilderness from Horseshoe Meadows, the most prominent being the Cottonwood Pass Trail, which begins at the end of the road immediately after the Golden Trout walk-in camp. The trail travels west, climbing to Cottonwood Pass (elevation 11,200 feet), where it intersects the Pacific Crest Trail. From the pass, the PCT travels north toward the John Muir Wilderness and south into the Golden Trout Wilderness. Or continue westward on a trail to Big Whitney Meadow, where there are several good campsites.

The Cottonwood Pack Station also offers horseback trips into the backcountry. For more information, phone (760) 878-2015.

Talk about a scary drive: The road to Horseshoe Meadows literally forms the letter "Z" up the side of the Eastern Sierra—it is easily seen when driving south on U.S. 395. The campgrounds are at an elevation of 10,000 feet; expect chilly nights.

Directions: From Lone Pine, drive 3.5 miles west on Whitney Portal Road. At Horseshoe Meadows Road, turn left and drive 19 miles. Be extremely careful and turn off the air-conditioning to avoid overheating while climbing the road. **Contact:** Inyo National Forest, Mount Whitney Ranger District, (760) 876-6200. **Locator:** KENNEDY MEADOWS.

MOUNTAIN HOME STATE FOREST

This is the sole entrance to the Golden Trout from the western Sierra. It's also fairly remote (see the section on Mountain Home State Forest in this chapter on page 155). The easiest access point is from the day-use parking lot just above the parking lot for the Hidden Falls Campground. The Redwood Crossing Trail follows the North Fork of the Middle Fork of the Tule River upstream—an especially picturesque stretch of water surrounded by giant sequoia trees. At 1.5 miles, the trail passes out of the state forest and into the Golden Trout. The trail ultimately crosses into Sequoia National Park; hikers can follow a network of trails all the way to Mineral King.

Directions: From Porterville take Highway 190 east for 18 miles and turn left on County Road J37. Drive 30 miles until J37 ends at the park. Follow the signs to Hidden Falls or Moses Gulch Campgrounds. The roads in the forest are unpaved, but are maintained just well enough to accommodate cars. **Fees:** Access is free. **Maps:** Maps are available at the ranger station in Balch County Park, which is located along the paved road in the middle of the state forest. **Pets:** Dogs are permitted, but should be leashed. **Contact:** Mountain Home State Forest, (209) 539-2855. **Locator:** MOUNTAIN HOME STATE FOREST.

• FEATURED TRIP •

UPPER KERN PLATEAU AND THE DOME LAND WILDERNESS

In Sequoia National Forest, northeast of Kernville

Looking for a campsite in the Sierra Nevada, a bit off the beaten path but still accessible by car?

Three words: Upper Kern Plateau.

The plateau constitutes the land to the east of the Kern River, south of the Golden Trout Wilderness, and west of the Dome Land Wilderness. Located entirely within Sequoia National Forest, the plateau is covered by millions of firs, pretty meadows, granite domes, and clear mountain streams.

The Upper Kern Plateau is also a good place from which to launch a trip into the Dome Land Wilderness, which is everything the plateau is, but more. What makes the Dome Lands special are its granite domes, peaks, and towers, often seen on ridges.

The Dome Land Wilderness covers 94,695 acres, most of which is above 7,000 feet in elevation. Like the plateau, the wilderness area is crisscrossed by mountain streams and trails. Wildflowers sprout here in the early summer, and finding a backcountry camping spot will be no problem, since the wilderness area does not receive heavy visitation.

In the past we have combined a rafting trip on the Kern River with camping in the plateau. Here's our itinerary: After work on Thursday night, we made the three-hour drive from L.A. to Kernville, where we spent the night in a motel. On Friday we took a half-day rafting trip, from 10 A.M. to 2 P.M. After lunch, we jumped in the car and made the 90-minute drive to Horse Meadow Campground.

There are 33 sites at the campground, most of which are large and some of which back up to a small creek. Facilities include fire rings with grills, picnic tables, piped water, and chemical toilets housed in what are commonly known as outhouses. Note: There are no garbage cans or dumpsters and it's necessary to pack out garbage. Bring plastic garbage bags!

Despite it being a Friday afternoon in early June, half of the campsites were still unoccupied. We chose a large site that backed up to a house-sized pile of boulders—perfect for scrambling about on. The redneck ratio at the campground was low: No boom boxes were heard, nor did we see any broken beer bottles on the ground. As evening fell, one gent in the adjacent site pulled out a guitar, which he plunked around on for a couple of minutes before dutifully following his womanly companion into their tent.

On Saturday morning we drove from Horse Meadow over a series of bumpy, narrow Forest Service roads to the trailhead for Manter Meadow; the trailhead is located on the eastern side of Big Meadow on Forest Service Road 23S07. There is a small parking area and Forest Service bulletin board at the trailhead. We could write all the directions in the world here, but you will never find it without the Sequoia National Forest map.

The trail meandered through the forest and then begin to rise. And rise. And rise some more. We hoofed it up the side of the mountain in an hour or so, panting thanks to the heat (80 degrees or so) and the elevation (7,500 feet).

At the top of the ridge is a sign indicating you're entering the Dome Land Wilderness. Looking up at a higher ridge on the left, it's easy to see where the wilderness area got its name. Granite domes.

The trail then wound its way downhill all the way to a ranger station at Manter Meadow, which was temporarily unoccupied. We hiked around the meadow's perimeter, eventually finding the perfect rock on which to picnic. After a few salami sandwiches followed by a nap, we hoofed it back up and over the hill to the car. During the entire day, we saw just five other people.

We returned to the campground and rested a bit, before taking a walk down to the Salmon Creek Trail, which begins just downhill from the campground entrance at the end of a short gravel road. The trail meanders through one corner of the meadow and then hooks up with Salmon Creek. You can try fishing in the creek, which the Forest Service swears is stocked. The only thing we saw were six-inch or smaller brook trout that were easily spooked.

Both the creek and the trail cut through a small canyon for almost five miles before ending at Salmon Creek Falls. Unfortunately, the falls can't be seen from the trail because they are in a precarious place—a cliff. No big deal. We took in the sunset from the boulders overlooking Salmon Creek. The gurgling stream and the wind blowing through the trees provided the soundtrack.

On Sunday morning we broke camp and start back to L.A. But first we stopped in Kernville and spent some time lying in the cool grass of the town's riverside park and eating ice cream cones. We watched some kayakers, fished a bit (unsuccessfully), and, finally, watched our dog roll in something really disgusting.

She seemed happy as a clam, so we rolled down the windows for the ride home. Thankfully, the temperature in the Central Valley was only 105.

Directions: From Kernville to Horse Meadow Campground, take Mountain Road 99 north for 19 miles and make a hard right onto Sherman Pass Road just before the Johnsondale Bridge over the Kern River. Sherman Pass Road winds uphill for five miles. At Cherry Hill Road (Forest Service Road 22S12), turn right and follow it for 10 miles to Horse Meadow Campground. If you stay on Sherman Pass Road, you can continue to the Black Rock Ranger Station and the other campgrounds. **Fees:** Day-use parking is free. All campgrounds are free except for Horse Meadow, which charges $6 per night. **Maps:** We recommend two maps: the AAA Tulare County Map, available through AAA and at many bookstores, and the Sequoia National Forest Map, available at the Sequoia National Forest, Cannell Meadow Ranger Station in Kernville (at 105 Whitney Road) or by sending a check for $4 to USDA-Forest Service, Attn: Map Room 807, 630 Sansome Street, San Francisco, CA 94111. **Best time to visit:** Late spring, early summer, and early fall are the best times to camp and hike on the plateau. Always expect chilly nights because of the elevation. And be aware that the mosquitoes can be brutal up here in late spring and early summer—especially during patches of warm weather. Bring a full bottle of bug repellent and, if particularly susceptible to bites, head netting. July and August days can bring daytime temperatures in the 90s, but very agreeable nights. The plateau is inaccessible in the winter; the Forest Service closes Sherman Pass Road when the snow starts falling. **Pets:** Dogs are permitted. They'll love it! **Campgrounds:** There are three developed campgrounds in the Upper Kern Plateau: Horse Meadow, Troy Meadows, and Fish Creek. All three are near creeks and have piped water and outhouses. You can also pitch a tent off trail in the Dome Land Wilderness, although you have to backpack in and out. You don't need a permit to camp, but you do need a permit to have a campfire. Permits can be obtained at the U.S. Forest Service, Cannell Meadow District Office in Kernville. **Mountain biking:** There's a ton of very good and very hard mountain biking, including lots of single track, in the Kern Plateau. Most of the better trails are found in the Black Rock area, which is north of Sherman Pass Road. The Cannell Meadow Ranger District has a four-page trail guide, available at the Forest Service office in Kernville. Two outfitters, Mountain & River Adventures (760-376-6553) and Sierra South Mountain Sports (760-376-3745) offer guided tours. **Contact:** Sequoia National Forest, Cannell Meadow Ranger District, (760) 376-3781. **Locator:** UPPER KERN PLATEAU AND THE DOME LAND WILDERNESS.

• FEATURED TRIP •

MOUNTAIN HOME STATE FOREST

Tucked in a quiet corner of the Western Sierra

A rule of thumb in California: Where there are big trees, such as giant sequoias or redwoods, there are people.

Thousands and thousands of people, many of whom will be bearing the weapon of choice preferred by many a modern tourist: the recreational vehicle. Those who escape being steamrolled by RVs on the roads—studies have shown there are three people on the planet who can competently drive a motor home—might actually make it to the trailhead.

But the trailhead is a dangerous place, too. Here, the modern tourist emerges from the cocoonlike RV and subjects himself to nature. To protect himself, the modern tourist carries a sidearm: the camcorder. The camcorder rarely appears in a holster; rather, it appears to be surgically attached to the modern tourist's eye socket. In the manner of a blind person drunk on turpentine, the tourist stumbles around the grove of big trees, pointing the camcorder only at things that don't move.

After taping 10 hours of raw footage of the same tree, the modern tourist quickly retreats back to his RV, where he can rewind the tape and review the scenery. This is important. Anything not preserved on videotape may not have actually happened.

The above scene takes place every

summer in Yosemite, Sequoia, and Kings Canyon National Parks, where most of the giant sequoia trees are found. Go see for yourself. If, by chance, you are reading this book while driving in a motor home and you're wearing plaid shorts and dark socks, read no further.

As for the rest, we'll let you in on a little secret: Mountain Home State Forest. Located 30 miles from off-the-beaten-path, the forest is the place to see giant sequoia trees and avoid the summertime crowds. Yes, there will be other people in the forest, but only a fraction of the throngs found in the nearby national parks.

The forest is set at an elevation of 6,000 feet, about 10 miles south of the Sequoia National Park boundary. The area was once heavily logged, but the state of California purchased the land from a lumber company in 1946, thus saving more than 5,000 old-growth sequoia trees. Parts of the demonstration forest are still logged by the state in order to promote sound forestry practices. But the emphasis is still on scenery.

There are some fabulous trails throughout the park, as well as two great campgrounds. There is also a lake stocked with trout, a pack station, and a beautiful stream, the North Fork of the Middle Fork of the Tule River, which is lined by sequoia trees and runs alongside the campsites. All in all, this is a fabulous place for a weekend camping getaway—and it's a place that few people in L.A. or San Diego know of.

Eight campgrounds are available within the park, the best being the Hidden Falls Campground and the Moses Gulch Campground.

Hidden Falls is situated on a bluff above the Tule River, at an elevation of 5,900 feet. The campground is of the walk-in variety. Visitors park their cars and then walk downhill to one of eight tent-only sites. The two farthest sites, numbers 7 and 8, are the best; they're a good 200 yards from the parking lot. The first two sites are not so great; they are next to the parking lot and outhouses, though they are roomier than the others. In 1996, brand-new bear boxes were installed at each of the sites.

Moses Gulch is about one mile downstream from Hidden Falls at an elevation of 5,400 feet. It, too, is a walk-in campground; most of the 10 sites are within 100 yards of the parking lot. A couple of the sites are just okay, but some are wonderful—a bit isolated and near the river. Bear boxes are also available.

Giant sequoias grace both campgrounds, and there are brook, brown, and rainbow trout in the Tule. The fish are small and the fishing is average, but the scenery makes up for lack of productivity. One guidebook we referred to before our visit warned of "roving bands of teenagers with fishing poles." After two days of failing to see such wildlife we lucked out on Sunday morning—the teenagers didn't appear to be dangerous (nor did they catch anything).

Any hiking in the forest? You bet. The best trail follows the Tule River, passing through both campgrounds. To the north, which is upstream, the trail follows a particularly beautiful stretch of the boulder-strewn river, with small waterfalls every 100 feet or so. Looming above the river are several peaks, including 9,331-foot Moses Mountain. At 1.5 miles north of Hidden Falls Campground, the trail comes to a junction with the Redwood Crossing Trail. It isn't marked, but if you follow the main trail as it bends away from the river, you will soon enter the Golden Trout Wilderness.

Directions: From Porterville take Highway 190 east for 18 miles and turn left on County Road J37. Drive for 30 miles until J37 ends at the park. Follow the signs to Hidden Falls or Moses Gulch Campgrounds. The roads in the forest are unpaved, but are maintained just well enough to accommodate passenger cars. **Safety tip:** Families with small children should camp at Moses Gulch instead of Hidden Falls. The bluff above the river at Hidden Falls is very steep in places; unsupervised children could fall. **Fees:** Camping at the state forest is free. **Maps:** Maps are available at the ranger station in Balch County Park, which is located along the paved road in the middle of the state forest. **Pets:** Leashed dogs are permitted. **Contact:** Mountain Home State Forest, (209) 539-2855. **Locator:** MOUNTAIN HOME STATE FOREST.

• FEATURED TRIP •

SOUTHWESTERN SIERRA NEVADA

Above Porterville and Springville, in the mountains

For reasons we don't entirely understand—but enjoy nevertheless—the southwestern Sierra Nevada receives little visitation from Southern Californians.

The area is huge and quite beautiful, featuring large rock formations, thick forests (with scattered groves of giant sequoias), beautiful mountain streams and rivers, plenty of hiking trails, and several good campgrounds.

It is roughly bordered by Sequoia National Park in the north, the Kern River to the east, Lake Isabella to the south, and the San Joaquin Valley to the west. Almost all of the land within those boundaries is comprised of the Sequoia National Forest with elevations ranging from 2,000 to 9,000 feet. As for development, there's not a lot up here—mostly some scattered retreats, communities, vacation homes, and campgrounds.

Access is easy. A good two-lane road called the Great Western Divide Highway does a kind of half-loop though the area; the highway is accessible from Springville in the north and California Hot Springs in the south. Although the road is open year-round, keep in mind that higher elevations often receive heavy snowfall in the winter. Always phone for road conditions before leaving home and, of course, have tire chains.

The best way to see the area is to spend a three-day weekend in the mountains. Here's how we do it: We leave after work on Thursday night and make the two-hour drive from L.A. to Bakersfield, where we bunk down in one of the two Best Westerns in town (both welcome our dog, Molly). Then, on Friday morning, after an artery-plugging and delicious breakfast at IHOP, we make the two-hour drive into the mountains. The idea is to get there early Friday afternoon in order to get a decent campsite. We don't recommend arriving on Saturday from Memorial Day to Labor Day, as campsites are hard to come by. Although Southern Californians don't visit here much, the flatlanders from the San Joaquin Valley know the area very well.

Most of the Forest Service campgrounds in the area follow a consistent theme: They're small, near a major trailhead, and some are adjacent to a stream stocked with trout by the state Department of Fish and Game.

1. REDWOOD MEADOWS AND LONG MEADOW CAMPGROUNDS

The best campground in the area is Redwood Meadows. It's just across the road from an impressive grove of giant sequoias known as the 100 giants. The largest tree here is 220 feet tall with a diameter of 20 feet at its base. In comparison, the General Sherman Tree in Sequoia National Park's Giant Forest is 270 feet tall with a diameter of 36.5 feet.

There are 100 giant sequoias in the main grove and an additional 168 trees spread out in the 355 acres that encompass the grove. A half-mile interpretive trail, called the Trail of 100 Giants, meanders through the trees with nice little signs explaining why the trees are so damn big.

As for the campground, which lies at elevation 6,500 feet, it has 15 spaces for tents or RVs. If Redwood Meadows is full (it's popular in the summertime), try the Long Meadow Campground, which is one mile north on the Great Western Divide Highway. Long Meadow has six sites for tents and RVs.

Each campground has fire grills, picnic tables, and pit toilets. Please note that Redwood Meadows has piped water, but Long Meadow does not—bring your own water.

Directions: From California Hot Springs take the Great Western Divide Highway north for 13 miles to the campgrounds. **Reservations:** Reservations are accepted at Redwood Meadows, but not Long Meadow. Phone (800) 280-CAMP/2267. **Fees:** Redwood Meadows is $12 per night. Long Meadow is free. **Contact:** Sequoia National Forest, Hot Springs Ranger District, (805) 548-6503. **Locator:** CALIFORNIA HOT SPRINGS.

2. PEPPERMINT AND QUAKING ASPEN CAMPGROUNDS

Going north from Redwood Meadows, the next two campgrounds are Peppermint (7,100 feet) and Quaking Aspen (7,000 feet). Peppermint sits next to Peppermint Creek, which receives trout plants—hike downstream to the best fishing holes. Quaking Aspen is also very pretty—just across the highway is Freeman Creek, where there is also some decent fishing (hiking downstream will eventually take you to the Freeman Grove of giant sequoias). Both campgrounds are well shaded. Facilities at each include fire grills, picnic tables, and vault toilets. Quaking Aspen has piped water, but Peppermint does not—bring your own water or a water filter/purifier.

There are several good hikes in the immediate area. The best hike is to the Needles, a collection of several rock outcrops that look like, well, needles. Your destination on this hike is a Forest Service fire-spotting tower that sits atop one of those needles.

Hikers are permitted to climb the tower via a series of wooden stairways built by the CCC during the Depression. The view of the Golden Trout Wilderness and the Kern River drainage is, to say the least, jaw-dropping. Before making the hike, phone the Tule River Ranger District at (209) 539-2607 to make sure the fire tower will be open.

To get to the trailhead from Quaking Aspen, drive south on the Great Western Divide Highway for just over one mile. Turn left onto Forest Service Road 21S05, which is unpaved. Drive almost three miles to the end of the road and park at the trailhead. It's two miles from the trailhead to the fire tower.

Directions: From Springville take Highway 190 east/south for 21 miles to Quaking Aspen. Continue south on the same road for two miles to Peppermint Campground. **Reservations:** Both campgrounds accept reservations, which are recommended during the summer. Phone (800) 280-CAMP/2267. **Fees:** Sites are $12 per night. **Contact:** Sequoia National Forest, Tule River Ranger District, (209) 539-2607. **Locator:** CAMP NELSON.

3. BELKNAP AND WISHON CAMPGROUNDS

The Belknap Campground is located on the outskirts of Camp Nelson, a small community in the woods consisting largely of summer retreats. The campground is right along the South Fork of the Middle Fork of the Tule River and is entirely shaded. The elevation is 5,000 feet. We like this campground a lot, although it does receive some through traffic, since there's a major trailhead at the end of the road.

It's a trail well worth taking, too. Though it has no official name, it is referred to on Forest Service maps as 31E30. The trail follows the Tule River, where there is some very good fishing. Within half a mile, the trail gently climbs into the McIntyre grove of giant sequoias. At one-half mile, the trail passes two side-by-side sequoias that are as big as they come.

The trail continues alongside the stream all the way to Quaking Aspen Campground, although there are several stream crossings en route. Don't try crossing in the spring, however; in June of 1998 this stream could easily kill you. Also, there are a couple of areas near the stream where the trail has eroded; watch your footing.

Belknap has 15 sites for tents or RVs. Facilities include fire rings, picnic tables, vault toilets, and piped water. As you drive into the campground, you'll pass a small grocery store that serves the community of Camp Nelson. It's a good place to buy all the things you forgot before leaving town.

Wishon Campground sits at an elevation of 3,000 feet, alongside the North Fork of the Mddle Fork of the Tule River. There are 35 sites, 26 of which can accommodate RVs. About half the sites are well shaded, the others are fairly exposed. Most of the sites do not afford much privacy; this is not the campground where you want to have bad neighbors.

Our advice is to visit Wishon anytime from Labor Day to Memorial Day—it's open year-round. Why? Wishon is the nearest campground to the San Joaquin Valley.

Let us repeat that. Wishon is the nearest campground to the San Joaquin Valley. It gets hits hard and, often on the weekends, is not exactly what you would call peaceful.

However, the campground is in a pretty location. Wishon receives heavy trout plants, and the river has hundreds of great fishing holes both upstream and downstream from the campground. These are hatchery fish, so there's nothing terribly challenging about catching one. Those with spin tackle should tie a swivel on to the end of their line and use a small hook (size 16 and up) with at least 18 inches of leader. Salmon eggs or Powerbait are the bait of choice here. Most fish are in the eight-inch range, although we've seen some 12- to 14-inchers get pulled from the stream.

There are a couple of hiking possibilities. From the campground, follow Wishon Road until it ends at a locked gate. The only people allowed to drive past the gate are residents of Doyle Springs, an exclusive little community about one-half mile north of the campground. Hike along the road to the entrance to town, where a sign points to a hiker's trail that climbs a ridge and skirts around the community. It's a new trail—hikers were formerly allowed to gain access upstream by hiking through town, but the rich folks got tired of that.

The trail climbs above Doyle Springs and eventually drops back to the river. Continue hiking upstream on Forest Service Trail 30E14 to get to some quieter fishing holes than the ones around the campground. Backpackers can also hike this trail all the way to Mountain Home State Forest.

The other option is to cross the river just upstream from Doyle Springs (don't try this crossing in high water) and follow the Jacobsen Trail (Forest Service Trail 32E11) to the Golden Trout Wilderness. It's a very pretty route through the forest and one that receives little traffic.

One important note about Wishon: Keep your eyes peeled for ensantina, better known as red lungless salamanders. These little critters are beautiful. They're also very slow and can often be found in the road. Watch your step and try not to run them over.

Directions: From Springville to Wishon Campground, take Highway 190 east for seven miles and turn left on Wishon Drive (if you pass the powerhouse, you've gone too far). Take Wishon Drive for four miles to the campground. It's a paved, but bumpy and narrow road. From Springville to Belknap Campground, take Highway 190 east for 15 miles. Turn right at the sign marking the turnoff for the campground. **Reservations:** Both campgrounds accept reservations, which are recommended during the summer. Phone (800) 280-CAMP/2267. **Fees:** Sites are $12 per night. **Contact:** Sequoia National Forest, Tule River Ranger District, (209) 539-2607. **Locator:** CAMP NELSON.

THE PONDEROSA

The Ponderosa is one of those little vacation-type mountain villages that have sprung up in the middle of nowhere. If you can't find it on the map, put your finger on Springville and follow Highway 190 until it turns into the Great Western Divide Highway.

This is a collection of 100 or so homes in the middle of the mountains. People come here to rent a cabin and still be able to say they're in the woods in the middle of nowhere. It's a cozy little place, especially for those who really need to get away from it all.

The Ponderosa Lodge rents out two large rooms and hosts the occasional wedding reception. Like everything else in the Sierra, the scenery is terrific. There's plenty to do, including hiking, fishing, horseback riding, cross-country skiing, and snowshoeing. The Trail of the 100 Giants is 10 miles south on the Great Western Divide Highway. Phone: Ponderosa Lodge at (209) 542-2579.

Forest Service Visitor Centers

There are Forest Service visitor centers in both Springville and California Hot Springs. Both are good places to purchase maps and get information on the area.

There's only one problem. We have often found that the Sequoia National Forest puts its least experienced ranger behind the visitors desk. For example, we stopped by the Tule River Ranger District, where a rather large man in a neatly pressed shirt manned the desk. To put it generously, he knew squat. He wasn't sure what roads were open, where the trails could be found, or which streams were stocked. He even admitted to having not done much hiking in the area.

Isn't it fun to see your tax dollars at work?

Directions: The Tule River Ranger District visitor center is located at 32588 Highway 190, three miles before entering Springville. The Hot Springs Ranger District visitor center is located on Route 4, in the town of California Hot Springs. **Maps:** To purchase a map through the mail, send $4 to the USDA-Forest Service, Attn: Map Room 807, 630 Sansome Street, San Francisco, CA 94111 and ask for the Sequoia National Forest map. The map can also be found in many higher-end sporting goods stores.

• FEATURED TRIP •

Rafting the Kern River
In the southern Sierra Nevada

Our guide's name was Buffy. She was blonde, she was buff, and she barked orders like a Marine drill sergeant. She was also quite generous. Near the end of our half-day of rafting on the Kern River, she asked if any of the six passengers might be interested in guiding the raft through the last series of Class III rapids.

Steve, under the misguided impression that he wasn't an idiot, volunteered. After successfully stumbling to the raft's rear, he began barking out a few orders.

"Forward!"

Everyone rowed forward.

"Right side backwards!"

The boat turned slightly to the right.

Easy enough.

The first set of rapids came and went with nary an incident. For at least a moment, it did appear that Steve actually knew what he was doing. As would be expected, his head swelled accordingly.

And, equally predictable, the next set of rapids wasn't so generous.

Kernville is about 70 miles south of Mount Whitney, the tallest peak in the continental United States at 14,495 feet. In the winter, storms slam into Whitney and the surrounding Sierra, blanketing them with snow. When spring arrives, the snow melts and much of that water south of Mount Whitney ultimately drains into one of four rivers: the Kings, Tulare, Kaweah, and the Kern.

The Kern descends straight south, cutting a narrow and deep canyon in the interior of the Sierra. Ultimately, the upper Kern River flows through Kernville and then Lake Isabella—where the river was dammed. Below the dam, the lower Kern River turns to the west, running through a gorgeous and steep canyon for 50 miles. Just east of Bakersfield the canyon abruptly ends and the river flows across gently rolling hills to Bakersfield.

White-water rivers are rated on a scale of Class I (easiest) to Class VI (unrunnable). In the rafting season, much of the Kern River is rated Class III (medium—some waves and holes) and IV (difficult—big waves and holes), enough to throw a scare into most reasonable people. In one 22-mile stretch of the upper Kern there are an astonishing 84 Class IV rapids. Translation: Wet and wild.

The U.S. Forest Service has granted permission to a handful of outfitters to run guided white-water trips on the river. Trips come in all shapes and sizes, including one-hour quickies, half-day and full-day runs, and overnight trips.

The outfitters offer trips on the lower Kern, the upper Kern, and the Forks of the Kern. Which to take?

The lower Kern is very scenic, but its water flows are dependent on releases from the Lake Isabella Dam. Most of the rapids are Class III, with some Class II and Class IV stretches. Two-day trips, including a night of camping, are very popular on the lower Kern.

The upper Kern tends to be wilder. Most of the rapids are Class III or Class IV. Unfortunately, this isn't a terribly long stretch of river; a half-day trip on the upper Kern often means running the same stretch of river three times—with bus trips back upstream.

The Forks of the Kern is the wildest available. The trip begins far upstream from the Johnsondale Bridge, and rafters descend an absolutely gnarly stretch of river—Class IV, V, and VI rapids are the rule, as are wet suits. Outfitters offer one- to three-day trips; many people enjoy the camping excursions because the scenery around the river is drop-dead gorgeous.

Rafting isn't cheap—it's one of the few sports that makes skiing look affordable. One-hour trips usually cost about $15 to $20, half days are in the $60 range, full days in the $100 to $120 range, and overnight trips about $200 to $300. In addition, expect rafting companies to solicit tips for their underpaid guides.

What can you expect from rafting? You're going to get big-time wet. But that's okay—temperatures can easily reach 100 degrees in Kernville in June and July. One other small item: There's a decent chance you might fall out of the raft. If that prospect absolutely scares you witless, don't go rafting.

People fall in all the time. Life jackets are mandatory and the rafting companies make all rafters sit through a lengthy safety lecture before the day begins. None of the companies has lost a customer yet.

The one thing you should bring, however, are Velcro-strapped rafting sandals, which are designed to come off of feet in strong current, preventing feet from getting stuck in between rocks on the river's bottom.

Speaking of falling in the river:

The next set of rapids was rapidly approaching. Buffy didn't seem too concerned. Steve did, hoping to steer the boat right, around the worst of them.

Only one problem. To the right was the riverbank. And someone, who obviously had a keen sense of humor, had built a home on this particular portion of the shoreline, complete with a concrete retaining wall.

The boat quickly fell into a current, which carried it straight toward the wall. If the raft hit the wall, the people sitting on the right side of the raft would have their day ruined—at the very least. Steve had several options here, and it's sufficient to say he chose the most undesirable: He froze.

At this point, Buffy finally came to the rescue, issuing a series of quick commands that somehow turned the boat back into the middle of the river. Afterward she shrugged.

It was, after all, just another afternoon on the Kern.

The Killer Kern

There's a ghoulish sign along Highway 178, just outside Lake Isabella, with a huge number painted on it. At last count the number was 182, which represented the number of people who have drowned in the Kern River since 1969.

That's an average of 10 per year and the reason why the Kern is sometimes referred to as the "Killer Kern."

However, not one of those people died while rafting with a company under permit by the Forest Service. Most died because they tried to swim in the river or tried to ride cheap inflatable rafts or inner tubes down the river. Many of those who died were children not adequately supervised or not wearing a life jacket, or people who were drinking alcohol.

The river's strong current is an obvious hazard. An equally fatal obstacle lies below the water's surface: rocks. Many drowning victims have gotten their feet stuck in the rocks and were subsequently pulled under by the current.

Directions: From downtown Los Angeles to Lake Isabella and Kernville, take Interstate 5 north through the Tejon Pass to Highway 99 north. Take Highway 99 for 23 miles, exiting to Highway 53 east. Drive seven miles and exit at Highway 184 (Patch Highway), turning left (north). Take Highway 184 to Highway 178 east. Drive 35 miles through Kern Canyon to Lake Isabella. From the lake to Kernville, take Highway 155 north until reaching Kernville. From San Bernardino and Riverside County to Lake Isabella, take Interstate 15 north to Highway 138 west. Take Highway 138 for 47 miles, exiting to Highway 14 north. Take Highway 14 for 75 miles, exiting to Highway 178 west. Continue 43 miles to the lake and then follow Highway 155 north to Kernville.

Lodging: Most people rafting the upper Kern choose to stay in Kernville, where most rafting parties gather before heading off to the river. Kernville has about a half dozen motels, all near the river. In the spring, the rooms are often reserved months ahead of time, especially on the weekends. If you are planning a June or July weekend trip, try making your reservations by April 1 or hope that you'll luck out with a cancellation at the last moment. We recommend Kern Lodge Motel, (760) 376-2223; River View Lodge, (760) 376-6019; Sequoia Motor Lodge, (760) 376-2535; and Kern River Inn Bed-and-Breakfast, located alongside Kernville's pretty riverside park, (760) 376-6750.

Rafting outfitters: The following outfitters are under permit from Sequoia National Forest to run rafting trips on the Kern River. Phone them for a free brochure or to make reservations. Chuck Richards' Whitewater, Inc., Lake Isabella, (760) 379-4444 or (760) 379-4685. Kern River Tours, Lake Isabella, (760) 379-4616 or (800) 844-RAFT from California, Nevada, or Utah. Outdoor Adventures, Wofford Heights, (800) 323-4234. Sierra South Mountain Sports, Kernville, (760) 376-3745 or (800) 457-2082. **Fees:** Prices for rafting trips range from $15 to $600, depending on the outfitter and length of trip.

Doing it yourself: The U.S. Forest Service, which administers the Kern River, does allow private citizens to raft the river in their own rafts. Only those with white-water guiding experience should even think about it. Permits are required between May 15 and September 15. Phone the Lake Isabella Visitor Center at (760) 379-5646 or the Tule River Ranger District at (209) 539-2607 for more information. **Best time to go:** Rafting season on the Kern usually begins after May 1, depending on the river's current, which is measured in cubic feet per second (CFS). If the CFS is more than 7,000 or so, the outfitters will often wait for the river to come down a bit. The season generally ends in late July or early August, depending on the previous winter's snowfall. **Contact:** Kernville Chamber of Commerce, (760) 376-2629 or (800) 350-7393. **Locator:** RAFTING THE KERN RIVER.

• FEATURED TRIP •

LAKE ISABELLA AND KERN RIVER FISHING

Draining the Mount Whitney watershed

Lee Penny worked 35 years on the docks in San Pedro and Long Beach. When he finally decided to retire in 1995, there was little doubt about where he and his wife, Sonia, were going to move: Kernville.

"About 28 years ago, a friend of mine said, 'Let's go fishing,'" says Penny. "He said, 'I'm going to take you someplace you're either going to like a lot or not like at all.' So we go up to Kernville and I say to him, 'what is there not to like?' You've got it all up here: The mountains, all the nice trails, the camping. And of course, you've got the river and the lake."

Sounds like a talking chamber of commerce brochure, huh? In fact, Penny's wife, Sonia, does work for the chamber of commerce. Still, Lee Penny has it right. The Kern River and Lake Isabella are one of Southern California's best 1-2 combinations when it comes to fishing, a bargain for only about a two-hour drive from Los Angeles.

The Kern River is known best for its white-water rafting, but there's nothing wrong with its fishing, especially in the 23-mile stretch between Johnsondale Bridge to the north and Isabella to the south. The river receives regular plants from the DFG, with most fish averaging about a pound.

Lake Isabella, too, is stocked regularly with trout, but also contains largemouth bass, crappie, bluegill, and catfish. There are plenty of boat rentals available.

FISHING THE KERN RIVER

"The secret to fishing the Kern," says Lee Penny, "is watching where the old-timers go and what they're fishing. You listen to them and watch them, you'll catch fish."

Fishing the Kern River, like fishing any stream, is a funny business and there are many variables that will determine your success—or lack of it.

Rule number one is using the right setup. Basically, you want to use very light line, two- or four-pound test maximum, with a sliding sinker, swivel, and 18-inch (or longer) leader. As for bait, Lee Penny prefers Powerbait. Others believe that salmon eggs are the way to go. Still others prefer artificial lures.

Late summer is the best time to fish the Kern. The river is low, allowing easier (and safer) access to its many pools. The water is also warm, meaning the fish are active.

Steve Haimwertz and his friends, all from the L.A. area, have mapped out much of the river over the years. "The more you fish the river, the better you'll do," says Haimwertz. "You have to know how to read the river for what the fish wants, which is protection. Look for undercuts, where the river is actually flowing underneath the banks, creating shady places where fish can retreat from the sun. Cast upstream from the depression, let your line drift down to it, let it sink, and see what happens."

Casting upstream is important because trout feed by facing upstream with their mouths open. The idea is to catch and eat anything floating downstream, which isn't an entirely terrible way to live.

"Rocks are good, too," continues Haimwertz. "Always walk upstream, not down; fish get scared if they see you walk downstream. Also, walking upstream gives you an opportunity to fish behind rocks. This is important because water brings food and oxygen, which swirls around the rocks. And that's what fish want. Faster-moving water and shelter."

On a recent trip to the southern Sierra, we spent the better part of the morning fishing the river with nominal success, but remember, we're lousy fishers. What we did find is that you can cover a lot of ground on the Kern. There are several campgrounds along Mountain Road 99 where you can park and walk to the river, as well as numerous other turnouts and grassy areas on the side of the road.

This is huge because river fishing demands that you cover as much ground as possible. Forget the stereotype of the fisherman sitting on a rock all day with his pole lazily in the water. Trout fishing is guerrilla warfare. Keep moving, keep quiet, stay low, have the right weapons, and hit as many pools of water as you can—even the unlikely looking ones.

"I've been hiking and fishing on the river and come across people who said, 'Don't bother going up there. There's no fish,'" says Haimwertz. "I went up there anyway and fished for half an hour and I came out with a 12-incher. Maybe they didn't give it long enough. Or maybe they didn't know what they were doing."

In fishing, time and know-how equals success.

Regulations: Only catch-and-release fishing is permitted on the Kern River north of the Johnsondale Bridge. Why? Because there are native California golden trout in there. Only barbless hooks are allowed and, yes, the rangers do check and write tickets for those who disregard this rule.

Camping: There are seven Forest Service campgrounds along the eastern bank of the Kern River, just north of Kernville on Mountain Road 99. The rule of thumb is the farther you get from Kernville, the nicer the campgrounds are: the southernmost campgrounds tend to be trashed by rowdy rednecks from the Central Valley partying it up on the river during the summer, especially on holidays. (Our advice: Stay away!) The rest of the time, we recommend either the Limestone or Fairview Campgrounds. Limestone has 22 sites for tents and

RVs (10 are tent only), and Fairview has 55 sites for tents and RVs. Facilities at both include fire rings, picnic tables, and outhouses. **Camping fees:** $8 per night. **Contact:** For more information, phone the Sequoia National Forest, Cannell Meadow Ranger District, (760) 376-3781. **Locator**: KERN RIVER.

LAKE ISABELLA

The tremendous spring runoffs that turn the Kern into an angry, snarling white-water river also hurts the fishing in the river. In addition, rafting on the Kern brings huge crowds to the area, causing traffic and crowds in Kernville and on Mountain Road 99.

During this time, Lee Penny simply heads to the lake instead. "You know, in the evening we'll go down to the lake with the Coleman lantern and lawn chairs and set up the fishing poles and take dinner with us, some cold drinks," says Penny. "We'll just sit back and relax and watch the sun set behind the mountains. It's peaceful, we shoot the breeze, we have a nice time."

If that's not enviable enough, Lee also catches his share of fish, typically taking the limit of five trout in anywhere from one to three hours. What's his secret?

Time. "I stick around until I catch something," says Lee, laughing. "I don't have anywhere I have to go. That's what we retired folks do."

Like in the river, Lee (who fishes from the bank, not a boat) uses lighter test with a sliding weight, sinker, and a 16-inch leader. The hook is usually smeared with Powerbait. He then puts his pole in a holder, sits back in his lawn chair, and waits for a bite.

Sounds easy, huh? Lee is the first to admit that not just anyone can drive down to the lake, wet a line, and expect Mr. or Ms. Trout to gladly offer themselves up for dinner. It's a big lake and Lee says you have to know where the good spots are. And, again, the good spots can be found by watching and talking to the old-timers.

So now your mission is complicated. First you have to fish for the old-timers and then you have to fish for the fish. How to find the old-timers? First, try getting up early and going for a walk around the lake. Or use some high-powered binoculars to scout the lakeshore. Maybe rent a boat for an afternoon and float around the lake, watching to see what other anglers are doing.

If you're spending a day or two at the lake, the fishing equation isn't all that much different from the river. Try as many places as possible, fishing both in the early morning and evening, when temperatures are cooler (daytime temperatures in late spring and summer often reach triple digits). Keep in mind, too, that Isabella gets a lot of attention for its bass fishing and it, at times, produces some prolific crappies, bluegills, and catfish.

If your luck poops out on the lake, drive up to the river. If your luck poops out up there, go back to the lake. Stay motivated: Count trout before you go to sleep. Do a fish dance. Pray. Pray some more. And in the evenings, keep your eyes peeled for those old-timers like Lee.

"Just sitting there at the lake, the water is rippling by, the sun is setting behind the mountains, and the sky is turning all the colors and you're just sitting there enjoying the beauty of it all," says Lee. "Well, all around is pretty much happy times."

Directions to Kernville and Lake Isabella: From downtown Los Angeles take Interstate 5 north through the Tejon Pass to Highway 99 north. Take Highway 99 for 23 miles, exiting to Highway 53 east. Drive seven miles and exit at Highway 184 (Patch Highway), turning left (north). Take Highway 184 to Highway 178 east. Drive 35 miles through the Kern Canyon to Lake Isabella. From the lake to Kernville, take Highway 155 north 11 miles and turn right at the bridge and cross the river. At Mountain Road 99, turn left (north). It's 19 miles to Johnsondale. **Lodging:** Several small towns can be found in the Lake Isabella/Kern River area. The ugly town of Lake Isabella is at the southern end of the lake, Wofford Heights is on the eastern shore, and Kernville is to the north. We recommend staying in Kernville at one of several pleasant motels: Kern Lodge Motel, (760) 376-2223; River View Lodge, (760) 376-6019; Sequoia Motor Lodge, (760) 376-2535; and Kern River Inn Bed-and-Breakfast, (760) 376-6750, which is located right alongside Kernville's shady and grassy riverside park. The Kern Lodge Motel allows pooches. For more information about accommodations, phone the Kernville Chamber of Commerce at (760) 376-2629 or (800) 350-7393. **Permits:** A California fishing license, available at all marinas, is required. **Maps:** We recommend the AAA maps of both Kern County and Tulare County, available through AAA and at many bookstores. **Boat rentals:** Boats of all types can be rented at one of three marinas serving the lake: North Fork Marina, (760) 376-1812; French Gulch Marina, (760) 379-8774; and Kern Valley Marina, (760) 379-1634. **Contact:** For information on the lake, contact Sequoia National Forest, Lake Isabella Ranger District, (760) 379-5646. For the Kern River north of the lake, phone Sequoia National Forest, Cannell Meadow Ranger District, (760) 376-3781. **Locator:** LAKE ISABELLA.

WHERE'S ALL THAT WATER COMING FROM?

The Kern River is the primary drainage of Mount Whitney, located 70 miles to the north of Kernville in Sequoia National Park. In 1954, the river was dammed at the tiny town of Isabella to form the largest reservoir in the state, Lake Isabella. When the lake is full, which it was at press time thanks to heavy rains and snowfall, it covers well over 500,000 acre feet. The water eventually winds up in the Central Valley, where it is used entirely for agriculture.

• FEATURED TRIP •

RED ROCK CANYON STATE PARK
Near Mojave

Highway 14 is the primary route used by Angelenos heading from the southland to the eastern Sierra. For an interesting antithesis to the alpine environs in the north, stop for a short hike in Red Rock Canyon State Park.

The park's main attraction, as the name implies, is a remarkable canyon of red rock, where the walls are striped both horizontally and vertically, highlighting many shades of red. The cliffs also appear to be folded, as if thousands of columns of rock were stacked every which way.

The canyon is easy to reach because Highway 14 was built right up the middle of it. The park covers

30,000 acres, much of which is backcountry. This is hard-core desert, with no formal hiking trails. There is, however, a network of sandy off-road trails running through various washes, which can be hiked. Watch for all-terrain vehicles, which are allowed to use the roads in some parts of the park.

The park's only "official" trail is a three-quarter-mile nature trail near the visitor center, located on the west side of Highway 14. There is also a network of footpaths around popular Hagen Canyon, as well as the Red Cliffs Area.

If heading north on Highway 14, the turnoff for the visitor center and Hagen Canyon is on the left and is well marked. The Red Cliffs Area is on the right-hand (east) side of Highway 14. Watch carefully for a small sign indicating a sharp turnoff and the parking area.

Directions: From Los Angeles take Interstate 5 north, exit onto Highway 14, and drive through Mojave. Red Rock Canyon State Park is about 20 miles north of Mojave. Follow signs to the turnoff for the Ricardo Campground and Visitor Center, which will be on your left. To access the Red Cliffs Area, watch for a not very well-marked turnoff on the right side of the road shortly after entering the park. **Fees:** Day use of the park is free. **Maps:** There are free trail maps at the visitor center. **Pets:** Pets are permitted in the campground but not on trails. This is a terrible place to bring a dog. **Camping:** There is a primitive campground with 50 sites for tents and RVs. Facilities include fire rings, picnic tables, piped water, and pit toilets. Fees are $7 to $9 per night. **Contact:** California Department of Parks and Recreation, Mojave Desert Office, (805) 942-0662. **Locator:** RED ROCK CANYON STATE PARK.

• FEATURED TRIP •

SPACE SHUTTLE LANDINGS
In the Mojave Desert

Designed as the world's first reusable spacecraft, the Space Shuttle has flown more than 75 missions since its first in April of 1981. During the shuttle's early days, landings at Edwards Air Force Base in the Mojave Desert were routine—as were the huge crowds who gathered to watch the shuttle return to Earth.

But in recent years, NASA has moved most of the shuttle landings to the Kennedy Space Center in order to save money and time between launches. Edwards is now used as a backup in case the weather goes sour in Florida. The problem is that NASA often doesn't make the final decision to land at Edwards until 12 to 24 hours in advance of touchdown time.

This poses a problem for spectators. Unlike the shuttle's early days, when the landings were scheduled well in advance, folks have to scramble to Edwards very quickly and often in the middle of the night since the landings typically occur just after sunrise.

For example, the shuttle *Atlantis* landed at Edwards in March of 1996 after a rendezvous with the Russian spacecraft *Mir*. Mechanical complications developed, coupled with bad weather in Florida, and the *Atlantis* ended up touching down at Edwards at 5:29 A.M.—less than 10 hours after NASA made the decision to relocate the landing.

How to see the shuttle land? First, keep an eye on the newspaper in order to track when the shuttle missions are scheduled (or rescheduled, as is often the case). Second, after the shuttle launches from Florida, frequently phone the NASA Space Shuttle 24-hour taped information hot line at (805) 258-3520. Third, if available, find the cable channel on your television that has around-the-clock coverage of NASA's Mission Control. It's not quite Seinfeld, but it can be very informative.

If the shuttle is going to land at Edwards, the base allows spectators to gather at a fence in the northeast section of Rogers Lake beginning 24 hours ahead of the scheduled landing. Once at the site, the only amenity offered is portable toilets. There is no shade, which can be a huge problem on hot days—remember, you're sitting smack dab in the middle of the Mojave Desert. The only luxury is the vendors the base allows into the parking area.

The viewing area is three to five miles from the runway where the Space Shuttle lands, but visibility is usually very good and unobstructed. Having binoculars is advisable.

About 10 to 15 minutes before the shuttle touches down, people in Los Angeles and the surrounding metropolitan area will sometimes hear a sonic boom as the shuttle, using the atmosphere to brake, slows from 25 times the speed of sound to its landing speed, which is about 220 miles per hour.

When the shuttle lands at Edwards, it is lifted into something called "the cage," which holds the shuttle off the ground while it undergoes inspection. After the shuttle clears inspection, a modified Boeing 747 airplane is rolled under the cage and the 450-million-pound spacecraft is bolted to the plane's top for its return flight to Florida. A landing at Edwards and the flight back to Florida costs in excess of $1 million. NASA also dispatches more than 200 technicians from the Kennedy Space Center to Edwards to inspect the shuttle.

Directions: From Palmdale take Highway 14 north, exit at Avenue J, and turn right. Continue on Avenue J for about 11 miles and turn left onto 140th Street. Take 140th Street onto the base grounds and turn right onto Avenue B/Mercury Avenue. Follow the road until it ends at the viewing area. There will be plenty of signs along the way. **Fees:** Viewing is free. **Maps:** Having an AAA map of either California or Kern County is advisable. Maps should be available at many bookstores, as well as AAA offices. **Contact:** NASA Space Shuttle 24-hour information (taped), (805) 258-3520. **Locator:** SPACE SHUTTLE LANDINGS.

19
SANTA BARBARA COUNTY

• FEATURED TRIPS •

JALAMA BEACH 175
SAN RAFAEL WILDERNESS 176
FIGUEROA MOUNTAIN 178
BIKING THE WINE
   COUNTRY 180
LAKE CACHUMA 182
SANTA YNEZ RIVER VALLEY 184
HIKING GAVIOTA PEAK 186

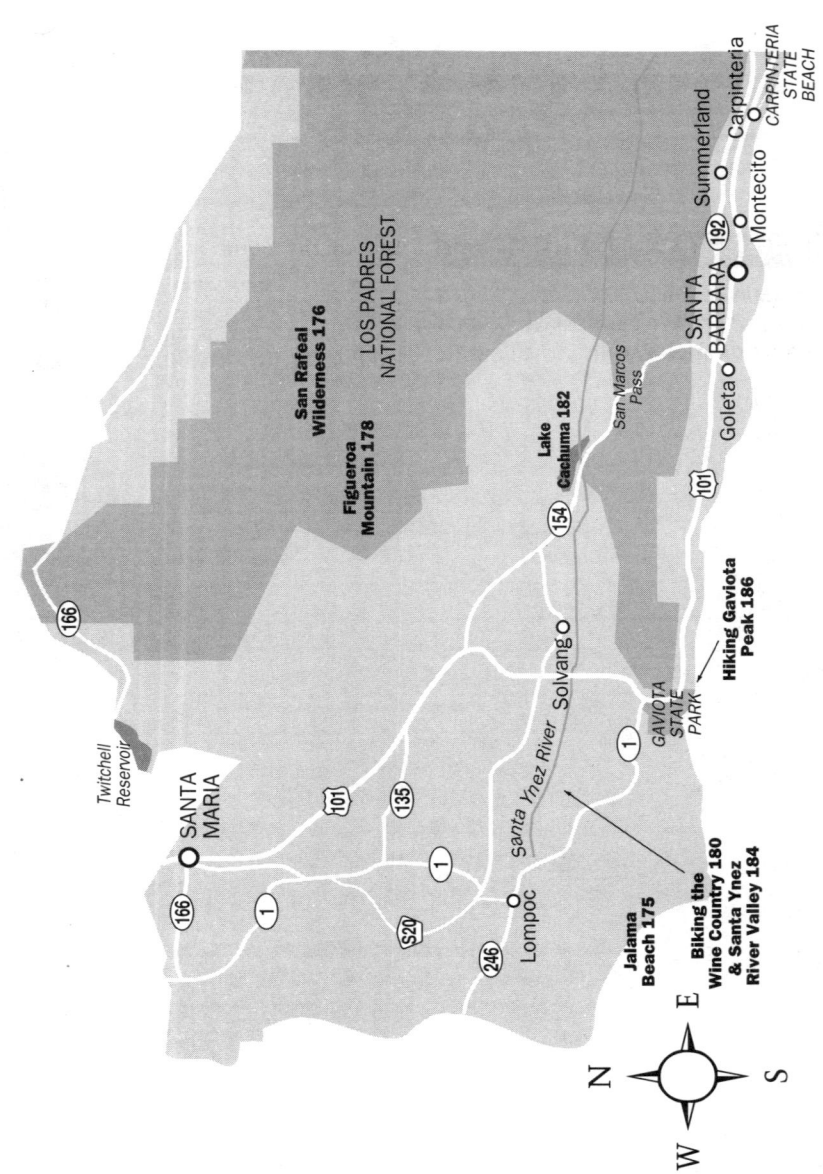

Santa Barbara County

• **FEATURED TRIP** •

JALAMA BEACH
West of Lompoc, on the Central Coast

This is the Jalama Burger: A perfectly grilled one-third-pound piece of beef covered with a smattering of ranch dressing and a thick slice of red onion. A big fat slice of tomato sits atop the burger, which is wedged inside a grilled sesame seed bun.

The burger is best consumed with perfectly seasoned french fries. It is well advised that when eating this perfectly constructed sandwich, you add a certain aesthetic appeal by sitting at a picnic table on the beach. Squishing of the toes into the sand is encouraged. Also recommended: cold beer, purchased for just a few coins at the Jalama Beach Market.

The Jalama Burger is the best burger in the United States, west of Mammoth Lakes. It is a fitting bit of serendipity, then, that Jalama Beach lives up to its namesake burger. The beach is damn near perfect.

What's not to like? Jalama has it all: a sometimes sandy, sometimes rocky beach two miles in length, plenty of shells and rocks for those who collect, interesting tidepools, good surf casting, great sailboarding and surfing, and a pleasant campground. It's also not a bad place to go for a dip.

And if you have a dog, Jalama Beach is one of the rare beaches in the state that allow pooches. Our chocolate Lab, Molly, pretty much decided this beach is as good as it gets. There were countless perfect sticks to carry, seabirds to chase, and great piles of kelp to roll around in—to complete her transformation to smelly dog. Best of all, there weren't any lifeguards around eager to drop an $80 fine on us.

On top of all this, Jalama Beach is also the most remote beach in the state—no other beach is farther from Highway 1. Jalama Road, the lone road to the beach, leaves Highway 1 about 13 miles north of Gaviota and then winds its way for 14 miles through the Santa Ynez Mountains, past hilly ranches, green and golden fields of grass and oak-shaded creeks. It's the kind of drive that explains precisely why you left Psoriasis, Alabama, in your Ford Pinto, vowing never to return.

What a wonderful beach to walk. Most of the beach sits under tall bluffs. The sand is sprinkled with lots of driftwood and rock shelves. On the northern end, high tide is slowly whittling away sea caves in the bluffs. At low tide, the intrepid beach hiker can walk south past Tarantula Point (a major surfing area) to the point where the beach disappears completely, becoming a series of seawalls leading toward Point Conception, which marks the transition from warm southern California to colder central coast waters.

The campground at Jalama Beach is not world class, geared more for RVs than for tents. On the other hand, the beach's remote location means it will be quiet. There is plenty of beach to walk—we recommend going when the moon is full. The concession stand and grocery store next to the campground is convenient and there are flush toilets and showers, always a major plus for the Reluctant Camper.

As we were leaving the beach one day, a parachute with a man attached (or the other way around) came up and over a bluff. The sport is called paragliding, and the idea is to use a parachute to ride in the air. The man found a nice piece of air and sat there, like a seabird looking down at a particularly choice chunk of land. Or maybe he was looking at the burger stand, licking his lips in anticipation.

IF IT LOOKS LIKE A MISSILE, SOUNDS LIKE A MISSILE . . .

. . . it probably *is* a missile, from Vandenberg Air Force Base, located directly to the north of Jalama Beach. The base occasionally fires test missiles or rockets carrying satellites. When doing so, they usually publish warnings of the upcoming launch in area newspapers ahead of time. Launches typically occur in the middle of the night.

Directions: From Santa Barbara take U.S. 101 north for 35 miles to Gaviota, exiting to Highway 1 north. Take Highway 1 for 13 miles and turn left on Jalama Beach Road. Stay on Jalama Beach Road for 14 gorgeous miles until it ends at the beach. **Fees:** The day-use fee is $3.50 per car. Dogs are an additional $2. **Maps:** The AAA map of Santa Barbara County is best; it's available through AAA and at many bookstores. **Pets:** Dogs are allowed, but they must be leashed. **Camping:** There are 110 sites for tents or RVs right near the beach. Facilities include flush toilets, showers, picnic tables, fire grills, and a small grocery store. No reservations are taken. Fees range from $14 to $18 per night. **Fishing:** Surf casters take note: Jalama Beach is in a coastal transition zone that extends from north of Jalama south to Point Conception. Here, two underwater biologic communities meet—the Oregon and California Provinces. That translates to a lot of food for fish, which explains why some 27 fish species can be found in the area, including perch, kelp bass, and surf perch. One fishing tip: Watch bird activity and keep your bait weighted down. **Contact:** Jalama Beach County Park, (805) 736-3504. Weather and surf conditions, (805) 736-6316. **Locator:** JALAMA BEACH.

• FEATURED TRIP •

SAN RAFAEL WILDERNESS
In the far backcountry of Santa Barbara County

One major advantage of backpacking, even a short distance, is often little discussed: a sense of accomplishment.

Or, to put it another way, it feels good to know that even in this technology-driven world, it's possible to stuff everything one absolutely must have into a backpack and survive in the wild. Sure, the going gets tough—but would you rather feel guilty every time you look at a backpacker in a heroic pose on the cover of *Outside* magazine?

The San Rafael Wilderness covers 148,170 acres in eastern Santa Barbara County. It is one of six wilderness areas in Los Padres National Forest. Wilderness areas are designated by Congress and exist in order to preserve things just as they are. That means no new roads are allowed to be built, nor is anyone allowed to construct new buildings. All mechanized vehicles and tools of any sort, including mountain bikes, are forbidden.

The land in San Rafael features canyons and gorges, meadows and forests, chaparral-covered hillsides, and lots of exposed sandstone. It's nothing like the Sierra; in fact, it resembles a wilder, larger version of what the Santa Monica Mountains must have been at one time (and still are, in places). Black bears and mountain lions still roam the land; the grizzly bear and California condor once lived here but are now gone. The Chumash Indians, it is believed, inhabited these parts 2,500 years ago. They remained until the late 1700s when the missionaries arrived to spread the word and take the land.

This is extremely rugged country and still receives little visitation, especially when compared to the Sierra. Much of the land has been protected as a "primitive area" since 1932, making it one of the oldest wildernesses in the nation. The wildflowers can be remarkable. And summers can be remarkably hot—with highs in the 110-degree range. We recommend visiting in spring or fall.

Visitors in the springtime, especially during a rainy year, need to be careful of stream crossings. In May of 1998, it was impossible to go west of the Potrero backcountry camp without risking your life on a dangerous crossing of Manzana Creek. We watched three preppy idiots from Santa Barbara try to throw a log over the creek. The log dropped three inches from the head of a three-year-old boy, then fell in the water and floated downstream. If the boy had been hit with the log, he would have suffered severe head trauma—at the least. A helicopter rescue landing in the area would have been impossible.

Access to the wilderness area begins at the NIRA Campground, which is accessible by car—it's a 60- to 90-minute drive from Santa Barbara. The NIRA camp was built by workers employed by the National Recovery Act during the Depression, thus the name.

The Manzana Creek Trail extends to both the east and the west from the campground. This trail forms the bottom half of a 40-mile loop around the interior of the San Rafael. Backpacking the entire loop typically takes about a week, according to rangers in the area. In the middle of the loop is the Hurricane Deck, a giant chunk of exposed sandstone that tilts out of the earth like a sinking ship. The area behind the Hurricane Deck is remote and visited much less often than the front side. The trail behind the deck follows the Sisquoc River.

Along the loop are 18 backcountry campgrounds, all of which are administered by the Forest Service. The closest backcountry campgrounds to the NIRA Campground—each about one mile away—are the Potrero Campground to the west and the Lost Valley Campground to the east. Those who don't want to lug their stuff too far can set up camp at either camp, both of which are perfectly nice.

As is always the case, the best campgrounds in the San Rafael Wilderness require more of a hike—no pain, no gain. If you hike west from NIRA, you'll first come to Potrero Campground at one mile, the Coldwater Campground at 2.5 miles, and the Manzana Schoolhouse Campground at 10 miles. The latter takes its name from an old schoolhouse used by early settlers, who later abandoned the area after deciding living in the middle of nowhere had its drawbacks. The Manzana Schoolhouse Campground is also near the confluence of the Sisquoc River and Manzana Creek, which flows best in the spring and early summer.

For those hiking east from the NIRA Campground, Fish Creek is about three miles away. The more popular Manzana and Manzana Narrows Campgrounds are 6.5 and seven miles to the east of NIRA, respectively.

Manzana Campground is located near the creek beneath a canopy of live oaks (shade!). Just one-half mile farther, the Manzana Narrows Campground is even better, sitting right alongside the creek. Here, the creek—you guessed it—narrows, forming a small canyon with swimming and fishing holes. The campground is also shaded by some dependable live oaks.

Manzana Creek is stocked with trout periodically. It's doubtful anyone will catch anything big, but with luck campers might land a few pan-sized fish to serve as a side dish or a little protein to throw in with the scrambled eggs at breakfast.

Remember, these are wilderness campgrounds, meaning there is a fire ring and sometimes a pit toilet. The wilderness area, like much of the Los Padres, is extremely fire-prone—be careful. Burning down the entire backcountry is not considered "leave no trace."

Also remember that there are black bears and mountain lions in the San Rafael Wilderness. They aren't seen often, but campers should still take the standard bear precautions: Don't leave food unattended and don't bring food into the tent.

Directions: From Santa Barbara take Highway 154 for 22 miles up and over the San Marcos Pass and continue past Lake Cachuma. Five miles past the entrance to the lake, turn right on Armour Ranch Road and drive 1.5 miles. Turn right on Happy Canyon Road and continue 11 miles to Cachuma Saddle, where the road becomes Sunset Valley Road (Forest Service Road 8N09). Drive six miles to the NIRA Campground. **Maps:** The AAA map of Santa Barbara County is the best road map of the area. A good trail map to the wilderness area is the Los Padres National Forest map, available at the visitor center in Goleta, or by sending $4 to the USDA-Forest Service, Attn: Map Room 807, 630 Sansome Street, San Francisco, CA 94111. USGS topo maps, available at high-end sporting goods stores, are often quite helpful. **Pets:** Dogs are permitted in the wilderness area. Watch for ticks and mountain lions, which might find Fido quite tasty. **Camping:** No reservations, fees, or permits are needed to enter and camp within the wilderness area. **Forest Service Visitor Center:** The closest Los Padres National Forest visitor center to Santa Barbara is located in Goleta. From downtown Santa Barbara, take U.S. 101 north for 8.5 miles and exit at Fairview. Turn right and then make an immediate left onto Calle Real and drive 1.5 blocks. The Forest Service office is located at 6144 Calle Real. For information, phone (805) 683-6711. **Contact:** Los Padres National Forest, Santa Lucia Ranger District, (805) 925-9538. **Locator:** SAN RAFAEL WILDERNESS.

• FEATURED TRIP •

FIGUEROA MOUNTAIN

Standing sentry over the Santa Ynez Valley

There's nothing like a relationship-threatening fight to jump-start an outdoor getaway:

"I thought you knew where we were going."

"Well it's not my fault you forgot the map."

"I wouldn't have forgotten the map if the kitchen table wasn't such a mess."

"The reason the table is such a mess is because I don't have anywhere else to put my stuff."

"Maybe you shouldn't have so much stuff."

"At least my stuff is important."

"Are you saying my stuff is junk?"

"I didn't say that. You're paranoid."

"You're about to drive off the road."

"Don't tell me how to drive."

"It's not my fault your driving stinks."

"Look who's talking."

"You can't take criticism either."

"$#%^ you."

At this point, you may have guessed that Figueroa Mountain is a bit off the beaten path. Actually, it's more like this: Go to off-the-beaten-path, turn left, and then keep going. And going. And then go some more.

The mountain is located in the northern inland corner of Santa Barbara County, which it's fair to say is remote. It's also quite pretty. Figueroa Mountain stands at an elevation of 4,528 feet and provides a beautiful view of the entire county—including views beyond the coastal range to the Channel Islands. The mountain also creates its own ecosystem that stands in stark contrast to the surrounding land. Whereas most of the Santa Ynez Valley is rolling grasslands dotted with oak trees, Figueroa Mountain is a mix of everything—live oaks, blue oaks, pines, firs, and some maple trees.

Figueroa is 11 miles from the main road, Highway 154—although the 11 miles feel more like 25 (and the perfect place to start an argument) as you wind your way through some very pretty, very remote ranchland and oil fields. The road then zigzags up the side of the mountain, where there is a network of trails and fire roads that provide for some good mountain biking. Our recommendation: If you are going to come all this way, plan on spending the night.

Your best bet is the Figueroa Campground, located near the top of the mountain within a pretty stand of pines. The campground has 33 sites for tents and RVs. Facilities include fire grills, picnic tables, and vault toilets—but no piped water. Reservations can be made by phoning (800) 280-CAMP/2267. Camping is six bucks per night.

Another campground, Davy Brown, can be found at the base of the mountain. It, too, is very pretty, located alongside Davy Brown Creek. The campground has 13 sites for tents and three for RVs. Facilities include fire grills, picnic tables, and vault toilets. There is no piped water. No reservations are accepted at Davy Brown, but camping is free. However, a Forest Service Adventure Pass is required.

A couple dozen hikes are available within the area. There is a short, paved interpretive trail from the Pinos Altos picnic area. It's hardly a workout, but the trail is worth taking just for the views of the surrounding county.

The one not to be missed is the Davy Brown Trail, which follows Davy Brown Creek from Davy Brown Campground to the top of the mountain. The trail is three miles long and it's as good as they come in Southern California. There are plenty of trees, some wonderful shale formations, and a pretty canyon to look at. The trailhead parking at the top of the mountain is on Mt. Figueroa Road, about one mile east of the campground on the left side of the road. At the bottom of the mountain, the trail can be accessed at Davy Brown Campground—pick a place to rock hop across the creek to the trail. Parking is limited within the campground; there is plenty of parking down Sunset Valley Road. Drive over the creek and park on the left side of the road, near the old horse corrals.

In the spring, the Davy Brown Trail is known for its views of wildflower displays on Figueroa's slopes. The mountain usually receives mention in Southern California newspapers each year for its showy wildflowers, but before making the long drive it's probably best to call the Forest Service first to make sure things are a-blooming (the spring of 1998 saw an awesome bloom). A long, fruitless drive to the mountain to show your honey-bunny wildflowers will definitely result in a relationship-threatening fight.

GREAT PLACE TO EAT

La Super-Rica in Santa Barbara was made famous by renowned cook Julia Child, who once said it's one of her favorite places anywhere for Mexican food. We suggest ordering an assortment of dishes, most of which are in the $2 to $3 price range. Hint: Don't miss the chorizo quesadilla. La Super-Rica is at 622 North Milpas Street, Santa Barbara, (805) 963-4940.

Directions: From Santa Barbara take Highway 154 over the San Marcos Pass and past Lake Cachuma. After passing through Santa Ynez, turn right onto Figueroa Mountain Road and continue for 11 miles, as the road twists and winds its way uphill. To reach the Davy Brown Campground, continue on for about six miles and turn left on Sunset Valley Road. Drive six miles to the campground entrance, which will be on your right.

Fees: A Forest Service Adventure Pass is available at ranger stations and most large sporting goods stores for $5 per day or $30 annually. **Maps:** The Los Padres National Forest map is available at ranger stations, large sporting goods stores, or by mailing $4 to the USDA-Forest Service, Attn: Map Room 807, 630 Sansome Street, San Francisco, CA 94111. **Pets:** Dogs are permitted, but must be under your control. **Contact:** Los Padres National Forest, Santa Lucia Ranger District, (805) 925-9538. **Locator:** FIGUEROA MOUNTAIN.

• FEATURED TRIP •

BIKING THE WINE COUNTRY
In the tranquil Santa Ynez Valley

Napa Valley may get all the press, but the Santa Ynez Valley is closer to home and has just as much quality for wine-loving Southlanders.

The problem with Napa Valley is that it was long ago trampled by tourists. It's Disneyland with grapes. The only thing missing is Mickey trying to pickpocket you at the front door.

"One of the things that's nice about Santa Barbara is that we aren't as crowded as the Napa Valley," a spokeswoman for the Santa Barbara County Vintners' Association dutifully reports. "We don't have hassles with people in Bermuda shorts and straw hats. We're much more slow paced."

We admit the Santa Ynez Valley is not exactly undiscovered. But it's still rural; the subdividers haven't gotten their slimy tentacles around it yet, nor have the freeway builders. Even the King of Weird, Michael Jackson, whose Neverland Ranch is in the valley, can't ruin the place.

The Santa Ynez Valley also produces some of the best wine in the state—Napa and Sonoma Counties included. Why? Look at a map. The Santa Ynez Mountains have an east-west alignment, which allows cool air from the Pacific Ocean to mix with the warm air of the inland valley. That's the kind of air wine makers love and it's the reason almost three dozen wineries are located in the valley.

Given the state of California's drivers—pathologically maniacal—there are few places left where we would recommend bicycling on the street. The Santa Ynez Valley is one of them. With the exception of two highly trafficked state highways, most of the roads in the heart of the valley are quiet, two-lane affairs.

In the spring, fall, and winter, the weather is perfect for biking (summers in the valley produce blast furnace heat). There are countless routes from which to choose, and many of the wineries are open to tasting. Most of the wineries also have picnic grounds, the perfect place to stop for lunch.

Before choosing a route, pick up a phone and dial the following number for the Santa Barbara County Vintners' Association: (800) 218-0881. The association will be glad to mail anyone interested a map and brochure of the valley wineries.

WHERE TO RIDE

There are easy to moderate rides between the towns of Los Olivos, Ballard, Solvang, and Santa Ynez. One easy to moderate route we like—rolling hills are the major obstacle—begins at Grand Avenue in Los Olivos. Head south on Grand. At 0.9 mile turn left on Alamo Pintado Road and ride for 1.3 miles to Baseline Road. Continue a few hundred yards farther to Carey Cellars, which will be on the left.

Some people also wind their way down Baseline Road to Refugio Road and then to the junction of Highway 246 and Highway 154, where the popular Gainey Vineyard is located. This is a good place to picnic.

For a strenuous ride featuring larger rolling hills, try this: Begin at Grand Avenue in Los Olivos. Ride north and turn left (west) onto Highway 154. Be careful: traffic moves quickly here. Ride 0.4 mile and turn right on Foxen Canyon Road.

As is plainly obvious on the map, you are now headed for the majority of the well-known wineries. From here, it's about six miles to the Fess Parker Winery, which is on the right. Another three miles beyond Fess's place is the Zaca Mesa Winery, on the left.

If you're not totally zonked at this point, an option on the return ride is to bear right on Zaca Station Road and ride an extra 1.6 miles to the well-known Firestone Vineyard.

Here are two other ideas—check them out on a map to see what you think:

Stick to Happy Canyon Road. It's mostly easy riding through very peaceful country. There are no wineries here, but it is quiet. When you hit the hill leading into the San Rafael Mountains, it's time to turn around. From Baseline Road to the hill, it's just over eight miles.

Another option, for those who enjoy the truly tacky: Los Olivos to the Danish community of Solvang. We highly recommend at least one visit to Solvang per lifetime. Years ago, some Danes settled here. Years later, and in need of a few dollars, they discovered that an easy way to get the tourist buses to stop is to build a few fake windmills and bakeries. This was obviously an idea whose time had come.

It should be noted that Solvang's population is slightly skewed toward the elderly. This isn't very PC, but what the hell, we'll say it anyway: People drive here like people drive in Miami Beach. Be careful when riding.

The route for this journey: From Los Olivos, take Grand Avenue to Alamo Pintado to Highway 246 west.

Après-tacky: For a genteel welcome back to reality after all that faux-Scandinavia, we highly recommend the beautiful Sanford Winery, on Santa Rosa Road halfway between Solvang and Lompoc. Nothing beats sipping their delicious pinot noir to the tunes of a live string quartet.

A Guided Tour

Adventours Outdoor Excursions in Santa Barbara offers guided bike tours of the wineries. There are several options, including single- and multi-day rides. Full support is offered for riders, meaning there's a van to shuttle them over more difficult stretches of road. Phone (805) 963-2248 for more information.

> **Directions:** From Santa Barbara to Los Olivos, take Highway 154 up and over the scenic San Marcos Pass (enjoying the view but keeping an eye on the road) and then past Lake Cachuma. Continue on Highway 154 for 11 miles and turn left at Grand Avenue in the tiny town of Los Olivos. Park along Grand Avenue or on one of the side streets in town. **Fees:** Most wineries offer tasting either for free or for a nominal charge. **Maps:** Phone the Santa Barbara County Vintners' Association for a free winery touring map. The AAA map of Santa Barbara County, available at most AAA offices and some bookstores, indicates some winery locations. **Note:** In the afternoon, wind often blows into the Santa Ynez Valley from the ocean. That means it's easiest to ride west in the morning, when there's little wind, and then ride east in the afternoon, when the wind is at your back. **Contact:** Santa Barbara County Vintners' Association, (805) 688-0881 or (800) 218-0881. **Locator:** SANTA YNEZ RIVER.

• FEATURED TRIP •

LAKE CACHUMA
Northeast of Santa Barbara

In the first week of February 1998, a much anticipated visitor finally arrived on California's doorstep. Except this visitor didn't bring a bottle of wine. Instead, Mr. El Niño—sponsored by California's roofing industry—walloped the state with a succession of three storms.

Our favorite statistic: In just the first eight days of February 1998, Santa Barbara received 12 inches of rain and the San Marcos Pass, the undisputed champion, received 21 inches of rain. In just eight days!

The pass is located where Highway 154 rises from Santa Barbara and then jumps over the Santa Ynez Mountains before descending into the Santa Ynez Valley. The 21 inches of rain explain exactly why motorists dropping into the valley see what they see: Lake Cachuma, one of the prettiest reservoirs in Southern California.

Cachuma, sitting on the valley floor, is a sea of blue surrounded by the golden, oak-studded hills of the Santa Ynez Valley. The lake, although far from natural, is the centerpiece of one of the most dramatic vistas in Southern California.

The lake is also the recreational capital of the valley, especially in the summer when temperatures routinely climb above 100 degrees Fahrenheit. Here's the catch: The lake provides drinking water for Santa Barbara, so there is no swimming or waterskiing allowed. That's why there's a huge swimming pool at the lake's entrance.

There is, however, very good fishing in the lake. There's also a large campground, perfect for families. A small grocery is located at the lake's headquarters and the campgrounds have showers and flush toilets. It's just over a two-hour drive to the lake from L.A.—and it's only 30 minutes from Santa Barbara. All in all, convenient and easy camping.

In fact, our first camping trip in California was at Lake Cachuma in the early spring. Daytime temperatures were in the 70s and the campground was about half filled. We were assigned a nice site in the Dakota Campground under a stand of live oaks. The water's edge was a couple hundred yards away, as were the bathrooms. The site also included a picnic table and fire ring, which had a few half-burnt logs already in it. There was no shortage of kindling nearby.

Cachuma is one of the best fishing lakes in the state (competing with Crowley Lake in the Owens Valley), compliments of heavy stocking by the Department of Fish and Game. More than 150,000 rainbow trout are tossed into the lake every year, joining a considerable population of Florida bass, catfish, crappie, bluegill, and redear perch.

The lake is huge—3,100 surface acres when full—and has four main coves, as well as plenty of smaller inlets. If you're fishing, do yourself a favor and rent a boat; a four-passenger boat with a small motor can be rented for about $50 a day. Pick up a free fishing map at the marina (where you can also purchase a fishing license), which shows areas off-limits to fishing, as well as the spots where different types of fish reside.

Hikers have all sorts of options. At the lake, we suggest trying the Sweetwater Trail, which begins at Harvey Cove and follows the lake's shore before climbing to an overlook of the area. A lot of folks bring their bicycles and pedal around the campgrounds.

Insider's tip: The rustic, beautiful Cold Springs Tavern sits just below the San Marcos Pass. Known for its setting, inexpensive pub food, relaxed atmosphere, and live music, Cold Springs is undoubtedly one of the best backcountry bars in the state.

To reach the tavern from the lake, take Highway 154 south toward Santa Barbara, cross the bridge and turn right at the sign for the restaurant, located at 5995 Stagecoach Road. Phone: (805) 967-0066.

CACHUMA'S BALD EAGLES

In the late 1980s, bald eagles migrating from the Pacific Northwest began wintering at Lake Cachuma after an absence of many years. If you're interested in seeing these magnificent birds, you can hop aboard a boat for an eagle-watching tour from December through the end of February. Our favorite fly-fishing instructor, the amiable and knowledgeable Neal Taylor, is a naturalist at the lake and conducts some of the tours. For more information about current eagle sightings, phone (805) 688-4658.

Directions: From Santa Barbara take Highway 154 up and through the San Marcos Pass. The entrance to the lake will be on the left, 25 miles after leaving Santa Barbara. **Fees:** There's a $5 day-use fee for the lake. **Maps:** Ask for a free map of the recreation area at the ranger gate. Free fishing maps are available at the marina. Having the AAA map of Santa Barbara County will help you find your way around. It's available at many bookstores and AAA offices. **Pets:** Dogs are allowed, but must be leashed. They are not allowed within 50 feet of the lake—the fine is hefty, so don't take your chances. **Camping:** There are 500 sites for tents and RVs, many with full hookups. All sites are offered on a first-come, first-served basis. Fees are $13 to $18 per night. **Contact:** Cachuma Lake Recreation Area, (805) 688-4658. **Locator:** LAKE CACHUMA.

• FEATURED TRIP •

THE SANTA YNEZ RIVER VALLEY

Just over the "hill" from Santa Barbara

The rugged backcountry of Santa Barbara County—the land behind the coast range—is crisscrossed by hundreds of streams. The largest and most important of these is the Santa Ynez River.

The river begins just west of the Santa Barbara County line, behind Rincon Peak and only a few miles from the headwaters of the Ventura River. While the Ventura flows to the southeast, the Santa Ynez begins a long journey westward.

A few miles into its voyage, the Santa Ynez is stopped by Juncal Dam to form Jamison Lake. Eight miles later, the river is stopped again, this time by Gibraltar Dam, forming Gibraltar Reservoir. This stretch of river, high above Santa Barbara, is called the Upper Santa Ynez River.

The river falls swiftly from Gibraltar Reservoir, and its valley begins to widen. This is the Lower Santa Ynez River, tumbling down toward the floor of the vast Santa Ynez Valley, where the river has been dammed to form Lake Cachuma, the primary source of drinking water for Santa Barbara County.

Not only is the river the lifeblood of the county in terms of water, but it also forms a huge artery of recreation, with a large network of campgrounds, trails, and swimming holes.

LOWER SANTA YNEZ

The Lower Santa Ynez River is beautiful. The banks are lined by oaks and steep mountains. Sandstone ledges are everywhere, many sitting in the riverbed. Swimming holes are found throughout—and, in the heat of summer, it seems everyone in the county is there, too.

The best swimming hole is found at the end of the road accessing the recreation area. Park at the Live Oak picnic area and walk one-half mile upstream. This is the area known as Red Rock. It is immensely popular and for good reason: it's one of the best natural swimming pools you'll find anywhere. When the ocean is freezing in the summer—as it is liable to be when Mr. El Niño isn't around—the Santa Ynez is the place to be. It should be noted that the river receives some trout plants and the fishing ranges from so-so to decent.

Most of the Lower Santa Ynez River accessible from Paradise Road lies within a concessionaire area. That means the Forest Service has leased the operation of the campgrounds and day-use parking lots to a concessionaire, who charges a fee. At press time, the fee is $3 to enter and park in the area, although discussions are under way to raise the fee to $4 (and, for the first time, implement an annual pass). Even those who have a Forest Service Adventure Pass must pay the fee to park within the fee area. As you might have guessed, this is a bizarre situation only the government could have created.

If hiking is your thing, there are numerous trails to choose from. Most head up the hills (there's nowhere else for them to go) for views of the valley. The trail we like continues to follow the river past Red Rock. This is the River Trail, also known as Forest Service Road 5N18. The trail goes uphill to Gibraltar Dam and follows the river all the way to the end of the reservoir, at the Mono Debris Basin.

A visit to the Lower Santa Ynez is good for a day trip from Santa Barbara—it's a 30-minute drive—or can be stretched into a weekend camping trip. The six campgrounds are similar to one another, but if we absolutely had to choose, we'd go with Los Prietos (38 sites for tents or RVs) or Paradise (15 sites for tents or RVs). Get there early and snag a site at the rear of the campground. Facilities at both camps include flush toilets, fire rings, picnic tables, and piped water. Reservations are not accepted. Fees are $8.50 per night.

Directions: From Santa Barbara follow Highway 154 for 10 miles up and over the San Marcos Pass. At Paradise Road, turn right and drive to the ranger booth. **Fees:** There's a $3 fee to enter the Santa Ynez River Recreation Area. **Maps:** The Los Padres National Forest map is available at the ranger station or in most large sporting goods stores. **Pets:** Dogs are permitted in the recreation area. **Contact:** Los Padres National Forest, Santa Barbara Ranger District, (805) 967-3481. **Locator:** SANTA YNEZ RIVER.

UPPER SANTA YNEZ

The crowds go to the Lower Santa Ynez because it's easily accessible. This is not the case with the Upper Santa Ynez, which requires a bit of mountain driving on a bumpy dirt road. There are four small car camps up here. The good news is that the camping is free. The bad news: There's no water. You must bring your own.

We recommend that those willing to make the drive at least stay the night. Be warned: This is rugged country. There are open fields of grass, shady boulder-lined creeks, oak-dotted hills, and, last but certainly not least, chaparral. Lots of it.

The Santa Ynez River can be accessed from all of the camps. As is the case in the lower river, there are plenty of great swimming holes and picnic spots. This is also true on the main tributaries, particularly Agua Caliente and Mono Creek. Southern California can be very dry, but you'll find more water here than at most places.

The four campgrounds, all for cars and tents only, are Juncal (6 sites), Mid Santa Ynez (6 sites), P-Bar Flat (3 sites), and Mono (9 sites). Facilities include fire rings, picnic tables, and vault toilets. Again, there's no water. Reservations are not accepted. At press time, there was currently no fee for these campgrounds (although this could change), but campers must have a Forest Service Adventure Pass, which costs $5 per day or $30 annually. Purchase an Adventure Pass at ranger stations, visitor centers, or most large sporting goods stores in Southern California.

We recommend the Mid Santa Ynez or P-Bar Flat Campgrounds, both under a pretty patch of oaks in an otherwise open area. The Pendola Ranger Station is adjacent to the Mid Santa Ynez Campground, convenient for getting directions to trails. Also, both camps are just down a short road leading to the Big Agua Caliente Hot Springs. At one time there was a resort here, but it burned down. The pool with piped water from the hot springs, however, remains. The downside to the hot springs is that everyone in Santa Barbara knows about it.

Feel the need to hike? Three trails are easily accessible from the Mid Santa Ynez and P-Bar Flat Campgrounds. They're what we call "round-trippers." Go as far as you like, then turn around and return.

From P-Bar Flat Campground, the Hildreth Jeepway begins in a meadow and travels north, allowing hikers views of the watershed. The Pendola Jeepway begins behind the Pendola Ranger Station and heads to the northeast, through the hills, eventually going all the way to Montecito Peak. The Agua Caliente Trail begins at the hot spring's parking lot and follows Agua Caliente Creek upstream into some pretty nifty sandstone canyons. Check out the swimming hole beneath the Agua Caliente Debris Dam, about one-half mile upstream from the hot spring.

Directions: From Santa Barbara take Highway 154 north for eight miles. At East Camino Cielo, turn right and drive 22 miles—the road is paved, then dirt. At Juncal Camuesa Road, turn left. Juncal Campground is near the intersection. Mid Santa Ynez and P-Bar Flat are nine and 10 miles, respectively, down Juncal Camuesa Road. **Fees:** Day users will need a Forest Service Adventure Pass, available at ranger stations and most large sporting goods stores. **Maps:** The Los Padres National Forest map is available at most ranger stations and large sporting goods stores. **Pets:** Dogs are permitted. **Contact:** Los Padres National Forest, Santa Barbara Ranger District, (805) 967-3481. **Locator:** SANTA YNEZ RIVER.

• FEATURED TRIP •

HIKING GAVIOTA PEAK
In Gaviota State Park, near Santa Barbara

The best way to see Gaviota State Park and surrounding environs is to make the moderately strenuous six-mile round-trip hike to 2,458-foot-tall Gaviota Peak, which offers a spectacular view of the coast and, often, the Channel Islands.

The hike begins in the state park on a steep fire road, which eventually bends back inland toward some beautiful ranchland on the backside of the park. In the winter and spring, this area is particularly green and lush, almost resembling the British Isles.

The trail passes another gate before rising sharply to the summit, which is actually within Los Padres

National Forest, not the state park. If you're lucky and it's exceptionally clear out, you can see all the way to 578-foot-tall Morro Rock, which is over 100 miles north of Gaviota. Even if "the rock" isn't visible, the view won't disappoint.

Directions: From Santa Barbara to the Gaviota Peak trailhead, take U.S. 101 north for 35 miles and exit at Highway 1 north. At the top of the exit ramp, make a hard right onto a small road paralleling the ramp. Continue several hundred yards until the road ends at the parking area. Self-register and pay the day-use fee at the gate. **Safety note:** Although rare, mountain lions have been seen in the park. Don't hike alone. **Fees:** The day-use fee is $2. **Maps:** Although most of the trail is on state park land, the best map of the area is the Los Padres National Forest map. It is available at many local sporting goods stores. Or, send $4 to the USDA-Forest Service, Attn: Map Room 807, 630 Sansome Street, San Francisco, CA 94111 and ask for the Los Padres National Forest map. **Pets:** Dogs are not permitted on trails within the state park. **Contact:** Gaviota State Park, (805) 968-1711. Los Padres National Forest, Santa Barbara Ranger District, (805) 967-3481. **Locator:** GAVIOTA PEAK.

20
VENTURA COUNTY

• **FEATURED TRIPS** •

MOUNT PINOS 191
OJAI VALLEY TRAIL 192
SESPE WILDERNESS 194
ANACAPA ISLAND 196

SANTA CRUZ ISLAND 198
SAN MIGUEL, SANTA
   BARBARA, AND SANTA
   ROSA ISLANDS 200
POINT MUGU STATE PARK 202

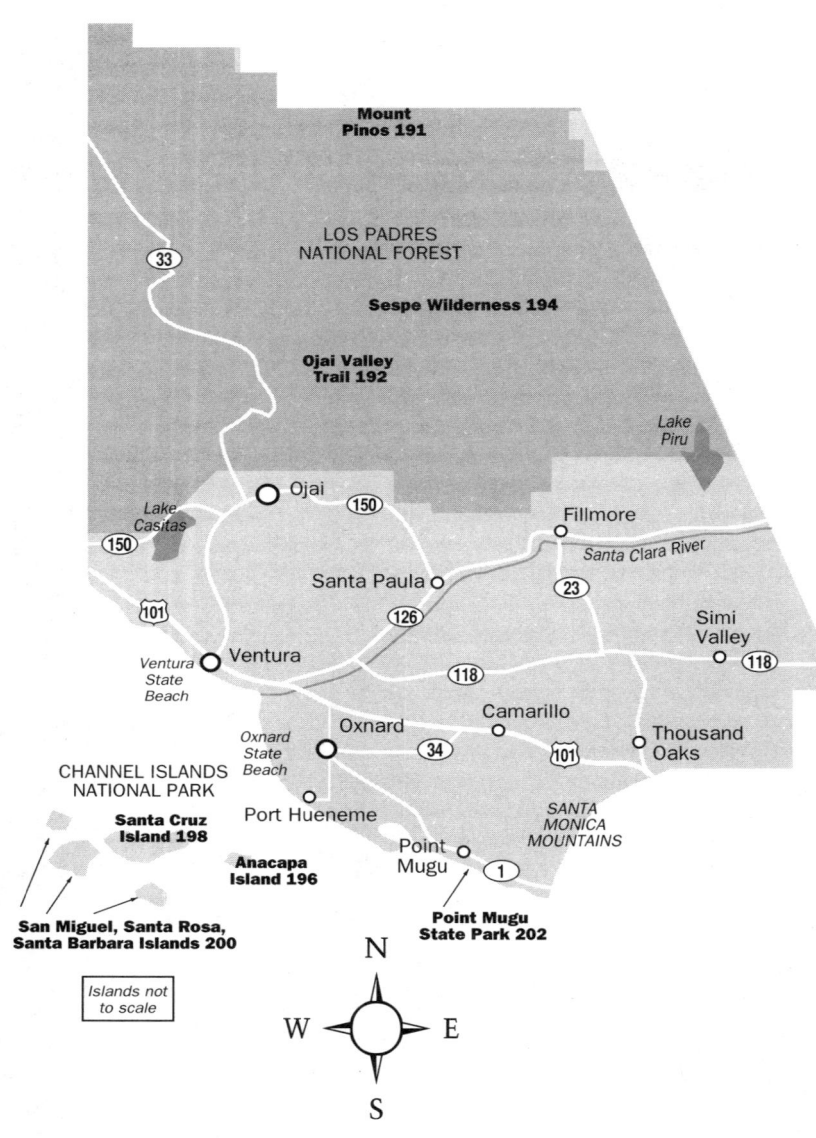

VENTURA COUNTY

• FEATURED TRIP •

MOUNT PINOS

In north Ventura County, near the Grapevine

The Tejon Pass is infamous for snagging every weather problem imaginable: freezing rain, sleet, snow, and the kind of high winds that blow tractor trailers onto their sides. The rainstorms that hit Los Angeles during the winter are often snowstorms in the Tejon Pass, forcing the closure of Interstate 5 either by choice or by wreck.

Whenever this happens, the L.A. TV news programs send some poor reporter to stand in the cold and report a nugget of wisdom, something along the lines that the rain is wet or the snow is cold or the ice is slippery. It's TV at its finest.

Not too far from this infamous section of the highway is a mountain that benefits greatly from the storms: Mount Pinos. With an elevation of 8,831 feet, it's the highest point in Ventura County and the tallest mountain west of I-5. Because of its elevation and western location, Pinos snags those storms and ends up blanketed by snow. The result: good cross-country skiing and snowshoeing. For those living in Ventura or Santa Barbara Counties, the San Fernando Valley or even L.A.'s Westside, Mount Pinos is also relatively easy to reach.

There is a large network of ungroomed trails covering Mount Pinos, most of which wind their way through thick forests of pine. Don't worry about the lack of grooming: the area receives enough usage from devoted skiers that schussing on most trails isn't very difficult.

The area receives heavy use on weekends. Typically, Los Padres National Forest rangers stop motorists at the bottom of the mountain—chains or snow tires are often required throughout the winter. It is a nine-mile drive from the chain-up area at the bottom of the mountain to the top. On several visits to the mountain, we've chained up in relatively mild weather—temperatures in the 40s—and then arrived at the top, where it was snowing.

The best skiing can be found at the top of the mountain, accessible from the Chula Vista parking area at the end of the road. There is a small store selling maps, as well as several outhouses. Pay attention: Just behind the outhouses is the beginning of the Condor Summit Road, the popular trail leading to the Pinos summit.

Initially, the trail is virtually all uphill, although the climb is not terribly difficult for those in decent shape. Eventually, after a mile or so, the trail levels out and heads toward the summit. We hear the view of the adjacent Chumash Wilderness is wonderful. Every time we have visited, we find ourselves staring out at clouds, which have descended upon the mountain with unfortunate timing.

Another trail we recommend is the Northridge Overlook, which splinters off the Condor Summit Road, just after the locked gate (about 100 yards from the outhouses). This trail is a bit more level initially, wandering through the forest. It's an absolutely beautiful place when it's snowing—a real alpine environment just a 90-minute drive from the ocean.

One of the great things about Pinos is that dogs are allowed on the trail. Our dog, Molly the chocolate Lab, lives

SEE COUNTY MAP ON PAGE 190

for a day on Pinos. One of her favorite tricks: riding on the back of our skis. Really.

SUMMERTIME ON MOUNT PINOS

Mount Pinos looks mighty fine during the winter, but the mountain is an equally fine summer retreat. The same trail from the Chula Vista parking lot to the summit—Condor Summit Road—can be hiked. The Vincent Tumamait trail begins at the end of Condor Summit Road and travels 3.25 miles to the top of nearby Mount Abel (8,283 feet).

There's also decent camping at two Forest Service campgrounds on Mount Pinos: the McGill and Mount Pinos Campgrounds. Facilities at both include fire rings, picnic tables, piped water, and vault toilets. Fees are $8 per night, and reservations are not accepted. For more information, phone the Los Padres National Forest, Mount Pinos Ranger District, at (805) 245-3731.

ASTRONOMERS BEWARE

Mount Pinos is, literally, closer to the stars than anywhere else in Ventura County. That's why it is a favorite of local astronomers, who informally gather throughout the year to gaze at the stars through telescopes that look anything but amateur. These suckers are huge! The public is welcome to come by and take a look—on clear nights it's usually a good bet the telescopes will be there.

Directions: From downtown Los Angeles take Interstate 5 north for 70 miles to the Frazier Park Road exit and turn left. Continue on Frazier Park Road for seven miles and turn right onto Cuddy Valley Road. Drive five miles and turn left on Mount Pinos Road. From there, either continue 10 miles up the road to the Chula Vista parking lot and ski center or park at one of the several marked trails alongside the road. **Navigating the Grapevine:** If the weather is at all spotty, listen to one of the Los Angeles news radio stations for information on closures along Interstate 5 between Santa Clarita and the Grapevine. Also bring tire chains, which will probably be needed after exiting the interstate or to make it to the ski center. Often rangers or highway patrol thin traffic to the top of the mountain by only allowing those with chains to continue. If you don't know how to put the chains on, then learn—because there may not be anyone around to help. **Fees:** Purchase a Forest Service Adventure Pass at a ranger station or most large sporting goods stores for $5 for a day or $30 annually. **Maps:** A trail map can be obtained for $1 from the ski center at the Chula Vista parking lot. **Ski rentals:** Cross-country skis and boots can be rented from many local ski shops or large sporting goods stores in Southern California, such as REI or Sport Chalet. Prices are typically very reasonable; you shouldn't pay more than $10 to $15 per day. **Contact:** Los Padres National Forest, Mount Pinos Ranger District, (805) 245-3731. **Locator:** MOUNT PINOS.

• FEATURED TRIP •

OJAI VALLEY TRAIL

East of Ventura, in the shadow of the Topatopa Mountains

The Ojai Valley begins in the foothills of the Topatopa Mountains and runs south to the city of Ventura. The valley's soil is fertile, making it the perfect place for orange trees to grow. The orange groves in the Ojai Valley were once so plentiful that a railroad was built in the late 1800s to haul the produce to Ventura and markets beyond.

Trucking helped kill the railroad in the twentieth century. In the 1980s, the old railbed was removed and converted to a nine-mile hiking, biking, and horseback trail. Today the trail parallels Highway 33 and runs 8.8 miles from Foster Park in the south to the charming village of Ojai in the north.

The paved trail is mostly flat with a few gentle, rolling hills. Although Highway 33 is often visible from the trail, the path sometimes disappears behind small hills or trees, allowing for quiet, unobstructed views of the Ojai Valley and the Topatopas. This is everything a bike ride in the country should be—easy, mellow, and relaxing.

How pretty is the valley? Well, you certainly don't have to be a Hollywood location scout to see why the Ojai Valley was chosen to serve as the location for Shangri-La in the 1937 film *Lost Horizon*.

In the movie, a plane crashes in the Himalayas and the survivors are rescued by the happy people of Shangri-La, where everything, as you might expect, is quite peachy. In one scene, the main character, a British diplomat named Robert Conway, looks out over the stunning Ojai Valley (stunning in black and white, that is), realizing that he has stumbled upon paradise lost, just as the rest of the world is heading into the toilet of World War II.

Shangri-La is a fairly difficult reputation to live down and many visitors head up to Ojai from Dante's Inferno, L.A., to spend the night at one of Ojai's inns or motels; the town has been a well-known retreat for city folk for many years. But Ojai isn't just an overnight destination. It's about a 90-minute to two-hour drive from the Central Coast or Los Angeles, meaning it's doable as a day trip.

Some folks like to leave their cars in Foster Park and pedal the 8.8 miles to the trail's Fox Street terminus, which is just two blocks from downtown Ojai. In town, you can lunch at one of the outdoor cafes or picnic in the oak- and sycamore-shrouded Libbey Park, located right across the street from Ojai's one-by-two-block downtown area. The city park, which is as pretty as they come, also hosts free concerts during the summer; check with the Ojai Valley Chamber of Commerce at (805) 646-8126 for dates and times.

In addition to the concerts, Ojai also hosts an annual classic music festival, which is usually held at Libbey Park's beautiful, woodsy amphitheater (next to the bike trail) during the first week of June. For information, phone the Chamber of Commerce.

Directions: From downtown Los Angeles, take U.S. 101 north to Highway 33 north, the last exit in Ventura. Follow Highway 33 north to Foster Park. To continue to Ojai, stay on Highway 33, following signs to town. From Santa Barbara, take U.S. 101 south to Highway 150 east. Follow Highway 150 for 18 miles and turn left on Highway 33. Continue to Foster Park or follow the signs on Highway 33 to town.
Fees: The trail is free and open to all hikers, bikers, rollerbladers, joggers, and equestrians. **Maps:** Ventura County maps are available at most large bookstores in California. Obtain a map of the trail by phoning the Ventura County General Services Agency

at (805) 654-3951. **Pets:** Dogs are allowed but must be leashed. **Horse rentals:** Guided one-hour trail rides are available through the Ojai Valley Inn for about $40. For more information, phone the inn's stables at (805) 649-5552. **Contact:** Ojai Chamber of Commerce, 338 East Ojai Avenue, P.O. Box 1134, Ojai, CA 93024; (805) 646-8126. **Locator:** OJAI VALLEY TRAIL.

• FEATURED TRIP •

SESPE WILDERNESS
Deep within Los Padres National Forest

Bordered roughly by Interstate 5 in the east, Highway 33 in the west, Santa Paula Ridge in the south, and Lockwood Valley Road in the north, the 220,500-acre Sespe Wilderness is unusually rugged, even by California standards. On a cloudy day, with the peaks barely hovering over the mountains, the place looks downright eerie when viewed from Interstate 5.

The Sespe can be divided into three areas: the higher elevations over 4,000 feet where there is Sierra-type scenery; the upper part of the Sespe River, from Lion's Camp toward Hot Springs Canyon; and the lower Sespe, where the river forms many deep pools. Boulders the size of houses line parts of the river and palm-sized turtles are often seen. The Chumash Indians called the turtles "sespe."

The Sespe Hot Springs, 17 miles from Lion's Camp, are located on a tributary of the Sespe and are the hottest hot springs in the state, sometimes reaching temperatures of 220 degrees. Needless to say, bathers must sit downstream a way to make sure they don't get scalded.

For all its glory, the interior of the Sespe doesn't get that many visitors. It wasn't declared a wilderness area until 1992; what kept it wilderness for all the preceding years was its ruggedness.

"You could come up here and see 30 cars at the trailhead at Lion's Camp and then go down there and not see anyone all day," says John Boggs, a ranger with the U.S. Forest Service since 1969 who has hiked every trail in the wilderness.

There are more than a dozen primitive campgrounds spread out around the interior. Those interested in backpacking or hiking the Sespe on their own and needing some tips should phone the Los Padres National Forest, Ojai Ranger District office.

GUIDED HORSEBACK TRIPS
Tony Alvis got his first glimpse of the Sespe Wilderness back in the late 1960s. Having heard that the Sespe Hot Springs were sensational and having an interest in the hot springs of the West, Alvis decided to check out the Sespe for himself.

Twenty-five years later, it's fair to say that he has never really left the Sespe, having found a career in the rugged backcountry which constitutes 18 percent of Ventura County's acreage. Shortly after acquiring his first horse, Alvis began to lead guided trips into the Sespe, a job he has often performed to great acclaim. Over the years, Alvis and his guided trips have received mention in virtually every newspaper in California, *Outside* magazine, *Men's Journal*, and a slew of other publications.

Alvis' description of the Sespe goes like this: "Well, it's real primitive. It has a lot of history from the Indians, starting with the grizzly bears. The Indians followed those bears all through the mountains—grizzlies were the rulers up there. They're gone, but there's still plenty of black bears. And the condors, well, they survived up there from prehistoric times all the way into this century.

"It was never very populated by man, just a few travelers, some horse thieves, and hermits who tried to hide up there. And there's the river [Sespe Creek]. It's the last free-flowing river in Southern California and steelhead trout still spawn there. There have been guys who wanted to dam it over the years, but 33 miles of the river are protected. They could still dam it down near Fillmore, though. They do that, it would be like damming the Grand Canyon."

Alvis' horseback trips can be tailor-made for anyone interested. Some people only go for a few hours; others go for several days. Needless to say, the longer you go, the more you see. The longer trips usually enter the Sespe from Lion's Camp, near Highway 33, and then head down the river before climbing back uphill to reach the hot springs.

Alvis brings along several burros to carry everyone's packs, as well as camping supplies; the only thing he asks customers to bring are hats and canteens. Camp is often set up on beaches right on the Sespe, which abounds with swimming holes—at some points the creek is almost 100 feet across. For food, Alvis often brings along a cook (sometimes even a Thai cook!) to produce some rather elaborate backcountry meals. As for your rear end, Alvis' horses walk, not trot, meaning that pretty much anyone who can withstand more than an hour a day in the saddle can take the trip.

Yes, we know this sounds like an advertisement, but think of it as a ringing endorsement. We haven't encountered anyone who speaks of Alvis in anything less than glowing terms. Although his trips are a bit on the cushy side for the seasoned backcountry hiker, they allow people to see more of the wilderness area than they probably would on foot. And you'll learn more about the land. Alvis aptly, fluently, and willingly wants to tell you the land's story.

The fact is Alvis' trips cost some money, potentially up to $125 per person per day for an overnight trip. That's not cheap. Certainly, you can see the Sespe quite adequately on foot while backpacking for a couple of days through the wilderness.

Perhaps the best thing about a trip with Alvis into the Sespe is that you can find yourself sitting in the saddle believing it could be 1898 or 1998. The horses cross Sespe Creek several times, with water up above your stirrups occasionally, and they also walk across the edge of cliffs overlooking the Sespe Canyon. Sometimes the horse is right on the edge of a drop-off, an experience some riders find unnerving. "Let me put it this way," says Alvis. "I don't want to lose you or the horse."

It was on Mother's Day a few years back that Alvis and a group of riders came to one of those overlooks rising above the Sespe. Everyone looked down and saw a mother bear and her two cubs playing in the creek. Reflecting on that moment some time later, Alvis says, "This is just one of those little ecosystems that's somehow surviving in a world of acid rain and pollution."

Directions: There are several trailheads leading into the Sespe Wilderness. The most popular begins at Lion's Camp and leads to a trail along Sespe Creek. From Ojai to Lion's Camp, take Highway 33 north for 15 miles and turn right on Sespe Creek Road. Drive for three miles until reaching Lion's Camp. **Fees:** Hiking and backpacking in the Sespe are free, but a Forest Service Adventure Pass is needed to park at the trailhead. The passes are $5 for a day pass or $30 for an annual pass, good in Los Padres, Angeles, San Bernardino, and Cleveland National Forests. Passes are available at all Forest Service visitor centers and most large sporting goods stores. Alvis' rates vary depending on the length of the trip. For an overnighter, he typically charges $125 per person per day. All camping equipment and food are provided. **Maps:** The Los Padres National Forest map is available at most ranger stations and at most large sporting goods stores. Or, send $4 to the USDA-Forest Service, Attn: Map Room 807, 630 Sansome Street, San Francisco, CA 94111 and request the Los Padres National Forest map. **Pets:** Dogs are permitted in the Sespe Wilderness but are not allowed on Alvis's trips. **Contact:** Los Padres National Forest, Ojai Ranger District, (805) 646-4348. Tony Alvis Los Padres Wilderness Outfitters, (805) 648-2113. **Locator:** SESPE WILDERNESS.

• FEATURED TRIP •

ANACAPA ISLAND

In Channel Islands National Park

After spending the afternoon hiking on Anacapa Island, we were enjoying a lazy boat ride around the isle before heading back to Ventura.

The boat had just swung around the famous Arch Rock at the island's southern tip and was chugging its way toward Anacapa's backside when the man with the binoculars stood up and screamed, "Stop the boat!"

His tone suggested we had either just rammed a rare Southern California iceberg or were about to be boarded and robbed of our Instamatics by Black Beard. To keep his eyes from bugging out, he had the binoculars pressed into his skull. Finally, he explained himself: "It's an American oystercatcher!"

There, perched on a rock some 50 yards away, was an ordinary-looking white and black bird with a red beak. The bird appeared nowhere near as excited as the birder, who was now hyperventilating.

Meanwhile, the birder's friend had pulled out his dog-eared Audubon guide, flipping blindly through the hundreds of pages before producing a drawing of the American oystercatcher. Patiently, the friend explained that American oystercatchers are rarely found in the area. This one had probably wandered up the coast from Baja after breeding. "Are the oysters up here better?" asked Steve, who believed he had just asked a perfectly reasonable question.

"They don't eat oysters," the birder snapped, acting as if we had just asked the sum of two plus two. "They eat mussels. Very, very small mussels."

Well, excuuuuuse me.

We drew two conclusions from this encounter. One, bird-watchers are a strange breed (more on this later in the book). Two, Anacapa is a bird-watcher's paradise.

Our friend the American oystercatcher was just a speck in a sea of brown pelicans, seagulls, cormorants, falcons, and hawks, among others. In fact, the three Anacapa isles are one of the foremost breeding sites for Western gulls in the entire United States. Even those who know nothing about birds—a group that includes us—will probably enjoy the sheer numbers of the little winged fellows on and around Anacapa.

Anacapa, of course, is one of the five islands that comprise Channel Islands National Park (along with Santa Rosa, Santa Barbara, Santa Cruz, and San Miguel). By far, Anacapa is both the most accessible and least expensive of the islands to visit, located only 14 miles from Ventura.

Anacapa actually consists of three narrow islands, known officially as West Anacapa, Middle Anacapa, and East Anacapa, with the latter open to visitation. All three islands are basically craggy and rocky mountains rising out of the sea. For those who like trivia: Anacapa and the Channel Islands are the only islands in the national park system.

Unless you have a boat, the only way to get here is via an excursion with Island Packers, the park service's designated concessionaire. At press time, the full-day trip will put a $37 dent in an adult wallet, $20 in a 12-and-under pocket.

When the seas aren't too heavy, the boat ride is a thrill. It's almost guaranteed that passengers will see seals, sea lions, and dolphins during the crossing of the Santa Barbara Channel. If luck is on your side from December to May, you may also get a glimpse of blue sharks or, hopefully, gray whales migrating either from the Arctic to Mexico or vice versa.

Much of Anacapa has actually been eroded away, leaving 100-foot-tall cliffs all the way around the isle's perimeter. It's so steep, in fact, that the only path from the sea to the island's rolling terrain is a climb of 154 stairs from the small dock where the boat lands. For those in decent shape, no problem. For those just finishing their third pack of the day, a little advice: Go to the rear of the line.

Once on the island, there's just enough hiking to keep people busy for an hour or so—a national park volunteer leads a guided tour, which we recommend taking. Another great way of passing the time is to have a seat at the appropriately titled Inspiration Point, which overlooks the other two Anacapa isles.

One final recommendation: Consider a visit in November, when the boat returns from the island as the sun sets. It's quite a sight—almost as good as seeing an American oystercatcher.

Directions to Island Packers in Ventura Harbor: From all points north or south, take U.S. 101 to Ventura and exit at Victoria. Take Victoria south and turn right onto Channel Islands Boulevard. Drive over the bridge and turn left at Harbor Boulevard. Drive one-quarter mile. Island Packers is on the left in the Marine Emporium, next to Tug's restaurant. **Directions to the Channel Islands National Park Visitor Center:** Exit U.S. 101 at Victoria and turn left. At Olivas Park Drive, turn right. After Harbor Boulevard, Olivas Park runs straight into Spinnaker Drive. The visitor center is located at the end of the road, alongside the harbor. **Note:** The ride to Anacapa can sometimes be rough. Inquire about conditions ahead of time. If you're prone to seasickness, either take an appropriate antinausea medication or reschedule your trip for when the seas are more calm. **Fees:** Island Packers offers a variety of packages to Anacapa. The full-day trip with an island landing is $37 for adults and $20 for kids 12 and under. **Maps:** For a free map of the Channel Islands, contact Channel Islands National Park, 1901 Spinnaker Drive, Ventura, CA 93001; (805) 658-5730. **Pets:** Dogs are not allowed to make this trip. **Clothing tip:** Bring a windbreaker and a sweater; the boat crossing can be chilly and the island can be windy. **Contact:** Channel Islands National Park, (805) 658-5730. Island Packers, (805) 642-7688 for information and (805) 642-1393 for reservations between 9 A.M. and 5 P.M., seven days a week. Island Packers Web site: www.isle.net/~ipco. **Locator:** ANACAPA ISLAND.

WHERE'S THE COLONEL?

The most noticeable thing about Anacapa's environment to the casual eye: the thousands of chicken bones that cover the island's terrain. It seems that many of Anacapa's gulls get the munchies in the dead of night and fly to the mainland, where they raid the Oxnard dump, which apparently has no shortage of chicken bones. By daybreak, the gulls return to Anacapa and scatter the bones everywhere.

• FEATURED TRIP •

SANTA CRUZ ISLAND
In Channel Islands National Park

This popular island, the largest of the Channel Islands, has undergone dramatic changes in the last two years. A large part of Santa Cruz, about 6,200 acres, was once a private ranch. But in the last two years, the National Park Service has completed its long-planned takeover of the ranch and is now beginning a massive restoration of the environment, which has been severely harmed by overgrazing.

Actually, 90 percent of the island is owned and set aside as a preserve by the Nature Conservancy. The NPS takeover of the ranch means that the other 10 percent of the island will be devoted to hikers. Landing fees for private craft will be reduced and the campground will be expanded. Native vegetation will also benefit greatly. All in all, it's a good deal for everyone involved.

A good friend, *Asbury Park Press* reporter Tim May, an ex-Californian, is nuts for Santa Cruz Island. He's visited often and he generously filed this report for us about a recent visit:

We hauled our butts out of bed early on a Saturday—about 6 A.M.—and drove to Ventura Harbor. There, clumps of outdoorsy-looking people clad in multi-pocketed shorts, hiking boots, and fleece pullovers stood around gripping their coffee cups for dear life. It was very apparent that few of us bound for Santa Cruz had showered recently. But for the $125 that Paddlesports (a Ventura outfitter) charges for the trip, that was someone else's problem.

About 30 people were making the trip to Santa Cruz Island. Some, like us, were going kayaking. Others were either staying at a bed-and-breakfast on the island or just camping and hiking. Finally, after a gentle three-hour ride in the boat, we got our first view of the contours of Santa Cruz Island, which is 24 miles from shore.

Soon we saw a rocky gray shoreline, tall yellow grass, and a series of steeply rising hills beyond. As our boat approached we saw sharp, sheer cliffs reaching up several hundred yards to the left and right of a small, clear green cove. At the bottom of the cliffs, frothy waves and currents had pounded sea caves, crags, and ribbon-line canyons deep into the rock. We would soon investigate these sites in ocean kayaks.

After mooring and motoring to shore in a succession of dinghy trips, we split up: non-kayakers trudged a short distance to the island's 100-year-old bed-and-breakfast, the Scorpion Ranch (which was destroyed in storms in late 1997). Campers (including us) quickly dumped our equipment at a couple of campsites carved into a hillside looking southeast over the cove.

My friend Angie and I then marched to a shed, where we each picked out a light, plastic kayak. Our guide divvied out wet suits, life vests, helmets, and paddles. It was little surprise that Angie wound up with a pink kayak, pink helmet, and purple life vest. If she were heading to the moon, she would have arrived in a color-coordinated space suit with matching boots.

After a 20-minute primer on how to handle the kayaks and maneuver inside the caves, we launched. Our first exercise involved falling out of our kayaks and climbing back in. It was an icebreaker in every sense of the word.

We paddled a short distance up the shoreline, gazing at the high, forbidding cliffs that leaned over us. The water was clear to a depth of about 15 feet. We entered our first cave, leaning back and passing, limbo style, into a large chamber with stalactites reaching down menacingly, forcing us to slalom around them. One of the guides' assistants went in ahead of us with a spelunker's lantern bound to her helmet to light the interior.

After about two hours of paddling in and out of a variety of caves and cracks, we entered a quiet, narrow inlet. Our guide encouraged Angie and me to take a peek below with our masks and snorkels—we were the only ones who had brought such gear.

We were awed immediately. A profusion of brilliant purple and blue and black urchins littered the walls that framed the inlet. We saw bright orange garibaldi fish swish through, and millions of butterfly-shaped mussels everywhere. An enormous halibut passed by, and sea snails sucked hungrily on treelike strands of kelp. We made a note to return the next day.

After getting back to the cove and setting up camp, we had a light dinner, downed a bottle of chardonnay, and set off on a hike up the hills to catch the sunset from the top of the island. On the way, we passed some of the many shaggy sheep that roam the island and spotted a few cat-sized island fox. We spent a very happy couple of hours not saying much and looking out to sea—a haze had lifted to reveal miles of blue, white-capped ocean.

The next day, we opened the tent flap and spied a solitary sea lion fishing in the cove. We watched him for a while, ate a breakfast of cereal, and embarked on a long hike, our packs laden with snorkeling equipment, bottled water, and lunch, heading out to the little inlet we had discovered the day before. We were not disappointed and spent several hours snorkeling around the inlet, marveling at the variety of life beneath us, without another human being in sight.

That evening, the boat from Ventura came to retrieve us and the few others who stayed at the bed-and-breakfast. The captain of the ship stopped and turned off course for a while to chase a pod of dolphins. We smiled all the way back home.

Directions to Island Packers in Ventura Harbor: From all points north or south, take U.S. 101 to Ventura and exit at Victoria. Take Victoria south and turn right onto Channel Islands Boulevard. Drive over the bridge and turn left at Harbor Boulevard. Drive one-quarter mile. Island Packers is on the left in the Marine Emporium, next to Tug's restaurant. **Directions to the Channel Islands National Park Visitor Center:** Exit U.S. 101 at Victoria and turn left. At Olivas Park Drive, turn right. After Harbor Boulevard, Olivas Park runs straight into Spinnaker Drive. The visitor center is located at the end of the road, alongside the harbor. **Fees:** Round-trip transportation by boat to Santa Cruz by Island Packers is $47. Prices for kayak tours vary. **Maps:** For a free map of the Channel Islands, contact Channel Islands National Park, 1901 Spinnaker Drive, Ventura, CA 93001; (805) 658-5730. **Pets:** Dogs are not allowed on Santa Cruz Island. **Contact:** Channel Islands National Park, (805) 658-5730. Island Packers, (805) 642-7688 for information and (805) 642-1393 for reservations between 9 A.M. and 5 P.M., seven days a week. Island Packers Web site: www.isle.net/~ipco. Paddlesports, (805) 899-4925. Kayak tours are also offered by Aqua Sports (in Goleta), (805) 968-7231, and Adventours Outdoor Excursions (in Santa Barbara), (805) 963-2248. **Locator:** SANTA CRUZ ISLAND.

• FEATURED TRIP •

SAN MIGUEL, SANTA BARBARA, AND SANTA ROSA ISLANDS
Off the Ventura County coast

During the heyday of whale hunting, in the early 1800s, hunters couldn't always find whales. In desperation, these hunters would often turn their attention to elephant seals, whose blubbery skin also contained valuable oil. By the end of the 19th century, it is believed that fewer than 100 elephant seals had survived—and nearly all were living on a small island off Baja California, Mexico.

The latter half of the 20th century has been much kinder to the elephant seals. San Miguel Island, part of Channel Islands National Park, often hosts thousands of elephant seals each year. In addition, five other species of seals can be seen on San Miguel during the mating season, including the harbor seal, California sea lion, stellar sea lion, northern fur seal, and the Guadalupe fur seal. San Miguel is the only place in the world in which six species of seals can be found together.

Now the downside. First, sea lions throughout Southern California had a terrible time in 1997–98, compliments of El Niño. As the sea became warmer and warmer, the food that sea lions rely on became harder and harder to find. Adult lions had to swim farther to find food, often leaving juveniles behind. Thousands of lions starved to death and hundreds others were rescued up and down the California coast.

It should also be noted that it takes

a four- to five-hour boat ride to reach San Miguel. By comparison, Santa Barbara Island and Santa Rosa Island are just a stone's throw away; Santa Barbara requires a three-hour boat ride and Santa Rosa is a three- to three-and-a-half-hour boat ride.

With no roads or conveniences, these three islands are even more remote than some of the deserts in Southern California. Those who camp on San Miguel or Santa Barbara in the late spring or early fall may even find themselves the isle's only inhabitants. The camping, of course, is completely primitive—as it should be.

SAN MIGUEL ISLAND

The island can be visited through Island Packers, which is under contract with the National Park Service to ferry visitors to and from the Channel Islands. Island Packers offers one- and two-day excursions to the island; guests sleep on the boat on the overnight trip.

One benefit of the overnighter is that it goes around the island's backside to Point Bennett, a sandy beach where the sea lions can be found. If you choose to camp on San Miguel, Point Bennett is a 15-mile round-trip hike from the campground.

For those planning to camp on the island, transportation can be arranged through Island Packers. A free camping permit must also be obtained from the National Park Service.

Campers should take caution because this can be extremely difficult camping. High winds can be a problem and there is no water available—it must be packed in. For those looking for an adventure, this is it.

SANTA BARBARA ISLAND

Our pal Tim May is nuts for the Channel Islands. Not only has he extensively kayaked Santa Cruz's coastline, but he recently signed up for an excursion through the Learning Tree University in Los Angeles, which allowed him to "swim with the seals."

The class went like this: A bunch of people from all walks of life and with varying snorkeling skills (from none to experienced) took a boat out to tiny Santa Barbara Island, which covers only one square mile of land. Just offshore, they put on wet suits and plopped into the 60-degree water—it was summer.

Looking underwater, they could hear the sound of approaching seals. Suddenly—boom!—the sea lions were swimming among the snorkelers, stopping to sniff their faces. Some of the sea lions were eight feet long.

That's how the class spent the rest of the morning and the afternoon before turning around and heading back to Ventura. Not a bad way to spend a day, huh?

SANTA ROSA ISLAND

Santa Rosa is 15 miles long, 10 miles wide, and covers 53,000 acres, making it the second largest of the Channel Islands (Santa Cruz is the largest).

However, Santa Rosa is kind of half in, half out of the national park. When the park service purchased the island in 1986 from the Vail and Vickers Company, it agreed to allow Vail and Vickers to continue ranching and hunting on the land for 25 years. Part of the agreement stipulated that visitors could only see much of the ranch if accompanied by a park ranger.

Santa Rosa is best suited for day use, and there are three interesting hikes worth taking. Keep in mind, too, that island fox, feral pigs, mule deer, Roosevelt elk, horses, and cattle all inhabit the island. In case you're wondering, the answer is yes, those who choose to camp here have to pig-proof their campsite before retiring for the night. Luckily, pigs aren't quite as wily as California black bears. Putting food in a cooler will do the trick.

Directions to Island Packers in Ventura Harbor: From all points north or south, take U.S. 101 to Ventura and exit at Victoria. Take Victoria south and turn right onto Channel Islands Boulevard. Drive over the bridge and turn left at Harbor Boulevard. Drive one-quarter mile. Island Packers is on the left in the Marine Emporium, next to Tug's restaurant. **Directions to the Channel Islands National Park Visitor Center:** Exit U.S. 101 at Victoria and turn left. At Olivas Park Drive, turn right. After Harbor Boulevard, Olivas Park runs straight into Spinnaker Drive. The visitor center is located at the end of the road, alongside the harbor. **Fees:** A day trip with Island Packers to Santa Rosa Island costs $62 per adult; a day trip to Santa Barbara Island is $49, and a two-day/two-night trip to San Miguel and Santa Rosa is $215. Prices for campers requiring transportation are higher; phone Island Packers for more information. Camping is free on the islands, but you must obtain a permit from the National Park Service. In spring of 1998, Truth Aquatics began running trips to Santa Rosa and San Miguel Islands from Santa Barbara. A day trip costs $75 per adult, and a two-day trip is $252 per adult. Truth Aquatics' boats have sleeping compartments. **Maps:** For a free map of the Channel Islands, contact Channel Islands National Park, 1901 Spinnaker Drive, Ventura, CA 93001; (805) 658-5730. **Pets:** Dogs are not permitted to make any of these trips. **Contact:** Channel Islands National Park, (805) 658-5730. Island Packers, (805) 642-7688 for information and (805) 642-1393 for reservations between 9 A.M. and 5 P.M., seven days a week. Truth Aquatics, (805) 963-3564. Learning Tree University, (818) 882-5599. **Locator:** CHANNEL ISLANDS NATIONAL PARK.

• FEATURED TRIP •

POINT MUGU STATE PARK
Where the Santa Monica Mountains plunge into the sea

Feeling a little blue about your relationship with the wheel? After spending your last paycheck, you rear-ended a Ferrari—in your Geo Metro.

Maybe a fellow motorist pulled a Jack Nicholson and tried his five-iron on your windshield.

Your commute eats time like the Jolly Green Giant eats green beans.

The I-5 is clogged, the 210 is worse.

Bad talk radio. Brain-shaking headaches. Spilled coffee in your lap.

Blech.

It is time to rectify the situation, to see living proof that the wheel isn't necessarily a bad thing. Yep, that's right, it's time to load the mountain bike into the car and drive (sorry, it is Southern California) straight to Point Mugu State Park. And there you're going to ride that bicycle of yours from the mountains straight down to the sea for 8.8 glorious, congestion-free miles.

The wind will blow back your hair. The park's famous sycamore trees will keep you cool. The scenery will soothe your brain. You may even become a person again.

Point Mugu (pronounced Ma-goo, as in Mister), located north of Malibu, is where the Santa Monica Mountains finally meet the sea. The park, which covers over 15,000 acres, features rolling hills, the jagged 3,000-foot-plus Tri-Peaks of the Boney Mountains (where it has snowed just five miles from the ocean!), several grassy meadows, and two gorgeous canyons, Sycamore and La Jolla, with creeks that flow year-round.

And then there is the biking. Our favorite ride is the aforementioned 8.8-mile trek on the Sycamore Canyon Trail from Rancho Sierra Vista at the park's northern boundary all the way to the Pacific Coast Highway and the sea in the south.

Five words explain why this is our favorite ride: It is virtually all downhill. After a short climb from the parking lot at Rancho Sierra Vista, the paved trail drops over 1,000 feet in the first two miles and then gently descends for another six miles to the ocean. As our wise friend Trevor the Canuck points out, "Check your brakes, eh." If your brakes fail, trust us, it will be a ride neither you nor the paramedics will ever forget.

After the initial drop, the paved trail becomes a dirt fire road and ambles alongside Sycamore Creek for the next six miles, passing countless sycamore tree savannas and a handful of grassy meadows. The trail also crosses the creek several times. If it has been raining and the creek is high, be careful and walk your bike across. If it's summer or fall and the creek's depth is less than a foot, put the bike in low gear and get wet.

What makes Point Mugu unique is the fact that it's one of the few mountainous areas where riders of any skill level can bike. If going uphill just isn't your thing, then do the downhill ride from Rancho Sierra Vista or enter the park at the PCH and stick to the approximately six-mile, mostly level portion of Sycamore Canyon. If you're interested in trying a little uphill action, turn around and try riding back up to Rancho Sierra Vista. It's a ride your lungs will be talking about for years to come.

There are numerous trails that splinter off the Sycamore Canyon Trail, most of which head up into the hills. There's some serious mountain biking on these ridges, where there are both steep and wide fire roads and "single track," which are dirt foot trails just wide enough to accommodate a single bike tire.

Ultimately, the Sycamore Canyon Trail ends at the Sycamore Canyon Campground, where a hose near the ranger's booth is available to wash down your bike, and possibly yourself. Beyond the ranger's booth is the PCH and, across the road, Sycamore Canyon Beach, the perfect place to wind down your day or rest before turning around and conquering the trail in the other direction.

A tip for one-way downhill riders from Rancho Sierra Vista to the Pacific Coast Highway: Either shuttle with two cars or have someone drop you off at Rancho Sierra and then pick you up later at Sycamore Canyon. It sounds inconvenient, but if you know where you're going it's no trouble at all.

Here's how to set up a shuttle:

You'll need two cars. First, follow the directions below to the Sycamore Canyon Campground and trailhead, which is accessible from the PCH. Park one of the cars, for free, on the side of the road, just after the campground entrance.

Then, take the second car—along with your mountain bikes—and follow these directions from Sycamore Canyon to Rancho Sierra Vista: Take the PCH north, exit at Las Posas Road, and turn right. Drive three miles and turn right on Lewis Road. Go one mile, turn right on Potrero Road, go seven miles, and turn right on Reino Road. Drive one-half mile to the entrance to Rancho Sierra Vista, which will be on your left. Park in the dirt parking lot. The trail starts at the far end of the lot, past the outhouses.

When you reach the PCH, load the bikes back onto the first car and go pick up the second car.

RETURN OF THE MONARCHS

Point Mugu State Park is renowned for its annual visits from the orange- and black-winged monarch butterfly, which usually makes its annual pilgrimage to Point Mugu in October, sometimes blanketing parts of Sycamore Canyon. The monarch is a wise guy: It eats poisonous milkweed, meaning that whatever eats the monarch is in for a case of possibly lethal indigestion. Humans do the same thing, but we call it Jack-In-The-Box.

WHALE OF A PARTY

Point Mugu State Park's annual whale festival is held each March. The festival features entertainment, food, and information booths. There's also whale watching. In March, the whales are returning from their winter migration point in Mexico and often pass close to Mugu. For more information, phone the park.

Directions to Rancho Sierra Vista:

From the San Fernando Valley, take U.S. 101 west to Lynn Road and turn left. Drive to Reino Road and turn left. At Potrero Road, turn right. The entrance to Rancho Sierra Vista is a dirt road on your left. **Directions to the Sycamore Canyon Trailhead:** From Santa Monica, take the Pacific Coast Highway north for 32 miles. The entrance to the campground and day-use parking lot is well marked on your right. **Fees:** Parking at Rancho Sierra Vista is free. Day-use parking at Sycamore Canyon is $6. There is some limited, free parking along the PCH at Sycamore Canyon. **Maps:** Maps of the park are available at the ranger's booth at the entrance to Sycamore Canyon. Maps are also available at the National Park Service's Santa Monica Mountains Recreation Area visitor center in Agoura Hills. **Pets:** Dogs are not allowed in the park, except for the campground, where they must be leashed. **Camping:** Sycamore Canyon Campground—which we rate as just okay—is located at the park's entrance and has 54 sites for tents or RVs. Facilities include picnic tables, fire grills, piped water, and flush toilets. Just a couple of miles up the road on the Pacific Coast Highway is Thornhill Broome State Beach Campground, with 84 sites for tents or RVs. The campground is right behind the beach, but too close to the noisy highway. Facilities include picnic tables, piped water, and pit toilets. For more information about the campgrounds, phone (818) 880-0350. Reservations for both are available through PARK.NET at (800) 444-PARK/7275. Fees range from $10 to $18 per night. **Contact:** California Department of Parks and Recreation Point Mugu State Park Ranger's Office, (805) 986-8591. **Locator:** POINT MUGU STATE PARK.

21
LOS ANGELES COUNTY

• FEATURED TRIPS •

ANGELES NATIONAL FOREST 208
WILDLIFE WAYSTATION 214
SKIING AND SNOWBOARDING THE
  SAN GABRIEL MOUNTAINS ... 215
MALIBU CREEK STATE PARK ... 218
PARAMOUNT RANCH 221
RED ROCK CANYON PARK AND
  THE STUNT HIGH TRAIL 222
TOPANGA STATE PARK 223
GRIFFITH PARK'S HORSE
  TRAILS 226
GRIFFITH PARK OBSERVATORY
  AND TELESCOPE NIGHT 227
LOS ANGELES COUNTY
  BEACHES 229
PALOS VERDES PENINSULA 231
SOUTH BAY BIKE TRAIL 234
BACKBONE TRAIL 236
CATALINA ISLAND 237
STONEY POINT 239

LOS ANGELES COUNTY—SOUTH

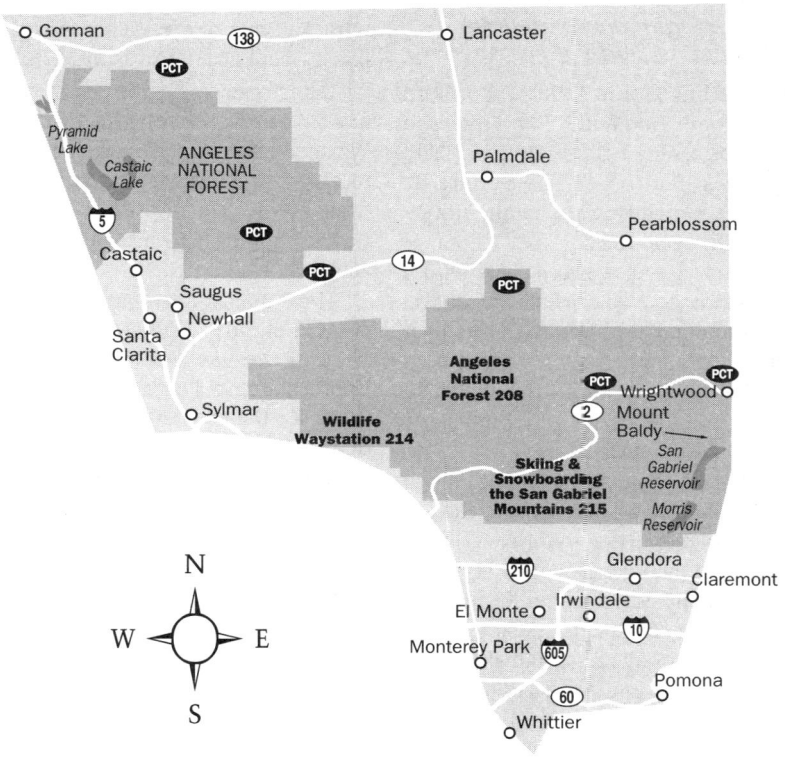

Los Angeles County—North

• FEATURED TRIP •

ANGELES NATIONAL FOREST
Covering the San Gabriel Mountains, north of Los Angeles

Seattle has Mount Rainier, Portland has Mount Hood, and San Francisco has the Golden Gate. Denver? The Rockies. Santa Fe? The Sangre de Cristos. Anchorage? Denali. Honolulu? Diamond Head.

These are all western cities with a signature view. And what view do we, the inhabitants of Los Angeles, most often see?

A brown curtain of impenetrable muck that makes our air resemble the lungs of Joe Camel.

What a sham and a shame. When the smog lifts, or blows out to the sea or the desert (tag—you're it!), the view that emerges is world-class. The vista of the San Gabriel Mountains towering over the city is so grand it makes up for all the strip malls, parking garages, and drug-laden politicians down below. Consider this: Most of L.A. is at or near sea level. The San Gabriels are a wall of rock behind the city, with its tallest peak, Mount Baldy, standing 10,064 feet high.

The San Gabriels boast more impressive statistics. The range travels the entire width of the county, from east to west, a distance of some 60 miles. The San Gabes, as they are known to the locals, cover one-fourth of L.A. County's acreage. The mountains are among the steepest in the nation, and a surprising amount of wildlife lives within them—black bears, mountain lions, bighorn sheep, and trout, to name just a few.

When Pacific storms slam into the mountains, as they did repeatedly in the winter of 1997–98, some of the most concentrated rainfall in the nation often follows. In his famous essay "Los Angeles Against the Mountains," John McPhee wrote, "The oddity of this is about as intense as the rain."

Take, for example, the day of January 25, 1969, when the National Weather Service's Big Tujunga Station recorded 11.52 inches of rain in a 24-hour period. During those same 24 hours, it rained 3.43 inches at the Los Angeles Civic Center.

The Angeles National Forest was created mainly to protect the watershed of the San Gabriels. The San Gabriels are not just a good source of water for the Los Angeles area, but a deadly one, too. In 1938, the rain would not stop falling. Debris flows and floods descended from the San Gabes, killing dozens of people in the valleys below.

Because of its proximity to L.A., the Angeles is the most visited national forest in the country; 29 million visitors dropped by to say hello in 1995. With elevation comes cooler temperatures, as well as that blessed water. In the summer, the forest is one of the valves where steam from the city is let off—for both the good and the bad.

There are hundreds of miles of hiking trails here, as well as 28 campgrounds, five ski resorts, and the famous Mount Wilson Observatory. There are enough trails and hikes to easily fill an entire book.

So, we're going to pick eight hikes that are representative of what the San Gabriels have to offer. Four of the hikes can be accessed from the front range—the communities below the mountains, such as Altadena, Monrovia, Glendora, and Claremont. The other four are found within the range, accessible by the Angeles Crest Highway, also known as Highway 2.

The highway was built during the Great Depression and is an engineering marvel. It begins in La Canada, in the San Gabriel Valley, at an elevation of 1,300 feet. Then, for the next 52 miles, the highway cuts through the mountains, sometimes reaching elevations of 7,000 feet and higher. Finally, on the north side of the range, the highway descends to the village of Wrightwood and then spits motorists out into the Mojave Desert.

How scenic is the Angeles Crest Highway? There are some stretches where one can look outside the car windows and see the land on one side rise 2,000 feet and the land on the other side fall 2,000 feet. Just to put that in perspective, the entire elevation change in the state of Iowa is only 1,130 feet. Motorists, as would be expected in L.A., sometimes drive over the edge. The lucky ones are found within a week.

The best map for all of the following hikes is the Angeles National Forest map, available at Forest Service ranger stations, as well as most sporting goods stores in the L.A. area. Or, purchase maps by mail by sending $4 to the USDA-Forest Service, Attn: Map Room 807, 630 Sansome Street, San Francisco, CA 94111; request the Angeles National Forest map. The Tom Harrison Recreation Map of the San Gabriel Mountains is a topographic trail map available at most outdoor stores.

Use of the Angeles National Forest was free until the spring of 1997, when the U.S. Forest Service began its "Adventure Pass" pilot program. Basically, the Forest Service wasn't getting the money it needed from Congress to run its recreation programs—although it gets plenty of money from Congress to run its very unprofitable logging programs. What to do about this dilemma?

Stick it to hikers! The Adventure Pass is now required to park anywhere within the Angeles, Cleveland, San Bernardino, or Los Padres National Forests. A day pass is $5, and an annual pass good for use in all four forests is $30. Passes can be purchased at any ranger station, as well as most Los Angeles area sporting goods stores.

5 HIKES FROM THE ANGELES CREST HIGHWAY

1. SWITZER FALLS TRAIL

This is a great hike for out-of-towners visiting L.A. because the trail offers a smorgasbord of just how pretty—and wild—the San Gabes can be.

The trail begins at the Switzer Falls Picnic Area, which can be accessed from the Angeles Crest Highway (Highway 2). The picnic area sits alongside the Arroyo Seco, a pretty creek that winds through the mountains all the way to Pasadena. The trail begins at the bridge over the creek and follows the creek downstream for one mile. The trail crosses the creek every few hundred yards, which in the springtime requires some boulder hopping and balancing beam routines on fallen logs.

At one mile, the trail reaches Switzer Campground, a backcountry camp with a half dozen sites and small fire stoves. This is also the location of one of the many backcountry resorts that dotted the San Gabes in the early 20th century. The Forest Service removed the last remnants of the resort in the 1950s.

Switzer Falls is just downstream from the campground, meaning you have to hike around the falls—do not attempt to follow the creek all the way to the falls. This is one of those places where people get themselves killed or mangled on a fairly regular basis. To hike around the falls, follow the marked trail across the creek. The trail now climbs a ridge, which provides awesome views of the canyon below and, to the east, Mount Disappointment. After another half mile, the trail reaches a junction: the Gabrielino Trail leads to the right, the trail to the falls to the left. Go left.

The trail travels another one-half mile, descending back to the creek below the falls. This is a great picnic spot, and those who get there early get the best spot.

Directions: From La Canada take Highway 2 north for 10.5 miles to the Switzer Falls Picnic Area and turn right (the entrance to the picnic area is just beyond the Clear Creek Ranger Station). There are three parking lots—you want to park in the one at the bottom of the canyon, where the picnic area and trailhead are located. Otherwise it's a long walk down (and back up) to the trailhead. **Fees:** Purchase a Forest Service Adventure Pass for $5 a day or $30 annually. **Contact:** Angeles National Forest Supervisor's Office, (626) 574-5200. **Locator:** LA CANADA.

2. BLUE RIDGE TRAIL

The Blue Ridge Trail begins across from the Big Pines Visitor Center, just west of Wrightwood on the Angeles Crest Highway.

The trail climbs a canyon situated between the two mountains of the Mountain High Ski Resort. It rises gently—and sometimes not so gently—for 2.5 miles before terminating at the Blue Ridge Campground and the bottom of a ski lift. Here the trail also joins the Pacific Crest Trail, overlooking the Sheep Mountain Wilderness in what can fairly be termed a spectacular view, especially at sunset. The entire hike is within the forest and it's a great place for a much needed fall color fix. When done hiking, grab a coffee or spirits in Wrightwood, just a few miles away.

Directions: From Wrightwood drive south on the Angeles Crest Highway (Highway 2) for two miles. There is parking available in a lot across from the Big Pines Visitor Center. **Fees:** Purchase a Forest Service Adventure Pass for $5 a day or $30 annually. **Contact:** Angeles National Forest Supervisor's Office, (626) 574-5200. **Locator:** WRIGHTWOOD.

3. BURKHART TRAIL

The Burkhart Trail begins at the Buckhorn Campground, located roughly in the middle of the range. The trailhead has its own parking lot at the far end of the campground. From the parking lot, follow the trail into a broad, forested canyon. Below you, to the right, is a pretty creek with a great (and popular) swimming hole. Stay on the trail, which soon begins bending to the left, still high above a canyon. After one mile, the now rocky trail begins switchbacking down an exposed ridge to Cooper Canyon. At the creek, surrounded by forest, the trail crosses the creek and intersects with the Pacific Crest Trail—a distance of almost two miles from the trailhead. The forest floor is lush down here, a far cry from some of the sunbaked mountains above. The PCT follows the creek—we suggest choosing a picnic spot along the creek and taking a breather before the march back up the trail. There are even some small trout in the creek.

Directions: From La Canada take the Angeles Crest Highway (Highway 2) for 34 miles and turn left into the poorly marked Buckhorn Campground. Drive through the campground to the trailhead parking lot. **Fees:** Purchase a Forest Service Adventure Pass for $5 a day or $30 annually. **Contact:** Angeles National Forest Supervisor's Office, (626) 574-5200. **Locator:** LA CANADA.

4. SILVER MOCCASIN TRAIL

The Silver Moccasin Trailhead is behind the Chilao Visitor Center, on the Angeles Crest Highway. The trail, built by and for Boy Scouts, is 53 miles long, traveling in a north-south direction through the mountains before terminating at 9,399-foot Mount Baden-Powell (named for the founder of the Boy Scouts). Trekking the entire trail is a bit much for a day hike; we recommend enjoying a bit of the trail from the visitor center. The forest, unlike the lower reaches of the mountains, is actually a forest up here, with conifers, boulders, and small creeks.

Directions: From La Canada take the Angeles Crest Highway (Highway 2) for 27 miles to the Chilao Visitor Center. **Fees:** Purchase a Forest Service Adventure Pass for $5 a day or $30 annually. **Contact:** Angeles National Forest Supervisor's Office, (626) 574-5200. **Locator:** LA CANADA.

5. MOUNT BADEN-POWELL TRAIL

The Mount Baden-Powell Trail is popular because of the view from the 9,399-foot summit. Not only does the summit provide a darn good vista of the surrounding San Gabes, but it also supplies an interesting view of the Mojave Desert, just below. The trailhead is in the Vincent Gap parking area on the Angeles Crest Highway, about 10 miles south of Wrightwood. It's a four-mile hike to the summit with an elevation gain of almost 3,000 feet. Ye-ow. Bring all the essentials (see page 288), especially plenty of water, a hat, and a windbreaker. And an extra lung. Get an early start and avoid this hike on especially hot days.

Directions: From La Canada take the Angeles Crest Highway (Highway 2) north for 53 miles. Park at the Vincent Gap parking area on the right side of the road. **Fees:** Purchase a Forest Service Adventure Pass for $5 a day or $30 annually. **Contact:** Angeles National Forest Supervisor's Office, (626) 574-5200. **Locator:** WRIGHTWOOD.

4 HIKES ON THE FRONT RANGE

1. MILLARD CANYON

Millard Creek cuts a beautiful canyon through the mountains, tumbling out of the range just above Altadena. From the Millard Canyon Campground, a trail follows the creek three-quarters of a mile upstream to 50-foot Millard Falls, a popular picnic spot. For those so inclined, the trail continues above the falls. How to get there? A hundred yards downstream of the Millard Canyon Campground, a footpath branches uphill to the right. Go up the trail. At one-half mile the trail intersects the Sunset Ridge fire road. Turn left. Walk 300 yards. Watch for the Sunset Ridge Trail to branch off to the left. Take it. Watch for another trail branching to the left, heading down to the creek. Take it. Ta da! Hike as far upstream as you like, allowing time to return. An old gold mine, Dawn Mine, is located along the stream at an elevation of 3,100 feet. Look, but don't enter. Note: Stay out of this canyon during and immediately after rainfall. It's a gusher and it could kill you.

Directions: From Pasadena drive north on Fair Oaks Boulevard. At Loma Alta, turn left. At Chaney, turn right. Follow the road into the hills. At the gate, turn left and drive downhill to the parking lot. Note: the lot is usually filled by weekend afternoons. **Fees:** Purchase a Forest Service Adventure Pass for $5 a day or $30 annually. **Contact:** Angeles National Forest Supervisor's Office, (626) 574-5200. **Locator:** PASADENA.

2. STURTEVANT FALLS

Any John McPhee fans out there? This hike along Big Santa Anita Creek provides a good view of the flood control measures installed by Los Angeles County following the disastrous 1938 flood. The trailhead begins at the Chantry Flats Ranger Station. Follow the paved road downhill into the canyon. The road eventually narrows to a trail as it follows Big Santa Anita Creek upstream. As you'll see, the creek flows over a series of crib structures. The county flattened the creek between the structures, which serve as a series of steps. The way it works: Massive debris flows and floods will dissipate their energy over the "steps," instead of picking up energy traveling down a steep canyon. Hmmmm. Numerous cabins line the creek—they're leased by the Forest Service to those willing to risk the cabins ending up on Foothill Boulevard following a huge storm. At 1.75 miles, the trail dead-ends into 50-foot-high Sturtevant Falls. Enjoy! If you want to go farther up the canyon, a side trail splits off from the trail one-third of a mile below the falls.

Directions: From Arcadia take Santa Anita Avenue north into the mountains. After some serious twisting and cliff-hugging, it will dead-end at the Chantry Flats Ranger Station. **Fees:** Purchase a Forest Service Adventure Pass for $5 a day or $30 annually. **Contact:** Angeles National Forest, Arroyo Seco Ranger District, (818) 790-1151. **Locator:** PASADENA.

3. MOUNT LOWE

Mount Lowe tops out at 5,603 feet, sitting right above Altadena. The mountain is best known for the Mount Lowe Railway, which clung to the side of the mountain earlier this century, delivering visitors to Ye Alpine Tavern. The railroad was considered, in its time, to be one of the engineering marvels of the world—until fire and flood contributed to its demise in the 1930s. The railway's grade is still there, along with historical markers and photos along the trail.

There are numerous ways to the top, depending on what level of steepness you are comfortable with. Most common: Take Chaney Drive from Altadena. Park along the road on Sunset Ridge—after passing through the gate (which is closed from 10 P.M. to 6 A.M.). Follow the Sunset Ridge fire road and continue past the water tanks. Go under the power lines. Approximately two miles into the trip, the fire road joins the old railroad bed. At five miles, you pass the Mount Lowe Campground, site of Ye Alpine Tavern. Keep going up the fire road, around the hairpin turn. Look for a trail leaving the right side of the trail. This is the East Summit Trail. Follow it to the summit. From the trailhead to the summit is a distance of seven miles with an elevation gain of 3,520 feet The summit on a clear day gives a view that perfectly demonstrates the lay of the land in the L.A. area. To the east, the Verdugo Mountains, the San Fernando Valley, and the spine of the Santa Monica Mountains. To the south, the entire L.A. Basin—directly south are Palos Verdes and Catalina. With binoculars, the Queen Mary can be seen—it's in Long Beach. To the west, Mount Wilson and Mount Baldy and, on a really clear day, Mount San Gorgonio. This is a great hike in the winter, especially after a storm. Expect wind and cooler temperatures near the top. Bring the essentials (see page 288).

Directions: From Pasadena drive north on Fair Oaks Boulevard. At Loma Alta, turn left. At Chaney turn right. Follow the road into the hills. At the gate, bear to the right and then park alongside the road. **Fees:** Purchase a Forest Service Adventure Pass for $5 a day or $30 annually. **Contact:** Angeles National Forest, Arroyo Seco Ranger District, (818) 790-1151. **Locator:** PASADENA.

4. MOUNT BALDY

Here's a perfect early fall or late spring hike, best navigated on low smog days. Why? When it's clear out, the view from Mount Baldy—and this is a money-back guarantee—will blow you away.

Mount Baldy is the tallest point in the San Gabriels, as well as Los Angeles County, at 10,064 feet. There are several ways to the top, but we'll give you the most common.

Park at the Mount Baldy Ski Resort and take the ski lift up from the lot. The lift is open on weekends during the summer. At the top of the lift, follow the fire road until it ends and the trail to the summit begins. Those afraid of heights will not enjoy this stretch of trail—there are some places along the ridge that seemingly drop straight into hell.

The trail climbs through the forest and eventually reaches the summit just over three miles from the top of the ski lift—with an elevation gain of 2,600 feet. The view? What view? Right. To the north, there's the Mojave Desert and, beyond that, the Sierra Nevada. To the south, all of the Los Angeles metropolitan area. To the east, Mount San Gorgonio and Mount San Jacinto. To the west, the Pacific Ocean and Catalina Island.

Do not go on this hike without the essentials—especially a windbreaker and/or rain suit. Go slow—chances are you woke up at sea level. Wear sturdy boots. Don't forget a camera. And don't forget to check the camera's batteries before leaving.

Directions: From Claremont take Mount Baldy Road until it ends at the Mount Baldy Ski Resort ski lift. Park and take the lift to the trail. **Fees:** Purchase a Forest Service Adventure Pass for $5 a day or $30 annually. **Contact:** Angeles National Forest, Mount Baldy Ranger District, (818) 335-1251. **Locator:** MOUNT BALDY.

CAMPING THE ANGELES NATIONAL FOREST

There are 28 Forest Service campgrounds in the Angeles National Forest, all accessible by car. Dozens of other primitive campgrounds are accessible only to backpackers or equestrians.

We'll be totally honest: We won't camp in the Angeles. We've heard too many horror stories and seen too many campgrounds vandalized. The sad truth is that the forest attracts a lot of trash from the city—we're talking people, not garbage. All in all, we'd rather drive the extra three hours to the Sierra than deal with some of the yahoos in the campgrounds here.

If you're going to camp, stick to one of the following, which are the nicer campgrounds in the Angeles: Buckhorn, on Angeles Crest Highway about 10 miles north of the Chilao Visitor Center; Blue Ridge, on the Angeles Crest Highway three miles west of Wrightwood; Lake, on Big Pines Highway about five miles west of Wrightwood; Monte Cristo, on the Angeles Forest Highway, about 10 miles west of the Angeles Crest Highway; and Coldbrook, on Highway 39 about 18 miles north of Interstate 210 in Asuza.

No reservations are necessary at any of the campgrounds. Fees range from $5 to $10 per night. For more information, phone the Angeles National Forest Supervisor's Office at (626) 574-5200.

Visitor Centers

Two visitor centers can be found along the Angeles Crest Highway. The Chilao Visitor Center is located on the Angeles Crest Highway, 27 miles from La Canada. The Big Pines Visitor Center is also on the Angeles Crest Highway, two miles west of Wrightwood. Rangers are on hand to give directions to trailheads. Maps and Forest Service Adventure Passes are also available for purchase.

Ranger Stations

Angeles National Forest Headquarters
701 North Santa Anita Avenue
Arcadia, CA 91006
(626) 574-1613

Mount Baldy Ranger District
110 North Wabash Avenue
Glendora, CA 91740
(626) 335-1251

Arroyo Seco Ranger District
Oak Grove Park
Flintridge, CA 91011
(818) 899-1900

Tujunga Ranger District
12371 North Little Tujunga Canyon Road
San Fernando, CA 91342
(818) 889-1900

The Dark Side of the Forest

Every year it's pretty much a sure bet that at least a half dozen bodies will be found in the Angeles National Forest. Most are victims of crimes committed down below in L.A.; the forest makes for a convenient dumping ground. There have also been vandalism problems at some of the campgrounds. The high-use areas, such as San Gabriel Canyon, can produce obscene amounts of trash—a single snow play area can accumulate one ton of trash in a weekend.

A Great Place to Eat

At the end of a day in the Angeles National Forest, many hikers and bikers (as in Harleys) stop for dinner or drinks at the popular Newcomb's Ranch, located near the Chilao Visitor Center on the Angeles Crest Highway. Newcomb's specializes in pub grub served in a very casual, rustic atmosphere. Phone: (626) 440-1001.

• FEATURED TRIP •

Wildlife Waystation
Within Angeles National Forest

There's your everyday zoo, and then there's the Wildlife Waystation, a bird of quite a different feather. This is readily apparent upon pulling up to this dusty outpost where the wolves can be heard howling, the peacocks squawking, and the lions roaring.

Located in the northeastern San Fernando Valley, in a rugged canyon in the Angeles National Forest, the Wildlife Waystation's 160 acres are home to hundreds of recuperating and abandoned wild and exotic animals. The group's goal is to get these creatures back on their paws and to place the animals into either a suitable home or release them back into the wild.

The public can get up close and personal to this slice of exotica on the Waystation's popular Sunday tours, which are held the first and third Sunday of every month, weather permitting. Guides take visitors past spacious cages, explaining how each animal wound up here while constantly reminding parents not to let their youngsters get too close. The tours typically last two hours.

This is more than just a few animals for show. The Waystation has everything from bears to boas and cougars to cockatoos. Lions have come from as far away as New Zealand and as close as Angeles National Forest, which is right in the backyard.

There's also a petting zoo and a pen of pygmy goats that kids (the human kind) love to feed before the tour. Educational demonstrations using some of the animals are scheduled throughout the day at a special stage area on the grounds.

Most of the animals are castoffs from zoos as well as from pet owners who bought or smuggled exotic animals only to discover they were in way over their heads. For example, in late 1995, a federal raid on a privately owned Idaho animal shelter found 27 tigers, lions, and ligers (a tiger-lion mix) living in horrid conditions. Within a few days, the Waystation had dispatched a caravan of trucks to retrieve the cats and bring them back here. Other rescue highlights include a pair of Siberian tigers rescued from an Irish farm and 1,000 chickadees saved from a cargo hold at LAX.

The Wildlife Waystation is a charitable organization run by a small paid staff and a large army of volunteers, who are put through a step-by-step training program. Those interested in a tour should visit the Waystation or phone the number below for more information. It is advisable to make reservations at least two weeks in advance.

Directions: From Interstate 210, exit at Osborne Street and go north. After Osborne Street turns into Little Tujunga Canyon Road, continue to drive north for five miles to the Wildlife Waystation. **Fees:** A minimum $7 donation is requested for adults, $3 for children ages 2 to 12. **Maps:** Pick up a *Thomas Brothers Guide to Los Angeles* or the AAA map of Los Angeles County. **Pets:** Dogs are not allowed. **Contact:** For tour times and reservations, phone the Wildlife Waystation, (818) 899-5201. **Locator:** WILDLIFE WAYSTATION.

• FEATURED TRIP •

SKIING AND SNOWBOARDING THE SAN GABRIEL MOUNTAINS

30 miles north of downtown Los Angeles as the crow flies

Skiing and snowboarding in the San Gabriel Mountains is a mix of the old and the new. The five resorts in the San Gabes have been around for years in one form or another. Some are getting better, others are crawling toward the millennium.

As is always the case in Southern California, the weekday rule applies: He/She who findeth a way to avoid the slopes on weekends will have the better skiing experience. Traffic is light and crowds are down. Best of all, the slopes aren't littered with snowboarders and snowboarder wannabes, sprawled every which way.

5 SAN GABRIEL SKI RESORTS

1. MOUNTAIN HIGH

This is the largest, and the best, of the San Gabriel ski resorts, at 205 acres with 11 chairlifts—which puts it in the same class as Snow Summit, Bear Mountain, and Snow Valley in the San Bernardino Mountains.

There's one big difference, though. For those living in Los Angeles or the San Fernando Valley, Mountain High can be reached in 90 minutes or less. It takes at least an hour longer to reach the San Bernardino resorts from L.A. And, on weekends especially, the traffic getting to and from Big Bear can reduce one to tears.

Mountain High actually sits on two mountains, which are not connected by either ski lift or trails. Instead, skiers have to take a shuttle bus back and forth from the bases of Mountain High East and Mountain High West. It's a pain, but the buses run often and the ride takes five minutes or less.

Mountain High East is, in our humble opinion, the best place to ski or snowboard in the L.A. metropolitan region. The wide, intermediate Gold Coast drops one mile from the top of the mountain. About halfway down, the Sundance run splits off to the right, offering several steeply pitched runs to the bottom. After a good dumping—and there were several in 1998—this is intermediate skiing at its best. The funny thing is that the west side gets overwhelmingly crowded while the east side often receives few visitors (on weekdays—weekends and holidays are another story).

Mountain High was, thankfully, purchased prior to the 1997–98 season. The previous owners were letting the place go to seed and the new owners, a corporation, are pumping some much-needed money into the mountain's facilities. They are also hiring employees whose prime qualification is not being young and stoned. Another plus: Unless it is snowing, tire chains are rarely required on Highway 2. The road is plowed often.

Directions: From downtown Los Angeles take Interstate 10 east to Interstate 15 north. Exit at Highway 138 west and drive to Highway 2 west. Drive three miles past the village of Wrightwood to Mountain High East. From the San Fernando Valley and Santa Monica, take Interstate 405 north to Interstate 5 north to Highway 14 (Antelope Valley Freeway) north, exiting at Highway 138 east. Drive 37 miles to Highway 2 west. Drive three miles past the village of Wrightwood to Mountain High. **Note:** In 1997–98, Mountain High offered $28 lift tickets, a real bargain. The tickets could be purchased at Ralph's grocery stores. **Contact:** Mountain High, (760) 249-5477. **Locator:** WRIGHTWOOD.

2. MOUNT WATERMAN

At one point on the Angeles Crest Highway, you'll pass a ski lift that pretty much goes straight up the side of a mountain with a little ski run underneath it. The run looks scary as hell—certainly not the kind of thing a beginning or low intermediate skier can even begin to contemplate.

Actually, most of the ski terrain is on the other side of the ridge. It also bears mentioning that locals love this place. Why? Because skiing Mount Waterman, in many ways, is skiing as it was 20 or 30 years ago, before the snobs moved in. Weekday crowds average 350 to 400 people and weekends rarely attract more than 1,500 skiers. In other words, Mount Waterman has precious elbow room.

Mount Waterman is best suited to expert skiers, with 60 percent of the runs labeled as advanced. Beginners and less than confident intermediates might not be comfortable on a good share of the terrain here and might be better off spending a little more for the gentle terrain down the road at Mountain High or Ski Sunrise.

The lift from the road takes skiers to the top of the mountain, where Mount Waterman's lodge and concession stand are located. From there, several trails lead downhill to Mount Waterman's other two lifts. For sure, it's a quiet place, nestled in the forest. Two owners, who bought the place just before Christmas in 1995, promise more improvements—even though many of Waterman's clientele feel few improvements are necessary.

There is one problem: Mount Waterman doesn't have snowmaking. It needs big storms to open and there have been huge stretches in the last few winters when the mountain was closed. Always, always phone first to inquire about skiing and driving conditions.

Directions: From the 210 freeway, exit to Highway 2 north. Drive 30 miles. The parking area and chairlift for Mount Waterman is opposite the entrance to Buckhorn Campground. **Contact:** Mount Waterman, (626) 790-2002. **Locator:** LA CANADA.

3. MOUNT BALDY SKI AREA

The rap on Mount Baldy has always been that the potential often outweighs the reality.

Here are the statistics: The base is at an elevation of 8,600 feet, and top to bottom the resort has a vertical drop of 2,100 feet, making it the ski area with the most vertical drop in Southern California proper. The longest run is 1.5 miles and Mount Baldy has four chairs servicing 27 runs.

So what's the problem? Mount Baldy faces south—toward the winter sun. And it gets windy. The sun and wind combine to form ice. Old lifts and limited snowmaking mean that Mount Baldy needs a really good day to be worth the effort. There is also not much beginner's terrain. The terrain is 40 percent advanced and 40 percent intermediate.

Snowboarders are allowed and there is a half-pipe. The ski resort is hoping the Angeles National Forest will approve an expansion that will add eight ski lifts accessing north-facing runs. For now, when the conditions are ideal, Mount Baldy's great. But, on a less than ideal day, it can be a tough day, too.

Directions: From downtown Los Angeles take Interstate 10 east for 28 miles to Indian Hill Boulevard and turn left, heading north. At Foothill Boulevard, turn right. At North Mills Avenue, turn left. North Mills Avenue turns into Mount Baldy Road. Go to the end of the road, where the parking area for the ski resort is found. **Contact:** Mount Baldy Ski Area, (909) 981-3344. **Locator:** MOUNT BALDY.

4. SNOWCREST AT KRATKA RIDGE

At just 58 acres, this is the smallest of the San Gabriel ski areas. Formerly known as Kratka Ridge, the resort was purchased in 1994 and the new owner is concentrating on the snowboard crowd because there just isn't enough ski terrain here to compete with the bigger resorts in the area. By the time you read this, the resort will have most likely removed one of the last single-seat chairlifts remaining in the country. The resort doesn't have snowmaking, so be sure to phone first for snow and driving conditions.

Directions: From Interstate 210, exit to Highway 2 north. Drive 31 miles. The parking area and chairlift for Kratka Ridge is just past Mount Waterman on the right side of the road. **Contact:** Snowcrest at Kratka Ridge, (626) 440-9749. **Locator:** LA CANADA.

5. SKI SUNRISE

This is another tiny resort that doesn't get much ink. The ski area is small, at 100 acres, and has mostly friendly terrain. Throw in affordable prices and Ski Sunrise becomes a decent place to take kids who are new to skiing. One of our friends still drops in here after work when the after-school crowds start to clutter up Mountain High.

Directions: From downtown Los Angeles take Interstate 10 east to Interstate 15 north. Exit at Highway 138 and drive 8.6 miles, then turn left on Highway 2 (Angeles Crest Highway) west. Drive through the village of Wrightwood, continue four miles, and turn right on Table Mountain Road. Drive one mile to Ski Sunrise at the end of the road. **Contact:** Ski Sunrise, (760) 249-6150. **Locator:** WRIGHTWOOD.

TIRE CHAINS

The easiest way to make sure you always make it to the ski resort is to always carry tire chains. It also helps if you know how to put them on. Our recommendation: Bring a piece of old carpet or something to put on the ground so that you don't have to lie in slush while wrestling with the chains—a good way to ruin the day before it starts.

STAY ON THE TRAILS

As tempting as it may seem, pay attention to those "no out-of-bounds skiing" signs. The terrain in the San Gabriel Mountains is steep and not very hospitable when it's cold and dark out. In February 1998, a 14-year-old snowboarder went off-trail at Mountain High. He was rescued after spending a week in the wilderness. Tragically, he died several days later, the result of an infection. Even with all the publicity, two more snowboarders disappeared just one week later when they decided to take an off-trail excursion at Snowcrest. They were quickly rescued, but as of press time were facing misdemeanor charges for skiing outside the resort's boundary.

• FEATURED TRIP •

MALIBU CREEK STATE PARK

In the Santa Monica Mountains, north of Malibu

Our favorite time to visit Malibu Creek State Park is the few hours before and after a winter storm. Blue sky and brilliant clouds produce a golden light. The hills are bright green—the direct opposite of the crispy brown appearance they take on during the summer. The jagged peaks and exposed rock glisten with moisture, disappearing in and out of the clouds. Malibu Creek's level rises dramatically, gushing through a narrow gorge and then out to sea.

There are often few people out, and this largely undeveloped tract of the Santa Monica Mountains looks like something from the past—before millions of people descended upon the area. It's easy to see why Hollywood has so embraced the park as a filming location: 20th Century-Fox owned most of the park's property from 1946 to 1972, when the state purchased the land. The park served as Korea for *M*A*S*H* and earth in *Planet of the Apes,* as well as the location for *How Green Was My Valley,* the Oscar winner for best film in 1941.

The park is large, covering 6,000 acres. It literally begins at the sea, where Malibu Creek flows into the ocean. The parkland then follows the creek up through Malibu Canyon and into the primary section of the park, bordered by Malibu Canyon Road on the east and Mulholland Highway to the north. Malibu Creek and its tributaries cut a swath through the park, forming narrow gorges.

The park is particularly great for hikers because there's plenty well worth seeing.

One obvious hike is from the parking lot to the old *M*A*S*H* set, where both the movie and the TV show were filmed. From the parking lot, take Crags Road, which follows Las Virgenes Creek to its confluence with Malibu Creek. The trail then goes to the visitor center, crosses Malibu Creek on a bridge, and then continues for a mile or so to the set, continuing to follow the creek.

Only one problem: A wildfire burned down the set in 1982, forcing the show's producers to alter the plot of the final episode (the 4077th had to bug out as the result of a fire). There are a couple of burned out jeeps left at the site as well as the somewhat overgrown helicopter landing pad. Climb the pad and look to the east: this is the same view of the mountains shown from the point of view of Radar O'Reilly during the show's opening sequence each week.

The hike to the *M*A*S*H* set is very popular, as it should be. For those looking for someplace less traveled, we recommend the Mesa Peak fire road, which skirts the park's southern boundary for 6.3 miles. (It is also part of the Backbone Trail, which will one day travel the length of the Santa Monica Mountains.) This is fairly tough hiking with a lot of ups and downs. There are two trailheads: On Malibu Canyon Road, there is a parking lot for Tapia Park, immediately south of the bridge over Malibu Creek. Follow the trail to the locked gate and the fire road. There is also a parking lot and trailhead at the end of Corral Canyon Road.

The Malibu Creek area of the park, near the visitor center, gets a lot of use, for good reason—it's a very neat place. The Rock Pool can be a great swimming hole when the water level is up (don't allow children to dive). Kids may also want to try their hand at fishing at Century Lake, formed by Century Dam on Malibu Creek. The lake was once the centerpiece of a country club in the early part of the century. But the lake is now silting up and becoming a meadow—some people want to see it dredged, others want the dam removed. In any case, the lake has rainbow trout, bass, bluegill, sunfish, catfish, and crayfish. Children under 16 are allowed to fish without a fishing license. Bring a net because there's no limit on netting crayfish, which can be used as bait for bass.

Many an Angeleno had his or her first camping experience at the park. Although the campground may not be the prettiest to grace our fine planet, it's better than would be expected for a place so close to the city. The campground has had occasional problems with rowdies from the city in recent years, but the park rangers keep close tabs and the vast majority of nights here are peaceful ones.

There are 50 sites available for tents or RVs up to 18 feet long. The fee is $15 per night on weekdays, $16 on weekends, plus $5 for an additional car. For reservations, phone (800) 444-PARK/7275. Facilities include fire grills, piped water, flush toilets, and showers.

Directions: From Woodland Hills take U.S. 101 west, exit at Las Virgenes Road, and turn left. Drive six miles to the park entrance, which will be on the right after crossing Mulholland Highway. From Santa Monica take the Pacific Coast Highway north and turn right on Malibu Canyon Road. Take Malibu Canyon Road through the S turns and tunnels for eight miles. The entrance to the park will be on the left, just before the intersection with Mulholland. **Fees:** Day-use parking is $5. **Maps:** Obtain a free map at the ranger's booth at the entrance to the parking lot. **Pets:** Dogs are allowed in the campgrounds, but not on the trails. **Contact:** California Department of Parks and Recreation, (818) 880-0367. **Locator:** MALIBU CREEK STATE PARK.

THE SOUTHERN STEELHEAD

In August of 1997, the National Marine Fisheries Service (NMFS) listed the southern steelhead as an endangered species. The southern steelhead is closely related to the Pacific salmon. Like the salmon, it is an anadromous fish—it is reared in freshwater streams, migrates to sea, and then returns to its native streams to spawn.

The southern steelhead could once be found up and down the Southern California coast. But its habitat has shrunk dramatically this century and now, according to the NMFS, Malibu Creek is the fish's southernmost habitat.

Although steelhead have been found in Malibu Creek over the years, there's a problem: Rindge Dam, a 100-foot-high structure, was built on the creek in the 1920s, just 2.5 miles upstream from the ocean. Many scientists feel that the dam is blocking critical upstream habitat that the steelhead needs to reproduce. Complicating matters further, the creek's water quality is questionable, as is its water quantity—in the summer, urban runoff is overwhelming Malibu Lagoon, the place where the steelhead prepare for the transition to salt water.

A small group of scientists has been calling for the removal of Rindge Dam for the last 15 years. It has, of course, been the source of considerable controversy. The dam completely filled with silt long ago—the state decommissioned the dam in 1967—and it serves no real purpose. However, taking the dam down is a costly proposition. Various aspects of dam removal have been studied, but there is no comprehensive study looking at the historical use of the creek's downstream and upstream habitat by the southern steelhead.

In January 1998, the U.S. Army Corps of Engineers began a reconnaissance study to determine whether the Malibu Creek watershed is deserving of an environmental restoration project. If the Corps determines that dam removal is a good project, it could still be anther decade before funds are located to pay for demolition and the subsequent environmental rehabilitation of the creek.

Meanwhile, the fate of the southern steelhead hangs in the balance, as does that of dozens of other species of steelhead and salmon. Dams, logging, agriculture, urbanization, and pollution have taken a toll on the West's once abundant natural fisheries. Malibu Creek is a small part of the West, but one that could play a pivotal role in the future of our natural fisheries.

• FEATURED TRIP •

PARAMOUNT RANCH
In the Santa Monica Mountains

One of the best places for a family picnic in the Santa Monica Mountains is the National Park Service's Paramount Ranch, just down the road from Malibu Creek State Park.

The main attraction at the ranch is a movie and TV set for an old Western town, complete with all the trappings—a little jail, an old-time saloon, a general store, troughs for horses at every corner, a blacksmith, stables, a train station, and a steam engine. Best of all is a little church on a nice grassy lawn sprinkled with a few big trees. It's the perfect place for a rowdy crowd to throw a rope around a convict's neck or, on a more pleasant note, have a cold meat loaf sandwich.

The set has been here for decades and most recently has been used as the main set for the popular CBS television program *Dr. Quinn, Medicine Woman,* starring Jane Seymour. The show films at Paramount Ranch off and on from August through March but remains open to the public every day—even when filming. When filming is going on, members of the public are asked to behave themselves and not take photos or videos.

Paramount Ranch was originally purchased by Jesse Lasky, then the main man at Paramount Pictures, in 1921. Under financial pressure, Paramount sold out in 1952. Sporadic filming continued at the ranch, which became the setting for several TV shows, most notably *The Cisco Kid,* which starred Leo Carrillo, who has a beach named after him down in Malibu.

After undergoing a typical showdown with real estate developers in 1980, when Paramount Ranch almost became a subdivision, a new sheriff, by the name of the National Park Service, came to town. That's why the place still exists.

In addition to the town, the park also offers some short hiking trails, all suitable for children. The shortest of these is the Coyote Canyon Trail, which begins behind the railroad station and climbs to a ridge that provides a nice view of the Western Town before returning to the area behind the town.

National Park Service rangers give free guided tours of the park called "From Set to Screen" every other Saturday morning. In the summer, the park service also shows black-and-white silent films under the stars. Phone the number below for the current schedule.

Directions: From Woodland Hills take U.S. 101 west and exit at Kanan Dune Road, turning left (south). Drive one mile and turn left onto Cornell Road. Continue two miles. The park entrance will be on the right. From Santa Monica, take the Pacific Coast Highway north to Malibu Canyon Road and turn right. Drive five miles on Malibu Canyon and turn left onto Mulholland. Continue three miles and turn right onto Cornell Road. The park entrance will be on the left. **Fees:** Entry is free. **Maps:** The park is small enough that you don't need a map, although a rough map of the park and its trails can be obtained at the Santa Monica Mountains National Recreation Area Visitor Center in Agoura Hills. **Pets:** Dogs are allowed in the park, but they must be leashed. **Contact:** National Park Service, (818) 597-9192 extension 201. **Locator:** PARAMOUNT RANCH PARK.

• FEATURED TRIP •

RED ROCK CANYON PARK AND THE STUNT HIGH TRAIL

In quiet Old Topanga and Cold Creek Canyons

The parking lot for 190-acre Red Rock Canyon Park has exactly four spaces. Actually, calling it a parking lot is a stretch. It's really more a patch of grass at the side of the road where people just happen to leave their cars.

Of course, Red Rock Canyon Park doesn't need a parking lot. That's because no one knows about the place—many people who live in Topanga don't even know it exists. We first heard about it from a woman at the market, who described it as this mythical place where "you can actually take dogs on a great hike." This sounded pretty good because there aren't too many places to walk dogs in Topanga Canyon; Steve once got spanked with a $78 ticket for walking our dog, Molly, in Topanga State Park.

Finding the patch of grass is relatively easy—it's right off the much-traveled Old Topanga Canyon Road. But then visitors have to say good-bye to their beloved automobiles and hike about one-third of a mile down Red Rock Canyon Road to get to the park, which isn't visible from Old Topanga Road.

The park is a gem. The canyon, formed by Red Rock Creek, is dominated on both sides by huge, towering masses of red sandstone that have been sculpted by wind and weather. A fire road follows the creek halfway through the park before the road begins climbing toward a ridge high above the canyon.

Hikers can reach the ridge in 30 to 45 minutes, where they'll find a spectacular vista of Red Rock Canyon to the south and Cold Creek Canyon to the north, as well as the Santa Monica Mountains beyond. Sunsets here are particularly awesome as the mountains are silhouetted by the sun. The sandstone in Red Rock Canyon resembles a pink lightbulb.

From the ridge above Red Rock Canyon Park, hikers can choose to continue to the fire road to the left, which goes downhill to Stunt Road, where the trail crosses the road into a small parking lot. Or they can follow the fire road to the right, which allows for other great vistas of the mountains. (The latter is the Calabasas Peak Motorway, one of many fire roads bulldozed into the mountain over the years. In the case of this road, it just happens to meander at the top of the ridge all the way to Woodland Hills in the San Fernando Valley.)

From the top of the parking lot, by the fence, a foot trail winds quickly down to Stunt Creek, one of the nicer boulder-lined creeks in the Santa Monicas—it sometimes flows well into summer. If the water isn't too high, you may want to hike down the creek, which can be a real hoot. Or choose a boulder and picnic. Dogs are welcome on the Stunt High Trail, too, and chances are they'll probably fall in love with the place. As per usual, watch out for poison oak and rattlesnakes.

The trail meanders alongside the creek for a bit and then cuts back to the left, following one of the creek's tributaries uphill a bit. The trail splits to the left again at the entrance to a UCLA study area that's closed to the public. From that point, the trail switchbacks up the side of the hill before meeting Stunt Road again near the top of the mountain.

Some folks choose to start their hike at the Stunt High Trail—certainly it's not necessary to hike both the Stunt High Trail and Red Rock Canyon. But done together, the two trails provide a good workout and take hikers to relatively quiet corners, both high and low, of the Santa Monica Mountains.

For those a little more adventurous, here's an alternative hike in Red Rock Canyon Park. Just after entering the park, you'll pass a house on the left side of the road, which belongs to the park's ranger. Just a few steps beyond the house, a small trail takes hikers across Red Rock Creek to the northern part of the park, where there are some sandstone bluffs just begging to be climbed. Another little side trip: Climb the sandstone tower along the fire road leading to the top of the ridge. It's on the left side of the trail and you can't miss it.

Directions: From Santa Monica take the Pacific Coast Highway north for six miles and turn right on Topanga Canyon Boulevard. Drive approximately five miles to the village of Topanga and turn left over the bridge onto Old Topanga Canyon Road. Drive about two miles, then turn left onto Red Rock Canyon Road, immediately parking in the grassy area on the right side of the road next to the creek. Walk down Red Rock Canyon Road until it turns into the park. **Fees:** Access and parking are free. **Maps:** Try the *Thomas Brothers Guide to Los Angeles*, which is available at most bookstores and large retail stores. Or pick up a map of Los Angeles County, available through AAA or at most bookstores. **Pets:** Dogs are permitted but should be leashed. **Contact:** Mountains Conservancy Foundation, (310) 589-2400. **Locator:** RED ROCK CANYON PARK.

• FEATURED TRIP •

TOPANGA STATE PARK
North of the Pacific Palisades

We love little-known facts. So here is yet another one: Topanga State Park, covering almost 10,000 acres of the rugged, chaparral- and oak-studded Santa Monica Mountains, is the largest park within a city in the entire United States. Topanga is much larger than even Central Park in New York City or Lincoln Park in Chicago.

Even more astonishing: Angelenos grossly underuse the park. There are times when there are more passed-out winos in Central Park than there are visitors in all of Topanga State Park. We used to live right next to the park and found that most of our trendoid friends down the road in L.A. had never even heard of the place. Incredible!

The park is surrounded by the Los Angeles basin to the south and east, the Pacific Ocean to the west, and the San Fernando Valley to the north. The park's topography consists mostly of three parallel canyons—Topanga, Santa Ynez, and Rustic. The vegetation is a mix of chaparral-covered hills and, on the canyon floors, lush forests surrounding seasonal creeks.

There are also some wonderful rocky outcrops at the top of the hills, most of which offer great panoramas of the park. It's mind-boggling to think most of the park is actually within L.A.'s city limits because there's not one coffee shop, juice bar, or yoga center within sight.

Hiking or mountain biking is the way to go for most of the park's visitors. There are 35 miles of trails and fire roads (mountain bikes are restricted to the fire roads), accessible from various spots in the Pacific Palisades, the San Fernando Valley, and Topanga Canyon. The park is very hilly, so it helps to be in shape. This means there are some absolutely hair-rising descents for mountain bikers. Wear a melon protector.

The park's main headquarters—called Trippet Ranch—is located in Topanga Canyon. There are a small nature center and a picnic area that we rate a five on a scale of 1 to 10. Most of the trails and fire roads can be accessed from the Trippet Ranch parking lot. Follow the fire road uphill, where it joins another fire road. The road passes under a stand of oaks, bends gently to the right, and then deposits you at a three-way junction of fire roads with a signboard pointing out the different trails.

We recommend these three popular trails:

The Santa Ynez Trail begins just uphill from the aforementioned junction and then winds 800 feet downhill into the wooded Santa Ynez Canyon. When finally reaching the canyon floor, the trail follows a seasonal creek to the 15-foot Santa Ynez Falls. This is a great hike with some nice panoramas of the Santa Ynez Valley and some atypically lush scenery on the canyon floor. There is one drawback, of course: What goes down must later come up.

The trail/fire road to the Parker Mesa overlook—a distance of three miles or so—meanders on a ridge above Topanga Creek and the S-turns of Topanga Canyon Road until finally reaching the vista. There's a great view of Santa Monica Bay and the Los Angeles basin, especially after a smog-clearing rain. The L.A. coast all the way to Palos Verdes is easily visible, as is downtown L.A. and the sometimes snowcapped San Gabriel Mountains. Out to sea looms Catalina. This is a great hike to take out-of-town guests who still need convincing that L.A. is a pretty good idea, although not always a terribly well-executed one.

The Musch Trail winds through a shaded hillside to a fork at a fire road. Left goes up to Eagle Rock (picnic spot!) and right goes down to Eagle Springs. The trails join together again at "the Hub," a junction of four major trails in the park. From here it's possible to hike all the way to Will Rogers State Beach in the Pacific Palisades via the Rogers Trail or to take the Temescal fire road downhill to Mulholland Drive in Woodland Hills. If you turn around and head back to park headquarters, it's about six miles round-trip.

No matter which trail you hike, be on the lookout for wildlife. Topanga State Park is home to coyotes, mule deer, red-tailed hawks, rattlesnakes, numerous types of lizards, tarantulas, and—according to our former plumber, Septic Tank Steve—at least one mountain lion. It's fairly common to see mule deer in the area around the giant trail signpost.

MOONLIGHT SERENADE

Full moon have you riled up? Go for a moonlight hike in Topanga State Park. The park is mostly sheltered from the lights of the city, and the fire roads are nice and wide. It's possible, in fact, to read a book by the light of a full moon on some of the trails. Of course, bring a flashlight and watch where you're stepping—equestrians frequent these trails.

BACK TO THE SIXTIES

We recommend entering the park in Topanga Canyon, for no other reason than it's off the beaten path and the canyon's relatively new and wealthy residents haven't yet completely squashed the canyon's hippie-ish charm left over from the 1960s.

Today much of the canyon's hippie heritage has metamorphosed into a small but faithful New Age movement. The Inn of the Seventh Ray is a renowned and beautiful restaurant along Topanga Creek that's known for its organic meals. In the small stores and shacks nearby, one can find all the incense and crystals necessary to satisfy one's soul.

EATING IN TOPANGA

Rocco's, one of our favorite Italian restaurants in all of L.A., is located in Topanga. The pizza is excellent, as is the aglio-olio. Portions are huge and the restaurant gladly serves grimy hikers. Rocco's is located on Topanga Canyon Road, next to the Topanga Post Office.

Directions: From Santa Monica take the Pacific Coast Highway north for six miles and turn right at Topanga Canyon Boulevard (Highway 27). Drive five miles, continuing through the village of Topanga. At Entrada Drive, turn right. Go uphill, pass the first unattended parking lot on the left, and follow the signs on Entrada Road to the park entrance. From the north and the San Fernando Valley, exit U.S. 101 at Topanga Canyon Boulevard (Highway 27) south. Drive eight miles, make a hard left turn uphill at Entrada Road, then follow the above directions. **Fees:** There's a $5 day-use fee per automobile. Some free parking is usually available on the streets near the park entrance.
Maps: A small hiking map is provided with admission. The Tom Harrison map of the Santa Monica Mountains East can be purchased at outdoor stores; there are central and west versions as well. **Pets:** Dogs are not allowed anywhere in the park.
Recommended reading: Anyone who spends a lot of time in Topanga State Park or the Santa Monica Mountains should pick up a copy of *Milt McAuley's Hiking in Topanga State Park*, which is available at many bookstores in L.A. McAuley has spent a lifetime hiking every square inch of the Santa

Monica Mountains and he offers insight into almost every foot of the trail. **Camping:** A small, self-registration primitive campground is accessible to backpackers. **Contact:** Topanga State Park, (310) 455-2465. **Locator:** TOPANGA STATE PARK.

• FEATURED TRIP •

GRIFFITH PARK'S HORSE TRAILS

Crisscrossing the park from the Valley to Hollywood

In a city so thoroughly obsessed with—and held prisoner by—the automobile, it's hard to believe that right smack dab in the middle of L.A. there's a place where a wee bit of the Old West survives.

The place is Griffith Park, which is to Los Angeles what Central Park is to New York City. That means drug deals, people doing nasty things in the brush, and a couple of dead bodies every so often. But that's just the downside. The upside is that the park also has 50 miles of horse trails, many of which offer spectacular views of Los Angeles, the San Fernando Valley, and the San Gabriel Valley.

The park itself doesn't rent horses to the general public, but there are several liveries just outside the park's borders which rent horses for trail rides. For the ordinary citizen who doesn't own a major multinational corporation, this makes Griffith Park the most accessible and affordable place to saddle up in the L.A. area. It also gives riders the chance to travel across a tiny piece of L.A. in the same manner most people trafficked the city before the introduction of the Mercedes Benz.

Griffith Park covers 4,000 acres and stretches from Los Feliz in the Los Angeles basin across the Santa Monica Mountains to the 134 freeway in Glendale and Burbank. On the north side of the 134 freeway is the Los Angeles Equestrian Center, which is home to more than 1,000 privately owned horses, frequent riding competitions, and the Traditional Equitation School (known as TES).

Four liveries handle most of the business for Griffith Park and they all typically rent horses for between $10 and $15 an hour; some stables will allow you to keep the horses out longer than others. Each of the stables also has special morning, sunset, or moonlight rides that may be offered outside of the stable's regular hours and regular prices. One note to adventuresome parents out there: Most of the stables offer birthday parties for kids who are both big enough and old enough to ride.

For those who have never ridden before, all of the stables offer brief lessons in basic horsemanship. Not that much horsemanship is needed. The truth is many of the horses used for trail rides aren't exactly the pick of the litter—it's not like someone is going to plop you down on Secretariat by accident. If you can sit, you can probably ride. For those who are still scared silly by the horses, all of the liveries offer the services of a guide at an additional cost.

A riding trail circles the entire Los Angeles Equestrian Center and connects to a bridge over the Los Angeles River, followed by a tunnel under the 134 freeway. Just like that, riders are in Griffith Park. Most riders hang a right after the second tunnel and head up one of the fire roads into the Hollywood Hills.

A popular destination in Griffith Park and one we highly recommend is the Skyline Trail, which straddles the top of the mountains dividing the San Fernando Valley from the rest of the L.A. basin. The trail, depending where you are on it, allows for views of the basin from downtown L.A. to the sea on some days, as well as views of the San Fernando and San Gabriel Valleys—with the beautiful San Gabriels in the background.

Keep in mind, though, that it takes a good 90 minutes to two hours to reach the top of the hill and that some of the stables only allow two-hour rentals. There is also the possibility that your horse will walk for an hour and then stop, having decided that it's time to return to the stable and eat. We've had such horses and there is little anyone could do to convince them that it's really in their best interest to haul their and our lazy butts up yet another hill.

There's one other thing easily seen from the park: all the freeways crisscrossing Los Angeles. A sign of progress, maybe, but it also kind of makes you wish we had stuck with the horses.

PLACES TO RENT HORSES

Griffith Park Horse Rentals, Burbank: (818) 840-8401.
Circle "K" Stables, Burbank: (818) 843-9890.
Bar "S" Stables, Glendale: (818) 547-0203.
Sunset Ranch, Hollywood: (213) 469-5450.

TRADITIONAL EQUITATION SCHOOL

The Traditional Equitation School at the Los Angeles Equestrian Center is one of the largest riding schools in the United States. Every year, thousands of students from in and around L.A. take lessons through TES.

An excellent introduction to TES is through UCLA's continuing education program. At press time, a horsemanship class costs $200, which includes two classroom sessions and seven one-hour riding lessons.

Students learn basic grooming—they groom and saddle their horses before and after lessons—as well as the basics of riding. There are also more advanced classes for those who already ride. Lessons in both Western and English styles are offered.

The riding lessons are taught in groups, with typically anywhere from a handful to 10 riders per group. They emphasize basic horsemanship, such as posting, trotting, and cantering. Those students who want to move on can sign up for another class at the end of the seven weeks.

The classes make a great gift, especially for horse lovers who believe that horseback riding lessons are beyond their means. Phone: UCLA Extension, (310) 825-9971.

Directions to Griffith Park: From downtown Los Angeles, exit U.S. 101 at Hollywood Boulevard and turn right. At Western Avenue, turn left. Follow Western uphill and around a sharp right turn—the road is now called Los Feliz Boulevard. At Fern Dell Road, turn left into Griffith Park.
Locator: GRIFFITH PARK.

• FEATURED TRIP •

GRIFFITH PARK OBSERVATORY AND TELESCOPE NIGHT
In the Hollywood Hills

High up in the Hollywood Hills, on telescope night at the Griffith Park Observatory, a man leaned over his eyepiece, squinting at a small dot of light that was only billions of light-years away. Adjusting the lens, he stood up straight and calmly announced he had found Saturn.

Once a month, from April to November, amateur astronomers from the Los Angeles Astronomical Society, as well as other stargazers, gather on the observatory's front lawn for a star party. Telescopes both big and small are hauled out of cars and minivans and pointed at the heavens above. As one astronomer puts it, "I guess we do it just to see what the hell is out there."

The astronomers are also there to share their telescopes with members of the public, often giving passionate discourses on the stars. "We're here for you," said another astronomer, as we checked out some craters on the moon.

Telescope night is a tradition dating back 25 years and a good, clear night can attract up to 50 telescopes from across the Southland. One guy might aim his telescope on the blinding white light of the moon, guiding you across lunar craters; the next guy, on the star N-57. Someone else might take a stab at Jupiter and its four moons. When the Shoemaker-Levy 9 comet collided with Jupiter in July 1994, many of the telescopes were capable of picking out the subsequent and spectacular color changes in Jupiter's appearance.

The setting for telescope night couldn't be any more perfect. Griffith Park Observatory, built in 1935, sits atop Griffith Park, perched in the hills above Hollywood. Not only can you see billions of light-years into space from the observatory, you can see the entire Los Angeles basin, which is a starscape of its own at night.

The observatory's main attraction is its own 12-inch Zeiss refracting telescope, housed under one of the building's three domes. The Zeiss is open to free public viewing; the telescope is usually aimed at different points in space throughout any given night. The Zeiss is also one of the largest telescopes available for public use anywhere in the country.

There is usually no more than a 10-minute wait to take your turn and walk up a few short stairs to the huge telescope's eyepiece. Even on a cloudy night in November, Saturn was still easily visible through the telescope—although the rings could only be seen as a line bisecting the planet. How big is this telescope? Saturn is 850 million miles from Earth—a distance so great that its light takes 75 minutes just to reach us.

Directions: From downtown Los Angeles, exit U.S. 101 at Hollywood Boulevard and turn right. At Western Avenue, turn left. Follow Western uphill and around a sharp right turn—the road is now called Los Feliz Boulevard. At Fern Dell Road, turn left into Griffith Park. Fern Dell turns into Western Canyon Road. Continue uphill, following signs to the Griffith Park Observatory. **Fees:** Telescope night is free, as is parking at the observatory. Admission to the observatory's Hall of Sciences is also free. **Observatory hours:** From June through September, 12:30 P.M. to 10 P.M. daily. From October through May, 2 P.M. to 10 P.M. Tuesday through Friday and 12:30 P.M. to 10 P.M. Saturday and Sunday. **Pets:** Not encouraged—do you want Fido lifting his leg at a $5,000 telescope? **Contact:** Los Angeles Astronomical Society, (213) 673-

7355. Griffith Park Observatory, (213) 664-1181. Sky reports, (213) 663-8171. Web site: www.griffithobservatory.org. **Locator:** GRIFFITH PARK.

• FEATURED TRIP •

LOS ANGELES COUNTY BEACHES

Where the sea meets the traffic

Aesthetically speaking, the beaches of Los Angeles County may not be the best in the world. At the very least, however, L.A.'s beaches can be termed interesting, as well as famous, compliments of the funny-looking folks in Hollywood.

Every weekend in the summer, thousands of people come to the beaches in L.A. to find a respite from the heat and, of course, to see the freaks. We've seen it all at the beach, including dolphins, sea lions, a dead beached whale (a bit odorous), topless women, and bottomless men. It ain't always pretty, but it's almost never boring.

1. ROBERT H. MEYER STATE BEACH, MALIBU

These three small beaches, known as Malibu's pocket beaches, are the treasures of the northern Malibu coast. From north to south, they are El Pescador, La Piedra, and El Matador State Beaches. All three are in hidden coves, requiring a descent from the parking lot via stairs.

El Matador, with its stony shoreline and rock arches, is the most scenic of the trio, as well as the most secluded—keep an eye or two peeled for Naked People! Dogs were permitted on these beaches (the only ones in L.A. County where dogs were allowed) until two years ago. The state inexplicably banned pooches in January 1997. Our dog, Molly, has one thing to say to state beach officials: "I poop in your general direction."

Directions: From Santa Monica take the Pacific Coast Highway north for 25 miles, past Trancas Canyon. El Matador will be the first beach, with the parking area on your left. If you continue north, you'll find the parking areas for La Piedra and El Pescador within a mile, also on the left. **Fees:** Parking is $3. There is limited free parking on the northbound side of the PCH; be careful of traffic. **Contact:** California Department of Parks and Recreation, (818) 880-0350. **Locator:** ZUMA BEACH COUNTY PARK.

2. ZUMA BEACH, MALIBU

Welcome to king of the beaches, L.A. style. This famous beach is often quiet until the summer, when suburban kids flock to its wide, flat expanse. Surfers and bodyboarders bow to its surf (warning—experience required). Legions of Valley-ites seek respite from . . . the Valley.

This huge white-sand beach has concessions, volleyball courts, a playground, and tons of parking. The traffic can be the making of the Devil, but once the car is parked, the beach is so big there's plenty of room for everyone.

Directions: From Santa Monica take the Pacific Coast Highway north for 21 miles, to the entrance to the parking lot. There is limited free parking on the PCH (good luck). **Fees:** Parking is $5. **Pets:** Dogs are not permitted. **Contact:** Los Angeles County Beaches and Harbors, (310) 457-9891. **Locator:** ZUMA BEACH COUNTY PARK.

3. Point Dume State Beach, Malibu

Point Dume is a low-key alternative to nearby Zuma Beach. This secluded beach is also a scenic spot from which to whale watch, while rock climbers test their skills on Point Dume's cliffs. Surfers like the surf's steep break, especially at Westward Beach. Swimming in the western portion can be dangerous because the surf breaks in shallow water.

Directions: From Santa Monica take the Pacific Coast Highway north for about 21 miles and turn left on Westward Road. Drive to the end of Westward and park. **Fees:** Parking is $5. **Pets:** Dogs are not permitted. **Contact:** Los Angeles County Beaches and Harbors, (310) 457-9891. **Locator:** Point Dume State Beach.

4. Malibu Lagoon State Beach, Malibu

Best known to surfers as Surfrider, this beach is classic Malibu. A 10-acre lagoon formed by the beach is home to a rare salt-marsh habitat of birds and fish. Low tide exposes rocks on the ocean side of the lagoon, forming tidepools with crabs, urchins, anemones, and other creatures. This is an extremely popular beach and an often congested area of the Pacific Coast Highway. Parking can be scarce.

Directions: From Santa Monica take the Pacific Coast Highway north for 12 miles, following the signs to the parking area. There is limited free parking on the PCH. **Fees:** Day parking is $6. **Contact:** California Department of Parks and Recreation, (818) 880-0350. **Locator:** Malibu Lagoon State Beach.

5. Will Rogers State Beach, Santa Monica

This popular family beach lies at the base of Temescal Canyon, just below the upscale Pacific Palisades, and offers a playground and volleyball nets. At three miles in length, it is the second-longest beach in L.A. County. *Baywatch* is often filmed at the lifeguard station between Temescal Canyon Road and Chiquita Road.

When swimming, stay away from a storm drain located a few blocks north of the Santa Monica city limit. Pollution is a problem, especially during the 72 hours following a rainstorm. Throughout the county, rain, as well as tons of trash, washes into Los Angeles' flood-control channels, many of which empty themselves out at the beach.

Following a 1998 winter storm, we took a walk on Will Rogers Beach and found the following items: eight tennis balls, three beer cans, one unopened prophylactic, a super ball, a Taco Bell hot sauce packet, 13 plastic bottles for various soft drinks/mineral water, one large plastic trash bag filled with trash, various plastic utensils (including chopsticks), two hubcaps, one plastic shovel, a dog collar, two coffee mugs, and hundreds of unidentifiable plastic items.

Directions: From Santa Monica take the Pacific Coast Highway north for three miles. At Temescal Canyon Road, turn left into the beach parking lot. If you turn right, there is free parking available on Temescal Canyon Road (good luck!). **Fees:** Parking ranges from $5 to $7. **Contact:** Los Angeles County Beaches and Harbors, (310) 305-9546. **Locator:** Will Rogers State Beach.

6. Santa Monica State Beach, Santa Monica

Funky Santa Monica Pier bisects this popular area, which along with neighboring Venice Beach, claims tanning and people-watching as its primary activities. These beaches make a good resting point when biking or rollerblading on the South Bay Bike Trail. Keep in mind that the closer you get to Venice, the better the people-watching. In the summer of 1997, El Niño had water temperatures here cranked up to bathtub levels. It was great.

> **Directions:** Access is available at the ends of both Pico Boulevard and Ocean Park Boulevard in Santa Monica. **Fees:** Parking ranges from $5 to $7. **Contact:** Los Angeles County Beaches and Harbors, (310) 305-9546. **Locator:** SANTA MONICA STATE BEACH.

7. Manhattan and Hermosa Beaches

Beach volleyball reigns at both Manhattan and Hermosa, where pro tournaments attract crowds of 10,000 and more. There are about 50 nets for public use. Bike rentals are available at both beaches, which the South Bay Bike Trail passes. A scenic walkway called The Strand parallels the beaches and draws walkers galore, especially on weekends. We've read that these side-by-side beaches supposedly epitomize the singles scene, Southern California style, whatever exactly that means.

> **Directions:** The beaches can be accessed from Pier Avenue or Manhattan Beach Boulevard. **Fees:** Metered parking, with some free parking available on local streets (good luck). Beach access is free. **Contact:** Los Angeles County Beaches and Harbors, (310) 305-9546. **Locator:** MANHATTAN BEACH and HERMOSA BEACH.

Sailing

On summer weekends, there's a steady stream of sailboats heading in and out of Marina del Rey. How to join the crowd? Take sailing lessons. We recommend the affordable lessons offered through UCLA, which has a sailing center in the marina.

Contact for Lessons

UCLA Extension, (310) 825-9971.

City of Los Angeles Parks and Recreation's Pacific Aquatic Center, (310) 765-5391.

Bluewater Sailing, Marina del Rey, (310) 823-5545.

California Sailing Academy, Marina del Rey, (310) 821-3433.

Calypso Charter & Sailing, Marina del Rey, (310) 821-3433.

Southern California Boat Club, (310) 822-1912.

Kayaking

These days it's increasingly common to see that surfers have some company on the Southern California coast: kayakers. Those interested should consider taking lessons. The Southern California Boat Club offers classes out of Marina del Rey; phone (310) 822-1912. For those really into the kayak scene, the California Kayak Friends is a statewide club that covers all the bases. Check out their Web site at: www.ckf.org

• **FEATURED TRIP** •

Palos Verdes Peninsula
Between Los Angeles and Orange Counties

Palos Verdes and La Jolla look like twins separated at birth.

La Jolla, which is just north of San Diego, and Palos Verdes, part of the L.A. metropolis, are almost identical in appearance despite being about 100 miles apart. Both feature rolling hills, coastal pine trees, and a long downhill drive to the tall cliffs—some as high as 300 feet—which drop into the ocean. Both are developed, but neither resembles the relentless strip mall sprawl that covers much of L.A.

Nor does the mostly residential Palos Verdes Peninsula go out of the way to make itself a tourist destination. If Palos Verdes had a motto, it might be: "Thanks for visiting, but we'd rather you not." Thousands of years ago the peninsula was actually an island separated from the North American continent. Today it still is an island, metaphorically speaking, for the moderately wealthy and stinking rich.

However, there are some excellent getaways on the peninsula if you just poke around a bit; specifically, there's some perfectly great whale watching, picnicking, hiking, and mountain biking.

Here are three places to visit in Palos Verdes, all within 10 minutes of one another by car:

1. Point Vicente Park and Whale Watching Area

This small, grassy, and very pretty park sits high atop a cliff that drops straight down into the ocean. It's a wonderful place to have a picnic, watch the sunset, and, of course, whale watch: Point Vicente is regarded as the best whale-watching spot on the peninsula and in the L.A. area.

In fact, volunteers for the American Cetacean Society use Point Vicente as a spotting area during the gray whale's migration season, which runs from December though May. During January and February, the peak months for whale sightings, gray whales have been seen as little as a third of a mile to half a mile offshore. Volunteers have also seen baby whales riding their mothers' backs here, as well as all kinds of typical whale behavior, such as spouting, breaching, and spy-hopping.

Does that guarantee that you'll see a whale? No, but your chances are better here than anywhere in L.A. Our suggestion is to pack a picnic and a pair of binoculars. The best way of spotting the whales is to keep an eye on the whale-watching boats just offshore. When the boats stop or start circling, it means Moby Dick has not yet left the building.

Directions: From Los Angeles International Airport, take Interstate 405 south to the exit for Hawthorne Boulevard south. Follow Hawthorne south for 10 miles until it dead-ends into Palos Verdes Drive South. Turn left and drive one mile. The entrance to the park will be on your right. **Fees:** Entrance to the park is free. Admission to the whale interpretive center is $2 for adults, $1 for children. **Maps:** The best map available of the Palos Verdes Peninsula is in the *Thomas Brothers Guide to Los Angeles*, which can be purchased in most area bookstores or large retail stores. **Pets:** Dogs are allowed in the park, but must be leashed. **Contact:** Point Vicente Park, (310) 377-5370. **Locator:** Rancho Palos Verdes.

2. Del Cerro Park and the Unnamed Trail

Del Cerro Park itself is a tiny patch of green that sits high in the hills above Point Vicente. The views are magnificent, but the really good stuff is right around the corner.

Just 200 yards past the park's entrance, Crenshaw Boulevard dead-ends at a huge gate with a dozen or so padlocks on it. Beyond the gate is a fire road that makes a slow, long descent until it U-turns and then zigzags around the hills for seven miles. The trail isn't on official parkland, but it is open to the public. This is great hiking terrain because you can just about always see the ocean. The mountain biking here is good, but only for the hardy since it's very hilly.

> **Directions:** From Los Angeles International Airport, take Interstate 405 south to the exit for Hawthorne Boulevard south (also known as County Road N7). Drive eight miles south on Hawthorne Boulevard and turn left on Silver Spur Road. At Crenshaw Boulevard turn right and continue on Crenshaw until it ends at a locked gate. Park either on the street or in the parking lot in Del Cerro Park, on the right 200 yards before the gate.
> **Tip for picnickers:** A great, albeit popular, spot is underneath a patch of pines at the bottom of the first U-turn. The view of the sea is in the poetry-inspiring category, especially during the golden hour before sunset. **Fees:** Access is free. **Pets:** Dogs are allowed, but should be leashed. **Contact:** No phone number is available. **Locator:** RANCHO PALOS VERDES.

3. MALAGA COVE AND BLUFF COVE

Malaga Cove is the terminating point for the wide, sandy beaches that stretch across the South Bay from Malibu to Redondo. At Malaga, the beach hangs a hard right and turns into the rocky coastline that signals the beginning of the Palos Verdes Peninsula's southwesterly journey out to sea.

Malaga Cove presents several exploring opportunities. At low tide, there is some decent tidepooling right beneath a private resort that sits above the beach. If you want to head to wide and sandy Torrance Beach, it's just 100 yards to the north. Surfing is also very popular at Malaga, while Torrance Beach is a good Boogie-board area—just be careful to not eat Biff's surfboard.

At low tide—and we mean low—Malaga Cove can also serve as a good launching point for a two-mile hike to Bluff Cove, which is farther south on the peninsula. As you hike to the south, the cliffs begin to rise to an eventual height of 300 feet or so. You'll pass through Flat Rock Point with its huge boulders before happening on the cove, which resembles some of the wild coastline that is more typical in Central and Northern California.

Bluff Cove, like Malaga, is popular with the surfer dudes who can sometimes be territorial if they think another Biff is preying upon their waves.

> **Directions:** From Los Angeles International Airport, take Interstate 405 south and exit to Hawthorne Boulevard south. Drive five miles and turn right onto the Pacific Coast Highway. At Palos Verdes Drive North, turn left. Follow the road straight through the confusing intersection with Palos Verdes Drive West. At the stop sign by Malaga Cove Plaza, turn right on Via Corta, which quickly turns into Via Almar. Turn right on Via Arroyo and then turn left on Paseo Del Mar. Park along the street. The trail to the beach begins just across the street from the school soccer field. **Fees:** Access is

free. **Pets:** Dogs are not allowed on the cove or beach. **Locator:** PALOS VERDES ESTATES.

WHERE'S THE INSTAMATIC?

There are also some tremendous views available from the peninsula.

Straight out to sea is Catalina Island, just 17 miles away. On really clear days the casino in Avalon can even be seen with binoculars.

One of the best and most photographed views of downtown L.A. framed by the San Gabriel Mountains, can be found along Crenshaw and Hawthorne Boulevards.

South of the peninsula are similarly fetching views of San Pedro, Long Beach, and the Orange County coastline.

From Malaga Cove, on Palos Verdes' north side, the entire South Bay can be seen—sometimes all the way to Point Dume in Malibu.

• FEATURED TRIP •

SOUTH BAY BIKE TRAIL
Along the Los Angeles coastline

Dear Diary,

Today we're going to ride our bicycles on the South Bay Bike Trail, which stretches 22 miles along the coastline from the Pacific Palisades all the way south to Redondo Beach.

The path is accessible anywhere along the coast between the Pacific Palisades and Torrance Beach, but today we're going to start in the Palisades and ride south.

In the words of the Metropolitan Transit Authority—the schmoes trying to build the subway—this is a Class I bike trail because it provides a separate right-of-way for bicyclists and rollerbladers.

We park the car on Temescal Canyon Road for free and then cross the Pacific Coast Highway to the trail, which appropriately begins (and ends) at the snack bar counter. Having just consumed three triple-coffeeless-sideways-cappuccinos at Starbuck's, we're also very thankful there is a public rest room here, as well as dozens of other rest rooms along the trail.

Will Rogers State Beach is just one mile into our journey. This is the *Baywatch* beach. For those not in the know, *Baywatch* is a syndicated television show in which models in revealing swimsuits, posing as lifeguards, help beachgoers solve serious problems in their lives. For example, in one dramatic episode, a large-breasted lifeguard prone to wedgies helped a psychologically damaged jockey get over his fear of horses. Not surprisingly, *Baywatch* is the most watched television show on the planet and, possibly, the universe.

Our second stop is at the recently fixed-up Santa Monica Pier. The pier is home to a roller coaster, Ferris wheel, merry-go-round, assorted carnival games (such as shoot the basketball through the impossibly small hoop), various food stands, and, of course, skeeball. Little known fact: Sugared, fried elephant ears could possibly have some nutritional value.

Stop number three is in Venice, which has the greatest number of freaks west of New York's East Village. We walk the bikes along the asphalt "boardwalk," hoping to catch a glimpse of the guy who juggles chain saws. Instead, we see three dogs wearing sunglasses and pith helmets and one person wearing nothing at all. We also stop to have a hamburger across from a man—apparently a vegetarian—selling T-shirts that show the McDonald's arches accompanied by the phrase "McS——."

Then we head to Muscle Beach, the infamous outdoor weightlifting area right along Venice Beach. Lifters actually have to try out in order to earn the right to work out here. Little known fact: If it takes you two hands to lift the handle on the gate around the gym, you flunk.

Next stop: Fisherman's Village in Marina del Rey, which is along the trail on Fiji Street. Of course, no real, smelly fisherman would ever dare be found here—this is Marina del Rey. Nevertheless, it's a nice collection of shops, restaurants, and bars, in a kind of contrived way.

About a mile after crossing the marina's main channel, we arrive at Dockweiler State Beach, one of the emptiest strands of beach in the South Bay. This might just have something to do with the fact that the beach is located smack dab at the end of LAX's two runways—making the trail an excellent place to see the underbelly of a 747 up close and personal.

Another four miles of pedaling brings us to Manhattan Beach, one of L.A.'s premier beach communities, with a very nice pier, beach, and a small strip of businesses just one block uphill from the trail. It's the perfect place to lock up the bike, hike uphill one block, and have a bite at either Starbuck's or a brunch at The Kettle, one of those restaurants that has pretty much everything imaginable on the menu. However, in the spirit of getaway books, we keep on pedaling.

Through Hermosa Beach, the trail loses its exclusive status and borders Hermosa Avenue for a bit before arriving in Redondo Beach, which stretches to the beginning of the Palos Verdes Peninsula. From the Redondo Beach Pier, it's possible to look north and, if it's clear out, see all the way to Catalina Island to the west and Point Dume to the north. It's a beautiful view with just one problem: the distance between us and the car is now 22 miles.

The return trip's main observation is that of an unusual bike trail phenomenon: We have been pedaling against the wind the entire trip, one of the trail's quirks. One of these days, someone should do something about that.

Directions: You can access the South Bay Bike Trail anywhere along the Los Angeles coastline from Temescal Canyon Road in the Pacific Palisades all the way south to Redondo Beach. Parking is available in city lots from $5 to $10; there is also metered parking in places along the way as well as free street parking. Remember, the early bird gets the parking space. **Fees:** Use of the trail is free. **Maps:** Obtain a free map of the trail from the Metropolitan Transit Authority by calling the Los Angeles County Bike Map Hotline, (213) 922-5622. **Pets:** Dogs are permitted on the trail but must be leashed. They are not permitted on the beach. **Bike and skate rentals:** They are available at dozens of shops and stands all along the route, located at the major intersections and parking lots. **Contact:** Department of Los Angeles Parks and Recreation, (213) 485-5555. L A. County Department of Public Works, which maintains the trail, (626) 458-3941. **Locator:** Between PACIFIC PALISADES and REDONDO BEACH.

• Featured Trip •

BACKBONE TRAIL
In the Santa Monica Mountains

Beginning at Point Mugu in southern Ventura County and ending at Will Rogers State Beach in the Pacific Palisades, the 60-mile-long Backbone Trail spans much of the Santa Monica Mountains.

What will you see on the Backbone Trail? Pretty much everything. There are ocean views from 2,000 feet above sea level, the tallest peak in the Santa Monicas, waterfalls in Zuma Canyon, the rugged high country of Malibu Creek State Park, spectacular views of Cold Creek Canyon, and equally mesmerizing vistas of Los Angeles from the rocky, chaparral-covered hills of Topanga State Park. It is not inconceivable that one day people will visit Los Angeles not to go to Disneyland but to hike the Backbone Trail.

As is the case with any civic project, the Backbone has an interesting history. Until the last 30 years, the Santa Monica Mountains were basically up for grabs to anyone who had the money to buy some land and the gusto to build on it. That began to change in the 1960s and '70s, when it became evident that not protecting the mountains would one day result in the Santa Monicas becoming paradise paved into a parking lot.

As large chunks of the mountains were incorporated into three state parks (Point Mugu, Malibu Creek, and Topanga), an idea that had been floating around for years slowly became reality: to connect all of the mountains' parks with a single trail. Together, the National Park Service (which administers the Santa Monica Mountains National Recreation Area), the Mountains Conservancy Foundation, and the Santa Monica Mountains Conservancy began buying up parcels of land, trying to come up with a patchwork on which the trail could be built.

The first parcel of land for the trail was purchased in 1978, and surveying for the trail's location got under way five years later. Finally, in late 1997, funding was secured by Congressman Brad Sherman (D-Woodland Hills) to finish the trail.

A good place to find maps or plan your Backbone Trail excursion is the National Park Service Visitor Center in Agoura Hills. If you're thinking of trying to hike the entire trail, we suggest you also purchase Milt McAuley's "Guide to the Backbone Trail" (1990, Canyon Publishing Company, Canoga Park, CA), which provides an almost footstep-by-footstep account of everything you'll see along the way.

Directions: To reach the National Park Service Visitor Center in Agoura Hills, exit U.S. 101 at Kanan Road and go south. At Agoura Road, turn right. The visitor center is located at 30401 Agoura Road, Suite 100, in an office complex on the right side of the road. **Fees:** Use of the trail is free. There is a $5 charge for parking in the state parks. **Maps:** Trail maps and topographic maps of the Santa Monica Mountains are available at the NPS Visitor Center. **Pets:** Dogs are allowed on the Backbone Trail with the exception of the portions of the trail that pass through state parks. **Camping:** There are no designated wilderness camps (yet), but backpackers can overnight it in Point Mugu State Park, Malibu Creek State Park, and Topanga State Park. **Contact:** Santa Monica National Recreation Area, (818) 597-

9192. **Locator:** Between Point Mugu State Park (see Ventura County map on page 190) and Pacific Palisades.

• Featured Trip •

Catalina Island
14 miles out to sea, west of the Palos Verdes Peninsula

It's easy to see the Catalina Island that everyone sees: the T-shirt shops and ice-cream parlors of Avalon, the campgrounds of Two Harbors, and the buffalo that inhabit some of the space in between.

But very few people ever see the real, untouched, pristine Catalina. The Catalina where electric eels and eagle rays drift lazily in the water or a school of barracuda drifts by, giving a scuba diver little notice. Maybe even a sea lion will whoosh past, on some kind of underwater errand for his mate. A friend of a friend of ours (yes, we're stretching it—but it's a good story) once saw a whale while diving near Catalina, describing it as "kind of like seeing a house move by underwater."

Catalina is the number one diving and snorkeling destination in the state. While it rarely offers the bathtub-type conditions of Hawaii, Mexico, or the Caribbean, there are some very good diving and snorkeling spots—if you know where to look. Even the novice snorkeler who doesn't want to venture too far offshore can easily see plenty of the fish most associated with Catalina—the garibaldi, a bright orange fish that looks like a moving construction pylon.

Ninety-nine percent of the people who dive and snorkel on Catalina do so on the warmer and calmer waters of the leeward side of the island, the side that faces Los Angeles and is thus protected from the wide-open Pacific Ocean. Of course, in Catalina warm means water temperatures in the 50s and 60s. In other words, divers will need a wet suit. As for snorkelers, water temperatures are higher on the surface where the sun is shining, so in the summer, a bathing suit will likely suffice.

The latest rage for divers and snorkelers is to rent an ocean kayak and paddle around to different diving spots. This is very possible, not to mention easy, because today's ocean kayaks allow the passenger to sit above the water. For example, divers or snorkelers can paddle out to a kelp bed, tie on to the kelp, and then make a dive. "It definitely takes some practice, but it's not difficult," says Dave Long, director of diving and aquatics for the West End Dive and Kayak Center in Two Harbors.

The island of Catalina is basically a two-city affair. Avalon is the touristy little resort town that most people go to. It's nice, almost charming after a couple of drinks, but a certain level of schmaltz hangs over it like the smog hovering over L.A.

Two Harbors, which is on the island's isthmus, has a campground, a marina, a bar, and very little else. Two Harbors is also closer to the better dive spots on the island, with the waters around two of those locations easily accessible to kayakers: Isthmus Reef and Bird Rock. Good snorkeling can also be found along the shores of the cove. Watch for lobster, kelp bass, and garibaldi.

On a recent trip to Avalon (to attend a wedding at the botanic gardens—not a bad idea, by the way) we rented a kayak and some snorkeling gear and quickly paddled out to Lover's Cove Marine Preserve, just east of the boat landing. After swimming around and spying some garibaldis, we reversed direction and headed back across Avalon's harbor toward the Casino (it was a casino and ballroom back in the 1930s but now serves mostly as a movie theater), which sits on a point.

At the end of the point is the popular Underwater Park, the only underwater city park in the country. Divers can wade into the park from the Casino parking lot, although they have to negotiate some slippery and jagged rocks first. Catalina Divers Supply, one of the local dive shops, keeps a truck at the Casino to rent and refill air tanks.

We landed the kayak on some nearby rocks and swam over to the park (there is no boating allowed through the Underwater Park). Under us were the Little Casino reefs and some rocks, where octopuses sometimes gather. At various points around the reef were four small shipwrecks, including the *Sue-Jac*, a 65-foot schooner that went down in 1980. We also saw divers feeding the garibaldis.

From there, we worked our way down the coastline heading west. There were many small gravel beaches along the way, where we landed the kayak and swam out to nearby rocks or kelp beds, the kind of place where sea life often congregates. Sometimes a couple of fish would swim by, sometimes they wouldn't. The water tended to be a little chilly, but there were numerous gravel beaches where we could plant ourselves on a rock and get some sun.

Later, as we prepared to board a boat heading back to L.A., we passed a karaoke bar in Avalon. Unlike the tourists bellowing "I Will Survive," we relished the thought that, for a few minutes, we had looked below the island's surface for a glimpse of the whole picture.

DIVE SHOPS AND BOATS

Argo Diving, Avalon, (310) 510-2208.

Catalina Divers Supply, Avalon, (310) 510-0330 or (800) 353-0330.

Catalina Scuba Luv, (310) 510-0330 or (800) 262-DIVE.

West End Dive and Kayak Center, Two Harbors, (310) 510-0303 extension 272.

KAYAK RENTALS

Descanso Beach Ocean Sports, Avalon, (310) 510-1226.

West End Dive and Kayak Center, Two Harbors, (310) 510-0303 extension 272.

Wet Spot Rentals, Avalon, (310) 510-2229.

GENERAL INFORMATION

Directions: Catalina Island is accessible by either private boat or, for the rest of us, by passenger boat. Catalina Express runs to Avalon and Two Harbors from San Pedro, Redondo Beach, and Long Beach. Phone: (310) 519-1212. Service is also offered between Avalon and Two Harbors, so you can check out both ends of the island. Catalina Cruises runs to Avalon from Long Beach. Phone: (800) 888-5939. Catalina Passenger Service runs between Avalon and Newport Beach. Phone: (714) 673-5245. **Fees:** Boat service ranges from $28 to $40 round-trip. It is free to snorkel or dive in the waters off Catalina. However, you will pay to get a space on a dive boat or to rent diving or snorkeling equipment. **Maps:** Diving maps are available at all of the dive shops on the island. **Contact:** Catalina Visitors Bureau, (310) 510-1520. **Locator:** CATALINA ISLAND.

• F E A T U R E D   T R I P •

STONEY POINT
In the San Fernando Valley

In the far northwestern corner of the San Fernando Valley lies a 300-foot-tall pile of boulders affectionately known to the rock climbing crowd as Stoney Point.

Half covered with graffiti and half covered with climbers, Stoney Point is L.A.'s best-known natural jungle gym. In fact, Stoney Point is the place where Patagonia founder Yvon Chouinard learned to climb before he went on to develop the equipment that would revolutionize the climbing industry.

For the amateur climber, Stoney Point is a great place to hone technique, as well as meet other climbers. At the base of the hill are several dozen large boulders, some with vertical faces of 10 feet or so—the perfect kind of rock upon which to practice free climbing skills.

Stoney Point is also a regular destination of area rock climbing clinics and classes, which are available from both individual guides or large sporting goods stores, such as Adventure 16.

How seriously do area climbers take Stoney Point? A couple of years ago, the producers of the Steven Seagal epic *Under Siege 2* decided to shoot some additional footage at Stoney Point. They painted some of the rocks to cover graffiti and match colors with an earlier location shoot in Colorado. This threw local climbers into a tizzy because the paint made the climbing on some of these popular boulders downright impossible and, more importantly, it amounted to the trashing of sacred climbing ground. One climber, quoted in the *Los Angeles Times*, compared the painting of the rocks to desecrating the Washington Monument.

Directions: From downtown Los Angeles take U.S. 101 west for 23 miles to Topanga Canyon Boulevard, exit north, and drive five miles. Stoney Point is on the right, one-half mile after crossing Chatsworth Boulevard. Parking is available on the street. **Fees:** Access is free. **Pets:** Permitted, but it's a bad idea, as there's too much broken glass. **Note:** Adventure 16 offers one-day climbing classes at Stoney Point. For more information, phone (310) 473-4574. **Contact:** Los Angeles County Department of Parks and Recreation, (213) 485-4851. **Locator:** STONEY POINT.

22
SAN BERNARDINO AND RIVERSIDE COUNTIES

• Featured Trips •

BIG BEAR LAKE 244
SAN BERNARDINO MOUNTAINS .. 245
SKIING AND SNOWBOARDING
   THE SAN BERNARDINO
   MOUNTAINS 248
JOSHUA TREE NATIONAL
   PARK 251
MOJAVE NATIONAL PRESERVE .. 254
SNOWSHOEING IN THE SAN
   JACINTO MOUNTAINS 258
SAN MATEO CANYON 260

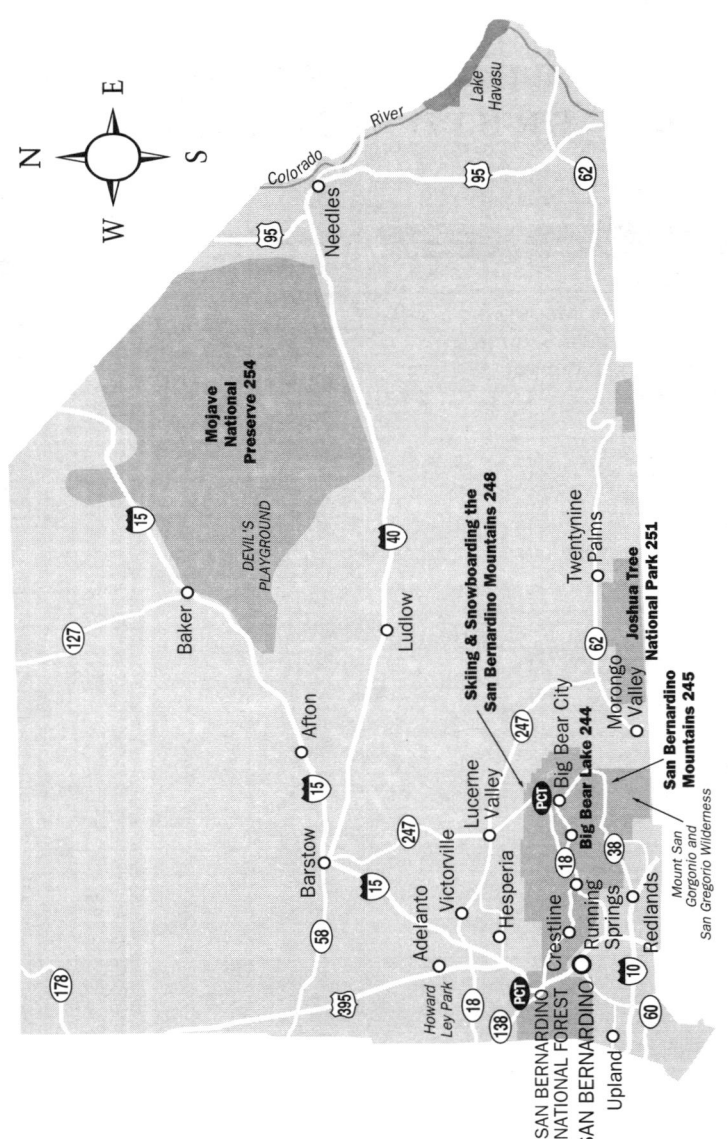

SAN BERNARDINO COUNTY

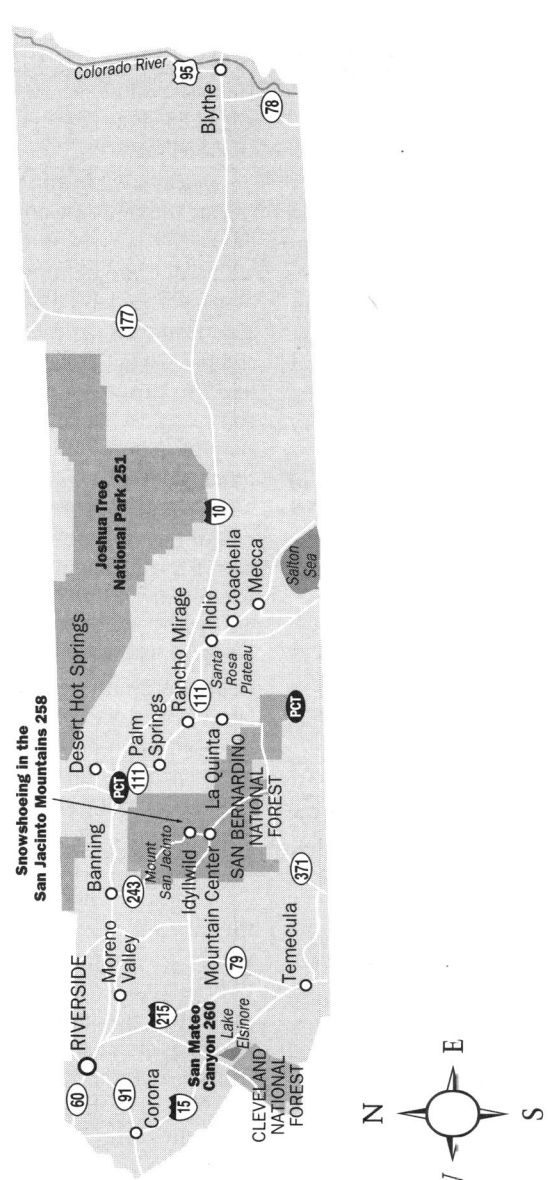

RIVERSIDE COUNTY

• FEATURED TRIP •

BIG BEAR LAKE
In the mountains north of San Bernardino

By the Fourth of July every year, the land to the north and south of the San Bernardino Mountains is nothing short of a blast furnace. The heat can fry the proverbial egg on the sidewalk or melt ice cream quicker than you can say "Chunky Monkey." Naturally, the local residents insist that it's a "dry heat."

The saving grace, the capital of cool (literally), and the primary oasis for the sunbaked people below is 3,000-acre Big Bear Lake. The lake, which is actually a reservoir, sits in a basin in the San Bernardino Mountains at an elevation of 6,738 feet. Surrounding the lake are mountains covered with pine trees and boulders. All in all, a rather picturesque scene.

The area has become quite a draw over the years. The south side of the lake has no shortage of rental cabins and motels, as well as the cute town of Big Bear Lake. Two large ski resorts, Snow Summit and Bear Mountain, are on the north-facing slopes just east of town.

Although Big Bear gets a dumping of snow every so often, the chamber of commerce likes to brag about the abundant sunshine—about 300 days of the year. This makes the lake a good place to have what we like to call a boating opportunity.

Boats are the thing at Big Bear Lake, whether it's a canoe (our preference), kayak, sailboat, motorboat, jet ski, pontoon boat, paddleboat, bass boat, rowboat, or toy boat. There are eight marinas at the lake and between them you can pretty much rent whatever type of boat it is you prefer. There's certainly no shortage of space to paddle about: the lake has 23 miles of shoreline.

On days when the water is calm, we like the canoeing and fishing at Big Bear. The lake is stocked regularly with trout and is known as a better-than-average bass fishery. The lake is also home to catfish, bluegill, and crappie. That's one of the reasons we like the canoe—it permits us to get some exercise while not catching a variety of fish in many different places on the lake.

Our favorite spot is on the eastern end of the lake, down toward the airport. It's usually quieter here (the lake is popular with the water-ski and jet ski crowd), with more moorings and beaches. The western end of the lake near the dam is equally scenic, as steep slopes with pine trees and boulders spill right down to the water. We like to paddle along the lake's shores, only crossing the lake at its narrowest parts. Motorboats usually monopolize the middle of the lake.

A word of advice: Try to get out on the lake for sunrise one morning. It will be cool out, thanks to the elevation, but it's well worth it. The lake is quiet, the mountains very pretty. As you float about surrounded by mountains, the only sound may be your paddle slicing through the water. Any day that starts like that should turn out to be a good one.

MARINAS
For all your boating needs, try one of the following:

Big Bear Marina, (909) 866-3218.
Gray's Boat Landing, (909) 866-2443.
Holloway's Marina, (800) 448-5335.

Lighthouse Trailer Park, (909) 866-9464.

North Shore Landing, (909) 878-4386.

Pine Knot Landing and Marina, (909) 866-2628.

Pleasure Point Boat Landing, (909) 866-2455.

Directions: From Los Angeles take Interstate 10 east for 60 miles to Redlands, exiting at Highway 30 north. Take Highway 30 to Highway 330 north and then continue 15 miles up and into the mountains to Running Springs. In Running Springs, follow Highway 18 east for 12.5 miles to Big Bear Lake. **Fees:** Canoe rentals usually run between $20 and $30 per day. All types of rental boats are available for an assortment of times and prices. **Lodging:** For referrals, phone the Big Bear Lake Resort Association at (909) 866-7000 or visit their Web site: www.bigbear.net. Phone the Big Bear Chamber of Commerce at (909) 866-4607 or (909) 866-4608. **Contact:** Any of the above marinas. The lake is administered by the Big Bear Municipal Water District, (909) 866-5796. **Locator:** BIG BEAR LAKE.

• FEATURED TRIP •

SAN BERNARDINO MOUNTAINS

Up and above smoggy San Bernardino

Over the years the town of San Bernardino has taken its lumps. Once a quiet town disconnected from Los Angeles, San Bernardino has since become a symbol for every urban problem imaginable, including violent crime, pollution, and joblessness. The smog that perpetually hovers over the sunbaked town is often the worst in the nation.

Many problems, of course, were imported from the L.A. metropolis, whose sprawl consumed the 60 miles between the two cities. What a shame. If San Bernardino had remained small and sleepy, it might be known today as a peaceful burg with the majestic San Bernardino Mountains serving as a backdrop.

The San Bernardino Mountains begin at Interstate 15 in the west and extend eastward to the town of Banning. Covering most of the range is the San Bernardino National Forest (the forest also covers the San Jacinto Mountains; see page 258), which includes the mountain towns of Big Bear Lake, Running Springs and Forest Falls.

Within the mountains are hundreds of miles of hiking trails, many of which have trailheads near the resort towns. The trails we like the best are the ones at high elevation, where the alpine forest sometimes bears a similarity to the Sierra Nevada—including the fact that bears do live there. The following are just a few of those trails:

1. COUGAR CREST TRAIL

If you're spending a weekend at Big Bear Lake and only have time for a little hiking, the Cougar Crest Trail is the trail not to be missed. It's a fairly moderate climb most of the way, is easily accessible, allows dogs (yes!), and offers a great view of Big Bear Lake and the surrounding mountains. If Big Bear isn't receiving much snow during the winter, this is also a year-round hike: we hiked it on New Year's Day 1996 in T-shirts and jeans.

The trail begins at the parking lot for the Cougar Crest Trailhead, just past the ranger station on Highway

38. You'll climb gently uphill, following a creekbed until the path narrows and begins a few gentle switchbacks to the trail summit.

Most folks stop here and head back down to their cars. However, if you have the time, follow the Cougar Crest as it circles around to the backside of the mountain. You'll soon pass a gnarled tree, which could be from the land of Oz and seems to say, "Are you saying my apples aren't what they ought to be?" If so, sit down and catch your breath. The altitude's getting to you.

Directions: The trailhead is located on Highway 38 about one-half mile west of the Big Bear Ranger Station. **Locator:** BIG BEAR LAKE.

2. PACIFIC CREST TRAIL

If you have always dreamt of hiking the PCT, here's the perfect opportunity: the PCT stretches across the crest of the mountains directly north of the lake. The easiest way to the PCT is to take the Cougar Crest Trail, which is described above.

The sign at the Cougar Crest Trailhead claims it's two miles to the PCT, but we think it's more like three (then again, we always believe it's more than what's posted). Once you're on the PCT you basically have two choices: turn left and continue 2,000 miles to Canada or turn right and settle for the relatively short jaunt to Mexico.

Just kidding. The PCT is actually going in an east-west direction here as it traverses the San Bernardinos. Both directions are perfectly interesting, but a westward journey (turning left onto the PCT from Cougar Crest) will take you a little deeper into the wilderness and provide views of the thoroughly unsettled northern part of the San Bernardino Mountains.

If heading east, you may want to branch off to the right on the trail leading to Bertha Peak. You'll get the same view you saw earlier from Cougar Crest, except you're now quite a bit higher.

For those planning on spending a night in the wilderness, there are trail camps in both directions from Cougar Crest. To the west, there's Little Bear Springs Trail Camp; to the east is Doble Trail Camp. As the crow flies, neither camp is far from the towns of Big Bear Lake and Big Bear City. Still, they feel a world away. (For more information on the Pacific Crest Trail see page 11.)

Directions: Take the Cougar Crest Trail (see above). **Permits:** A wilderness permit, which you can get for free at the Big Bear Ranger Station on Highway 38, is needed for overnight stays on the Pacific Crest Trail. **Locator:** BIG BEAR LAKE.

3. WOODLAND TRAIL

This is one of those interpretive trails with the little signs telling you about the geography of the land—you know, the kind of stuff that makes you realize you slept through Earth Science in high school. This is an easy, pretty 1.5-mile hike, suitable for all ages and abilities.

Directions: The trailhead parking lot is located on Highway 38 about 200 yards west of the intersection with Stanfield Cutoff. **Locator:** BIG BEAR LAKE.

4. CASTLE ROCK TRAIL

As you first enter Big Bear from the west, you'll probably notice the huge boulders by the side of the road. We're talking boulders the size of houses. The appropriately titled Castle Rock Trail climbs uphill to one big mama of a boulder called Castle Rock. The views of the lake and surrounding area are as stunning here as they are anywhere. The rocks are cool, too.

Directions: The trailhead parking area is located in a clearing along Highway 18 about one mile east of the Big Bear Dam. Or, to put it another way, just west of Talbot Drive. **Locator:** BIG BEAR LAKE.

OTHER HIKING OPTIONS

The above is just a sampling. Other, more rugged areas you may want to ask rangers about are the Deep Creek basin, which begins near Lake Arrowhead (see "Hot Springs" on page 95), as well as the Siberia Creek Trail and the Pine Knot Trail, which are both to the south of Big Bear Lake. Just to whet your appetite: the Siberia Creek Trail has a section that drops 2,500 feet in just two miles.

YELLOW POST CAMPING

Scattered throughout the San Bernardino Mountains around Big Bear are about 30 yellow post camping sites. These are individual campsites, accessible by unpaved Forest Service roads. Most of the sites can be reached by a regular passenger sedan. Facilities at each site include only a fire ring and a picnic table. There is no piped water or rest room facility. There is also no fee; this one's on the U.S. Forest Service.

The obvious advantage of these sites is that you don't have to put up with a campground filled with people, yet you also don't have to backpack into the wilderness. Of course, there's a catch. Reservations are not accepted and the 30 sites are often taken in the summer months; it helps if you arrive early on a weekday.

To get a site, you will need to visit the Forest Service's Big Bear Ranger Station in Big Bear Lake and get a visitor permit. The rangers will then give you directions to your yellow post site, which you may occupy for up to two weeks.

For more information, phone the San Bernardino National Forest, Big Bear Ranger District, at (909) 866-3437.

SAN GORGONIO WILDERNESS

The 59,000-acre San Gorgonio Wilderness, which includes 11,499-foot-tall Mount San Gorgonio (the tallest peak in Southern California), is south of Big Bear Lake. The area is most easily accessed from Highway 38, which runs between Redlands and Big Bear. The two best entry points to the wilderness are from either the Barton Flats Campground area or the mountain village of Forest Falls. For more information on the trek to San Gorgonio peak, flip to page 7.

Directions for all San Bernardino Mountains listings: From Los Angeles to the San Bernardino National Forest Big Bear Ranger Station, take Interstate 10 east for 60 miles to Highway 30 north. Exit to Highway 330 north and drive 15 miles to Running Springs, and then exit to Highway 18 east. Take Highway 18 for 12.5 miles to Big Bear Lake. Bear left onto Highway 38 and drive five miles to the ranger station, which will be on the left. **Fees:** A Forest Service Adventure Pass is available for purchase at ranger stations and most large sporting goods stores for $5 per day or $30 annually. **Maps:** The San Bernardino National Forest map is sold at ranger stations and most large sporting goods stores. Or send $4 to the USDA-Forest Service, Attn: Map Room 807, 630 Sansome Street, San Francisco, CA 94111 and ask for the San Bernardino National Forest map. **Pets:**

Dogs are allowed. **Note:** Late afternoon lightning storms occasionally hit Big Bear Lake during the summer. Keep an eye on the weather, even if it seems nice out. If thunderheads start rolling in, get back to low ground pronto. **Contact:** San Bernardino National Forest, Big Bear Ranger District, (909) 866-3437. **Locator:** SAN BERNARDINO MOUNTAINS.

• FEATURED TRIP •

SKIING AND SNOWBOARDING THE SAN BERNARDINO MOUNTAINS

North of San Bernardino

8:00 A.M.: Wake up after oversleeping an hour and realize you have no clean shirts to wear to work.

8:03 A.M.: Realize lack of clean laundry is actually a divine signal: Work is not in the stars for you today.

8:07 A.M.: With a clothespin on your nose and speaking through four paper towels, leave a message on your boss's voicemail. Pause in mid-message for simulated vomiting sounds.

8:30 A.M.: Join the brigade of unemployed actors and screenwriters for a cup of joe at the local coffee shop. So, you realize—this is what 90 percent of L.A.'s population does instead of going to work.

8:45 A.M.: After the girl operating the cappuccino machine refuses your bumbling advances, decide to go skiing.

11:30 A.M.: You are on the slopes. A snowboarder named Gink collides with you and then actually stops to apologize and help you up. You immediately realize you have entered a dimension in time and space that has little to do with reality.

Although much of the above scenario might have little to do with reality, it remains true that some very good skiing and snowboarding is just two and a half to three hours from the beach (depending on traffic, of course). And, while it may be true that skiing and sliding in the San Bernardino Mountains may lack the allure of Aspen or the grandeur of Mammoth, the truth is that when the conditions are right, the skiing can be pretty darn good. Even when the conditions aren't so good, it sure beats working.

One word of warning: The tape-recorded snow condition phones maintained by the resorts sometimes tend to embellish. When a snow phone message claims there is "five feet of snow," even when a storm hasn't moved through in weeks, assume that it means there's five feet of snow in one stray drift—and a couple of inches of man-made stuff everywhere else.

All four resorts offer ski and snowboard rentals, as well as lessons.

1. SNOW SUMMIT

This is the most popular ski resort in Southern California with 31 runs and 11 lifts, including two high-speed quads. Three of the runs are over a mile in length and beginners or intermediates can ski from the summit to the lodge—a major plus. Total vertical drop is 1,200 feet.

The resort cut its adult lift ticket prices to $32 for the 1997–98 season, a wise move. The resort has always attracted large crowds and the discount will surely help. But that's also the problem; this place can be ungodly crowded, even when ticket sales are cut off to limit crowds. Do yourself a favor and come on a weekday.

In the right conditions—plenty of snow and smaller weekday crowds—Snow Summit can be a great place. The views of the lake are sensational. Also try the night skiing, which is usually available Friday and Saturday nights and holidays. It's a little chilly sometimes, but riding the chair over a dark forest of pines on a clear night is a real kick.

One of the things we like about Snow Summit is that it has a top-to-bottom run for beginners, called the Summit Run. Alongside that trail is the Miracle Mile, an intermediate-rated run that's terrific fun, when not too clogged with skiers. We also recommend that skiers try the west side of the mountain off chairs 1, 5, 6, 7, and 10—hit the Timber Ridge run.

The resort has historically been extremely popular with 'boarders. There are three freestyle parks, including a sensational top-to-bottom affair called Westridge Freestyle Park.

One note: In 1997–98, Snow Summit continued its popular "Ski Free on Your Birthday" program. You'll need to present a valid photo ID.

Directions: From Los Angeles take Interstate 10 east for 60 miles to Redlands, exiting to Highway 30 north. Take Highway 30 to Highway 330 north and then continue 15 miles up and into the mountains to Running Springs. In Running Springs, follow Highway 18 east for 12.5 miles to Big Bear Lake. Drive through Big Bear Village and turn right on Summit Boulevard. **Special note:** Lift ticket reservations are suggested for weekends and holidays. Phone (909) 866-5841.

Contact: Snow Summit, (909) 866-5766. **Snow reports:** Los Angeles County, (310) 390-1498; Orange County, (714) 972-0601; Inland Empire, (909) 866-4621; San Diego County, (619) 294-8786; San Fernando Valley, (818) 242-0032. Web site: www.snowsummit.com. **Locator:** BIG BEAR LAKE.

2. BEAR MOUNTAIN

Bear Mountain doesn't have as many runs as its archrival Snow Summit, but it is 600 feet taller. Generally speaking, there is a bit more expert-level terrain here than at Snow Summit. Total vertical drop is 1,665 feet.

The layout is a bit different, too, with the resort encompassing runs down three different peaks. Bear Peak is the tallest and steepest—the resort gives it a double black diamond rating. We give it a single black.

Unlike Snow Summit, Bear Mountain didn't cut its lift ticket prices for the 1997–98 season; it's still $42 for an all-day adult lift ticket. What a joke: Mammoth, which is over 10 times the size of Bear Mountain, is $47.

The resort is best for intermediates and advanced skiers—there is relatively little beginning terrain when compared to Snow Summit or Mountain High, the best of the San Gabriel resorts. Intermediates will enjoy the Exhibition run (from the Silver Mountain lift) and the Expressway run (from the quick Big Bear Express Quad), while advanced skiers will like Geronimo, the double black run from the top of 8,805-foot Bear Peak. Views of Big Bear Lake are superb; there is also some off-trail skiing in the trees (please be careful).

Shredders will enjoy the Outlaw Snowboard Park, which includes a double barrel half-pipe.

SAN BERNARDINO AND RIVERSIDE COUNTIES

Directions: From Los Angeles take Interstate 10 east for 60 miles to Redlands, exiting to Highway 30 north. Take Highway 30 to Highway 330 north and then continue 15 miles up and into the mountains to Running Springs. In Running Springs, follow Highway 18 east for 12.5 miles to Big Bear Lake. Continue through Big Bear Village, past Summit Boulevard, and turn right onto Big Bear Boulevard. **Contact:** Bear Mountain, (909) 585-2519. Web site: www.bearmtn.com. **Locator:** BIG BEAR LAKE.

3. SNOW VALLEY

Snow Valley doesn't look like much of a resort from the road, but somehow the folks here figured they have 235 acres of slopes, as compared to 230 acres for Snow Summit and 195 for Bear Mountain. Much of the terrain is hidden from the road, as are many of the 14 lifts. Total vertical drop is 1,098 feet.

Most of the runs are blues (intermediates) and blacks (advanced), although the beginner with a fire in her or his belly won't have much problem with the blues. Generally speaking, Snow Valley lacks some of the long runs you'll find at its above rivals, but as compensation the resort has some fun advanced runs (into a small bowl at the top of Slide Peak, its highest point). Snowboarders have the run of the entire place and also have a half-pipe and terrain park about 1,300 feet in length to themselves.

One of the resort's key selling points is its location: It's only five miles east of Running Springs on Highway 18, making it much easier to get to and exit from when compared to Bear Mountain and Snow Summit.

Snow Valley is perfectly okay, but if we're going all the way to Big Bear, we'll go the extra miles to either Bear Mountain or Snow Summit.

Directions: From Los Angeles take Interstate 10 east for 60 miles to Redlands, exiting to Highway 30 north. Take Highway 30 to Highway 330 north and then continue 15 miles up and into the mountains to Running Springs. In Running Springs, follow Highway 18 east for five miles to the ski resort, which will be on the right. **Contact:** Snow Valley, (800) 680-7669. Web site: www.aminews.com/snowvalley **Locator:** RUNNING SPRINGS.

4. BIG AIR GREEN VALLEY

Formerly known as Ski Green Valley, this small resort changed its name when it banned skiers and became a snowboard-only facility for the 1993-94 season.

Situated on 40 acres above picturesque Green Valley Lake, with 500 feet of vertical, the resort has just three lifts, including a poma and tow rope. There's a half-pipe, too, but call first and make sure "Big Air" has "big snow"—there's no snowmaking.

Directions: From Los Angeles take Interstate 10 east for 60 miles to Redlands, exiting to Highway 30 north. Take Highway 30 to Highway 330 north and then continue 15 miles up and into the mountains to Running Springs. In Running Springs, follow Highway 18 east to the town of Arrowbear Lake. Turn left onto Green Valley Road, which continues to the resort. **Contact:** Big Air Green Valley, (909) 867-2338. Snow report, (909) 867-2338. **Locator:** RUNNING SPRINGS.

GENERAL INFORMATION

Tips: If you're going skiing in Big Bear on the weekend, be prepared: traffic can be miserable. One Sunday last winter, it took us two hours to drive from Snow Summit to Running Springs, a distance of just over 10 miles. So leave early—try to arrive at resorts by 8 A.M. Or, if you're going later, consider taking Highway 38 from Redlands. It's longer, but often less trafficked. **Note:** Chains are often required during and after storms in the San Bernardino Mountains. Always have chains in the car—just in case. **Lodging:** The Big Bear area has hundreds of motel rooms in all shapes, sizes, and levels of cheesiness. For information, phone Big Bear Lodging and General Referrals at (909) 866-7000.

LESS LIKELY THAN MIDDLE EAST PEACE

Unfortunately, it seems likely that there will be peace in the Middle East before skiers and snowboarders learn how to get along.

We're skiers, so our view of the problem may be a little biased. Our view: Most snowboarders are a bunch of lame-brained grungeoids who either don't look, or care, where they are going.

This is relevant because the San Bernardino resorts are teeming with 'boarders. They're sprawled at the tops of the runs (where they strap up), they're sprawled on the hills (where they've fallen), and they're sprawled all around the lift lines (where they sit with typically blank-faced expressions).

Much of this is the result of aggressive marketing to 'boarders by the resorts, especially Snow Summit. It wouldn't be much of a problem if the Ski Patrol actually ski patrolled more aggressively and was more willing to throw a few of these folks off the mountain.

That would be good for both skiers and other snowboarders alike. Of course, the problem is that it would be bad for business.

THE LANGUAGE OF SNOWBOARDING

Dude: Anyone who snowboards.
Going big: Making huge vertical jumps on the snowboard.
Kiss snow: To fall face-first into the snow.
Stoked: To be enthusiastic.
Grom: A little kid.
Maggots: Snowboarders who get in over their heads on a difficult hill.
Park zoos: Crowded parking lots at ski resorts.
Posers: People who buy all the snowboarding gear just so they look cool, but are really bad snowboarders.
Rip: To shred or tear up the hill on your snowboard.

• **FEATURED TRIP** •

JOSHUA TREE NATIONAL PARK

North of Palm Springs, in the Morengo Valley

"Rrrrbleckh . . ." gasped our friend Ralph. "I think I'm stuck."

Ralph was wedged between two immense granite boulders in one of many huge rock piles in Joshua Tree National Park.

Ordinarily this wouldn't be much of a problem. Except this was the early days of winter and the sun was about to set. The lunar-like landscape had already turned into a very real painted desert. The silhouettes of thousands of Joshua trees, all seemingly in different poses, added a flair of drama to the scene—as if the trees were watching our little predicament.

"Suck in your big, fat gut," suggested a member of our small group.

"Can't," said Ralph. "Had that burrito as big as my head for lunch."

Ralph had gotten himself in his current situation because we had spent the afternoon "bouldering." Bouldering is a form of rock climbing with the main difference being that you don't really have to know what you're doing. Simply put, bouldering means scrambling about on big rocks. And, as it happens, Joshua Tree has more piles of big rocks than anywhere else in Southern California.

Joshua Tree is also one of the premier technical rock climbing locations in the nation—the park offers more than 3,000 ascents for all levels of climbers. Should you ever take a rock climbing class, there's a very good chance a field trip could land you here, about 90 minutes north of Palm Springs and pretty much out in the middle of nowhere.

Of course not everyone wants to hang off of cliffs on ropes, even if it really is a swell time. But anyone with a pair of good hiking boots can climb a boulder. Even better: Rent some rock climbing shoes at an outdoor store.

The ranger at the park's gate, who will gladly separate you from some of your money, can easily point you toward the better bouldering spots in the park. The best places include Jumbo Rocks, Sheep Pass, and the Hidden Valley areas. All three are right along the main road through the park with convenient, well-placed parking areas.

It feels strange to proclaim one pile of rocks better than another, but the rock pile not to be missed is the Wonderland of Rocks, accessible from a trailhead at the Hidden Valley Campground. The trail cuts between two boulder piles, which is also the indicator that you have now entered the Wonderland of Rocks. Why is it a wonderland? Well, because there are rocks everywhere.

The short trail winds through the rocks until it arrives at Barker Dam, a relic from the early part of the century when ranchers grazed cattle in the park. There's still water behind the dam and the small pond has become the dumping ground for hundreds of goldfish. Twentynine Palms Marine Base is nearby, and when the soldiers get transferred, take a guess as to where their fish go.

The pond is surrounded by more of the Wonderland of Rocks, some of which are climbable and some of which are not. The best way of choosing a route is to not do anything too stupid. In other words, keep it simple and don't climb up anything that will be too difficult to climb down. Not only is being rescued by park rangers embarrassing, but it could result in a hefty fine.

If you're on the rocks in the Barker Dam area, keep an eye out for wildlife. Earlier in the day, we had seen a desert bighorn sheep pass right in front of a large and noisy church group. The group was a lot more excited than the sheep, which slowly ambled along the rocks until the people finally walked away.

So whatever happened to good ol' Ralph? Well, it turns out he wasn't stuck after all. He claimed he was just "joshing" us. What a guy. We laughed all the way down the road through the transition zone from the Mojave Desert to the Colorado Desert (not quite as interesting as you're led to believe) to the Pinto Basin, a flat and desolate desert that stretches for miles with nothing in sight.

And then we dropped Ralph off and kept right on driving. We were just kidding, of course.

CAMPING

Joshua Tree National Park has nine campgrounds, most of which are set against some very neat piles of rock. Winter nights can be very chilly—remember to bring sleeping bag pads in addition to an inflatable pad. Anyone with a telescope should bring it because the night skies put on quite a show.

Facilities at the campgrounds include fire rings, picnic tables, and pit toilets, with the exception of Black Rock Campground, which also has flush toilets. Note that ONLY Black Rock and Cottonwood Campgrounds have piped water. If you stay at the other camps, you must bring your own water.

Seven of the camps have individual family campsites available on a first-come, first-served basis. Only the Black Rock and Indian Cove Campgrounds take reservations for individual sites; reservations can be made through PARK.NET: (800) 444-PARK. Reservations are advisable for weekends from October to April. If you really like bouldering, we especially recommend the Jumbo Rocks, Hidden Valley, Ryan, or Indian Valley Campgrounds, all of which are set against good climbing spots. The Indian Cove and Black Rock Campgrounds charge a fee of $10 per night. Cottonwood's fee is $8 per night. All other campgrounds are free.

Directions: From downtown Los Angeles take Interstate 10 east for 99 miles to the Highway 62 exit, about 45 miles past San Bernardino. Take Highway 62 north for 26 miles to the town of Joshua Tree or go 15 miles farther to the town of Twentynine Palms. Each town has a well-marked entrance to the park. From San Diego take Interstate 15 north to Highway 60 east. Take Highway 60 to Interstate 10 east. Exit at Highway 62 north. Take Highway 62 north for 26 miles to the town of Joshua Tree or go 15 miles farther to the town of Twentynine Palms. **Fees:** A $5 entrance fee admits you to the park for seven days. **Maps:** A free map is provided upon entry to the park. **Pets:** Dogs are allowed in campgrounds only. Due to cactus and little shade, this is a terrible place for pooches. **Rock climbing:** For those interested in formal instruction in rock climbing, there are several guides who teach a variety of classes at Joshua Tree. Classes are offered throughout the year and are especially popular on weekends from fall through spring. For more information and to receive a pamphlet, phone the following outfitters: Joshua Tree Rock Climbing School, (800) 890-4745; Vertical Adventures, (714) 854-6250; First Ascent Climbing Services, Inc., (800) 325-5462. **Best time to visit:** October through April, when temperatures are usually mild during the day and cold at night. The park is empty in the summers, when temperatures are usually well over 100 degrees. **Keys View:** Don't miss this panoramic vista at an elevation of 5,185 feet at the southern end of the park. The view is straight south, encompassing the San Jacinto Mountains and the Coachella Valley. When it's clear, it's possible to see for over 100 miles, all the way to the Salton

SAN BERNARDINO AND RIVERSIDE COUNTIES

Sea and the Mexican border. **Contact:** Joshua Tree National Park, (760) 367-7511. **Locator:** JOSHUA TREE NATIONAL PARK.

THE CACTUS THAT BITES

A note of caution for those who go off trail on the desert floor: This is a desert. There are many types of cactus here and they all have one thing in common: sitting or standing on them hurts.

It is especially agonizing to get nailed by the cholla cactus, of which there are several types in the park. When hiking off trail or bouldering, never put your foot anywhere without looking. If nailed by the cholla cactus, the best way to remove the needles is with a fork.

TWENTYNINE PALMS

Besides being the title of one of Robert Plant's best songs, Twentynine Palms is also one of the most depressing towns in Southern California.

The town is best known for being the home to Twentynine Palms Marine Base, which is a possible explanation as to why the town seemingly has more tattoo parlors per capita than any other city in the nation.

Twentynine Palms, as well as the town of Joshua Tree, has a fair number of low-priced motels. We recommend the 29 Palms Inn, a funky collection of adobe-style cottages, all of which have fireplaces. Phone: (760) 367-3505. The inn also serves an outstanding brunch on the weekends in a cute dining room/bar. If the inn is full, try the always reliable Best Western, also in Twentynine Palms. Phone: (760) 367-9141.

• FEATURED TRIP •

MOJAVE NATIONAL PRESERVE
East of Barstow, in the Mojave Desert

The California deserts see plenty of sunshine, but they had never seen a day as bright as October 31, 1994.

On this day, almost 3,000 miles from the Joshua trees, sand dunes, cinder cones, and canyons of the preserve, President Bill Clinton signed into law the Desert Protection Act. With one fell swoop of a pen, Death Valley and Joshua Tree were upgraded from national monuments to national parks. At the same time, the former East Mojave National Scenic Area, under the administration of the Bureau of Land Management, was converted to the Mojave National Preserve, under control of the National Park Service.

What exactly is the difference between a national preserve and a national park? National preserves still allow some private ventures, such as ranching or mining, within their boundaries. However, no new ventures are allowed. Thus, the land remains protected as the national treasure that it is.

Many people opposed the bill. And many of those people, mostly Republicans, were elected into the Congress and the Senate just one week after President Clinton signed the Desert Protection Act. Within the next year the Contract with America was unveiled and it became glaringly obvious to everyone that the Desert Protection Act would never have made it past Newt Gingrich's hatchet.

For as much that has been said and written about the act—there are many who would like to see it repealed—relatively few people have ever seen the preserve. To most, the Eastern Mojave Desert is a no-man's-land, void of popular attractions such as Badwater and Dante's View in Death Valley.

Although the land remains relatively free of people, there is beauty everywhere. This is especially so in the winter, when cooler temperatures prevail (sometimes so cool that it snows) and the low-angle light brings out the many subtle colors of the high desert. As for geological features, the Mojave is stocked: There are spectacular caves, the world's largest forest of Joshua trees, lava tubes, twisty and narrow five-foot-wide canyons, four mountain ranges, and a resurrected railroad town. And that is just the short list.

More than anything, the Mojave Desert has space. You can pull to the side of the road on any given day and wait a real long time for another car to pass. Out here in the desert the constraints of time and space, which are often so overwhelming in the city, seem to dissipate.

Like Death Valley, the greatest challenge to the average park visitor is the preserve's size, combined with the fact there is only one "official" day-use hiking trail. If cars feel like an intrusion at some of California's other national parks, they are an absolute necessity here. It's the only way to begin to see even a small slice of the preserve.

However, those with cars should be warned: Don't just start driving the lesser known unpaved backroads of the preserve for the fun of it. A ranger once got her high-clearance four-wheel-drive vehicle stuck so badly in the sand that she had to hike three hours to the nearest phone. When the tow truck finally hauled her truck back to civilization, the bill was a cool $1,000.

Accessing the Mojave from Baker

The best starting point for the northern portions of the Mojave Preserve is the tiny desert town of Baker, on Interstate 15. If you're driving on the interstate, it's a town you literally can't miss. A couple of years back, in a fit of self promotion, the town spent $750,000 constructing a 134-foot thermometer next to the freeway. The joke is that 134 degrees is the highest temperature ever recorded at Death Valley, located one hour north of the town.

What Baker lacks in looks, it makes up for in practicality. It has its share of cheap motel rooms as well as the Mojave Information Center, which is at the base of the great thermometer. The center is staffed by National Park Service rangers and is a good place to stop before entering the preserve. Baker also has one of the few good roads heading into the preserve, Kelbaker Road.

Heading south on Kelbaker Road from Baker, the first item of interest you'll encounter are the cinder domes, on the left (east) side of the road. If it's still early in the morning, go for a walk; wandering where there are no trails in this big desert will either give you the heebie-jeebies or give you the feeling the rest of the world is very, very far away.

Continuing down Kelbaker Road for another 16 miles will land you at the old Union Pacific Railroad Depot. The depot is no longer used, but the tracks are still very active—big freight trains often rumble past.

To the west of the depot, at the end of a four-mile unpaved road, are the Kelso Dunes, also known as the Devil's Playground. An hour or so of difficult hiking leads to the top of the 700-foot-tall sand dunes, which are among the prettiest and most remote dunes in the state. The dunes are best known for the thunderlike sound the sand makes as it shifts about. Bring a lunch tray and try riding down the dune's sides.

A piece of advice: It's easy to lose one's bearings in the sand dunes. Bring a compass and the knowledge to use it.

THE PROVIDENCE MOUNTAINS

The Providence Mountains State Recreation Area is in the south-central portion of the preserve and is administered by the state, not the NPS. The area has three campgrounds, two established hiking trails, and Mitchell Caverns, which is the big tourist draw. Take note that it's easier to reach this area of the park from Interstate 40.

The trails can be found at the Hole-in-the-Wall area, where there is a campground. The first trail leaves the picnic area and descends through a canyon of volcanic rock. The narrow, tight canyon requires some boulder hopping and pulling yourself up with iron rings that were drilled into the rock years ago. It's serious Indiana Jones–type scenery.

An equally interesting trail leads from Hole-in-the-Wall to Mid Hills, which also has a small campground. The entire trail is seven miles long, although you can get a nice glimpse of the desert landscape and plant life by just hiking a couple of miles.

The main attraction in this part of the park is the 1.5-mile guided hike through Mitchell Caverns, a limestone cave with all sorts of fascinating limestone rock formations. The cave is open daily (except holidays) from Labor Day to Memorial Day. Arrive at least 30 minutes before the tour is due to depart. Groups of 10 to 25 people must have a reservation; for current tour times, phone the state recreation area at (760) 928-2586.

SPELUNKING

Mitchell Caverns is open to guided tours for the public. But Mitchell's companion cave, Winding Stairs, is open only to proven cavers, also known as spelunkers.

"It's more exciting than a guided tour to get on your hands and knees and wallow in the mud of a dark cave for a while," says Mojave National Preserve ranger Kirstin Talken, an amateur caver whose sister was married in a cave. "Although sometimes you come out a different color than when you went in."

How to get involved in spelunking? Contact the National Speleological Society (NSS), the nation's largest organization devoted to the exploration of caves, and find out how to contact the local NSS grotto (chapter).

You'll find the NSS on the Internet at www.caves.org.

CAMPING

There are two developed campgrounds in the Mojave National Preserve—Mid Hills and Hole-in-the-Wall—and one in the Providence Mountains State Recreation Area.

Providence Mountains Campground, near Mitchell Caverns, has six sites for tents or RVs and is administered by the state. Facilities include fire grills, picnic tables, piped water, and flush toilets. Reservations are not accepted. Fees are $12 per night plus $1 for pets.

The Mid Hills Campground has 26 sites for tents and RVs, about 20 miles north of Mitchell Caverns. The campground is at an elevation of 5,500 feet and is set among pinyon and juniper trees—trees in the desert! Facilities include fire grills, picnic tables, vault toilets, and limited piped water; bring plenty of bottled water. Reservations are not accepted, and fees are $10 per night.

Hole-in-the-Wall Campground has 35 sites for tents and RVs. The campground is at an elevation of 5,000 feet, on Essex Road, about 28 miles north of Interstate 40. Facilities include fire grills, picnic tables, vault toilets, and limited piped water. No reservations are accepted, and fees are $10 per night.

Directions: To Baker from downtown Los Angeles, take Interstate 10 east to San Bernardino, exiting to Interstate 15 north. Drive 120 miles to Baker, exiting at Highway 127. Turn left, cross the freeway, and then turn right toward the big thermometer behind the Bun Boy restaurant, where you will find the Mojave Information Center. To enter the park, recross the freeway and head south on Kelbaker Road. It's 34 miles to Kelso Dunes. Note: You can also take Interstate 40 west from Barstow for 77 miles, exiting at Kelbaker Road and turning left to reach the dunes OR exiting at Essex Road and turning left to reach Mitchell Caverns and the Providence Mountains State Recreation Area. **Fees:** Day use of the preserve is free. **Maps:** The AAA map of San Bernardino County is perfectly adequate and is available at many bookstores or AAA offices. For more detailed maps of particular areas, ask to see the list of USGS maps available at the Mojave Information Center.

Pets: Dogs are allowed but must be leashed. Note: This is an unforgiving environment for most dogs—too much sun. **Contact:** Mojave Desert Information Center, (760) 733-4040. Mojave National Preserve, (760) 255-8801. Providence Mountains State Recreation Area, (805) 942-0662. Baker Area Chamber of Commerce, (760) 733-4469. **Locator:** MOJAVE NATIONAL PRESERVE.

PICTURE TIME

The once volcanic Cima Dome is located on Cima Road in the middle of the park. The dome is a 1,500-foot-tall mound, heavily covered with Joshua trees. The trees are particularly photogenic, especially at the golden hour after sunrise and preceding sunset.

NO FREE HBO

The Mojave is littered with the remains of old mining and cattle towns. One town that has survived is Nipton, located on Highway 164 in the eastern section of the preserve about 10 miles from Interstate 15.

The town was once a railroad watering spot on the line between L.A. and Salt Lake City. Today, many of the town's buildings remain standing. One is a four-room bed-and-breakfast called the Hotel Nipton. If you're looking for peace and quiet, look no further. Phone the Hotel Nipton at (760) 856-2335.

GENERAL PATTON'S TURF

To prepare his troops for combat in North Africa in World War II, General George Patton established 11 desert training camps in the Mojave Preserve. Most of the camps were near the California-Arizona border; there are still places where 55-year-old tank tracks have been preserved in the dirt.

SNOWSHOEING IN THE SAN JACINTO MOUNTAINS
Up and above Palm Springs

All across Southern California there are billboards for the Palm Springs Aerial Tram. The picture on the billboards usually features the big red tram cheerfully swinging uphill, with awestruck tourists breathlessly enjoying the adventure.

Well, the good news is that truth in advertising is still alive. The tram ride is great—and there is no doubt the tram is nothing less than an amazing feat of engineering (not to mention chutzpah).

Consider this: In just 10 minutes, the tram leaves the desert floor in Chino Canyon at an altitude of 2,643 feet. After ascending straight up the mountain, including a couple of agonizing drops over cable towers, the tram deposits passengers at the mountain station, elevation 8,516 feet.

In other words, this ain't no ordinary ski lift. The bottom of the tram sits in a dry, gravel-filled desert. The top of the tram lands at a mountaintop area covered with boulders, pine trees, gurgling creeks, and, in the winter, snow. It's hard to imagine anywhere else in the world where such a startling change in ecosystems can be experienced so quickly.

The cross-country skiing up here is tough—the snow can be spotty and the trails are not groomed. But it's an absolutely great place to try snowshoeing, not to mention a popular one. Just down a trail from the tram station is the Nordic Ski Center, which rents cross-country skis, snowshoes, and sleds.

One of the reasons snowshoeing has had a resurgence in popularity in recent years is the snowshoes themselves. They have been drastically redesigned and are now much easier to use. In the old days, snowshoes were made of wood and were often three to five feet long. Walking in them required hikers to alter their stride. It was clumsy and difficult.

Not anymore. Today snowshoes are made of lightweight metals, such as aluminum. They're also much smaller, typically no more than two feet long and 10 inches wide. Nor do they require any special type of stride. If you can walk, you can snowshoe. Underneath some snowshoes are metal teeth that help you dig in when climbing hills.

WHERE TO GO SNOWSHOEING

The tram station is within the boundaries of Mount San Jacinto State Park, which is surrounded by the San Bernardino National Forest. Here's what to do: From the Nordic Ski Center, follow the signs to the Long Valley Ranger Station. Here, you'll need to fill out a wilderness permit—it's free and the ranger can give you trail information. Trail maps are also available for the bargain-basement price of 25 cents.

The 2.1-mile trail to Round Valley Campground begins right in back of the ranger station, climbing gently along a small creek. After crossing the creek, the trail switchbacks up a hill and then follows a ravine to the campground. If there has been plentiful snow, you'll find this hike to be a winter wonderland of pines, boulders, gurgling creeks, and the quiet of the big forest. It's also a good workout—dress in layers (avoiding cotton), making it easier to get comfortable.

A great little side trip is the Desert View Trail, which overlooks the Coachella Valley and Palm Springs below. It's also possible to see 60 miles away to the southern boundaries of Joshua Tree National Park.

One of the great things, too, about hiking up here in the winter is that you can come back in the summertime and hike or backpack on the same trails. Even when it's 115 degrees in Palm Springs, the temperatures up here are much milder—although the sun can be very strong, as it always is at high altitudes.

Over 100 miles of trails crisscross the top of the San Jacintos. There are eight campgrounds accessible by car (from the western side of the mountain) and four hike-in camps. One of the best views in the country is also here: Mount San Jacinto stands at 10,804 feet and offers a view of Southern California that will not soon be forgotten. (For more information on hiking to the peak, please see page 10.)

Keep in mind, also, that the wilderness area can be accessed from the alpine village of Idyllwild, located on the mountain's western side.

Upon returning to the tram's Mountain Station for the ride back down the tram, you may want to reward yourself with a drink at the upstairs bar, which offers outstanding alpine scenery and views of the desert floor, over 7,000 feet below. The prices are sky-high, but then again, so are you.

Camping

A number of drive-in campgrounds access the San Jacinto area from Highway 243 near Idyllwild. We recommend either the state park's Stone Creek Campground or Idyllwild Campground.

Stone Creek has 50 sites for tents and RVs. Facilities include fire rings, picnic tables, piped water, and pit toilets. Reservations can be made by phoning PARK.NET at (800) 444-PARK. Fees are $11 on weekend nights in the summer and $9 on weekdays.

Idyllwild Campground has 31 sites. Facilities include fire rings, picnic tables, piped water, flush toilets, and showers. Reservations can also be made through PARK.NET at (800) 444-PARK. Fees are $14 on weekend nights during the summer, $12 on weekdays.

The Round Valley Campground, located near a pretty meadow, is accessible by backpacking 2.1 miles from the top of the Palm Springs Aerial Tram. A wilderness permit is needed; permits can be reserved up to 56 days in advance by mail or in person. The address is P.O. Box 308, Idyllwild, CA, 92549, c/o Mount San Jacinto State Park. During the high season, rangers recommend you get a permit at least 10 days in advance of your visit.

Facilities at Round Valley include piped water and pit toilets. No fires are allowed, so you'll need to bring a stove. Camping at Round Valley is free. For more information, phone Mount San Jacinto State Park, (909) 659-2607.

Directions: From downtown Los Angeles take Interstate 10 east for 95 miles, exiting at Highway 111 heading south to Palm Springs. Drive nine miles on Highway 111 and turn right on Tramway Road. Continue four miles to the tramway station. From San Diego take Interstate 15 north to Interstate 215 north to Interstate 10 east. Exit at Highway 111 heading toward Palm Springs. Drive nine miles and turn right on Tramway Road. Continue four miles to the tramway station. **Fees:** At press time, Palm Springs Aerial Tram tickets are $16.95 for adults and $10.95 for children ages 5 to 12. There is a discount for AAA members. Use of Mount San Jacinto State Park is free. Snowshoes can be rented both by the hour and the day. **Pets:** Dogs are not allowed on the tramway, nor are they permitted in the state park. **Note:** To avoid a wait at the tram, get there early in the day. **Contact:** Palm Springs Aerial Tram, (619) 325-1391. Snow conditions, (619) 327-6002. Mount San Jacinto State Park, (909) 659-2607. **Locator:** MOUNT SAN JACINTO.

IDYLLWILD

At an elevation of 5,200 feet, Idyllwild is a cute little town on the western side of the San Jacintos. There's plenty to do for the outdoor oriented. Many of the trails into the national forest and state park begin near the town—including the 2.6-mile Ernie Maxwell Trail, which begins at Humber State Park. Some good fishing can be found at Lake Hemet, nine miles south of town on Highway 74.

Idyllwild hosts an outdoor jazz festival every August. Phone (909) 659-3774 for date and ticket information. There are cabins, motels, and bed-and-breakfasts in town, as well as nearby campgrounds.

Directions: To reach Idyllwild from downtown Los Angeles take Interstate 10 east for 83 miles, exiting at Highway 73 south. Drive 25 miles on Highway 73. **Contact:** For information, phone the Idyllwild Chamber of Commerce at (960) 659-3259. Or visit the Web site at www.idyllmtn.com. **Locator:** IDYLLWILD.

A COUPLE OF BIG ROCKS

When hiking from Idyllwild, it's hard to miss two big rocks sticking out of the side of the mountain: Suicide Rock and Tahquitz Rock (also called Lily Rock). Both are very popular rock climbing sites; Suicide Rock has more than 250 climbing routes on it. Of course, you have to be experienced to climb either rock, and there's no better way to learn than to take a lesson. For more information about rock climbing classes, phone Idyllwild's Nomad Adventures at (909) 659-4853.

• **FEATURED TRIP** •

SAN MATEO CANYON
In Cleveland National Forest

How many times do you think one dog could chase the same stick into the same swimming hole in the same creek without tiring of the game?

By our estimation, 102. We should know. The owner of this dubious accomplishment is our chocolate Lab, Molly. In fact, Molly liked San Mateo Canyon so much we might never have left had Steve not taken her favorite stick and broken it into little tiny pieces.

It doesn't take a genius to see why dogs or hikers like this place so much. The nine-mile-long canyon, carved by San Mateo Creek, is one of the larger watersheds for the Santa Ana Mountains. The creek eventually cuts a swath across the northern part of Camp Pendleton before draining into the ocean at San Onofre State Beach.

Although the creek dries up in the summertime, enough water passes through the canyon during the winter to keep it lush year-round. Those willing to hike four miles from the trailhead will also find some dandy boulders, swimming holes, and picnic spots that are no secret to local hikers.

The trail begins at the parking lot at the end of Tenaja Road. From here, hikers follow a fire road down Tenaja Canyon to Fisherman's Camp. This is an indication to just how strong the fish population was in Southern California. Southern steelhead, listed as a federally endangered species in August 1997, were once reared in these waters. After reaching adulthood, the anadramous fish would swim out to sea before returning to their native creeks to spawn. Habitat degradation is the primary reason for the southern steelhead's demise.

Just below Fisherman's Camp, Tenaja Creek spills into San Mateo Canyon. The San Mateo Trail follows San Mateo Creek downstream—although there are places the trail virtually disappears, compliments of winter storms.

Along the way, tributaries spill into the creek, each often having its own side canyon. Both the Bluewater Trail and Creek join the San Mateo from the north. Bluewater, one of the major tributaries, also makes for plentiful rock scrambling. The Bluewater Trail travels quite a way upstream, where it makes a loop within the San Mateo Wilderness, one of the four wilderness areas in the Cleveland National Forest. Wilderness areas have been set aside by the U.S. Congress to exist as places that continue to be wild—touched by man, but untrammeled. Consider yourself privileged to visit such a place.

Four quick safety notes: 1) Stay away from the canyon during and immediately after a rainfall; 2) never, ever dive into a swimming hole; 3) keep a close watch on kids if you're allowing them to swim here; and 4) keep your eyes peeled for poison oak—there's a lot of it.

Directions: From Lake Elsinore take Interstate 15 south for six miles, exiting at Clinton Keith Road and turning right. Take Clinton Keith Road for seven miles and turn right on Tenaja Road (Forest Service Road 7S01). Continue to the trailhead at the end of the road. **Fees:** Purchase a Forest Service Adventure Pass ($5 per day or $30 annually) at ranger stations and most large sporting goods stores. **Maps:** The Cleve and National Forest map can be purchased at ranger stations or most large sporting goods stores. Or mail $4 to the USDA-Forest Service, Attn: Map Room 807, 630 Sansome Street. San Francisco, CA 94111 and ask for the Cleveland National Forest map. **Pets:** Dogs are permitted. Bubba will love it! **Contact:** Cleveland National Forest, Trabuco Ranger District, (909) 736-1811. **Locator:** SAN MATEO CANYON.

23
ORANGE, SAN DIEGO, AND IMPERIAL COUNTIES

• FEATURED TRIPS •

CASPERS WILDERNESS PARK ... 266
CRYSTAL COVE STATE PARK 268
SAILING ORANGE COUNTY 269
SAN JUAN TRAIL 270
PALOMAR MOUNTAIN
  STATE PARK/PALOMAR
  OBSERVATORY 271
CUYAMACA RANCHO
  STATE PARK 273
ANZA-BORREGO DESERT
  STATE PARK 275
SAN DIEGO DEEP-SEA
  FISHING 278
SAN DIEGO HOT AIR
  BALLOONS 280
TORREY PINES STATE
  RESERVE 282
SAILBOARDING MISSION BAY ... 283
BATES NUT FARM'S
  GREAT PUMPKINS............... 285
IMPERIAL SAND DUNES 286

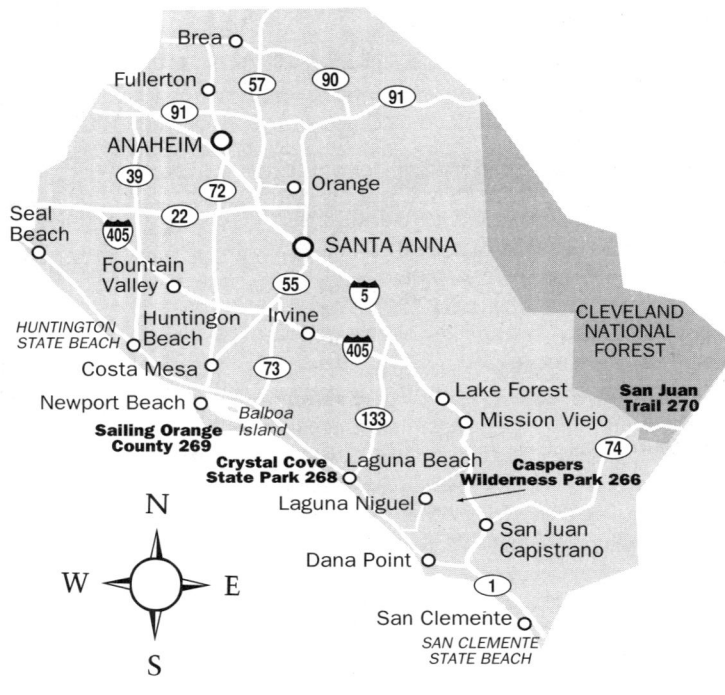

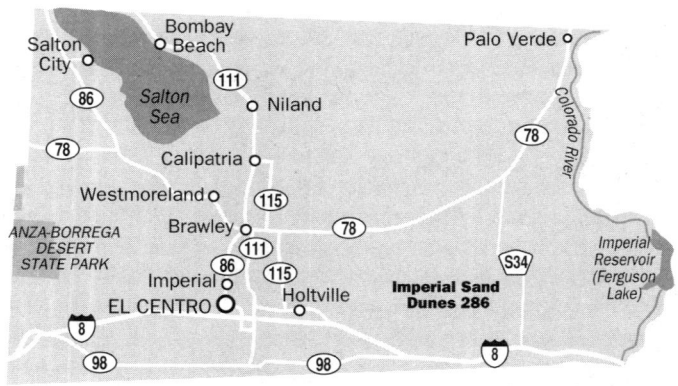

ORANGE AND IMPERIAL COUNTIES

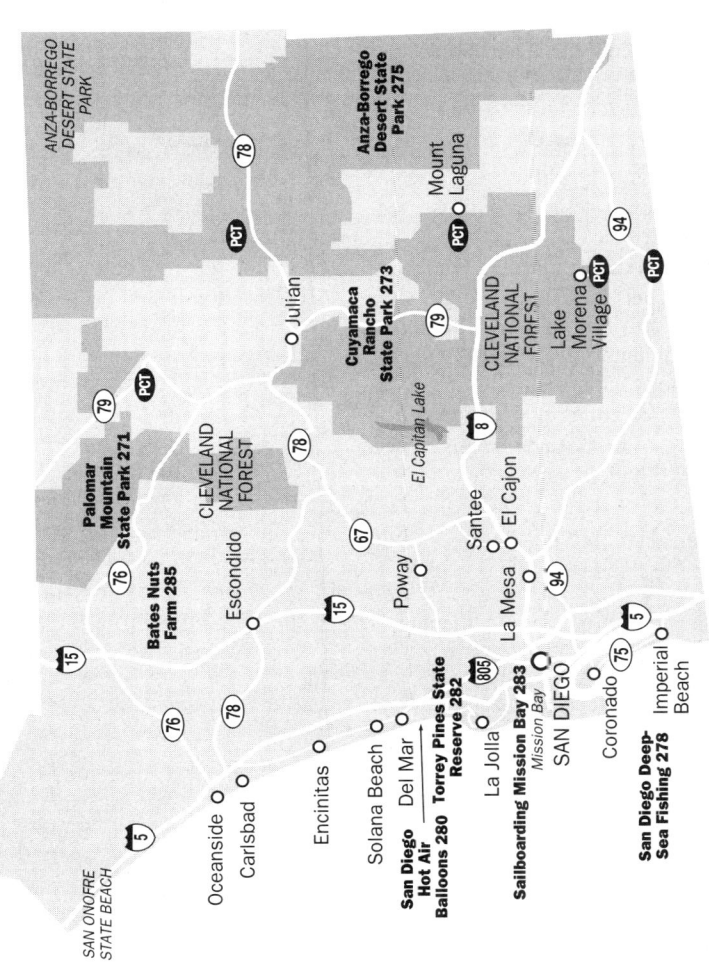

SAN DIEGO COUNTY

• FEATURED TRIP •

CASPERS WILDERNESS PARK
On the Ortega Highway, east of San Juan Capistrano

Some of the most pleasant scenery in Orange County is within easy reach of tons of people, yet most of those people will never see it.

Why? Because, for more than a decade, there has been no getting around the association between mountain lions and Ronald W. Caspers Wilderness Park—whether it's a deserved association or not.

In 1986, in the space of just half a year, two children were attacked in the park. One of those children, a five-year-old girl, was left partially blind and paralyzed as a result of the attack. Her family sued Orange County and reached an out-of-court settlement of $1.6 million in 1992. That's when the county, wary of any further litigation, closed the entire park to children.

It stayed that way until August of 1995, when the county reopened the picnic grounds and playground portion of the park to children. Two more years went by until the park was completely reopened to children. In late 1997, park officials also ended the practice of making adults sign waiver forms whenever they entered the park. The forms protected Orange County from being sued should a mountain lion attack.

The voluminous number of signs about mountain lions posted in the park can, as would be expected, manage to somewhat freak out even the seasoned hiker. The ranger who greeted us at the entrance gate didn't help matters by saying, "Don't worry about it. It's not like there's a mountain lion waiting for hikers behind every rock."

But is there really any reason for adult hikers to worry?

Not particularly. Yes, there are obviously mountain lions in the area—as there have been for hundreds, probably thousands, of years—but the lions are rarely seen. When they are seen, the lions generate a lot of attention from the press, which tends to make the lion population sound larger than it is. The truth is that people who take the proper precautions are almost guaranteed of not seeing a mountain lion. The most important precaution: Hike with a partner.

The park is as pretty as they come—we think it offers the best scenery in Orange County. The picnic area and campground are scattered in several grassy meadows surrounded by sycamore trees. The park is rarely crowded, so getting a picnic table, grill, or campsite is not exactly difficult.

Most of the hiking trails begin at the Old Corral picnic area; have the ranger give you directions from the front gate. The Nature Trail Loop is a pleasant little 0.7-mile jaunt that begins in a heavily forested part of the park and then leads across a dry wash to a meadow filled with prickly pear cactus, providing for an interesting juxtaposition of vegetation types.

Midway through the Nature Trail is a well-marked junction with the Dick Loskorn Trail, which heads uphill and merges with the East Ridge Trail. From this point, there are some great views of the park below and the Santa Ana Mountains beyond.

For those looking for a good loop hike, make a right turn from the Dick Loskorn Trail onto the East Ridge Trail. Continue to the marked Star Rise

Trail, turn right, and walk downhill to the Bell Canyon Trail (it helps to have a map, of course). Head right and you'll find yourself back at the Old Corral picnic area. All in all, it's a 3.5-mile hike that takes anywhere from 90 minutes to two hours to finish.

Directions: From San Juan Capistrano, take Highway 74 (the Ortega Highway) east for 7.5 miles to the park entrance, on the left. **Fees:** The day-use fee is $2 per car on weekdays and $4 on weekends. **Maps:** Ask for a free trail map from the ranger who greets you at the front gate. **Pets:** Dogs are not allowed in the park. **Camping:** The park has four very nice campgrounds, including camps for equestrians and groups. The campground for families and individuals has 42 sites. Facilities include picnic tables, charcoal grills, flush toilets, and showers, but no RV hookups. Camping is $12 per night and is available on a first-come, first-served basis. Spring is the busiest season; temperatures can hit triple digits at the park in the summer. For information, phone the park at the number below. **Special note:** Children under 18 years of age are only allowed in the picnic areas and campgrounds. **Contact:** Ronald W. Caspers Wilderness Park, (714) 728-0235 or (714) 728-3420. **Locator:** CASPERS WILDERNESS PARK.

WHAT'S FOR DINNER?

When we car camp, we sometimes make a meal at home and then reheat it at camp. Yeah, it's cheating a bit, but so what? It's convenient, especially after a long day hike.

Steve's Brown Dog Chili is based on Cincinnati's infamous chili. Make the chili a couple of days ahead of time and then bring the entire pot in your cooler. To reheat, put the pot on a grill over a medium fire. To prevent burning the chili, add two cups of water during reheating and stir often. Serve with saltines or, better yet, corn bread for dipping. To do it right, top a bowl of chili with grated cheddar cheese.

INGREDIENTS

1 big yellow onion
1 tablespoon olive oil
1 pound ground beef
1 28-ounce can crushed tomatoes
1 15-ounce can kidney beans
McCormack's Chili Powder or Gebhardt Chili Powder
Ground cumin
Cocoa powder (Nestlé's or hot chocolate mix will do fine)
Ground cinnamon
Allspice
Garlic powder
Sugar
Salt

1. Chop up the onion and cook for five minutes in a frying pan in olive oil.
2. Add the ground beef and brown thoroughly.
3. In a large pot, put the crushed tomatoes and the kidney beans (drain and wash the beans first).
4. Drain the grease from the meat and onions and then dump the meat into the pot with the sauce.
5. Add 4 tablespoons chili powder, 2 tablespoons ground cumin, 1 teaspoon cocoa powder, 1 teaspoon cinnamon, 1 teaspoon allspice, and 1 teaspoon garlic powder.
6. Cover and simmer on low heat for 90 minutes, stirring occasionally.
7. Add another 2 tablespoons chili powder, 1 tablespoon ground cumin, 1 teaspoon sugar, and 1 teaspoon salt. Simmer uncovered

for 30 minutes, stirring occasionally.
8. Allow to cool for 30 minutes. Then cover and refrigerate.

• FEATURED TRIP •

CRYSTAL COVE STATE PARK
Along the coast, north of Laguna

When Californians think of beach communities, cities such as Santa Monica, Santa Barbara, Laguna, and La Jolla are usually at the top of their list. And for good reason. These tony communities set the standard not just for California, but for much of the nation.

In comparison, there is the tiny village of Crystal Cove. Tucked under the bluffs in Crystal Cove State Park, Crystal Cove is comprised of 45 small beach houses, many of which date back to the 1930s and 1940s. Some of the cottages are in great shape; others look like Moby Dick just spit 'em out. The village is a remnant of old California, when there were miles of undeveloped coastline and living near the beach was accessible to those less than very wealthy.

The cottages are privately owned, but they sit on state parkland—the state purchased Crystal Cove State Park from the privately held Irvine Company in 1979. The state then began terminating the leases on the cottages in 1995, hoping to renovate the houses and rent them to the public for short-term stays.

Not a terrible idea, except that the rentals will be on the pricey side. And, the state has been lollygagging about with their plans; there's a chance some of the cottages may fall into such disrepair that renovation is hopeless. The result has been one hell of a controversy. Our advice: See Crystal Cove sooner instead of later since the state could very well bungle its planned renovation of the village.

The state park encompasses much more than the beach, although the three-mile-long beach is its highlight. The beach sits under bluffs and has some of the best tidepooling in the state. (For more information on tidepooling, please see page 78.)

Just off the beach there is an underwater park, meaning that everything above and below the ocean's surface is protected under state law. To take things a step further, park officials are also building—if that's the right word—an underwater trail around Split Rock, located at the southern boundary of the park. Just so it's clear: Do not attempt to use the underwater trail without scuba equipment.

The Pacific Coast Highway bisects the park, separating the beach and the bluffs from Crystal Cove's considerable backcountry. The backcountry actually has its own parking lots on the inland (east) side of the PCH.

Crystal Cove's most popular hike is the El Moro Canyon Trail. It begins at the El Moro parking area near the rest rooms. From there, the trail gently winds up El Moro Canyon for three miles before terminating at some private property. Along the way, the trail crosses a creek and passes through a beautiful section lined by oaks and sycamores. Hikers can then make their retreat on the El Moro Trail, or turn right and head toward Mono Ridge, which climbs high above El Moro Canyon in a path back toward the sea. This is a longer and more strenuous alternative.

The park is also very popular with

mountain bikers, although many of the trails are short and very steep; the Poles Trail climbs 400 feet in just one-quarter mile. We hiked down it and saw no fewer than five bikers sprawled at various points praying to the gods of oxygen.

Directions: From Laguna Beach drive north on the Pacific Coast Highway (Highway 1) for four miles. For the backcountry parking lot, turn right at the stoplight in front of El Moro School and drive uphill to the visitor center. For beach access, turn left from the PCH into one of the park's beach parking lots. Follow the marked trails to the beach. **Fees:** There's a $5 day-use parking fee. **Maps:** A small map is provided with paid admission. **Pets:** Dogs are not permitted in the park. **Contact:** Crystal Cove State Park, (714) 494-3539. **Locator:** CRYSTAL COVE STATE PARK.

• FEATURED TRIP •

SAILING ORANGE COUNTY
Off Newport Beach

There is a widely held perception that sailing is the domain of only the rich and the very rich. Anyone who has ever been to Newport Beach Harbor in Orange County knows this perception is, in fact, the truth. If you think skiing is expensive . . . you ain't spent nothing yet.

Luckily, there are ways to make the sport a bit more affordable. In sailing's defense, it's a pursuit well worth spending money on. There is no other form of boating like it. Harnessing the wind and using it to good effect is both a physical and intellectual challenge—and it provides a good history lesson, too: sailboats were around 3,000 years before Christ.

Small sailboats can typically be rented for $25 an hour or so at such places as Balboa Boat Rentals in Newport Beach. Patrons will be quizzed on their sailing knowledge. If they don't pass, they don't sail. And the answer is no: We are not going to give you the questions ahead of time.

The most cost-effective way to learn to sail is to take lessons through a local college. Residents of Orange County are particularly lucky because Orange Coast College, located on Newport Bay, has one of the best sailing schools in the country—about 5,000 students take sailing classes at the school each year.

Orange Coast College offers a beginning sailing class for just $85, which includes 20 hours of class time, about 18.5 hours of which is spent on the water. By the end of the class, students should be familiar enough with tacking and jibbing to competently sail a 14-foot dinghy around Newport Harbor. It should be noted that UC Irvine also offers sailing classes through its recreation department.

The next step at Orange Coast is a class titled Intermediate Lidos, in which working the helm and sail trim are stressed. Students can then move up to a series of "shields" classes, to learn how to sail 27- to 30-foot keel boats. Depending on one's previous experience, five or six different classes should get sailors to the point where they can successfully make the 30-mile trip from Newport Harbor to Catalina Island.

For those interested in making longer voyages at sea, learning how to navigate is a must, even in this day of the global positioning system. Orange Coast also offers navigation classes in the evenings. The history of sea navigation is really quite interesting (you'll be fascinated to learn how smart people were a thousand years ago and depressed that you feel so stupid today), and even rudimentary navigational skills are useful if you're interested in astronomy, hang gliding, serious backcountry hiking, or, in particular, learning to fly.

For those who have dreamt of one day sailing around the world, Orange Coast College has four 50-foot-plus sailboats that do just that. Advanced students can take classes to learn how to crew these boats and then sign up for multiweek voyages on the boats; destinations in 1996 included Antarctica, Tahiti, New Zealand, Hawaii, Mexico, the San Juan Islands, Vancouver, and Alaska, to name a few.

No, the trips aren't cheap. Prices range from $795 for a weeklong Newport Beach to San Francisco excursion all the way to $8,250 for a 33-day trip to Antarctica. Yes, it's a lot of money. But you'll probably get a lifetime of stories to tell, and we all know that whoever has the most stories when they go to the Big Harbor in the Sky, wins.

Rentals: Balboa Boat Rentals, Newport Beach, (714) 673-7200. **Sailing lessons:** Orange Coast College Sailing Department, Newport Beach, (714) 645-9412. UC Irvine Recreation Office, (714) 824-5346. **Locator:** NEWPORT BEACH.

• FEATURED TRIP •

SAN JUAN TRAIL
Up and into the Santa Ana Mountains

There are two kinds of mountain bikers. There's the hard core, an admirable species, who likes to punish herself or himself with steep, technical descents and heart-pounding, lung-collapsing ascents. These are the kind of people that are fun to watch on ESPN while eating take-out food.

At the other end of the spectrum is the soft-core mountain biker. This particular breed, of which we claim membership, will often take two cars to a mountain. One vehicle will be left at the bottom of the hill and the other will be used to deliver both rider and bike to the top of the hill. The point of this logistical exercise, of course, is to avoid challenging the more unpleasant symptoms of gravity.

The San Juan Trail in Orange County's Santa Ana Mountains will surely satisfy both lots. If you're one of those mountain bikers who have a taste for mind-bending pain, you can ride 11 miles up the San Juan Trail from the Ortega Highway to Blue Jay Campground, for a gross elevation gain of 2,620 feet. That's a lot. Or, if you're like us, you'll bring two cars, park one at the bottom, and then make the 25-minute or so drive to the top of the mountain.

The San Juan Trail, in terms of length and elevation loss, is one of the great descents in Southern California, along with Noble Canyon (2,600 feet in nine miles) in San Diego County and Sycamore Canyon in Point Mugu State Park (about 1,200 feet over 8.8 miles) in Ventura County. (For more on these two rides, see pages 31 and 202.)

Entirely within the Cleveland National Forest, the San Juan Trail is also one of the more popular rides, too. Check your speed often, as other bikers, hikers, and horseback riders use this single-track trail. Take caution because you'll find plenty of obstacles in your path, including rocks, roots, and patches of slippery decomposed gravel. We hereby order all readers to wear their melon protectors! Why? Once at a wedding reception, Steve sat next to a brain surgeon who told a wonderfully graphic story about a mountain biker who didn't wear his helmet.

The scenery on the San Juan Trail is classic Southern California, that is to say it's mostly sage with a few scattered oaks at the top of the trail (where the elevation is about 3,300 feet). If you feel like taking the ride a couple of times, you can add some variety by turning down the Chiquito Trail (to the left) and then riding about two miles and turning right onto the Viejail Trail, which will take you back to the San Juan Trail.

If you are pushing the envelope, you can make it from top to bottom in half an hour. However, there's a series of switchbacks at the lower part of the mountain, where you should be advised that sometimes the envelope often pushes back.

The San Juan Trail is just one of many trails crossing the mountains in an east-west direction. Other popular trails in the mountains include the Trabuco Canyon fire road and the Santiago Trail. Many routes do not allow for shuttles—meaning bikers have to go uphill before coming back down.

Directions: From San Juan Capistrano take Highway 74 (the Ortega Highway) east for 12 miles. At the San Juan fire station and Forest Service buildings, turn left and continue on a small road for less than a mile to the signed parking area at the trailhead. You can park one car here and continue to Blue Jay Campground by turning left (east) onto Highway 74 and driving for eight miles. At Forest Service Road 6S05, turn left and drive seven miles to the campground. **Note:** Don't park in the campground—you'll be ticketed. Use the small day-use parking lot just before the campground entrance. **Fees:** Purchase a Forest Service Adventure Pass ($5 per day or $30 annually) at ranger stations and most large sporting goods stores. **Maps:** The best map is the Cleveland National Forest map available at ranger stations and most large sporting goods stores. Or mail $4 to the USDA-Forest Service, Attn: Map Room 807, 630 Sansome Street, San Francisco, CA 94111 and ask for the Cleveland National Forest map. **Pets:** Dogs are permitted on the trail. **Contact:** Cleveland National Forest, Trabuco Ranger District, (909) 736-1811. **Locator:** SAN JUAN TRAIL.

• FEATURED TRIP •

PALOMAR MOUNTAIN STATE PARK/ PALOMAR OBSERVATORY

In north San Diego County, at the end of the Pauma Valley

At the junction of Interstate 15 and Highway 76, there's a little tangerine stand off to the side of the road. There's nothing else at this junction—no fast food, strip malls, jumbo gas stations, or truck stops. Just fresh tangerines.

For the next 20 miles, Highway 76 winds westward through the largely undeveloped Pauma Valley, past orange groves and ranchlands, eventually climbing to the point where it sits above the meandering San Luis Rey River. Up ahead stands Palomar Mountain, a 5,000-foot-tall behemoth looming over the valley floor.

The mountain, too, is beautiful and

largely undeveloped. For those living in San Diego or Orange Counties, it's also a perfect place for a weekend camping trip.

Most of the mountain lies within the Cleveland National Forest, with the exception of the Palomar Observatory and Palomar Mountain State Park. We recommend pitching a tent at the park's campground, which is set in a pretty little valley beneath the mountain's western ridge.

At an elevation of 4,700 feet, the campground sits in a forest of live oak, black oak, ponderosa pine, and huge, telephone pole-like incense cedar; some are so big they bring to mind redwood trees. The black oak and the poison oak combine to put on fall colors that are as pretty as can be found anywhere in San Diego County.

The campground isn't very large, with just 31 sites, 11 of which can accommodate RVs. Facilities include fire grills, picnic tables, piped water, flush toilets, and showers. Reservations are recommended on summer weekends, Easter through Halloween, and can be made through PARK.NET at (800) 444-PARK/7275. Fees range from $12 to $16.

One of the reasons the mountain is so lush is that it receives an average of 40 inches of rain per year—more than double the average amount of precipitation either Los Angeles or San Diego gets. A fair share of the precipitation takes the form of snow, which limits camping in the winter when nighttime temperatures routinely dip below freezing. Any time of year, be advised that the weather on Palomar is often totally unrelated to the weather elsewhere in the county.

There's no shortage of things to do on the mountain. The state park has several hiking trails, the nicest of which is called the Scott's Cabin Trail. The trail extends from the Cedar-Doane Trail near three-acre Doane Pond to the park entrance, a distance of approximately two miles. Naturally, Scott's Cabin is long gone. (Note: Doane Pond is the perfect place to take small children fishing since it is stocked regularly with trout. Fishing is catch-and-release only.)

Another trail in the area is a must: the Observatory Trail, which is in the Cleveland National Forest, about a six-mile drive from the state park. The two-mile trail begins near campsite 20 at the Observatory Campground and climbs 800 feet before ending near the Palomar Observatory. A stop at the observatory and its museum is a perfect respite before heading back down the trail.

An absolutely stunning place for a picnic—one of our top 10 places in Southern California—is back near the entrance to the state park. The Silver Crest Picnic Area is set under some spectacularly twisted, almost creepy oak trees. There are plenty of picnic tables scattered around the grove and even some old stone barbecues.

The best part of the picnic area is at its western edge, where a large outcrop of rock provides the perfect place to sit and look out at the length of the Pauma Valley. It's a fine place to watch a sunset, read a book, or enjoy one of the valley's tangerines.

PALOMAR OBSERVATORY

When construction of the Palomar Observatory was completed in 1948, its 200-inch Hale telescope was, at the time, the most powerful in the world. One of the observatory's landmark discoveries was that the universe is expanding.

The observatory is run by the California Institute of Technology and is open to tours. Visitors can look at the Hale telescope but unfortunately can't look through it. There is also a small museum.

The observatory is open from 9 A.M. to 4 P.M. on weekends only, except in July and August when it is open on weekdays from 9 A.M. to 4 P.M. For more information, phone (760) 742-2119.

Directions: From Temecula take Interstate 15 south for 11 miles, exit at Highway 76, and turn left (east). Drive on Highway 76 for 21 miles and then turn left onto County Road S6. Follow County Road S6 for seven miles, twisting and winding up the side of the mountain, and turn left onto County Road S7. Follow the signs for two miles to the entrance to Palomar Mountain State Park. **Fees:** Day-use parking is $5. Pets are $1 extra. **Maps:** The best map of the region is the Cleveland National Forest map, available at ranger stations or most large sporting goods stores. Or mail $4 to USDA-Forest Service, Attn: Map Room 807, 630 Sansome Street, San Francisco, CA 94111 and request the Cleveland National Forest map. **Pets:** Dogs are permitted in the state park campground and picnic areas, but not on any trails in the park. Dogs are permitted on the Observatory Trail and other trails in the Cleveland National Forest. **Biking:** Gravity Activated Sports, located in the town of Pauma Valley, offers guided bike rides down Palomar Mountain to either the Pauma Valley (a 5,000-foot descent in 16 miles) or Borrego Springs in Anza-Borrego Desert State Park (a 3,700-foot descent in 12 miles). The outfitter supplies the bikes, lunch, a support van, and a guided tour of the top of the mountain before the descent. For more information, phone (800) 985-4427. **Contact:** Palomar Mountain State Park, (760) 742-3462. **Locator:** PALOMAR MOUNTAIN STATE PARK.

• FEATURED TRIP •

CUYAMACA RANCHO STATE PARK

In the mountains beyond San Diego

Lord only knows what the wildlife was thinking. There we were, sitting on a bed of pine needles, admiring a rather stunning view of Rancho Cuyamaca State Park, when we fell asleep.

It was only 4 P.M. and it hadn't been that long of a day. Accompanied by our pal San Diego Mike, we had left San Diego about 10 A.M. ("early starts" is more a theory than a reality when it comes to us) and had arrived at the park in 90 minutes. It took another five minutes to register for a primitive campsite at Arroyo Seco in the park's backcountry. But before strapping on our backpacks, our stomachs kicked in with a request for lunch. So instead of huffing off to camp, we walked down to the Green Valley Picnic Area.

A short trail led us down to the Sweetwater River, which is really a small stream. The Sweetwater is lined with huge boulders, which serve grandly as substitute picnic tables. On a sunny rock, and with the sound of running water providing a backdrop, we munched our salami sandwiches. It took us about three seconds to decide this is one of the top 10 picnic spots in Southern California.

We left our car at the nearby Arroyo Seco Picnic Area and began our short hike to the campground on the Arroyo Seco fire road. The road dipped and went uphill a bit in places, but was never steep (thankfully). The scenery was drop-dead gorgeous as we passed through one bucolic meadow after another.

Most of Cuyamaca Rancho State Park is at an elevation over 4,000 feet—and we were seeing perfect evidence of it here. There were boulders, pines, manzanitas, oaks, and chaparral. The landscape even had a quasi-Sierra feel to it; we never expected to find this type of terrain this far south. We were even more shocked to learn that it snows at Cuyamaca most winters. (Cuyamaca means "the place where it rains." And snows, too, when it's chilly enough out. The park has a couple of snow play areas along Highway 79, which means it's toboggan time. Phone the park to check snow conditions before heading up from San Diego.)

After determining that we had the campground to ourselves—it was late March—we decided to occupy a group site set under a huge oak tree and half-surrounded by an rocky outcrops. On the other side of the rocks were a shallow ravine and trickling creek. The giant boulders were great to scramble around on. One huge boulder actually had the branch of an oak tree growing into it. How often is it possible to climb a rock and a tree at the same time?

Our only complaints: A pit toilet promised in the park brochure was nowhere to be found and campfires were not allowed—a common restriction in much of Southern California's backcountry. We had brought along a couple of small camping stoves, but a fire would have been enjoyable, especially that night, when the thermometer bottomed out at 34 degrees.

Back at Arroyo Seco, we set up our camp and took the usual inventory of things we had forgotten ("Hey, where's the can opener?") before heading up Airplane Ridge, where we sat down and looked east at the distant hills of the Cleveland National Forest. It was such a tranquil scene that all three of us fell asleep, right there along the trail. It's almost a shame no other hikers came upon the three sprawled bodies on the trail—it probably would have provided some talk around the campfire.

After dinner that night, we went for another hike to a nearby meadow. Up in the sky we found the comet Hyakutake. Even with a bright three-quarter moon, the comet and its tail could be seen clearly through binoculars.

We stayed in that meadow for a very long time, lying on our backs and staring at the heavens above. Nearby, some owls were hooting up a storm, either laughing at us shivering, happy humans or maybe enjoying the comet's spectacle, too.

Camping

Backpackers have two primitive campgrounds to choose from. In addition to Arroyo Seco, there is also a small primitive camp at Granite Springs on the park's eastern side. This camp is slightly higher, at 4,850 feet, and is also farther in, requiring a 4.5-mile hike on the East Mesa Trail. Campsites at both locations are available on a first-come, first-served basis year-round.

If you aren't into backpacking, the park has two fine drive-in campgrounds. The Green Valley Campground is near the Arroyo Seco trailhead. The Paso Picacho Campground is four miles north of the visitor center on Highway 79. Both have flush toilets, showers, charcoal grills, picnic tables, and a dump station for RVs. Paso Picacho, in particular, was one of the prettiest campgrounds we've seen in Southern California. Hint: Sites 41 through 45 are very nice, located on the campground's backside.

Drive-in campsites at Green Valley and Paso Picacho can be reserved by phoning PARK.NET at (800) 444-PARK/7275. Fees range from $12 to $14 per night. Dogs are $1 extra.

Lake Cuyamaca

Cuyamaca is a pleasant little lake, located on the park's northern boundary at an elevation of 4,620 feet. The main activity is fishing, with trout and bass the primary targets. A marina there rents out canoes and small motorboats. If you're going camping at the park, absolutely bring your pole and fishing license—dinner could be lurking in the lake.

Directions: From downtown San Diego take Interstate 8 east for 35 miles, exiting at Highway 79 north. Drive seven miles on Highway 79 to the entrance to the Green Valley Picnic Area and the Arroyo Seco Trail. To reach the camp visitor center, continue north on Highway 79 for two miles.
Fees: Day-use parking is $5. Primitive camping fees are $3 per person per night. **Maps:** An adequate map of hiking trails can be purchased at the visitor center for $1. A better map, also for sale at the center, is the Tom Harrison Cartography map of the state park. **Pets:** Dogs are permitted only in the developed drive-in campgrounds and picnic areas but must be leashed.

Special note: Mountain lions have been seen in this park, and a woman who was hiking alone here was killed by a mountain lion in 1994. Don't panic, be sensible, don't hike alone, and keep your children or dogs with you at all times. **Contact:** Cuyamaca Rancho State Park, (760) 765-0755. **Locator:** CUYAMACA RANCHO STATE PARK.

Gut Check

Try the seven-mile round-trip hike on the Lookout Trail from Paso Picacho Campground to the top of 6,512-foot-tall Cuyamaca Peak. The hike features an elevation gain of 1,700 feet, but should be manageable for those in decent shape. Needless to say, the views of the surrounding Cleveland National Forest are stunning.

• FEATURED TRIP •

Anza-Borrego Desert State Park
East of San Diego

In the middle of a hot March afternoon, our first impression of the desert town of Borrego Springs was "why?" Why put this town in the middle of a vast wasteland of dirt and rock? Why would anyone want to live here, baking day after day under a blistering sun?

The desert is a tricky place, not easily loved (read your Edward Abbey), a place where there is always more than meets the eye. For example, the park ranger at Anza-Borrego's visitor center will tell the average sweat-stained visitor that the park has only one "developed" trail nearby. But when the visitor shows a gleam in the eye and a willingness to explore—boom!—the ranger soon starts pointing out all the casual, often unmarked footpaths around the park.

The best desert trails, in our view, wind through narrow canyons where anything seems possible. Rock is fabulously twisted, as is the light. Even when the canyons have been explored—and most of them have—it's hard not to feel like the first person to ever set foot within.

One of our favorite hikes begins in the easy-to-miss parking lot for Calcite Mine, which can be found on the left side of County Road S22, just a mile before the microwave relay tower. The parking area, a generous term, holds only four or five cars max. A small signpost has a few paragraphs on the history of Calcite Mine. Most people pull over, read it, retreat to their cars, and drive on.

Don't let that be you. Hike down to the canyon floor on the 4x4 unpaved road to the left of the signpost. In five minutes, you're on the canyon floor, in a badlands of sandstone carved by water, eroded by wind, and perfected by the ages. Most people continue back up the other side of the road to the mine, which really isn't much to see. We recommend staying put and exploring the canyon floor.

The canyon runs east-west alongside County Road S22 and is used by four-wheel-drive vehicles occasionally—thus the sandy off-road trail running down the middle of the canyon floor. We recommend hiking to the left (west).

Down in the canyon, the sun beats down hard—even on this day in March the heat was relentless. Sunglasses, a baseball cap or bandanna, and extra water are absolute necessities. It doesn't take long to begin feeling grubby and sweaty, like a desert rat, as Edward Abbey used to write.

We found the first side canyon about 10 minutes after reaching the canyon floor. On the left was a 20-foot-long outcrop of rock. On the right was a very green, very short fern. Just past the fern and—ta da!—a very obvious foot trail splits off to the right.

At first the canyon was about 10 feet wide. We brushed our hands up against the sandstone and it literally turned back into sand and crumbled to the ground. We knocked on the sandstone, which responded with a hollow sound because it is porous—so porous, in fact, it soaks up most of the sound in the canyon, making things eerily quiet.

Soon, the canyon narrowed to about five feet and then began winding and twisting its way back toward the Santa Rosa Mountains. The canyon walls gradually grew taller. Smaller side canyons split off from both sides of the canyon, many of them leading deeper into the badlands. Most of these canyons come to dead ends, with inclines too steep to navigate.

The narrow canyons, formed and polished by flash floods, appear sculpted. One ended in a small cave. Down on our hands and knees, we peered into the cave and saw a spider's web that looked as if it was spun of heavy-duty thread. We decided not to enter the cave.

Desert canyons are like Oreo cookies. You can't have just one. Returning to the main canyon floor, we backtracked to the east, passing the 4x4 road where we entered the canyon. Again, more twisty canyons below the mine were found. At one point the canyon narrowed to the point where it was only large enough for one person to pass through.

By the time we returned to our car at the Calcite Mine turnoff, the sun was beginning to set. The badlands and the many canyons seemed to take the sun's rays and twist them into more shades of red than are imaginable. We sat on the hood of the car and gave serious thought to hiking back in. We were hot, we smelled, we were sunburned, we were desert rats. And like all good desert rats, we just wanted to head back down into the earth, where the desert never fails to answer the question "why?"

More Canyons to Roam

Just across County Road S22 is another network of badlands leading east to the Ocotillo Recreation Area; if the off-roaders aren't out in force, there is great hiking down here.

Bow Willow Canyon and Carrizo Canyon are two of many canyons worth hiking in the Carrizo Badlands, located in the southern section of the park. Both can be accessed from County Road S2—get a map of the state park and check canyon conditions with the rangers. The popular Rockhouse Canyon splits off from Carrizo Canyon.

Another nearby canyon worth checking out is Canyon Sin Nombre. The trailhead is about half a mile north of the Carrizo Badlands Overlook, also on County Road S2.

Near the visitor center in Borrego Springs is the trailhead to Cougar Canyon, which has a year-round stream. The historic Anza Trail follows the creek and is one of the few green spots in the park. The trailhead to the canyon is three miles from the Desert Gardens Picnic Area. Be warned, past the picnic area you should have four-wheel drive to continue any farther.

Wildflowers

Each spring, wildflower enthusiasts flock to Anza-Borrego for the annual bloom. The rainbow of colors includes yellow dandelions, white primrose and lily, purple verbena, red monkey flower, and scarlet ocotillo.

The problem, of course, is that the bloom can be unpredictable. The best wildflower blooms are preceded by rainy winters. Typically, the bloom begins at the lower elevations anywhere from late February through April.

For information, call the park's wildflower hotline: (760) 767-4684. Or send a self-addressed and stamped postcard to the park. About two weeks before peak bloom hits, you'll get the card in the mail. The address: WILDFLOWERS, Anza-Borrego Desert State Park, Box 299, Borrego Springs, CA 92004-0299.

Camping

As far as developed campgrounds go, your choice is limited to either Borrego Palm Canyon, near the visitor center, or Tamarisk Grove, 13 miles from the visitor center. Both have trees, which means shade. Both also have fire grills, picnic tables, piped water, flush toilets, and showers. Both camps are better suited for RVs. Both also fill up quickly on the weekends from October through May; for reservations, phone PARK.NET at (800) 444-PARK/7275. Fees are $16 on weekends, $15 on weekdays.

The park has several primitive campgrounds for backpackers. Culp Valley is at an elevation of 3,400 feet, set in the midst of a spectacular boulder field high above the desert floor. It's free with no amenities—fires are not permitted. The adventuresome would probably enjoy a night here. The Reluctant Camper would not.

Lodging

The village of Borrego Springs, located in the center of the park, has two motels and a hotel. We recommend either the more upscale La Casa Del Zorro Resort Hotel [Phone: (800) 824-1884] or the more modest Palm Canyon Resort Motel [Phone: (760) 767-5341].

One other option may be to stay in the charming little town of Julian, which is about 30 miles from Borrego Springs. Julian is known for its apples—every apple by-product on Earth can be purchased here. The Julian Lodge is a reasonable little motel along the town's main strip; phone (760) 765-1420.

A recommendation for visitors to Julian: Hit one of the bakeries for coffee and apple pie à la mode for breakfast. Talk about a pre-hike caffeine and sugar rush.

Directions: From San Diego to the park's visitor center, take Interstate 8 east to Highway 67 north, then drive 25 miles to the junction with Highway 78 east. Follow Highway 78 for 40 miles and turn left on County Road S3 (Yaqui Pass Road). Continue seven miles on County Road S3 and turn left on Borrego Springs Road. Drive for five miles to the traffic circle and turn left onto County Road S22 (Palm Canyon Road). Proceed one mile to the visitor center. From the visitor center to Calcite Mine, take County Road S22 (Palm Canyon Road) east for 19 miles. There is a small parking area for Calcite Mine on the left side of the road by a bulletin board—about one mile before the microwave tower. **Fees:** Entrance is free. **Maps:** A park service map can be purchased at the visitor center for $1. USGS topographic maps are also sold there. **Pets:** Dogs are permitted in the campgrounds, but not on the trails. Because of the heat and sun, this is a lousy place to bring your dog any time of year. **Best time to visit:** November through April. Expect triple digit temperatures on a daily basis from June through September, when you're better off going elsewhere. **Contact:** Anza-Borrego Desert State Park general information, (760) 767-5311. Visitor Center, (760) 767-4205. Wildflower hotline, (760) 767-4684. **Locator:** ANZA-BORREGO DESERT STATE PARK.

• FEATURED TRIP •

SAN DIEGO DEEP-SEA FISHING
Where the big fish lurk

All the world is not a stage, but all the world is, in certain parts of San Diego, a really big fish story. Whether it's a man bragging about the price of his new BMW or a starlet bragging about the size of her Demi Moores, it's all but a twist on the guy with his arms outstretched claiming "it was this big . . . really."

Want to hear a real fish story, fresh from the waters off San Diego? Here goes. One day, a mako shark is dragged aboard a party boat. One of the crew, a man named Doug Reed, cuts off the shark's head, as is usually done, and leaves the head on the boat's floor. One hour later, Reed picks up the head and it bites him. Reed even has the requisite scars on his hand to prove it.

Another one of Reed's stories: A woman from Oklahoma, who has never been deep-sea fishing before, catches a 46-pound halibut. The fish is pulled on board, where it flops around the deck. Its brutally sharp teeth snap like the monster in the film *Alien*. One of Reed's crewmates jumps on top of the fish and wrestles it into submission as the fish chews on his beard.

Next to south Florida, San Diego has some of the best deep-sea fishing in America. Why? Fish are cold-blooded creatures and thus crave warm water. It just happens that the water is nice and warm off Baja California, Mexico, to the south of San Diego. This puts large numbers of game fish within reach of San Diego's fleet of deep-sea charters.

Most half-day or full-day charters from San Diego stay within American waters. Fish caught during these trips include albacore, yellowtail, barracuda, rockfish, sheepshead, and calico bass. For those willing to take a longer trip deeper into Mexican waters, the variety of game fish increases to marlin, tuna, wahoo, grouper, and skipjack.

Want to know how good the fishing is? A gentleman aboard a Fisherman's Landing boat caught a world-record 395-pound tuna. In one recent issue of *Fishing and Hunting News*, there's a photo of a honeymooner posing next to the 300-pound blue marlin he just caught. On the preceding page is a photo of an angler out of San Diego standing with his shirt off, a 115-pound yellowfin tuna on one side and a 110-pound yellowfin on the other. That's what is commonly referred to as a Kodak Moment.

Anyone looking to pick a fight with a fish may just find it in the waters off San Diego. When these fish hit, it feels like a jet ski has grabbed the line and is running away at top speed. Those who don't react quickly and get the fish's head pointed at the boat are in for a long, and possibly losing, battle. Once a fish—even a three- or four-pound barracuda—gets its powerful tail pointed at you, it's like trying to catch a torpedo.

The trips work like this: Most of the large charter operations typically run both a morning and afternoon half-day trip, as well as a twilight run, which typically lasts about four to five hours. Most half-day trips are to local waters—one popular destination is the kelp beds just off Point Loma. Prices generally range from $20 to $30 per person.

Three-quarter day trips usually leave early in the morning and return 12 hours later. The chief advantage is that the boats have time to work southward toward the Coronado Islands. The price range is usually $40 to $60 per person. Full-day trips are even better. You board late at night and the boat departs. By the time passengers wake up the next morning, the boats are usually well into Mexican waters, looking for whatever it is they want to catch. The price range for these trips is $80 to $100 per person.

Those hoping to increase the odds of catching a monster fish should go on an extended cruise to Mexican waters. All the party boats offer private charters (very expensive) or mini-long range cruises in the $200 to $400 price range. Meals are usually included, as are bunk fees.

All deep-sea charters rent equipment, although some do charge for hooks; when making a reservation ask about this because finding a charter that will throw in all the tackle for free is a good way to save a few bucks. The crews aboard these boats are almost always very helpful because the boats need repeat business. Some of the charters will even clean your fish for free (patrons should always tip these guys). Other nominal fees that are sometimes tacked on are Mexican fishing licenses (if fishing in Mexican waters) and fuel surcharges. Ask ahead of time or be caught with your wallet out.

Good luck and may the fish be with you.

Deep-Sea Charters

Fisherman's Landing, San Diego Harbor, (619) 222-0391.

H&M Landing, San Diego Bay, reservations/information, (619) 222-1144; Daily catch report, (619) 224-2800.

Helgren's Oceanside & Islands Sportfishing Trips, Oceanside, (760) 722-2133.

Point Loma Sportsfishing, San Diego Bay, (619) 223-1627.

Seaforth Sportfishing, Mission Bay, reservations/information, (619) 224-3383; Daily catch report, (619) 224-6695.

• FEATURED TRIP •

San Diego Hot Air Balloons

Up, up, and away . . .

"So, you wouldn't happen to know any of those nuts who bungee-jump from hot air balloons?"

John Arnott smiled at the question. Sitting in the lobby of A Skysurfer Balloon Company in Del Mar on a sunny March day, Arnott appeared to be the definition of mellow. Slightly sunburned face, casually gray hair, the kind of guy who seems like he should be exactly what he is: an accomplished hot air balloon pilot.

"Some of my friends were into that," said Arnott. "In fact, I even did it once. I was terrified. I closed my eyes the whole way down. I wouldn't even dive. I held onto the cord in a standing-up position."

Even worse—if that's possible—the hot air balloon from which Arnott jumped was only 400 or so feet off the ground. The bungee cord was about 250 feet long. Instead of a merely harrowing jump into a river, as is often the goal in bungee jumping, Arnott and his buddies were intentionally trying to simulate a free fall from a hot air balloon to the ground.

We tell this anecdote for one purpose: To prove there are a lot of people out there who enjoy performing the macarena with the Grim Reaper as their dance partner.

On a much lighter note, hot air ballooning (in which passengers are highly encouraged to stay in the basket) is the big thing in Del Mar. The only horrifying thing about it is the price tag, which is typically anywhere from $100 to $150 per passenger, depending on the particular company.

Del Mar is a magnet for hot air balloons because of its great weather and the wide-open terrain to the east. Most balloon rides begin near the coast and then use the steady winds coming in from the ocean to propel them eastward, roughly following the San Dieguito River inland toward the town of Rancho Santa Fe, a distance of five miles, depending on the flight plan.

Typically, hot air balloon rides are offered both the hour after sunrise and the hour before sunset. People intent on photographing the coastline should take the morning flights, when the sun is at their backs. The sunset flights, as might be expected, offer incredible views with the bonus that you might actually be awake enough to enjoy it. Whatever riders do, they shouldn't forget cameras and plenty of film. According to Arnott, hot air balloons are the most photographed objects in the world. We have no evidence to dispute him.

Our friend Mike Zacchino, a San Diego native, recently took a ride in a balloon and reports: "Taking off was like being shot out of a cannon. One minute, you are standing in this tiny little basket, chatting to someone standing outside the basket. And then the pilot fires it up, the gorillas let go of the basket, and you're off like a bullet."

Balloon rides with four to eight passengers usually last about an hour. The rides are incredibly smooth because the baskets are very well balanced—in fact, hot air balloons are so stable they can actually bump against one another while in flight (called "kissing"), with no ill effects. Riders in balloons don't feel a breeze either, which makes sense—the balloon is moving the same speed as the wind. In fact, the only air movement passengers feel is when the pilot fires up the propane jets, which fills the balloon with the hot air that makes it rise.

Maybe the most amazing aspect of the ride is the sound. When the jets aren't being fired, the hot air balloon is a totally silent creature. Even at elevations of 4,000 or 5,000 feet, people and dogs on the ground can be heard talking and barking as the balloon flies over neighborhoods. Sound travels in all directions—when it travels straight up, there is nothing to disperse or interfere with the sound waves.

Most of the balloon companies offer champagne while in flight, a nice touch. Some of the charters ask passengers to help in both the set-up and tear-down of the balloon, which we recommend: it adds time to the experience and makes you feel like you're involved, even if you have no idea what you're doing.

BALLOON RIDE ALTERNATIVES

There are a couple of exceptional balloon rides worth noting. Sunrise Balloons, out of Temecula, takes passengers for rides over Anza-Borrego Desert State Park, whereas California Dreamin' Balloon Adventures, out of Palomar Airport in Carlsbad, offers rides near Palomar Mountain. Both Anza-Borrego and Palomar Mountain are nothing short of spectacular when viewed with one's feet planted firmly on the ground; from up above, well, let your imagination run with that for a while.

SAN DIEGO HOT AIR BALLOON CHARTERS

A Beautiful Morning, Del Mar, (619) 481-6225 or (800) 503-9901.

A Skysurfer Balloon Company, Del Mar, (619) 481-6800 or (800) 660-6809.

Balloon Flights, San Diego, (800) 558-5828.

California Dreamin' Balloon Adventures, Carlsbad, (760) 438-9550 or (800) 373-3359.

Sunrise Balloons, Temecula, (800) 548-9912.

HOW TO BECOME A PILOT

People interested in learning how to pilot a hot air balloon first need to take lessons from a pilot licensed by the Federal Aviation Administration. Virtually all pilots charge upwards of $100 an hour for these lessons.

Another way to learn is to volunteer to be on a hot air balloon company's crew. The pay is either zero or nominal, but volunteers learn a lot about ballooning and make good contacts within the ballooning community. Later, work could be exchanged for lessons, or perhaps a pilot will give a student a discount.

• FEATURED TRIP •

TORREY PINES STATE RESERVE
North of La Jolla, along the coast

A warning to any readers who happen to be botanists: The following will probably be offensive.

Torrey Pines State Reserve exists for one simple reason: To ensure the survival of the Torrey pine tree, the rarest of all pines in the United States. Although the Torrey pine was once found throughout Southern California, the trees have since fallen victim to urban development, insect infestation, wind, and pollution. The Torrey pine's habitat today consists of the reserve and Santa Rosa Island of Channel Islands National Park.

What does the Torrey pine look like? Imagine the average pine tree. Now, imagine the same tree after being sat upon by the Jolly Green Giant. That's a Torrey pine.

How seeing the Torrey pine up close and personal will float one's boat is to be determined. About all that we can tell you is that the Torrey pine, while an admirable species for its perseverance, doesn't quite leave one quaking in one's boots. We've seen the giant sequoia, and the Torrey pine is no giant sequoia.

But the reserve as a whole is out of this world. The entrance to the park leads straight to the mile-long beach, which sits under a tall sandstone. Up on top of the bluff is a rolling coastal landscape made up of a few scattered groves of the Torrey pines, chaparral, and other native plant species, such as the colorful monkey flower. Throughout the bluffs are a series of wide trails, two of which lead down to the beach and the ocean.

The Guy Fleming Trail, a two-thirds mile loop, features the most trees along with a nice walk along the top of the cliff with some stunning ocean views (something the reserve has no shortage of). The trailhead can be found alongside the road leading from the beach to the visitor center. There is a small parking lot on the right side of the road. If it's full, park at the visitor center and walk back down the road.

The Beach Trail leaves from behind the rest rooms that are located across the road from the visitor center. On the way down, turn right onto the Red Butte Trail, which travels to sculpted red sandstone that looks like the kind of mesa that might be found in Colorado. From Red Butte, the Beach Trail then switchbacks its way down the hill into a canyon before spilling onto the beach.

What's there to do once on the beach? Enjoy the sandstone cliffs, which appear artistic in their detail. Flat Rock, at the bottom of the Beach and the Broken Hill Trails, makes for great tidepooling. It's one of those beaches that's nice to take a walk; outstanding scenery is on either side.

In fact, we'd say the reserve features scenery so fine that it draws comparisons to Montana de Oro State Park, located over 200 miles to the north. Of course, most of the land in between Montana de Oro and Torrey Pines is either privately held, overdeveloped, or has the Pacific Coast Highway practically sitting upon the sand.

This reserve, just 10 minutes from San Diego, is the exception.

The reason? A funny-looking pine tree that just doesn't know how to give up.

Directions: From downtown San Diego take Interstate 5 north to Carmel Valley Road, exiting and turning left. Follow the road for 1.4 miles and turn left at County Road S21. Continue to the entrance to the reserve, on the right. **Fees:** Parking is $4. There is some free parking available on Torrey Pines Road, just north of the beach. **Maps:** A trail map is provided with paid admission to the reserve. **Pets:** Dogs are not permitted anywhere in the reserve. **Contact:** Torrey Pines State Reserve, (619) 755-2063. **Locator:** TORREY PINES STATE RESERVE.

• FEATURED TRIP •

SAILBOARDING MISSION BAY
North of downtown San Diego

The exceedingly well-organized recreation area at Mission Bay covers 4,600 acres and has a bit of everything: over 20 miles of beaches; trails for walkers, bikers, and bladers; and fantastic picnic lawns, fishing, sailing, and powerboating—in addition to several marinas, hotels, restaurants, and the infamous Sea World. If you wanted to paint yourself purple with white polka dots and stand on your head chanting "I am the egg man," well, the bay probably has an area for that, too.

On top of all this, Mission Bay is also known as the premier sailboarding spot in Southern California. As the inland valleys east of San Diego heat up each day, they begin to suck cool air in from the ocean. These prevailing winds usually hit Mission Bay in the afternoon and, like cuckoos on a cuckoo clock, the sailboarders come out in force.

"These guys want to go anywhere where there's wind," says Filipe Mesquita of CP Watersports, which offers sailboarding rentals and lessons in Mission Bay. "That's why they all go to the Columbia River Gorge. There's always great, strong winds there. Of course, there's all those barges in the river, too. That's why if you eat it up there and one of those barges is coming, well, you could be in trouble."

There are no such barges in Mission Bay. Unfortunately, there's just one other problem with sailboarding here: The sport, no matter where practiced, is difficult. One of our pals, *New York Newsday* writer Kelly Whiteside, once took a lesson in Hawaii and provides two tips: "One, never take a lesson when there are two good-looking surfers watching you and, two, consider learning how to jet ski instead."

How's that for a bit of encouragement, eh? The good thing about Mission Bay is that much of its water is protected from ocean waves and winds, which will make it much easier to learn. It also helps to take a lesson in the morning when the winds are usually calm, thus giving an advantage to the novice.

Of course, all novice sailboarders must take a lesson. CP Watersports, which is located in a small booth behind the San Diego Hilton in Mission Bay, offers a three-hour lesson for $50, as good a deal as you'll find. Anyone who can grasp the basics in three hours and manage a couple of turns without falling has done better than one of us.

Here are a few more tips: It helps to weigh over 110 pounds and to have an average amount of strength. Take lessons only on a beginner's board; it floats and is much longer and wider than an advanced board, which does not float. Beginners should use a small sail—something in the range of 3.5 square meters. Advanced sailboarders use larger sails to grab more wind. A beginner who grabs too much wind is a beginner going into the drink.

Beginner's boards also have footstraps, thus making it a little easier to stand up. It's easy to think the boom will provide something to hold on to, but the boom isn't stationary—it moves in every direction, often taking the sailboarder with it.

The general idea on a sailboard is to always keep the sail at a 90-degree angle to the wind; the fin on the bottom of the board then takes that wind and converts it to forward motion. Many people can learn to sail in a straight line without too much difficulty. The problems begin with tacking and beating.

Tacking is turning the board around. Without tacking, the novice sailboarder must place a humiliating collect phone call to the rental agency, reporting that she or he is stuck at the other end of Mission Bay.

Beating is sailing at a slight angle to a wind trying to push you away. Typically, learning how to beat is synonymous with falling and then having to remount the board. "Eighty percent of a beginner's energy is spent getting the board back upright and getting back on the board," says Filipe. "The most important thing I tell beginners is that if you feel like you're losing it, don't try to hold the sail. Instead, drop to your knees on the board and make sure you don't fall. Once you've regained your balance you can always get the sail back."

In three hours, a beginning windsurfer might begin to put everything together—the balance of staying on the board and manipulating the wind. Even if you spend the day serving as entertainment for beachgoers, surfers, picnickers, kite fliers, and hotel guests, at least you tried to be cool.

Directions: From downtown San Diego to CP Watersports, take Interstate 5 north for four miles and exit at Friars Road, turning left. Take Friars Road and turn right at Sea World Drive. Drive one block to East Mission Bay Drive and turn left. Drive about one mile to the Hilton hotel and park on the street. CP Watersports is on the bay behind the hotel. To reach the Dana Inn & Marina location, turn left on Sea World Drive. Continue to Ingraham Street and turn right. Continue to the entrance to Dana Inn & Marina, which will be on the left.
Fees: CP Watersports charges $50 for a three-hour lesson and $30 for a one-hour lesson. If you already know how to windsurf, you can rent a beginner's sailboard for $15 an hour/$45 for four hours or an advanced board for $20 per hour/$50 for four hours. If you have your own sailboard, day use of the beach is free. **Contact:** CP Watersports at the San Diego Hilton, (619) 275-8945 or (619) 276-4010 extension 2945. CP Watersports at Dana Inn & Marina, (619) 226-8611.
Locator: MISSION BAY.

SAILING

San Diego is one of the sailing capitals of the United States. Here are just a few places to rent sailboats in the San Diego area:

Action Sports Beach and Bay Rentals, Coronado, (619) 424-4466.

Bahia Resort Hotel Marina, Mission Bay, (619) 488-0551.

Campland, Mission Bay, (619) 581-4224.

Coronado Boat Rental, Coronado, (619) 437-1514.

CP Watersports (in the San Diego Hilton), Mission Bay, (619) 276-4010.

Mission Bay Sportscenter, Mission Bay, (619) 488-1004.

• FEATURED TRIP •

BATES NUTS FARM'S GREAT PUMPKINS
Near Escondido

This is a true story. A few years back a man brings his family to the Bates Nuts Farm near Escondido, hoping to purchase one of the farm's gigantic pumpkins. Out in the pumpkin patch, he picks out a real prize—a pumpkin that weighs more than 50 pounds. The pumpkin is so big he needs a wheelbarrow to carry it to his car.

Unfortunately, the unloading doesn't go quite as smoothly as the loading. When the man gets home, the pumpkin is dropped. It rolls down the driveway and into the street. Luckily, nothing is in the pumpkin's way, so there is no swath of destruction. But the pumpkin is utterly destroyed—imagine 50 pounds of orange glop—and the man, with his crying children in tow, drives all the way back to the farm to buy another huge pumpkin.

Come October, the Bates Nuts Farm sells pumpkins. A lot of pumpkins. On a typical weekday, anywhere from 500 to 1,000 schoolchildren may visit the farm to pick out a jack-o'-lantern. "It's just one school bus after another," says one of the farm's employees.

The pumpkins are popular, but they are not grown at the farm, which doesn't have enough land to grow ordinary, everyday pumpkins. Instead, the farm reserves its pumpkin patches for the "Big Macs," a strain of pumpkin that grows anywhere from 20 pounds to well over 100 pounds. Very impressive. (Just in case you're wondering, the world record is a 1,061-pounder, grown by the husband and wife team of Nathan and Paula Zehr of Lowville, New York, in 1996.)

How popular are the big pumpkins at the Bates Nuts Farm? Very. On the first weekend of October, when the farm usually opens the pumpkin patch for public harvest, so many people descend upon the place that the farm has a fleet of 75 wheelbarrows to help pickers get the pumpkins from the pumpkin patch into their cars. The larger pumpkins are usually knee-high and fat—really fat.

If you want a truly big pumpkin, follow the rules of fishing: The early bird gets the worm. And don't forget to stop at the cash machine. The farm charges 20 cents per pound for the huge pumpkins, meaning that a 150-pounder will put a $30 dent in your wallet. Is it worth it?

"They do make good conversation pieces," says Walter Bates, the third generation in his family to work the farm.

Directions: From San Diego, take Interstate 15 north for 33 miles, exit at County Road S6, and turn right. Drive for seven miles (County Road S6 will become Valley Center Road) and turn right on Wood Valley Road. Drive three miles to the farm, which will be on the left. **Fees:** Admission to the farm is free, but you do have to pay for pumpkins. **Pets:** Not permitted. **Contact:** Bates Nuts Farm, (619) 749-3333. **Locator:** BATES NUTS FARM.

• FEATURED TRIP •

IMPERIAL SAND DUNES
Along the Imperial Valley

The Imperial Sand Dunes are the largest network of dunes in the state, 40 miles in length, extending along the eastern edge of the Imperial Valley.

Once upon a time, in 1911, builders constructed a road made of elevated wooden planks. The road was only wide enough to accommodate one vehicle, so wooden turnouts were built to allow passing. Nowadays Interstate 8 cuts across the southernmost section of the dunes.

The dunes are best known for the tens of thousands of off-highway vehicle enthusiasts who flock to the site. As you might have guessed, the OHVs tear the place apart and the drivers manage to maim themselves in a variety of accidents (some of which are alcohol related). The BLM is in charge of the place, and the OHV lobby has worked hard to keep two-thirds of the dunes open to the off-roaders.

Hikers are best off in the Algodones Outstanding Natural Area, which is closed to off-roaders. There are plenty of dunes to climb within the natural area, also located near the Cahuilla Ranger Station.

Directions: From San Diego take Interstate 8 east for 113 miles and exit to Highway 86 north. Drive 14 miles and turn right onto Highway 78. Take Highway 78 for 25 miles. After crossing the Old Coachella Canal, the ranger station access road will be on the right. **Fees:** Access is free. **Pets:** Pets are permitted, but this is not a good place for pooches. **Contact:** Bureau of Land Management, California Desert District, (909) 697-5200. **Locator:** IMPERIAL SAND DUNES.

24
RESOURCES

• HOT TIPS •

**GETTING HOME IN
  ONE PIECE** 288
**PHOTOGRAPHING THE
  OUTDOORS** 295
OUTDOOR GIFT IDEAS 297

• RESOURCES •

**WILDERNESS AND
  ADVENTURE TRAINING** 299
**PARKS, PRESERVES, AND
  FORESTS** 303
PROTECTING THE WILDERNESS ... 306

• HOT TIPS •

GETTING HOME IN ONE PIECE

Here is our first rule of the great outdoors: All outdoor activities are greatly enhanced by arriving home either alive or with most, if not all, of your body parts in functioning order.

California, of course, offers an unparalleled variety of ways to put you in the hospital. Without going into great detail, drowning, hypothermia, heatstroke, altitude sickness, and snake bites are just a few of the threats to your health.

The good news is that almost every accident is preventable. It's just a matter of being prepared.

THE 10 ESSENTIALS

It's the nicest day of the year. Sunny skies, 70 degrees, not a trouble in the world . . . until someone sprains an ankle five miles from the trailhead and—surprise—it starts to rain. Making matters worse, it gets cold and dark.

There's an endless variety of ways hikers have had to spend an unplanned night in the backcountry. Although it may not be your idea of fun, such a night can be easily survived—if you just come prepared with the essentials. All of the following can easily fit inside a daypack or large fanny pack:

1. Extra food and water. A few Power Bars or candy bars will do. Don't hit the trail for a day hike without at least two quarts of water per person.

2. Medicine kit. It doesn't have to be a portable hospital, but the kit should include extra-strength pain reliever (because there's nothing worse than an altitude-related headache or surprise migraine), an antibiotic cream, rubbing alcohol, cotton balls, moleskin (for blisters), gauze and tape, scissors, tweezers, and an elastic bandage. It also doesn't hurt to have iodine (available at most high-end sporting goods stores), which can be used to kill bacteria in streamwater.

3. Waterproof matches in a waterproof container. It's also a good idea to have a tube of fire starter, as well as several long-burning candles.

4. A trail map waterproofed in plastic—a ziplock sandwich bag will do.

5. Compass. Sign up for a navigation course at a sporting goods store and learn how to use the compass and read topographic maps. It sounds dorky, but the best way not to get lost is to know where you are.

6. Waterproof rain suit. Not water resistant. Waterproof. The suit should be made of nylon and coated with a rainproof material, such as polyurethane or Gore-Tex. To test your suit, we recommend taking a shower in it.

7. Extra clothes. Nothing sucks heat from a body like cold, wet clothes. Don't forget extra socks, too.

8. Swiss Army knife. A knife with 101 functions is not necessary, but it is helpful to have a good blade, screwdriver, tweezers, and scissors.

9. Flashlight. Bring at least one extra bulb and a set of fresh extra batteries.

10. Sunglasses, a wide-brimmed hat, and sunscreen. There is more ultraviolet light at high altitude than there is at sea level, where most Southern Californians live.

BONUS ESSENTIALS

Toilet paper, since some emergencies cannot be prevented. And although many people may be morally opposed to it, we believe anyone who has a cellular phone should bring it along (make sure it's charged). Cell phones don't jibe with the spirit of the wilderness, but in a life-threatening emergency, we'd rather have the phone than feel good about our moral righteousness.

WEATHERING THE WEATHER

Always prepare for it to be hotter or colder than expected.

If you're camping in the Sierra—even during the summer—bring along a few extra layers. The worst thing that will happen is that you won't use them.

On a similar note, be prepared for severe heat. Here's one thing that happens all the time in Angeles National Forest. Joe Hiker and friends take one of those long trails downhill to a beautiful creek. Later, they have to ascend back up the trail, which is fully exposed to the sun. Joe Hiker stops and sits down, convinced he's having a heart attack. And the rangers have to be called in.

What to do? Wear a wide-brimmed hat, bring along plenty of sunscreen, and, of course, have plenty of water. Remember: What goes down must come up. Plan accordingly.

If it's hot where you are going and you're bringing your pooch along, please think about ol' Fido's safety. Many dark-coated dogs don't fare well in the sunlight when temperatures are over 70 degrees. And whatever you do, never leave your dog in the car in direct sunlight while you go on a two-hour hike. Roast dog is a delicacy in Korea. Here, it's criminal.

An equally deadly problem in the mountains is hypothermia, also known as exposure. The cold in the mountains has to be felt to be fully appreciated. Sometimes the cold comes out of nowhere, especially at night, when temperatures in the Sierra can plummet 50 degrees from the daytime high.

This is why it's important to dress in layers. Have an emergency pair of long underwear in a dry bag in your pack. If you get soaked and it's chilly out, change. Not later, when you're numb. Now, while your head is clear. And speaking of your head, everything your mother said was true. A great deal of heat is lost through an uncovered noggin, so have a warm hat that covers the ears. Bring some gloves, too, even if heading to the mountains in the summer. Frozen hands are useless hands—and you will want those hands if you somehow get stuck in a bad situation.

Another note about the mountains: Late afternoon thunderstorms are common, especially in the summer. If you get stuck in a lightning storm, the best place to be is in a forested area away from the tallest trees, which tend to act as lightning rods. Nor is it a good idea to be standing in open areas, where you are the lightning rod.

Two other reminders: Water conducts electricity, so get away from it during a thunderstorm and keep in mind, too, that a backpack with metal rods can be a portable lightning rod.

46 WORDS ABOUT BOOTS

There is nothing that will ruin an outdoor getaway quicker than ill-fitting boots. If purchasing new boots, buy them at least two weeks before hitting the trail. Spend as much time as possible breaking them in; the heavier the boot, the longer it will take.

RESOURCES

Crossing Streams

A good rule of thumb is that stream crossings, especially in the mountains, are always tougher than they appear. A common way for people to drown in the Sierra is to attempt to cross a stream swollen with snowmelt. Or, someone's dog jumps into a stream and can't get out. The dog's owner jumps in after the dog and both end up stuck. Don't underestimate the forces of water. It kills people every year.

What to do? Check maps for stream crossings ahead of time. Phone the rangers and ask for stream conditions. Scout out the smartest place to cross. Most important, always—ALWAYS—unstrap your daypack or backpack buckles before crossing a stream. That way, if the water knocks you down, the weight of the pack won't pull you under. Yes, you may lose your pack, but you'll save your life.

Must Have Water

The rule of thumb for water consumption is each person should have a gallon of water for every day spent in the field. The same goes for children and dogs.

Unfortunately, there is no creek water in Southern California that can be considered safe for drinking without treatment of some kind. Giardia isn't always present in creeks and streams, but there's a good enough chance it could be. What is giardia? Without going into great detail, contracting giardia basically means you and your toilet will be on a first-name basis for 10 days to two weeks.

What to do then? If camping, either bring your own water, boil water for three minutes (not always practical), or invest in a water purification system. There are many systems to choose from with all kinds of filters. Generally speaking, the less expensive models tend to break or become clogged quickly. Conversely, it probably isn't necessary to go high-end, unless you're planning to hike the entire Pacific Crest Trail.

We recommend going to a sporting goods store such as REI or Adventure 16, where the sales staff is knowledgeable. Take a look at all the models and decide which is best for your needs.

You, Your Pooch, and Ticks

This is a true story. An actor takes his German shepherd for a hike in the Santa Monica Mountains. That night, the actor and the dog curl up together in bed. The next morning, the actor wakes up and feels a lump on the end of his nose. A tick had crawled off his dog and burrowed itself into the actor's schnozz, meaning this was a man not ready for his close-up.

Unfortunately, ticks seem to like Southern California as much as, if not more than, people do. Basically, these little monsters hang from tree branches, hoping to catch a ride on a human limb or dog. Because ticks generally hang low to the ground, it's usually the dog they get.

The problem is, ticks just don't bite you and exit stage left. Using their heads, they bore into you as if you're Grandma's Jell-O mold. Their goal is to gas up on your blood. As if that's not bad enough, here's the really bad news: Some ticks are known to be carriers of either Lyme disease or, occasionally, Rocky Mountain spotted fever. We'll spare you the exact details of Lyme disease, other than to say it eventually causes you to totally deteriorate physically—and then go completely nuts.

Most tick bites are harmless. However, if the tick is in you for a long time—over a day—or you develop a splotchy red rash around the wound, then you should see a doctor immediately. Lyme disease is easily treated with antibiotics if it is caught early.

What to do if a tick feasts on you? Your best bet is to use a tick extraction kit, which can be purchased for about $10 at most local sporting goods stores. We have and endorse the Repel Tick Kit, which has never met a tick it couldn't repel. Repel also makes a good tick repellent.

Although it's hard to say why, the winter of 1997–98 was especially bad for ticks in the local mountains. One day we took our dog up to Paramount Ranch for a quick hour-long hike. That night, we pulled four ticks off her.

Ticks can usually be found on a dog's neck, ears, or belly. The best way to check for ticks is to roll the dog over onto its back and search everywhere. Don't just look—feel through its fur. It's also good to have a vet give your dog an annual Lyme disease vaccination.

Extracting a tick from a dog is the same as it is for a human. The Repel Tick Kit comes with a pair of spring-loaded tweezers. With those, you grasp the tick's rear and rotate it several times, either clockwise and counterclockwise. The tick's head then retracts, allowing it to be removed. The wound, which often causes a big red lump on a dog or human, should then be cleansed and treated with an antibiotic cream or ointment.

If you're worried the tick might be carrying a disease, keep the tick and have a medical lab run tests on it. Our tick kit even comes with a tick storage container.

RATTLESNAKE!

We know people who have hiked around the hills and deserts of Southern California for years and have never seen a rattler. We also know people who found a rattler in their driveway on the day they moved into their new home.

As common as rattlesnakes are, they really don't cause many problems and people are rarely bitten. However, if you have a dog that likes to romp around in the brush, then it's worth being extra careful. Rattlers will only mess with someone who messes with them—something unsuspecting pooches are rather accomplished at.

The best way to avoid rattlers is to simply watch where you are stepping. Stay on the trail and avoid heavy brush, where the snakes may be hiding. When venturing off trail, use a hiking stick and make some noise—this alone will usually scare away snakes. And, when rock climbing or bouldering, never put a hand into a place that can't be seen.

What to do if bitten? Well, freaking out completely and screaming "I'm gonna die!" isn't going to help matters. Nor is it true. The common myth is that humans have an hour to get antivenin, but the reality is that every snake bite is different. The amount of poison injected depends on the bite—sometimes hardly any poison is injected at all—and a particular person's reaction to the snake's venom.

The most important thing is to keep the victim relaxed and as immobile as possible. Movement allows the venom to enter the bloodstream more quickly. The victim should sit, relaxed and still, while someone else gets help. If the victim can make it back to the car, move the victim slowly and then go straight to the hospital. Do it calmly, quickly, and confidently.

There are various snakebite kits available at some outdoor stores or pharmacies, some of which have suction devices to help remove the venom from the bite. Our advice: Save your money. Over the years, many snakebite kits have caused just as many problems as they have solved.

BEWARE OF THE BIG BAD BEAR

In California, humans are more a threat to bears than the other way around.

The problem is food. No matter how many signs the forest or park administrators install, people still insist on leaving food out at their campsites. A bear finds the food and then returns time and again to the campground until it becomes a "problem bear." Problem bears are shot and killed.

How best to play it safe?

When leaving a campsite for the day, put all food in a bear-proof storage locker (which are becoming increasingly common at many popular campgrounds) or put the food in a car. Never place the food within sight in a car, since bears will pry open a window or hatchback to get at food they can see. If your cooler is visible through a hatchback window, throw a blanket over it. Bears recognize coolers and they know what they hold. Just watch one of those bear shows on the Discovery Channel sometime.

A bear's sense of smell is 1,000 times better than that of a dog. So, if there is food around, they'll find it.

If you catch a bear in the act of raiding your camp, try the old standby: bang pots and pans and make a lot of noise. Hopefully, the bear will leave, although you can count on the bear probably taking your food with him.

Whatever you do, never store food in your tent. Either hang it from a tree or put it in a bear-proof locker. Don't bring the clothes that you wore when cooking or eating into the tent.

If you encounter a bear on a trail, the same thing applies: Make noise. Don't approach the bear, and stay clear of any cubs. Black bears will likely not be interested in you anyway—they rarely give chase (grizzly bears, which are extinct in California, are a whole other story). In fact, if they know you are coming, they'll probably get out of your way without you even knowing they are there.

MOUNTAIN LIONS

The idea of mountain lions is often much scarier than the reality. The truth is that mountain lions are extremely shy and don't seem to care much for humans. Sightings of lions are rare—much more so than black bears—although sightings often attract the kind of hysterical press coverage that does no one any good.

Over the last decade various studies have tried to guess how many mountain lions are in the state. The number that most frequently shows up in the newspapers comes from the California Department of Fish and Game, which in 1996 estimated there were between 4,000 and 6,000 lions in all of California.

Trophy hunting of mountain lions in California was banned in 1972, and since then most researchers agree that the number of lions has risen and they are coming into contact with people more often. This is also probably due to habitat destruction and fragmentation, along with Southern California's increasing population.

Incidents between people and lions are rare, but they do happen. Between 1909 and 1994 there were no mountain lion attacks resulting in a fatality in California. Then, in 1994, two fatal attacks occurred. A 40-year-old woman was killed while jogging in Auburn State Recreational Area, which is about 45 miles from Sacramento in Northern California. Later, a 56-year-old woman was killed while hiking in Rancho Cuyamaca State Park, east of San Diego.

The deaths of both women attracted considerable media attention, as did three other mountain lion attacks on people that occurred from August 1994 through March 1995. But one year later, in March 1996, California voters rejected Proposition 197, which would have allowed limited trophy hunting of mountain lions, protected in the state for over 20 years. It was a brave decision, repudiating the powerful gun lobby—which many people feel unduly influences the California DFG.

What are the facts? In Southern California, lions are found in most of the major mountain ranges. They are often found on rural, undeveloped land where there's also a lot of deer. Generally speaking, the lion population seems to be most dense in the western Sierra.

Another statistic: People have a far greater chance of being hit by lightning than of being attacked by a mountain lion. Lions are night predators and are shy; they generally don't want to deal with humans. The evidence also tends to suggest that mountain lions attack victims that are small and seem susceptible. Of the nine verified mountain lion attacks on humans between 1986 and the present, four of the victims were children and two were the women who were killed.

The evidence suggests that the best way to avoid mountain lions is to not hike or bike alone in remote areas where they are known to exist. Chances are that a mountain lion will not attack more than one person.

Should you ever encounter a mountain lion, take the following steps:

Don't try to run away because this might trigger the lion's instinct to chase its prey. If you are hiking alone, don't power hike or jog. Mountain lions seem to take power hiking and jogging as a sign you are prey.

Wave your hands and shout; try to make it appear you are bigger than you really are. If children are with you, pick them up and put them on your shoulders so that it appears you are taller.

If the lion behaves aggressively, throw stones at it. Make eye contact and keep eye contact. Be aggressive.

If the lion attacks, fight back as hard as you can, using rocks, sticks, or whatever is handy.

Earthquake!

If the 1989 Loma Prieta and 1994 Northridge earthquakes taught us any lessons, it's that the almost-big-one can come at any time, including the time you choose for your great outdoor getaway.

Thus, it could never hurt you to have an earthquake preparedness kit in your car. Take a couple of hours and put it together—although you should remember to change the food supplies every six months.

What do you need? In no particular order: bottled water, extra clothes (jeans, T-shirts, a sweatshirt), boots that are safe to wear around broken glass, work gloves, a first-aid kit, blanket, flashlight, three sets of batteries for the flashlight, toilet paper, and a can opener.

As for food, you want the nonperishables. Nutrition bars, dried fruit, jerky, and crackers are all recommended. And three boxes of brown cinnamon Kellogg's Pop Tarts with frosting never hurt anyone. Important safety tip: Every six months, replace the Pop Tarts and other perishables. As for the old Pop Tarts, eat the entire box and wash them down with several bottles of Black Dog Ale.

Don't forget the dog. Keep extra doggy supplies (food, leash, boots, medication, rawhide) in your earthquake kit, also. Fido will be appreciative.

How Not to Get Lost

As you'll soon see, we have included directions to most of the destinations in this book. Therefore, it's impossible for you to get lost, eh?

Wrong, wrong, wrong. Even with great directions and all the right maps, it is almost certain that at some point you will become hopelessly lost. That's nothing to be ashamed of—as long as you can get yourself found.

AAA, including the Automobile Association of Southern California, publishes great county road maps and national park road maps, both of which we highly recommend.

We also like U.S. Forest Service maps, which are a necessity if you're headed out on any unpaved roads. These maps can be found at most outdoor stores, such as REI, Adventure 16, Sport Chalet, and Sportsmart. Or purchase maps by mail by sending $4 to the USDA-Forest Service, Attn: Map Room 807, 630 Sansome Street, San Francisco, CA 94111, and requesting whichever map it is that you want.

Trust us, getting the right maps is worth it. There is nothing worse than a relationship-threatening fight over directions. Remember, guys, in the history of mankind, there has never been a fight over directions in which the man's countless other faults weren't brought into play. Isn't that so, ladies?

Plants Not to Take Home to Your Mother

You have probably heard of the old saying about poison oak: Leaves of three, let it be.

Poison oak is prolific in many parts of Southern California, especially in canyons and lush areas. Basically, it's a green plant with three pointy leaves. Toward the end of summer, poison oak also has a tendency to turn red, one of the few chaparral plants to change colors.

If you stay on the trail, poison oak won't be much of a problem. However, if you have a dog that likes to snoop around (especially around creeks), watch where he's walking. Poison oak doesn't bother dogs, but the plant's oil tends to stay on a dog's fur, and then later rub off on the dog's owner.

What to do if stricken? Head to the pharmacy and try some of the various poison oak medicines. Most doctors recommend Calamine, which works for most people.

The other plants to avoid, of

course, are cacti. They come in a variety of shapes and sizes and it's fair to say none of them is terribly comfortable to sit upon.

Be especially aware of the "jumping" cholla cactus, which is basically a short, hairy cactus with whitish barbed needles. If you are walking past a cholla, it can actually reach out just a wee bit so that its needles brush up against you. Extracting a cholla cactus needle from a leg is, reportedly, excruciating.

Why Can't I Breathe?

Joe Ventura or Ronnie Reseda go hiking in the High Sierra. They're both in great shape—after all, they're unemployed actors who spend all day attached to exercise machines. But when they reach 11,972-foot Bishop Pass, they suddenly feel nauseous and have pounding headaches.

Starbuck's withdrawal? No. Altitude sickness, which can turn even the physically fit into a useless pile of quivering flesh. As you travel to higher elevations, the amount of oxygen decreases. But the body still needs oxygen to function. When the imbalance between oxygen taken in and oxygen needed reaches a high level, altitude sickness kicks in. Symptoms include severe headaches, nausea, dizziness, confusion, weakness, and violent fits of vomiting.

When traveling to high elevations, get there early enough to spend time acclimating to the thin air before setting off on a 15-mile day hike. Drink as much water as possible for a week—yes, a week—before your trip. Be a bladder with legs.

Barking at the Seals

Some folks have sea legs and others do not. There's no real rhyme or reason to it. Someone's 90-year-old grandma might do fine in heavy seas, while surfer Rock Stonebreaker is at the railing puking his guts up.

Those prone to seasickness should try Dramamine or any of the other over-the-counter anti-nausea medicines. Read the instructions because many of these medications need to be taken several hours in advance of the trip. Bring extra water because the medications tend to make some people thirsty.

One other word of caution: If someone gets sick on the boat, don't watch—resist the Beavis and Butthead inside! We've seen many a fine sailor stumble because, like Lot's wife in the Bible, they turned around and looked.

• **Hot Tips** •

Photographing the Outdoors

You know the routine. The photos from the big trip are ready. You rush to the drugstore. The envelope is ripped open in the store. The photos are overexposed. Underexposed. Scratched. Terrible.

You, the photographer, stand there, shuffling through the deck of stills time and time again. You are incapacitated. A pimply clerk is summoned to help you to the car.

What went wrong? How could this—bad photos of the Yosemite Valley—happen to you?

Here are a few tips:

1. Consider going manual. Manual cameras allow photographers to manipulate film speed, shutter speed, aperture, and focus—the tools that allow one to manipulate light. Automatic cameras, also known as "point and shoots," are often very good, but they

are designed to produce evenly exposed, competent photos—not artistic photos. Manual cameras have a light meter, making it easy to choose the proper f-stop and shutter speed.

2. Be patient. "Patience is perhaps the most essential element when photographing landscapes," says David Montesino, a professional freelance photographer. "This means setting up your shot. Absorb the scenery and seek out an angle that strikes you as the most interesting. Do not try to include everything in your shot. Try and frame your shot with a dominant element in mind. This will give you a much stronger image."

3. Get a tripod or unipod. A camera not on a tripod will produce a softer image than a camera on a tripod. A tripod also allows you to take photos of yourself in the outdoors with the self-timer. Unipods are one-legged tripods and can also help you keep the camera still. A great trick with a unipod is to use it as an extension of your arm. For instance, if you are standing at the railing of the Grand Canyon, you can grip the bottom of the unipod and hold your camera several feet over the railing, thus allowing for an unobscured shot straight down. Many lightweight tripods and unipods fold up enough to fit in a daypack.

4. Consider film speed. "I've found that low-speed film (25 to 64 ASA) is best used for landscape and scenery photos," says Montesino. "Low-speed films capture more subtle tones and shades better than faster speed films can. The main drawback is you need to have a tripod because you'll be shooting at lower shutter speeds and higher f-stops [which allow less light into the camera] with low-speed film. You should carry a roll or two of high-speed film with you in case you encounter wildlife. This will give you the flexibility to shoot low-light situations at relatively faster shutter speeds."

5. Try shooting black-and-white film, which is particularly good for outdoor photography. One of the difficulties with color film is that it has to come out perfectly to replicate reality. Black-and-white images tend to be more dramatic and artistic since they are taking color images and turning them into numerous shades of gray. Remember, too, that gray cloudy days often soften the light, allowing for bolder images with less contrast.

6. Experiment with longer shutter speeds in very low light situations. A tripod or unipod will also allow you to keep your camera steady for taking twilight shots at slower shutter speeds, such as 1/32, 1/16, or even 1/8 of a second. Hint: On the night of the full moon in the desert, try getting a shot of the moon above the landscape by using a lower f-stop and a lower shutter speed—maybe even two or three seconds. Manual cameras have a setting that allows you to keep the shutter open for as long as you please.

7. Play with the focus on manual cameras. Try shooting a close-up of a wildflower with an out-of-focus stream in the background.

8. Try to show movement. Keep the shutter open longer to show a waterfall cascading over a rock. Pan along with a skier, runner, biker, etc., keeping the shutter open a bit longer than necessary.

9. Shoot in the golden hours. This is the hour immediately following sunrise and preceding sunset. The best light is low angle light, which

makes landscapes appear more dramatic than the harsh light in the middle of the day.

10. Get film developed properly. When it's time to get your film developed, don't take it to the local supermarket, which will probably do a very poor job and scratch your negatives. Peruse your local yellow pages and find a professional film lab. Often, the prices are the same as the supermarket, but the quality will be much better.

11. Take a class. Wilderness photography classes are offered several times a year by Adventure 16. The Sierra Club conducts outings devoted especially to photography. Most community colleges and large universities offer photography classes through their adult or continuing education programs.

Glossary

FILM SPEED determines how quickly the film reacts to light. A variety of speeds are manufactured. The lower the number, the lower the film speed. Speeds of 100, 200, and 400 are most common for amateurs.

APERTURE determines the size of the opening through which light will pass before it hits the film. This is measured by f-stop. The lower the f-stop, the larger the hole. Aperture can be used to manipulate the depth of field. Generally, the higher the f-stop, the more depth of field.

SHUTTER SPEED dictates the amount of time that film is exposed to light.

FOCUS allows the photographer to adjust the camera so that it can take clear photos of objects that are varying lengths from the camera. The more depth of field, the more objects within the frame that will be in focus.

• Hot Tips •

Outdoor Gift Ideas

As you probably are aware, holiday shopping can be an unbearable nightmare when you don't know what it is you are shopping for.

Enter outdoor gifts. Even if the person in mind hasn't been camping or hiking in 29 years, he or she will probably like that you think the person is actually capable of doing an outdoor activity. And maybe your gift will prompt the recipient to get off his or her bottom and actually do it, too.

Beachgoers

First string: A stunt kite. Low-end models are usually $10 to $20. There's a list of kite stores in the "Kite Flying" section on page 49 in this book, but keep in mind that some of the larger toy stores, such as Toys-R-Us, have kites, too.

If all else fails: A boogeyboard. You can buy the low-end models for $15 to $20 at most large sporting goods stores. If worse comes to worst, the Styrofoam might make good packing material.

Bird-watchers

First string: Binoculars. They should have at least a 10x42 lens. Some of the better brands are Bushnell, Bausch & Lomb, Nikon, Pentax, and Zeiss. Get out the gold card: you can plan on parting with $100 to $200.

If all else fails: An audiotape of "Voices of the Peruvian Rainforest" ($11.95). When they say "voices," they mean bird voices. Order by calling the Los Angeles Audubon Society bookstore at (213) 876-0202.

RESOURCES

BOOKWORMS

First string: Edward Abbey's *Desert Solitaire* (Simon & Schuster), Abbey's account of a summer spent as a park ranger in the canyonlands of Utah. It's the kind of book that could potentially change someone's life.

If all else fails: A one-year subscription to *Outside* magazine. Get a subscription card out of a current issue or phone (800) 678-1131.

CAMPERS

First string: A gift certificate to an outdoor store. It makes you look thoughtful and the recipient can choose what he or she really needs.

If all else fails: A headlamp. Basically, it's a flashlight you wear around your head, allowing you to use both hands at night to do such things as fend off a bear, repair the hole in your tent, read, or find your way to the camp rest room. They typically run $28 to $40 at most large sporting goods stores.

DOG LOVERS

First string: A doggy backpack ($30 or so), available at some large sporting goods stores or through the Campmor catalog. Phone Campmor at (800) CAMPMOR to order.

If all else fails: Pooper-scooper, the gift that speaks for itself, is available at most pet stores.

HIKERS

First string: Try a panoramic camera, which takes extra-wide photographs—especially good for mountain views. Typically they run $20 to $30 at most camera stores.

If all else fails: A fanny pack with multiple water bottle holsters. Every time they take a drink, they'll think of you.

FISHERS

First string: A fly-fishing vest. If you wanna be cool, you gotta look cool. They're available at many tackle shops or large sporting goods stores.

If all else fails: A fishhook removal kit ($10) is available at most tackle shops.

MOUNTAIN BIKERS

First string: A cordless cyclocomputer with seven functions: speedometer, odometer, trip distance, average speed, elapsed time, maximum speed, and clock. It retails for about $60 at sporting goods stores or bike shops.

If all else fails: A helmet ($30 and up), so your favorite biker can take a few lumps on the noggin. Available at most large sporting goods stores or bicycle shops.

ROCK CLIMBERS

First string: Gift certificate for a rock climbing class. Phone your local climbing store (see the Rock Climbing section on page 17).

If all else fails: Gift certificate for climb-time at a local indoor climbing club. Check the Rock Climbing section on page 17 for a list of climbing clubs.

ROLLERBLADERS

First string: Wristguards and elbow and knee pads ($30 to $40). Try to find them all together in one package, which is cheaper than buying each of the pads separately. They're available at most sporting goods stores.

If all else fails: Lip balm ($1).

SKIERS

First string: The Ski Tote Pocket Tote (about $30), which is a handle that allows skiers to clamp their skis together and then carry them as if they were a suitcase. Even better, the Pocket Tote can then be locked to a rack, so no one walks off with your skis while you're having lunch. It's available at most major sporting goods stores.

If all else fails: Get one of those funny hats that make a skier look like a court jester in a Shakespeare production. These are easy to find at any ski shop or outdoor store and are usually $20 to $40. They're good for goofy holiday photos, too.

SURFERS

First string: One of those really big towels with Velcro on the edges so it stays closed while your favorite surfer changes out of his or her wet suit in front of all the traffic on the PCH. Check your local department store.

If all else fails: A can of surfboard wax ($3), available at your local surf shop.

SCUBA DIVERS AND SNORKELERS

First string: A super cheap underwater camera, which usually costs about $10. Try your local dive shop.

If all else fails: A laminated fish identifier card, which can actually be quite useful. Check your local dive shop.

PARENTS

First string: A Perky-Pet brand hummingbird feeder (about $20), available at most retail and pet stores.

If all else fails: Anything having to do with the weather.

THE PERSON IN THE OFFICE GIFT POOL YOU HATE

First string: Generic insect repellent ($5). They'll think they're protected until it's too late. Heh, heh, heh. Check your local supermarket.

If all else fails: Ski mask ($5). The recipient might get the message. Check your local retail store.

WILDERNESS AND ADVENTURE TRAINING

WILDERNESS TRAVEL COURSE (SIERRA CLUB)

In the Los Angeles area, the sporting goods stores are thriving in February. Winter sales result in a lot of business, but there's also a mad scramble for sleeping bag and tent rentals, even on the rainiest of weekends.

What gives?

The clerks at stores like REI and Adventure 16 know what's up—it's the annual Wilderness Travel Course, better known as the WTC, offered by the Angeles Chapter of the Sierra Club. The class is one of the most affordable, not to mention best, ways to learn basic backpacking and navigation skills.

The Angeles Chapter—the largest local branch of the Sierra Club—has been teaching the WTC (it was known as the Basic Mountaineering Training Course until the late 1980s) since the 1960s. Thousands of students have graduated from the course.

The class consists of 10 weekly meetings and four field trips. Topics covered include the 10 essentials, backpacking equipment, conditioning, basic mountaineering, map reading and navigation, mountain medicine, and snow travel. All of these come into play during the four outings.

The first field trip is a conditioning hike. And it's quite a hike. Steve's conditioning hike left Millard Campground (in Angeles National Forest) at

RESOURCES

7 A.M. and proceeded to climb to the top of Mount Lowe, a distance of six miles with an elevation gain of 3,850 feet. After an hour at the summit, the class made the return hike, returning to their cars by 6 P.M. A long day, but a lucky one. The previous day another class hiked for 10 hours in a torrential downpour.

The second field trip is a car camping excursion to Joshua Tree National Park, where navigation skills are practiced amid the park's boulder fields, which is where basic rock climbing moves are also taught.

The third trip is a day outing, emphasizing snow skills.

And the final trip is the granddaddy: Snow camp.

Snow camp is held in the Eastern Sierra. Typically, a bus deposits students at the trailhead about 9 P.M. At that point, students and instructors snowshoe and backpack their way into places like Onion Valley, South Lake, or North Lake. The weekend is spent hiking and navigating—and learning how to not become an ice cube.

How much does all of this cost?

In 1997, it was $183 for non-club members and $168 for club members. That is not a typographical error.

In all of the outdoors, the WTC may be the best bargain of them all, a real credit to the Sierra Club volunteers who have kept the school going for so long.

WTC classes will be held in four locations throughout the Southland in 1999, from January to March: Long Beach, the San Gabriel Valley, Orange County, and the Westside of Los Angeles.

Contact: Sierra Club Angeles Chapter, (213) 387-4287. Web site: www.edge-internet.com/wtc

OTHER EDUCATIONAL OPPORTUNITIES

Want to rock climb, but you don't know how? Always wondered what it would be like to navigate a sailboat using only the stars? Interested in lowering yourself into the sea in a shark cage in order to get up close and personal with Mr. Jaws?

The little-known secret to outdoor life in Southern California is that a great many classes are available from outfitters, local colleges, and environmental study centers. Classes are often very affordable ($100 and less) and are a great way to broaden your horizons, meet new people, and—gasp—have fun. Plus, you can't ask for a bigger classroom than the great outdoors.

Here are some places to look for outdoor educational opportunities:

ADVENTURE 16

Learn outdoor skills such as reading a compass, backpacking, rock climbing, first aid, outdoor photography, and even wilderness cooking on one of Adventure 16's numerous wilderness outings. The store, located throughout greater Los Angeles and San Diego, offers evening seminars, multi-day trips into the wilderness, as well as clinics and slide shows. There are six A-16 outdoor travel stores in Southern California; each has its own schedule of outings. Phone for details or visit one of the stores.

Contact: West Los Angeles, (310) 473-4574. Tarzana, (818) 345-4266. Costa Mesa, (714) 650-3301. San Diego, (619) 283-2374 and (619) 234-1751. Solana Beach, (619) 755-7662.

RESOURCES

CALIFORNIA POLYTECHNIC STATE UNIVERSITY—SAN LUIS OBISPO

The campus group Associated Students Inc. (ASI) sponsors outings for both students and nonstudents. Outings include day hikes, canoeing, camping, biking, cross-country skiing, backpacking, kayaking, and rock climbing. The outings also take place at a wide range of destinations, including Yosemite National Park, Santa Margarita Lake, Montana de Oro State Park, Pinnacles National Monument, and Monterey Bay.

Contact: ASI, at the Escape Route shop on campus, (805) 756-1287.

DESERT STUDIES CENTER

Located in the Mojave Desert town of Zzyzx, the center serves as a field station for California State University. The university uses the center for research, but the public can take weekend-long classes there; students live in dorm rooms at the center. Curriculum covers many aspects of desert ecology, from wildflowers to insects, birds, and bats. Tuition ranges from $140 to $200 and includes overnight lodging and five meals. Registration for the courses is available through Cal State San Bernardino's extended education program.

Contact: California State University San Bernardino extended education program, (909) 880-5975.

LEARNING TREE UNIVERSITY

"Encounter greater numbers of blue sharks and makos when they are on the prowl for their nighttime hunt!" reads the course description for "Shark Encounter—Night Voyage!" a class offered by Learning Tree in Chatsworth. How do you encounter the sharks? We'll give you a hint: Both you and the shark are in the water. Other classes include swimming with sea lions, elephant encounters, hiking the Santa Monica Mountains, and horseback riding.

Contact: Learning Tree University, (818) 882-5599.

LOS ANGELES DEPARTMENT OF PARKS AND RECREATION

The department's Pacific Aquatic Center offers courses in kayaking, canoeing, and sailing at urban locations such as Venice, Harbor City, and Marina del Rey. Classes run for about five weeks and are very affordable—none is over $200.

Contact: Pacific Aquatic Center, (213) 765-5391.

PACIFIC WILDERNESS INSTITUTE

The institute offers wilderness skills and adventure programs for hikers, skiers, and climbers. Cross-country and telemark skiing, mountaineering, rock and ice climbing, and wilderness navigation and survival are among the topics. Seminars and outings take place at Southern California mountains, as well as Mammoth Mountain, Lake Tahoe, and other Sierra locations. The institute is located in Orange.

Contact: Pacific Wilderness Institute, (714) 998-4596.

REI

REI offers free clinics and events at its five Southern California stores, located in greater Los Angeles and Orange County. Seminars cover everything from waterproofing footwear and fixing a bike flat to wilderness first aid for pets and slide shows on exotic locales. Phone REI for details or visit one of their stores.

Contact: Carson, (310) 538-2429. Northridge, (818) 831-5555. San Dimas, (909) 592-2095. Santa Ana, (714)

543-4142. Mission Viejo, (714) 348-1400.

SANTA BARBARA MUSEUM OF NATURAL HISTORY

The museum offers field trips in and around Santa Barbara County to introduce people to the natural environment. Some class subjects in the past year included tidepooling, whale watching, and bird-watching. The museum's Sea Center—located on Stearns Wharf in Santa Barbara—also partners with the Channel Islands National Marine Sanctuary throughout the summer to offer presentations on marine life from staff marine biologists.

Contact: Santa Barbara Museum of Natural History, (805) 682-4711. Sea Center, (805) 962-0885.

SIERRA CLUB

Besides the Wilderness Travel Course (WTC) on page 299, the Sierra Club offers hundreds of guided outdoor trips in California and around the world. Among them are many backpacking excursions into the Sierra Nevada, with many of the trips designed for beginner or intermediate backpackers. The club's quarterly trip list is available for $5 at some outdoor stores; or visit the Sierra Club's Web page at www.sierraclub.org.

Contact: Sierra Club Angeles Chapter, (213) 387-4287.

THE WILDERNESS INSTITUTE

A nonprofit organization in Agoura Hills, about one hour north of downtown Los Angeles, the Wilderness Institute offers instruction ranging from backcountry skills courses to mountain biking and rock climbing. The institute also conducts hikes and special natural history trips such as fossil finding. Tuition ranges from about $25 to $75.

Contact: The Wilderness Institute, (818) 991-7327.

UCLA EXTENSION

The nation's largest urban campus continuing higher education program offers a number of physical activities and outdoor recreation classes every semester. Classes are held at the main Westwood campus as well as at branches in Universal City, Santa Monica, and downtown Los Angeles. In addition to courses in fly-fishing, sailing, and horseback riding, the program also conducts wilderness rafting and hiking trips to Alaska. There's even a very popular field trip on horseback to see wild mustangs in the Inyo National Forest. Giddy-up! Tuition ranges from $200 to $2,125 for the Alaska trip.

Contact: For a catalog, phone UCLA Extension in Westwood at (310) 825-9971.

UNIVERSITY OF CALIFORNIA—IRVINE

The university's recreation office offers beginning to advanced sailing classes, as well as rock climbing classes.

Contact: UC Irvine Recreation Office, (714) 824-5346.

UNIVERSITY OF CALIFORNIA—RIVERSIDE

The university extension program offers classes through its natural and agricultural sciences departments. Recent offerings included field study of birds in Yosemite; a wild mustang ecological field program; field study of the San Andreas Fault; classes in the geological and natural histories of Death Valley, the Eastern Sierra, and Yosemite; and a frontier pack trip through Yosemite.

RESOURCES

Contact: UC Riverside Extension, (909) 787-4105 or (800) 442-4990.

• RESOURCES •

PARKS, PRESERVES, AND FORESTS

CALIFORNIA STATE PARKS

Southern California, from Monterey to the Mexican border, has 11 state parks and more than two dozen state beaches. Every type of environment in California is protected by the state system, including the coast, desert, mountains, rivers, and lakes.

Contact: California State Parks, Office of Information, P.O. Box 942896, Sacramento, CA 94296-0001; (916) 653-6995.

Anza-Borrego Desert State Park, P.O. Box 299, Borrego Springs, CA 92004; (619) 767-5311.

Crystal Cove State Park, 8471 Pacific Coast Highway, Laguna Beach, CA 926651; (714) 494-3539.

Cuyamaca Rancho State Park, 12551 Highway 79, Descanso, CA 91916; (619) 765-0755.

Gaviota State Park, 10 Refugio Beach, Goleta, CA 93117; (805) 968-1711.

Malibu Creek State Park, California Department of Parks and Recreation, 1925 Las Virgenes Road, Calabasas, CA 91302; (818) 706-8809.

Montana de Oro State Park, Los Osos, CA 93402; (805) 772-2560.

Morro Bay State Park, (805) 772-2560.

Mount San Jacinto State Park, (714) 659-2607.

Palomar Mountain State Park, c/o Cuyamaca Rancho State Park, 12551 Highway 79, Descanso, CA 91916; (619) 765-0755.

Point Mugu State Park, California Department of Parks and Recreation, 1925 Las Virgenes Road, Calabasas, CA 91302; (818) 880-0350.

Red Rock Canyon State Park, 1051 West Avenue M, Suite 201, Lancaster, CA 93534; (805) 942-0662.

Saddleback Butte State Park, Avenue J, 170th Street East, Lancaster, CA 93534; (805) 942-0662.

San Simeon State Park, (805) 927-2068.

Topanga State Park, 20829 Entrada Road, Topanga, CA 90290; (310) 455-2465.

NATIONAL PARKS

Most states in this country are lucky to have one national park. Southern California alone has five: Joshua Tree and Death Valley in the deserts, the rugged Channel Islands in the Pacific, and pristine Sequoia and Kings Canyon in the Sierra Nevada. Death Valley, with over 3.3 million acres, is the largest national park in the lower 48; and the Channel Islands are the only islands in the national park system. Southern California also is home to the Santa Monica Mountains National Recreation Area, which is located just minutes from the urban wilderness of La-La Land, and the Mojave National Preserve, which protects much of the desert lying between Interstate 15 and Interstate 40 in San Bernardino County.

Channel Islands National Park, 1901 Spinnaker Drive, Ventura, CA 93001; (805) 658-5730.

Death Valley National Park, Death Valley, CA 92328 (619) 786-2331.

RESOURCES

Joshua Tree National Park, 74485 National Monument Drive, Twentynine Palms, CA 92277; (619) 367-7511.

Kings Canyon National Park, Grant Grove, CA 93633; (209) 335-2856.

Mojave National Preserve, (619) 255-8801.

Santa Monica Mountains National Recreation Area, 30401 Agoura Road, Suite 100, Agoura Hills, CA 91301; (818) 597-9192.

Sequoia National Park, Ash Mountain, Three Rivers, CA 93271; (209) 565-3341. Sequoia Wilderness Office, (209) 565-3708.

NATIONAL FORESTS

The U.S. Forest Service protects resources such as foliage, forage, timber, water, wildlife, and areas boasting incredible scenery as well as a wide variety of ecosystems. Within the national forests are wilderness areas, where no mechanized vehicles or machines are allowed, including mountain bikes. Hikers and campers must sometimes obtain a free permit to enter such areas. Listed below are the headquarters for each national forest, as well as ranger stations, where information, maps, and Forest Service Adventure Passes can be obtained.

Contact: USDA-Forest Service, Office of Information, 630 Sansome Street, San Francisco, CA 94111; (415) 705-2874.

ANGELES NATIONAL FOREST

Supervisor's Office, 701 North Santa Anita Avenue, Arcadia, CA 91006; (818) 574-1613 or (818) 574-5200.

Arroyo Seco Ranger District, Oak Grove Park, Flintridge, CA 91011; (818) 899-1900.

Mount Baldy Ranger District, 110 North Wabash Avenue, Glendora, CA 91740; (818) 335-1251.

Tujunga Ranger District, 12371 North Little Tujunga Canyon Road, San Fernando, CA 91342; (818) 889-1900.

CLEVELAND NATIONAL FOREST

Supervisor's Office, 10845 Rancho Bernardo Road, Rancho Bernardo, CA 92127-2107; (619) 673-6180.

Descanso Ranger District, 3348 Alpine Boulevard, Alpine, CA 91901; (619) 445-6235.

Palomar Ranger District, 1634 Black Canyon Road, Ramona, CA 92605; (619) 788-0250.

Trabuco Ranger District, 1147 East Sixth Street, Corona, CA 91719; (909) 736-3002.

INYO NATIONAL FOREST

Supervisor's Office, 873 North Main Street, Bishop, CA 93514; (619) 873-2400.

Lone Pine Ranger District, P.O. Box 8, Lone Pine, CA 93545; (760) 876-6200.

Mammoth Ranger District, P.O. Box 148, Mammoth Lakes, CA 93456; (760) 924-5500.

Mono Lake Ranger District, P.O. Box 429, Lee Vining, CA 93451; (760) 647-3000.

White Mountain Ranger District, 798 North Main Street, Bishop, CA 93514; (760) 873-2500.

Interagency Visitor Center, located in Lone Pine on Baker Road at the base of the giant thermometer that is easily seen from the freeway; (619) 876-6222.

LOS PADRES NATIONAL FOREST

Supervisor's Office, 6144 Calle Real, Goleta, CA 93117; (805) 683-6711.

RESOURCES

Monterey Ranger District, 406 South Mildred Avenue, King City, CA 93930; (408) 385-5434.

Mount Pinos Ranger District, HC1 Box 400, Frazier Park, CA 93225; (805) 245-3731.

Ojai Ranger District, 1190 East Ojai Avenue, Ojai, CA 93023; (805) 646-4348.

Santa Barbara Ranger District, Star Route, Santa Barbara, CA 93105; (805) 967-3481.

Santa Lucia Ranger District, 1616 Carlotti Drive, Santa Maria, CA 93454-1599; (805) 925-9538.

SAN BERNARDINO NATIONAL FOREST

Supervisor's Office, 1824 South Commerce Center Circle, San Bernardino, CA 92408; (909) 383-5588.

Big Bear Ranger District, P.O. Box 290, North Shore Drive, Fawnskin, CA 92333; (909) 866-3437.

Front Country Ranger District, 1209 Lytle Creek Road, Lytle Creek, CA 92358; (909) 887-2576.

Idyllwild Ranger Station, P.O. Box 518, Idyllwild, CA 92349; (909) 659-2117.

Mountain Top Ranger District, P.O. Box 350, 28104 Highway 18, Skyforest, CA 92385; (909) 337-1104.

San Gorgonio Ranger District, 3471 Mill Creek Road, Mentone, CA 92359; (909) 794-1123.

SEQUOIA NATIONAL FOREST

Supervisor's Office, 900 West Grand Avenue, Porterville, CA 93257; (209) 784-1500.

Cannell Meadow Ranger District, P.O. Box 6, Kernville, CA 93238; (619) 376-3781.

Greenhorn Ranger District, 15701 Highway 178, P.O. Box 6129, Bakersfield, CA 93386-6129; (805) 871-2223.

Hot Springs Ranger District, Route 4, Box 548, California Hot Springs, CA 93207; (805) 548-6503.

Hume Lake Ranger District, 36273 East Kings Canyon Road, Dunlap, CA 93621; (209) 338-2251.

Tule River Ranger District, 32588 Highway 190, Springville, CA 93265; (209) 539-2607.

BUREAU OF LAND MANAGEMENT DESERT WILDERNESS AREAS

The Bureau of Land Management, commonly referred to as the BLM, administers 9.5 million acres of public lands in the Southern California deserts. The California Desert Protection Act, signed into law by President Clinton in 1995, protected 69 individual BLM areas covering 3.6 million acres of this land. Public access to these lands is free, but there's a catch. Most of these desert and mountain areas are undeveloped, which means there are no paved roads, no roads at all, or paved roads that even a high-clearance 4x4 might have trouble negotiating. To get more information, call the BLM and try to get your hands on a loose-leaf book printed by the bureau titled "BLM Wilderness Areas Maps and Information—California." This book gives vital statistics on all the wilderness areas and what might be found there, along with small-scale versions of the appropriate United States Geological Survey maps.

BLM SOUTHERN CALIFORNIA OFFICES

Barstow Resource Area, Barstow, (619) 255-8700.

California Desert District, Riverside, (909) 697-5200.

RESOURCES

El Centro Resource Area, El Centro, (619) 337-4400.

Needles Resource Area, Needles, (619) 326-3896.

Palm Springs-South Coast Resource Area, North Palm Springs, (619) 251-4800.

Ridgecrest Resource Area, Ridgecrest, (619) 384-5400.

Yuma District, Yuma (AZ), (602) 726-6300.

• RESOURCES •

PROTECTING THE WILDERNESS

California, bless her soul, has long served as a beacon for much of America, if not the world. She was considered a place where dreams came true, jobs were plentiful, and lives gone awry were salvaged. The state's overwhelming beauty and seemingly endless resources were just the icing on the cake.

In the last 150 years, California has grown from a remote outpost of the United States to its most populated state. There are still stretches of endless, undiminished beauty. But there is no denying that many of the state's resources have been greatly diminished. At the same time, the cities of Southern California continue to push outward, as if further development will solve the problem rather than add to it.

Which makes it more vital than ever to protect the wilderness that surrounds our cities in Southern California. If we fail to preserve some of our planet in its pristine state for future generations to enjoy and investigate, we rob the future of beauty and promise. And to do so is to rob the future of life itself. As Thoreau once said, "In wilderness is the preservation of the world."

PEOPLE TO CONTACT

Don't be shy about expressing your views when it comes to wild California. Many of the parks written about in this book were once slated for development. They became parks because someone—people like John Muir and David Brower—cared enough to speak up loudly. To express your views or comment on policy (or lack thereof), write:

President Bill Cinton, 1600 Pennsylvania Avenue NW, Washington, D.C. 20500. President's comment line. (202) 456-1111. E-mail: president@whitehouse.com

Vice President Albert Gore, Executive Building, Washington, D.C. 20500.

Governor Pete Wilson, Capitol Building, First Floor, Sacramento, CA 95814; (916) 322-9900 or fax (916) 445-4633.

Senator (CA) Barbara Boxer, 112 Hart Senate Building, Washington, D.C. 20510; (202) 224-3553.

Senator (CA) Diane Feinstein, 331 Hart Senate Building, Washington, D.C. 20510; (202) 224-3841.

RESOURCES ON THE INTERNET

When we first began working on this book, in 1995, the Internet was a relatively new phenomenon, geared more to industry and academia than the general public.

Talk about a revolution. In the last three years, government agencies, gear manufacturers, and publishers have embraced the Web. The result: More current information is at your fingertips than ever before. Especially welcome is our government's use of the Web—taxpayers have never been so close to government.

Want to know more about volcanic

RESOURCES

activity? Go the United States Geological Survey's Web site. Interested in forest logging policies? Go to the U.S. Forest Service's Web site and read the comments of service chief Mike Dombeck. Want to know more about the Glen Canyon Dam? The Bureau of Reclamation, too, has a good Web site (if slightly biased toward dams).

So much information is being put on the Web so quickly, it's hard to keep up. But, for the time being, here are some addresses that might be handy:

GOVERNMENT

Bureau of Land Management: www.blm.gov
Bureau of Reclamation: www.usbr.gov
California Department of Fish and Game: www.dfg.ca.gov
California Department of Parks and Recreation: www.cal-parks.ca.gov
Inyo National Forest Wilderness Reservation Service: www.sierrawilderness.com
National Marine Fisheries Service: www.nmfs.gov
National Park Service: www.nps.gov
National Oceanic and Atmospheric Administration: www.noaa.gov
U.S. Department of the Interior: www.doi.gov
U.S. Fish and Wildlife Service: www.fws.gov
U.S. Forest Service: www.fs.fed.us
U.S. Geological Survey: www.usgs.gov

WEATHER

National Weather Service Forecast Office: www.nwsla.noaa.gov
National Weather Service Western Headquarters: www.nimbo.wrh.noaa.gov
National Weather Service hourly updates: www.iwin.nws.noaa.gov/iwin/ca/ca/hourly.html
Sierra Nevada weather: www.mammothweb.com/updates/weather.html
Skiing snow reports: www.skinet.com/snowreport/california.html

ENVIRONMENTAL ORGANIZATIONS

Audubon Society: www.audubon.org
California Trout: www.caltrout.org
Ducks Unlimited: www.ducks.org
Earth First!: www.earth-first.com
Friends of the Earth: www.foe.org
National Outdoor Leadership Schools: www.nols.edu
Pacific Crest Trail Association: www.gorp.com/pcta
Sierra Club: www.sierraclub.org
The Nature Conservancy: www.tnc.org
The Wilderness Society: www.wilderness.org
Trout Unlimited: www.tu.org

PUBLICATIONS

Backpacker magazine: www.bpbasecamp.com
National Geographic Society: www.nationalgeographic.com
Outside magazine: www.outside.starwave.com

EQUIPMENT RETAILERS

Campmor: www.campmor.com
REI: www.rei.com

MANUFACTURERS

Jansport: www.jansport.com
Marmot: www.marmot.com
Patagonia: www.patagonia.com
W.L. Gore: www.gorefabrics.com

OTHER BESTS AND WORSTS OF SOUTHERN CALIFORNIA

Worst place to run out of gas:

Panamint Valley Road in the Owens Valley. Which will get to you first—the vultures or AAA?

Favorite affordable motel:

Buckeye Lodge in Three Rivers. A bear once rode a dumpster past this place. Need we say more?

Favorite unaffordable hotel:

Ritz Carlton Laguna Niguel. Almost inconceivable that we'll ever be able to afford it.

Favorite meal:

The burger stand at Jalama Beach.

Most romantic spot:

Tamarack Lodge in Mammoth Lakes. Being snowbound up here in a comfy little cabin with your honey bunny might not be a bad thing.

Favorite city:

San Luis Obispo. Charm galore and affordable with a beautiful downtown featuring real architecture and a river running through it.

Scariest town:

Inyokern. Makes nearby Ridgecrest look good.

Scariest town runner-up:

Twentynine Palms. Has more tattoo parlors per capita than any other city in the country.

Our dog's favorite place:

Mammoth Lakes, anytime of any day of the year.

Best place to celebrate New Year's Eve:

Furnace Creek Ranch in Death Valley. You don't have to worry about that Rose Bowl traffic.

Best thing to do with your parents visiting from out of town:

Whale watching. You'll be able to tell your kids how Grandpa threw up on a group of nuns.

Best way to celebrate your 40th birthday:

Skydiving. When your feet touch the ground and you're still among the living, 40 won't seem so bad anymore.

Scariest road:

The short drive to North Lake in Bishop Canyon. If you're riding shotgun, do yourself a favor and don't look down.

Best place to wet a line:

The Upper San Joaquin River in the Ansel Adams Wilderness. Whether or not you catch anything, you win.

The place that has never disappointed anyone we've met:

The Golden Trout Wilderness. The name alone sounds beautiful.

Best tip on how to start your campfire:

Burn this book. Immediately buy a new copy of the book upon returning home.

INDEX

INDEX

A

A Beautiful Morning 281
A Skysurfer Balloon Company 281
Abalone Cove 80
Abbott, Mount 4, 126
Abel, Mount 192
Action Sports Beach and Bay Rentals 285
Adams, Ansel, Wilderness 119, 121, 123, 125
Adventours Outdoor Excursions 87, 182, 200
Adventure 16 18, 239, 290, 294, 297, 299, 300
Adventures Unlimited 49
Agnew Meadows 12, **69,** 121, 123, 125
Agoura Hills, CA 31, 204, 222, 236, 302, 304
Agua Caliente Creek 185, 186
Agua Caliente Creek, Big Hot Spring **97**
Agua Caliente Debris Dam 186
Agua Caliente Trail 186
Air Adventures Skydiving, Inc. 47
Air Adventures West Skydiving Center 47
Airplane Ridge 274
Algodones Outstanding Natural Area 286
Alien (film) 279
Aliso, CA 32
Alper's Ranch 55
Alpine Experience 19
Alpine, CA 304
Alta Sierra, CA 93
Altadena, CA 208, 211, 212
Alvis', Tony, Los Padres Wilderness Outfitters **70,** 194, 195, 196
Amboy Crater **14**
American Cetacean Society 78, 232
Anacapa Island 73, 80, 196, 197, 198
 East 197
 Middle 197
 West 197
Anaheim Hills, CA 19
Ancient Bristlecone Pine Forest 92
Angeles Crest Highway **94,** 209, 210, 211, 214, 216
Angeles National Forest 12, 15, 18, 43, 196, **208,** 209, 213, 214, 215, 217, 289, 299, 304
 Arroyo Seco Ranger District 212, 213, 304
 Headquarters 214
 Mount Baldy Ranger District 213, 304
 Supervisor's Office 30, 210, 211, 212, 214, 304
 Tujunga Ranger District 304
Ansel Adams Wilderness 119, 121, 122, 123, 125
Antelope Valley Sportsmen's Club 68
Anza Trail 277
Anza-Borrego Desert State Park **15,** 65. 83, 95, 273, **275,** 277, 278, 281, 303
Aqua Sports 87, 200
Arcadia, CA 214, 304
Arch Rock 73, 196
Arcularius Ranch 55
Argo Diving 238
Arnott, John 280, 281

INDEX

Arrowhead Ranger District 98
Arrowhead, Lake 62
Arroyo Grande, CA 89, 108, 112
Arroyo Seco 209, 273, 274, 275
  Ranger District 212, 213, 214
Arroyo Seco Picnic Area 273
Arroyo Sequit 94
Arujo, Mike 61
Asbury Park Press 198
Ash Mountain 150
Aspendell, CA 130
Assembling California
  (J. McPhee) 12
Associated Students Inc. 301
Asuza, CA 214
Atlantis (space shuttle) 171
Atwell Mill **148,** 151
Audubon Society 72, 307
Automobile Association of
  Southern California 294
Avalon, CA 234, 237, 238
Avila Beach, CA 56, 95, 96, 108, **109,** 110
Avila Hot Springs and
  RV Park **95**
Avila State Beach 107, 110
Azalea **142,** 144
Azusa, CA 26

B

Backbone Trail 219, **236**
Backpacker (magazine) 307
Baden-Powell, Mount **211**
Baden-Powell, Mount,
  Trail **211**
Badger Pass Ski Area 23
Badwater Basin 10, 133, **135,** 255
Bahia Resort Hotel
  Marina 285
Bailey Geological Party 132
Baker Area Chamber of
  Commerce 257
Baker, CA 93, 97, 255

Bakersfield, CA 160, 164, 305
Balboa Boat Rentals 269
Balboa Island **51**
Balboa Pier 51
Balboa, CA 42, 52
Balch County Park 156, 160
Baldwin Lake Stables **70**
Baldy, Mount (*see also* Mount
  San Antonio) 7, 47, 90, 208,
  213, 217, 218
  Ranger District
    213, 214
Baldy, Mount, Ski Area 213, **217**
Ballard, CA 181
Balloon Flights 281
Banning, CA 245
Bar "S" Stables **70,** 227
Barker Dam 252
Barstow, CA 14, 254, 305
Barton Flats Campground 247
Bates Nuts Farm **285,** 286
Bates, Walter 285
Baywatch (tv show) 230, 234
Beach Trail (Torrey Pines State
  Reserve) 282
Beach Trails (bicycling, Orange
  County) **27**
Beachfront Horse Rentals **70**
Bear Creek Spire 4, 126
Bear Mountain 216, 244, **249,** 250
Bear Springs, Little,
  Trail Camp 246
Belknap Campground **162**
Bell Canyon Trail 32, 267
Benton Crossing 54, 125
Berner's Pack Outfit **69**
Bertha Peak 246
Best Western (Paso Robles) 103
Best Western (Bakersfield) 160
Best Western
  (Twentynine Palms) 254
Best Western El Rancho
  (Morro Bay) 104

INDEX

Best Western Holiday Lodge (Sequoia National Park) 150
Best Western, Shelter Cove Lodge (Pismo Beach) 108
Best Western, Shore Cliff Lodge (Pismo Beach) 108
Beverly Hills, CA 94, 135
Big Agua Caliente Creek 97
Big Agua Caliente Hot Spring 186
Big Air Green Valley (*see also* Ski Green Valley) 250
Big Bear Chamber of Commerce 26, 245
Big Bear City, CA 26, 30, 88, 246
  East 70
Big Bear Express Quad 249
Big Bear Lake 26, 30, 58, 62, 93, **244,** 245, 246, 247, 248, 249, 250
Big Bear Lake Resort Association 245
Big Bear Lake Trail **26**
Big Bear Lake, CA 70, 245, 246, 247
  Municipal Water District 245
Big Bear Lodging and General Referrals 251
Big Bear Marina 244
Big Bear Ranger District 246, 247, 248
Big Falls (Santa Lucia Wilderness) 111
Big Meadow 127, 157
Big Pine, CA (Inyo National Forest) 8
Big Pines Visitor Center (Angeles National Forest) 210, 214
Big Santa Anita Creek 212
Big Stump 144
Big Sur 105
Big Tujunga Station 208

Big Whitney Meadow 155
Birch, Steven, Aquarium 81
Bird Rock 237
Bishop Creek 130
  Middle Fork 129, 130, 131
  North Fork 128, 129
  South Fork 130, 131
Bishop Creek Canyon 69, 92, 126, **128, 129,** 130, 131
Bishop Creek Lodge 130
Bishop Pack Outfitters **69,** 128
Bishop Peak 17, 18
Bishop, CA 54, 58, 92, 125, 126, 128, 131, 304
Black Mountain 30
Black Mountain Road **30**
Black Rock Campground 253
Black Rock, CA 158
Blackrock Ranger Station 153
Blackrock Trail 5, 152, **154**
Bloody Mountain 4
Blue Jay Campground 270
Blue Lake **15,** 129
Blue Lake Trail 129
Blue Ridge Campground 12, 210, 214
Blue Ridge Trail **210**
Bluewater Creek 261
Bluewater Trail 261
Bluff Cove **233**
Bluff Trail 106
Bolsa Chica State Beach 77
Boney Mountains 203
Borrego Badlands 15
Borrego Palm Canyon 277
Borrego Springs, CA 273, 275, 277, 278, 303
Bow Willow Canyon 277
Box Lake 126
Boyden Cavern **13**
Bright Valley Farm, Inc. **70**
Broken Hill Trail 282

BOLD PAGE NUMBERS INDICATE MAIN LISTINGS

INDEX

Brown, Davy, Campground 179, 180
Brown, Davy, Creek 179
Brown, Davy, Trail 179, 180
Bryant, Rebecca 33
Buckeye Flat Campground 92, 147, **148**
Buckeye Tree Lodge 145, 150
Buckhorn Campground 15, 210, 214
Buckhorn Campground to Cooper Canyon (scenic hike) **15**
Bucks Lake 126
Burbank, CA 70, 226, 227
Bureau of Land Management (BLM) 11, 13, 14, 15, 254, 286, 305, 307
    Barstow Resource Area 305
    Caliente Resource Area 28
    California Desert District 286, 305
    El Centro Resource Area 306
    Needles Resource Area 306
    Palm Springs-South Coast Resource Area 3 06
    Ridgecrest Resource Area 306
    Yuma District 306
"BLM Wilderness Areas Maps and Information—California" 305
Bureau of Reclamation 307
Burkhart Trail **210**
Burnt Rancheria Campground 12
Buttonwillow, CA 84

C

Cabrillo Beach 78
Cabrillo Bike Lane **25**
Cabrillo Marine Aquarium 78, 79, 80
Cachuma, Lake 32, 54, 58, **72**, **182**, 183, 184
Cachuma, Lake, Recreation Area 72, 184
Cahuilla Ranger Station 286
Cajon Pass 62
Calabasas, CA 303
Calcite Mine 276, 277
California AIDS Bike Ride **32**, 33
California City Skydive Center 47
California City, CA 47, 84
California Department of Fish and Game 56, 59, 67, 68, 161, 183, 292, 307
California Department of Parks and Recreation 40, 80, 204, 220, 229, 230, 303, 307
    Mojave Desert Office 171
California Desert District 286
California Desert Information Center 14
California Desert Protection Act 305
California Dreamin' Balloon Adventures 281
California Hot Springs, CA **96**, 160, 161, 164, 305
California Institute of Technology 273
California Polytechnic State University 107, 301
California State Parks 36, 37, 73
    Office of Information 303
    Point Mugu Ranger Office 37
California State University San Bernardino 301
California State Water Project 62
California Trout 307
Camp Nelson, CA 162, 163
Camp Pendleton 260
Campland 285
Campmor 298, 307
Campo, CA 11

INDEX

Cannell Meadow Ranger District 6, 29, 153, 157, 158, 169, 170
Canyon Lodge 116, 117
Canyon Sin Nombre 277
Canyon View Group Camp **142**
Capitola Wharf **6**
Cardiff State Beach 81
Cardiff-by-the-Sea, CA 38
Cardinal Village Resort 130
Carlsbad, CA 281
Carlton, Mary Anne 146, 149
Carpinteria State Beach 6, **36**, 78, **79**, 80
Carpinteria, CA 36, 40
Carrillo, Leo 221
Carrillo, Leo, State Beach **37**, 40, **80**, 85, 94
Carrizo Badlands 277
Overlook 277
Carrizo Canyon 277
Carrizo Plain **12**, 13, **28**
Carson, CA 19, 301
Casa Vieja Meadows **5**, 6, 152, 153
Casino (Catalina Island) 238
Casitas, Lake **60**, 61
Caspers Wilderness Park (*see also* Ronald W. Caspers Wilderness Park) 32, 43, 91, **266**, 267
Castaic, Lake 61
Castle Rock Trail **246**
Catalina Divers Supply 238
Catalina Island 78, 213, 224, 234, 235, **237**, 239, 269
Catalina Scuba Luv 238
Catalina Visitors Bureau 239
Cayucos Beach Pier **56**
Cayucos, CA 56
Cedar Grove Pack Station **69**, 144
Cedar Grove Village, CA 69, 140, 141, 142, 143, 144
Cedar Grove 140, 141, 142, 144
Cedar Springs, CA 62
Cedar-Doane Trail 272
Century Dam 219
Century Lake 219
Channel Islands National Marine Sanctuary 302
Channel Islands National Park 36, **73**, 80, 83, 86, 87, 179, 186, 196, 197, 198, 200, 201, 202, 282, 303
Visitor Center 79
Chantry Flats Ranger Station 212
Chatsworth, CA 301
Cheeseboro Canyon 31
Chickenfoot Lake **4**, 126
Chilao Visitor Center 211, 214
Child, Julia 180
Chinatown (film) 124
Chino Canyon 258
Chino Hills State Park 32
Chiquito Trail 271
Chouinard, Yvon 18, 239
Chuck Richards' Whitewater, Inc. 166
Chula Vista, CA 21, 47, 191, 192
Chumash Wilderness 191
Cima Dome 257
Circle "K" Stables **70**, 227
Circle B Ranch Stables 70
Cisco Kid, The 221
Cisco Sportfishing 78
Claremont, CA 208
Cleveland National Forest 12, 43, 66, 94, 196, 209, 260, 261, 270, 271, 272, 273, 274, 275, 304
Descanso Ranger District 31, 304
Palomar Ranger District 304
Supervisor's Office 304
Trabuco Ranger District 261, 271, 304

INDEX

Cliffs at Shell Beach 109
Climbing Mount Whitney (W. Benti et al.) 8
Clinton, Bill 254
Close Encounters 44
Coachella Valley 253, 259
Coastal Trail (bicycling, Ventura County) **25**
Cold Creek Campground 121
Cold Creek Canyon 222, 236
Cold Springs **148,** 151
Cold Springs Tavern 183
Coldbrook, CA 214
Coldwater Campground 3, 4, 123, 177
Coldwater Creek 121, 123
Colker, David 32
Colorado Desert 252
Come Fly a Kite 52
Condor Summit Road Trail 21
Conejo Valley 31
Congress Trail **146,** 150
Convict Creek 59, 125
Convict Lake 54, **59,** 124
Convict Lake Resort 59
Cooper Canyon 15, 210
Corallina Cove 106
Corona del Mar, CA 80
Corona, CA 44, 96, 304
Coronado Boat Rental 285
Coronado Islands **27,** 279
Coronado, CA 27, 285
Corral Meadow 29
Costa Mesa, CA 18, 19, 300
Cottonwood Campground 155, 253
Cottonwood Pack Station **69,** 155
Cottonwood Pass 155
Cottonwood Pass Trail 155
Cougar Canyon 277
Cougar Crest Trail 12, **245,** 246
County Roads G-14 and G-19 **92**

Countyline State Beach **40**
Coyote Canyon Trail 221
CP Watersports 283, 284, 285
Crescent Meadow **15,** 145, **146**
Crescent Meadow Trail 146
Crestline, CA 62, 63
Crowley, Lake 53, **54, 58,** 59, 92, 124, 183
Crowley, Lake, Fish Camp 58
Crux 19
Crystal Cave **146**
Crystal Cove State Park **30,** 31, **80,** 268, 269, 303
Crystal Cove, CA 268
Crystal Crag 122
Crystal Lake **122**
Crystal Pier **57**
Crystal Springs 142
Cuyamaca Peak 275
Cuyamaca Rancho State Park 43, 65, **273,** 274, 275, 303
Cuyamaca, Lake 65, 275

D

Dade, Mount 4, 126
Dakota Campground 183
Dana Inn and Marina 57, 284
Dana Point 78, 81
Dana Point Marina 81
Dante's View **135,** 255
Darwin, Mount 131
Davy Brown Campground 179, 180
Davy Brown Creek 179
Davy Brown Trail 179, 180
Dawn Mine 211
Death Valley Junction, CA 93
Death Valley National Park 9, 10, 14, 15, 86, 92, 93, 97, **131,** 132, 133, 134, 135, 136, 254, 255, 302, 303
Death Valley Natural History Association 136
Death Valley, CA 303

INDEX

Deep Creek 247
Deep Creek Hot Springs **98**
Deer Lakes 125
Del Cerro Park **232**
Del Mar, CA 280, 281
Delano, CA 68, 84, 93
Descanso Beach Ocean Sports 238
Descanso Ranger District 31
Descanso, CA 70, 303
Desert Gardens Picnic Area 277
Desert Protection Act 254
Desert Solitaire (E. Abbey) 298
Desert Studies Center 301
Desert View Trail 259
Devil's Chair 13
Devil's Golf Course 135
Devil's Playground (*see also* Kelso Dunes) 256
Devil's Punchbowl **13**
Devil's Punchbowl County Park 14
Devils Postpile National Monument 12, 120, 122, 123
Devils Postpile Trailhead 121
Diablo Canyon 107
Dick Loskorn Trail 266
Disappointment, Mount 210
Disneyland 236
Doane Pond 272
Doble Trail Camp 246
Dockweiler State Beach 235
Doheny State Beach 38, 81
Dombeck, Mike 307
Dome Land Wilderness 82, 156, 157, 158
Dorn's Original Breakers Cafe 104
Dorst Campground **148**
Doyle Springs, CA 163
Duck Lake 125
Duck Pass 3
Duck Pass Trail 3
Ducks Unlimited 307
Dune Trail (Montana de Oro State Park) 105
Dunlap, CA 305

E

Eagle Rock 224
Eagle Watch Tours 102, 103
Earth First! 307
East Anacapa Island 197
East Big Bear City, CA 70
East Camino Cielo Road **29**
East Fork (campground, Rock Creek Canyon) 127
East Mesa Trail 274
East Mojave National Scenic Area 254
East Ridge Trail 266
East Summit Trail 212
Eastern Mojave Desert 255
EconoLodge (Mojave) 152
Ediza Lake 125
Edwards Air Force Base 51, 171, 172
El Capitan (Yosemite National Park) 18
El Capitan Lake **65**
El Capitan State Beach **36, 78**
El Centro, CA 306
El Matador State Beach 229
El Mirage Dry Lake Bed **51**
El Monte, CA 84
El Moro Canyon 268
El Moro Canyon Trail 268
El Pescador State Beach 229
Elsinore, CA 47
Elsinore, Lake 45, 47, 49, 94
Elsinore, Lake, Sports 49
Emerald Lake **121**
Emerson, Mount 128, 129, 131
Emigrant Junction, CA 133
Emigrant Campground **134**
Encinitas, CA 41, 81
Encino Reservoir 71
Encino, CA 94

INDEX

"Enviromap Guide to Seashore Life" 104
Eric's Tackle 57
Ernie Maxwell Trail 260
Escape Route 301
Escondido, CA 44, 95, 285
Etech 104
Expressway (ski run) 249

F

Fairview Campground 168
Fall Canyon **133**
Fast Times at Ridgemont High (film) 39
Fawnskin, CA 305
Featherly Regional Park 26
Federal Aviation Administration 281
Fess Parker Winery 181
Field Guide to the Birds of North America 71
Field Studies of California Birds II (UCLA class) 72
Fields of Honor 44
Figueroa Campground 179
Figueroa Mountain 82, 90, 179, 180
Fillmore, CA 195
Finicky Fish, The 104
First Ascent Climbing Services, Inc. 19, 253
Fish Bowl, The 104
Fish Creek 154, 158, 177
Fish Creek Mountains 15
Fish Shanty 104
Fisherman's Camp 261
Fisherman's Landing 78, 280
Fisherman's Village 235
Flat Rock 282
Flat Rock Point 233
Fleming, Guy, Trail 282
Flintridge, CA 214, 304
Flintstones (film) 14
Florence, Mount 153

Font's Point 15
Foothills (Ash Mountain) Visitor Center 147, 149, 150
Forest Falls, CA 9, 245, 247
Forks of the Kern 165
Fort Hunter Liggett 68
Fort Tejon 13
Foster's Pass 11
Four Jeffrey Campground 130
Franklin Lakes 125
Franklin Pass 149
Frazier Park, CA 305
Free Willy (film) 76
Freeman Creek 161
Freeman Grove 161
French Gulch Marina 170
Frenchman's Flat 55
Frenchy's Cove **80**
Fresno, CA 140, 144
Friends of the Earth 307
Furnace Creek Inn **135**
Furnace Creek Ranch **135**
Furnace Creek Visitor Center 136
Furnace Creek Campground **134**
Furnace Creek, CA 10, 133, 135, 136

G

Gabrielino Trail 210
Gainey Vineyard 181
Galley, The 104
Gardens of Avila, The 109
Garnet Lake 125
Gaviota Beach 78
Gaviota Pass 33
Gaviota Peak 97, 175, **186,** 187
Gaviota State Park 36, 97, 186, 187, 303
General Grant Tree 141
General Grant Tree Loop 143
General Sherman Tree 145, 146, 161

INDEX

General's Highway **92,** 145, 146, 147, 148, 150
"Geologic Auto Tour" (pamphlet) 13
George, Lake 23, 54, 120, 122, 123
Geronimo 249
Giant Forest 15, 92, 141, 145, 146, 147, 148, 149, 150, 161
Giant Forest Lodge 150
Giant Forest Village, CA 146
Gibraltar Dam 184, 185
Gibraltar Reservoir 184
Gibraltar Rock 18
Glacier Point 23
Glacier Point Road (cross-country ski trail) 23
Glen Canyon Dam 307
Glendale, CA 70, 226, 227
Glendora, CA 26, 208, 214, 304
Glenn Ivy Hot Springs **96**
Glorietta Park 27
Gold Coast 216
Golden Trout Wilderness 5, 6, 15, 82, 92, 147, 151, 152, 153, 154, 155, 156, 161, 163
Goleta Beach 78
Goleta, CA 70, 87, 178, 200, 303, 304
Goodwin Education Center 13, 28
Gorgonio, Mount 9
Gorman, CA 83
Granite Springs 274
Granite Staircase 19
Grant Grove 22, 140, 141, 142, 143, 144, 150
  Visitor Center 140, 144
Grant Grove Stables **70**
Grant Grove Village, CA 13, 22, 70, 140, 141, 142, 143, 144, 304
Gravity Activated Sports 273
Gray's Boat Landing 244

Great American Fish Company, The 104
Great Central Valley 116
Great Western Divide Highway 160, 161, 163
Greblo, Joe 48
Green Meadow 31
Green Valley Campground 274, 275
Green Valley Lake 62, 250
Green Valley Picnic Area **43**, 273
Greenhorn Ranger District 97
Greensfield, CA 32
Gregory, Lake **62**
Gregory, Lake, Regional Park 63
Griffith Park 88, **226,** 227, 228, 229
Griffith Park, Observatory **227,** 228, 229
Griffith Park Horse Rentals **70,** 227
Grover Beach 33
Grover City, CA 107, 108
Guided Mule Rides **70**
Guy Fleming Trail 282

H

H&M Landing 78, 280
Hagen Canyon 171
Haimwertz, Steve 168
Half Dome 17
Halfway Trail Camp 9
Hang Gliding Center, The 49
Harbor City, CA 301
Harmony Borax Works **135**
Harrison, Tom, Cartography (Recreation Maps)
  Cuyamaco Rancho State Park 275
  Mammoth High Country 4
  Mono Divide High Country 4, 131

BOLD PAGE NUMBERS INDICATE MAIN LISTINGS 319

INDEX

Sequoia and Kings Canyon National Parks 144, 150
San Gabriel Mountains 209
Harvey Cove 183
Hazard Canyon 31
Heart and Blood: Living with Deer in America (R. Nelson) 67
Heart Lake 126
Helgren's Oceanside & Islands Sportfishing Trips 280
Hells Hole Trail 152
Hemet, Lake 63, 260
Hermosa Beach **231,** 235
Hermosa, CA 25
Hesperia, CA 98
Hidden Falls Campground 155, 159, 160
Hidden Valley Campground 252, 253
High Adventure 49
High Creek Trail Camp 9
High Sierra Trail **146,** 147
Highway 127 **93**
Highway 155 **92**
Highway 33 **93**
Highway 76 94
Highway 76 **94**
Highway 78 **95**
Hilltop Horse Rental **70**
Hilton in Mission Bay 283
Hilton Lake
  Lower 126, 127
  Upper 126, 127
Hilton Lakes Trail 126
Hobo Campground 96
Hole-in-the-Wall Campground 256, 257
Holidays on Horseback **70**
Hollywood Hills 227
Hollywood, CA 70, 94, 219, 226, 228
Horse Meadow 29, 156, 157, 158
Horseback Adventures **69**

Horseshoe Lake 23, 120, 121, 125
Horseshoe Meadows 69, **155**
Horseshoe Meadows Equestrian Camp 155
Hospital Point 81
Hot Creek 92, 125
Hot Creek Hatchery 125
Hot Springs Canyon 194
Hotel Nipton 257
How Green Was My Valley (film) 219
Humber State Park 260
Humphreys Basin 128
Huntington State Beach 26, 27, **40,** 41, 57
Huntington Beach, CA 26, 27, 84
  Visitors Bureau 57
Huntington Pier 41, **57**

I

Idyllwild Campground 259
Idyllwild, CA 11, 18, 30, 63, 259, **260,** 305
  Chamber of Commerce 260
Idyllwild's Nomad Adventures 260
Imperial Beach 75
Imperial Sand Dunes **286**
Imperial Valley 286
Independence, CA 4, 5, 92
Indian Cove Campground 253
Indian Valley Campground 253
Indio, CA 84
Inn of the Seventh Ray 225
Inspiration Point 197
Intermediate Lidos 269
International Whaling Commission 77
IntraWest 120
Inyo County Parks 97

INDEX

Inyo National Forest 15, 120, 122, 125, 127, 128, 131, 152, 153, 302
  Interagency Visitors Center 304
  Lone Pine Ranger District 304
  Mammoth Lakes Ranger District 4, 59, 125, 304
    Visitor Center 125
  Mono Lake Ranger District 304
  Mount Whitney Ranger District 5, 9, 153, 155
  Supervisor's Office 304
  White Mountain Ranger District 4, 128, 130, 131, 304
  Wilderness Reservation Service 3, 8, 9, 307
Iris Meadow 127
Irvine Lake **64**
Irvine, CA 74
Isabella, Lake 97, 160, 164, 166, 167, **169**, 170
  Dam 165
Island Packers (transport to Channel Islands National Park) 73, 78, 86, 197, 198, 200, 201, 202
Islandia Sportfishing 78
Isthmus Reef 237
Ivanpah Lake 51

J

Jackson, Michael 181
Jacobsen Trail 163
Jail Canyon 10
Jalama Beach **35**, 36, 90, **93**, **175**, 176
Jalama Beach County Park 36, 176
Jalama Beach Road **93**
Jamison Lake 184
Jansport 307
Jayhawker Canyon *133*

Jennings, Lake **65**
Jim Wallace Skydiving School 45, 47
Joaquin River Valley 122
John Muir Trail 120, 141
John Muir Wilderness 3, 4, 8, 18, 119, 128, 147, 155
Johnson, Gary 49
Johnson, Karen 71
Jordan Hot Springs 5, 152, 154
  Campground 152
Joshua Tree National Park 17, 18, 43, 86, **251**, 252, 253, 254, 259, 300, 303, 304
Joshua Tree Rock Climbing School 19, 253
Joshua Tree, CA 254
Julian Lodge 278
Julian, CA 278
Jumbo Rocks 252
Jumbo Rocks Campground 253
Juncal Campground 29, 185
Juncal Camuesa Road **29**
Juncal Dam 184
June Lake 92, 118
June Mountain **117**, 118
June Mountain Ski Area 118
Junipero Serra Trail 32

K

Kaweah River 145, 148, 164
  Marble Fork 147, 148
  Middle Fork 145
Kayak Horizons 104
Kayaks of Morro Bay 103, 104
Kearsage Pass 5
  Trail 4, 5
Kearsage Peak 5
Kelso Dunes (*see also* Devil's Playground) 256
Kennedy Meadows 154, 155
Kennedy Space Center 171, 172
Kern Hot Spring **96**
Kern Lodge Motel 166, 170

INDEX

Kern National Wildlife Refuge 68
"Kern Plateau Mountain Bike Trail Guide" (pamphlet) 29
Kern Plateau, Upper **28,** 29, 156, 158
Kern River 8, **54,** 55, 147, 156, 160, 161, 164, 165, 166, 167, 168, 169, 170
   Rafting **164**
   South Fork 5, 154
Kern River Canyon 147
Kern River Fishing 167
Kern River Inn Bed-and-Breakfast 166, 170
Kern River Tours 166
Kern Valley Marina 170
Kernville, CA 29, 55, 92, 154, 156, 157, 158, 164, 165, 166, 167, 168, 169, 170, 305
   Chamber of Commerce 170
Kettle, The 235
King City, CA 305
Kings Canyon National Park 8, 11, 13, **22,** 23, **60, 69, 70,** 92, 128, **140,** 141, 142, 143, 144, 150, 159, 303, 304
Kings River 164
   South Fork 140, 141, 142
Kite Man 52
Kites Galore 50, 51
Kites, Etc. 52
Kratka Ridge 18, 218

L

L.A. Harbor Cruises 78
L.A. Harbor Sportfishing 78
La Canada, CA 94, 209, 210, 211, 214, 217, 218
La Casa Del Zorro Resort Hotel 278
La Jolla Canyon 37, 203
La Jolla Cove 81
La Jolla Shores 81
La Jolla, CA 49, **81,** 231, 232, 268, 282
La Piedra State Beach 229
La Quinta, CA 70
La Super-Rica 180
Laguna Beach, CA 80, 268, 303
Laguna, Mount 12, 31
Lake Arrowhead 62, 247
Lake Cachuma 54, 58, **72, 182,** 183, 184
Lake Cachuma, CA 32
Lake Campground (Angeles National Forest) 214
Lake Casitas **60,** 61
Lake Casitas Recreation Area 61
Lake Castaic 61
Lake Crowley **54, 58,** 59, 92, 124, 183
Lake Crowley Fish Camp 58
Lake Cuyamaca 65, 275
Lake Elsinore 45, 47, 49, 94
Lake Elsinore Sports 49
Lake Elsinore, CA 47
Lake George 23, 54, 120, 122, 123
Lake Gregory **62**
Lake Gregory Regional Park 63
Lake Hemet **63,** 260
Lake Hemet Municipal Water District 63
Lake Hemet Campground 63
Lake Isabella 97, 160, 164, 166, **167, 169,** 170
   Dam 165
   Visitor Center 167
Lake Jennings **65**
Lake Mamie 23, 54, 120, 123
Lake Mary 3, 23, 54, 120, 121, 123
Lake Mary Loop 23
Lake Mary Road (cross-country ski trail) 23
Lake Matthews 47

INDEX

Lake Morena Village, CA 66
Lake Morena **65**
Lake Morena County Park 66
Lake Nacimiento **59**, 103
Lake Perris
  26, 47, **63**, 64
Lake Perris State Recreation
  Area 26, **51**, 64
Lake Piru 55, **61**
Lake Pyramid 55, 62
Lake Sabrina 129, 130, 131
Lake San Antonio 58, 59, **75**,
  101, 102, 103
Lake Skinner 47, **64**
Lake Skinner County
  Park 64
Lake Tahoe 301
Lake Virginia 125
Lakeside, CA 74
Lamarck Lakes 128, 129
Lancaster, CA 68, 82, 303
Langley, Mount, CA 8
Las Cruces Hot Spring **97**
Las Vegas, CA 48
Las Virgenes Creek 219
Lasky, Jesse 221
Lassen National Park 11
Learning Tree University
  201, 202, 301
Lee Vining, CA 304
Leo Carrillo State Beach
  37, 78, 40, **80**, 85, 94
Lewellyn, Michelle 50
Libbey Park 193
Lighthouse Trailer Park 245
Lily Rock (*see also* Tahquitz
  Rock) 260
Limestone Campground 168
Lion's Camp 98, 194, 195
Little Bear Springs Trail
  Camp 246
Little Casino 238
Little Falls (Santa Lucia
  Wilderness) 111

Little Lakes Basin 4, 126, 127
Little Pothole Lake **4**
Little Round Valley
  Campground 10
Live Oak 184
Livery Stable, The 69, 108
Loch Leven Lake 129
Lodgepole Campground **148**
Lodgepole Visitor Center
  145, 146, 150, 151
Loma Prieta 293
Lompoc, CA 175, 182
Lone Pine, CA 7, 8, 92, 304
Long Beach Harbor 77
Long Beach, CA 76, 167, 213,
  234, 300
Long Lake 126
Long Meadow Campground
  150, **161**
Long Valley Caldera 116
Long Valley Ranger Station
  10, 11, 258
Long, Dave 237
Lookout Trail 275
Loop Nature Trail (Devil's
  Punchbowl) 13
Lopez Canyon 111
Lopez Creek 111
Lopez Lake 58, **110**, 111, 112
Lopez Lake Marina and
  Store 111
Lopez Lake Recreation Area
  110, 112
Los Angeles Aqueduct 124
Los Angeles Astronomical
  Society 228
Los Angeles Audubon Society
  71, 297
Los Angeles County
  Beaches and Harbors 40, 41,
    229, 230, 231
  Bike Map Hotline 25, 26
  Department of Parks and
    Recreation 25, 26, 239, 301

INDEX

Department of Public Works 235
Museum of Natural History 77
Los Angeles Equestrian Center 26, 227
Los Angeles Gay and Lesbian Community Service Center 32
Los Angeles River, 226
Los Angeles Times 239
Los Feliz, CA 226
Los Olivos, CA 181, 182
Los Osos, CA 303
Los Padres National Forest 29, 43, 58, 61, 68, 93, 97, 111, 176, 178, 180, 185, 186, 187, 191, 194, 196, 209, 304
   Monterey Ranger District 305
   Mount Pinos Ranger District 21, 73, 192, 305
   Ojai Ranger District 55, 98, 194, 196, 305
   Santa Barbara Ranger District 29, 97, 185, 186, 187, 305
   Santa Lucia Ranger District 111, 178, 180, 305
   Supervisor's Office 304
Los Padres, CA 70
Los Prietos 185
Los Robles Open Space 31
Loskorn, Dick, Trail 266
Lost Valley Campground 177
Lover's Cove Marine Preserve 238
Lowe, Mount **212,** 300
   Summit **43**
Lowe, Mount, Campground 212
Lowe, Mount, Railway 212
Lower Hilton Lake 126
Lower Morgan Lake 126
Lower Santa Ynez River **184,** 185
Ludlow, CA 14

Lytle Creek, CA 305

M

M*A*S*H 219
Mack Lake 126
Mahogany Flat 134
Mahogany Flat Campground 10, 133, **134**
Malaga Cove **233,** 234
Malibu Bluffs 51
Malibu Bluffs Park **51**
Malibu Canyon 219
Malibu Creek 219, 220, 221
Malibu Creek State Park 17, 18, **218,** 220, 221, 236, 303
Malibu Lagoon **73,** 220
Malibu Lagoon State Beach **40, 80,** 230
Malibu Pier 40
Malibu, CA 32, 37, 40, 51, 73, 80, 90, 94, 203, 218, 229, 230, 233, 234
Mamie, Lake 23, 54, 120, 123
Mammoth Creek 120, 123, 125
Mammoth Crest 121
Mammoth Lakes Basin 3, 4, 14, 18, 23, 54, 55, 59, 92, 117, 119, 120, 121, 122, **123,** 125, 126, 248, 249
   Main Lodge 116, 117
   Ranger District 4, 59, 124, 125
Mammoth Lakes Visitor Bureau 117
Mammoth Lakes, CA 19, 54, 55, 58, 59, 69, 116, 118, 119, 120, 121, 122, 124, 126, 129, 175, 304
Mammoth Mountain 12, **28, 116,** 117, 118, 119, 120, 121, 301
Mammoth Mountain Ski Resort 121, 122
Mammoth Mountaineering School 19
Mammoth Pass **121**

INDEX

Manhattan Beach **231,** 235
Manhattan Beach, CA 25
Manning, Frank 40
Manter Meadow 156, 157
Manzana Campground 178
Manzana Creek 177, 178
Manzana Creek Trail 177
Manzana Narrows Campground 178
Manzana Schoolhouse Campground 177
Marble Canyon **15**
Marble Falls 147
Marble Fork Trail **147**
Marina del Rey, CA 235, 301
Marine Institute 81
Mariposa County 23, 24
Marmot 307
Marsh Lake 126
Mary, Lake 3, 23, 54, 120, 121, 123
Mary, Lake, Road (cross-country ski trail) 23
Matilija Creek **55**
Matilija Dam 55
Matilija Wilderness Area 93
Matthews, Lake 47
Maxwell, Ernie, Trail 260
May, Tim 198, 201
McGee Creek 125
McGee Creek Canyon 69
McGee Creek Pack Station **69**
McGill Campground 192
McGrath State Beach **36,** 37
McPhee, John 208, 212
Mentone, CA 9, 305
Mesa Peak 219
Mesquita, Filipe 283
Mesquite Spring **134**
Metropolitan Transit Authority (Los Angeles) 26
Meyer, Robert H., State Beach **229**

Mid Hills Campground 256, 257
Mid Santa Ynez Campground 185, 186
Middle Anacapa Island 197
Middle Fork Bishop Creek 129, 130, 131
Millard Canyon **211**
  Campground 211, 299
Millard Creek 211
Millard Falls 211
Mills, Mount 4, 126
Milt McAuley's "Guide to the Backbone Trail" 236
Milt McAuley's *Hiking in Topanga State Park* 225
Minaret Falls 123
Minaret Mountains 116
Mineral King Pack Station **70**
Mineral King Valley 151
Mineral King, CA 70, 147, 148, 150, 151, 153, 155
Miracle Hot Springs **96**
Miracle Mile 249
Mission Bay 27, **51,** 283, 284, 285
Mission Bay Park **27**
Mission Bay Sportscenter 285
Mission Bay, CA 78, 280
Mission Beach 27
Mission Trails Regional Park 32
Mission Viejo, CA 19, 302
Mist Falls **141**
Mitchell Caverns 256, 257
Mohan, Geoff 33
Mojave Desert Information Center 255, 257
Mojave National Preserve 11, 62, 152, 171, 209, 211, 213, 252, **254,** 255, 256, 257, 301, 303, 304
Mojave, CA 170
Monache Meadows 5
Mono Campground 185
Mono Creek 185

BOLD PAGE NUMBERS INDICATE MAIN LISTINGS

INDEX

Mono Debris Basin 185
Mono Lake 14, 92
Mono Pass 126
Mono Pass Trail 126
Mono Ridge 268
Monrovia, CA 208
Montana de Oro State Park
 15, 31, 43, **79,** 103, **105,** 106,
 107, 282, 301, 303
Monte Cristo 214
Montecito Peak 186
Montecito, CA 70
Montecito-Sequoia Lodge 150
Montecito-Sequoia Nordic Ski
 Resort **23**
Monterey Bay 301
Monterey County
 Parks 75, 103
Monterey, CA 303
Montesino, David 296
Moorpark, CA 27
Moraine **142**
Morena, Lake, Village, CA 66
Morena, Lake **65**
Morena Lake
 County Park 66
Morengo Valley 251
Moreno Valley, CA 26, 51, 64
Morgan Lake
 Lower 126
 Upper 126
Morgan Pass Trail 126
Morgan, Mount 4
Mormon Rocks 13
Moro Canyon 30
Moro Canyon Trail 30
Moro Ridge 30
Morrison, Mount 59, 124
Morro Bay 33, 50, 56, **75,**
 103, 104, 105, 106
 Estuary 104
 Harbor Master's Office 56
Morro Bay State Park 75, 103,
 104, 303

Morro Bay, CA 51, 56, 76, 78,
 103, 104
 Chamber of Commerce
  75, 104
 City T-Pier **56**
Morro Rock 50, 103, 105, 187
Morro Strand State Beach **50**
Mosaic Canyon 132, **133**
Moses Gulch Campground
 159, 160
Moses Mountain 159
Mosquito Flat 126
Mosquito Flat Trailhead 4
Mount Abbott 4, 126
Mount Abel 192
Mount Baden-Powell 211
Mount Baden-Powell Trail **211**
Mount Baldy (*see also* Mount
 San Antonio) 7, 47, 90, 208,
 213, 217, 218
 Ranger District 213, 214
Mount Baldy Ski Area
 213, 17, 218
Mount Dade 4, 126
Mount Darwin 131
Mount Disappointment 210
Mount Emerson 128, 129, 131
Mount Florence 153
Mount Laguna 12, 31
Mount Langley, CA 8
Mount Lowe **212,** 300
 Summit **43**
Mount Lowe Campground 212
Mount Lowe Railway 212
Mount Mills 4, 126
Mount Morgan 4
Mount Morrison 59, 124
Mount Pinos **21, 72,** 73, **191,** 192
 Ranger District 21, 73, 192
Mount Pinos Campground 192
Mount San Antonio (*see also*
 Mount Baldy) 7, 47, 90, 208,
 213, 217
 Ranger District 213, 214

INDEX

Mount San Gorgonio 7, 9, 10, 30, 47, 213, 247
Mount San Jacinto 7, 10, 11, 15, 22, 30, 47, 213, 259, 260
  Ranger District 30
Mount San Jacinto State Park **10,** 11, **15, 21,** 22, 258, 259, 260, 303
Mount Thompson 131
Mount Waterman **216,** 217
Mount Whitney **7,** 8, 9, 10, 11, 92, 133, 146, 147, 164, 167, 170
  Ranger District 5, 9, 153, 155
  Zone 9
Mount Whitney, CA 8
Mount Williamson 17, 18
Mount Wilson 213
  Observatory 208
Mount Wilson Toll Road **30**
Mountain & River Adventures 29, 158
Mountain High Ski Resort 210, **216,** 217, 218, 249
  East 216
  West 216
Mountain Home State Forest **155,** 156, **158,** 159, 160
Mountain Station 259
Mountains Conservancy Foundation 223, 236
Mr. Paintball 44
Muir, John 10, 120, 146, 151
Muir, John, Trail 120, 141
Muir, John, Wilderness 3, 4, 8, 18, 119, 128, 147, 155
Mulholland Drive **94**
Mulholland, William 124
Musch Trail 224
Muscle Beach 235
Museum of Natural History 104

N

Nacimiento, Lake **59,** 103

National Aeronautics and Space Administration (NASA)
  Space Shuttle 172
  Mission Control 172
National Audubon Society 71
National Geographic 71
National Geographic Society 307
National Marine Fisheries Service 220, 307
National Oceanic and Atmospheric Administration (NOAA) 307
National Outdoor Leadership Schools (NOLS) 307
National Park Service 122, 136, 143, 147, 198, 201, 202, 204, 221, 222, 236, 254, 255, 256, 307
  Visitor Center 236
"National Park Service Backcountry Hikes" (pamphlet) 136
National Recovery Act 177
National Speleological Society 256
National Weather Service 208, 307
  Forecast Office 307
  Western Headquarters 307
Nature Conservancy, The 13, 28, 198, 307
Nature Trail Loop (Caspers Wilderness Park) 266
Needles, CA 306
Neverland Ranch 181
New Shady Rest 124
New York Newsday 283
Newcomb's Ranch 214
Newhall, CA 44
Newport Bay 269
Newport Bay, Upper 37
  Ecological Reserve and Regional Park **74**

BOLD PAGE NUMBERS INDICATE MAIN LISTINGS

INDEX

Newport Beach Harbor 27, 269
Newport Beach, CA
  37, 38, 74, 269, 270
Newport Dunes Park **37,** 38
Newport SeaFest Kite
  Festival 51
Nike Missile Site 32
Ninemile Creek, 152, 154
Nipton, CA 257
NIRA Campground 177
Noble Canyon **31,** 270
Nordic Ski Center 258
North Beach Campground 109
North Fork Marina (Lake
  Isabella) 170
North Grove Loop **141**
North Lake (Bishop Creek
  Canyon) 128, 131, 300
  Campground 128, 129, 130
North Lake Tahoe 24
North Palm Springs, CA 306
North Shore Landing
  (Big Bear Lake) 245
Northridge Overlook 191
Northridge, CA 19, 301

O

O'Connell, Terry 61
O'Reilly, Radar 219
Observatory (Palomar)
  Campground 272
  Trail 272, 273
Oceano Dunes State
  Vehicular Recreation
  Area 35, **107**
Oceano, CA 69, 108
Oceanside, CA 280
Ocotillo Recreation Area 277
Ojai Ranger District 98, 196
Ojai Valley 192, 193
Ojai Valley Inn 194
Ojai Valley Trail 29, **192,** 194
Ojai, CA 6, 29, 30, 55, 60, 90,
  93, 193, 194, 305

Chamber of Commerce
  29, 193, 194
Ojai's Shelf Road **29**
Olaine Lake 122
Old Corral Picnic Area 32, **43,**
  266, 267
Old Shady Rest 124
Old Topanga Canyon 222
Olde Port Beach 109, 110
Olde Port Inn 110
Onion Valley 4, 5, 15, 92, 300
Onion Valley, CA 60, 69
Orange Coast College 269, 270
Orange County
  EMA/Transportation 26, 27
  Regional Parks 74
Orange County Marine
  Institute 79, 81
Orange, CA 65
Ortega Highway **94**
Oso Flaco Lakes **60,** 108
Oso Flaco, CA 107
Ostrander Ski Hut 23
Outdoor Adventures 166
Outlaw Snowboard Park 249
Outpost Camp 8
Outside (magazine)
  176, 298, 307
Owens River 53, **54,** 55, 58,
  92, 124, 125
Owens River Gorge 18
Owens River Valley 5, 8, 58,
  116, 120, 131, 183
Oxnard State Beach 50

P

Pacific Aquatic Center 301
Pacific Beach 27
Pacific Coast Highway
  32, 35, 203, 204, 230, 234,
  268, 282
Pacific Crest Trail **11,** 12, 30,
  94, 98, 120, 121, 123, 154,
  155, 210, **246**

INDEX

Pacific Crest Trail Association 12, 307
Pacific Flyway 102, 103
Pacific Gas and Electric Company 103, 107
Pacific Palisades 25, 32, 223, 224, 225, 230, 234, 235, 236, 237
Pacific Wilderness Institute 301
Paddlesports 87, 198, 200
Painted Cave 18
Palisade Campground 127
Palm Canyon Resort Motel 278
Palm Springs Aerial Tram 10, 11, 21, 22, 70, 258, 259, 260
Palm Springs, CA 22, 70, 251, 252, 258, 259
Palmdale, CA 13, 51
Palomar Airport 281
Palomar Mountain 94, 271, 272, 273, 281
Palomar Mountain State Park 43, 87, 91, 94, **271**, 272, 273, 303
Palomar Observatory **271**, 272
Palos Verdes Estates, CA 234
Palos Verdes Peninsula 78, **80**, 213, 224, 231, 232, 233, 234, 235, 237
Panamint Mountains 9, 132, 134
Panamint Valley 9
Panther Peak 146
Parachutes Over San Diego 47
Paradise Campground 185
Paramount Pictures 221
Paramount Ranch State Park **43**, 94, **221**, 222
Parchers Resort 130
Parker Mesa 224
Pasadena, CA 30, 43, 209, 212, 213
Paso Picacho Campground 275
Paso Robles, CA 32, 33, 59, 69, 92, 101, 102, 103

Patagonia 239, 307
Patton, George 257
Pauma Valley 94, 271, 273
P-Bar Flat Campground 185, 186
Pear Lake 22, 60
Pearblossom, CA 14
Pelican Point 80
Pendola Jeepway 186
Pendola Ranger Station 186
Penny, Lee 167, 169
Penny, Sonia 167
Pepperdine University 51
Peppermint Campground **161**
Peppermint Creek 161
Perris Valley Skydiving 47
Perris, CA 47
Perris, Lake **26**, 47, **63**, 64
Perris Lake State Recreation Area **51**, 64
Perry, George 61
Peter Strauss Ranch State Park 94
Pine City Campground 123
Pine Creek Canyon 69
Pine Creek Pack Station 69
Pine Glen 124
Pine Grove 127
Pine Grove Campground 126
Pine Knot Landing and Marina 245
Pine Knot Trail 247
Pine Valley Stables **70**
Pine Valley, CA 70
Pinnacles National Monument 301
Pinos Altos 179
Pinos, Mount **21, 72,** 73, **191,** 192
   Ranger District 21, 73, 192
Pinos, Mount, Campground 192
Pinto Basin 253
Pinto Peak 133

INDEX

Piru Creek **55**
Piru, Lake 55, **61**
Pismo Beach 35, 108, 110, 112
Pismo Beach Pier 108
Pismo Beach, CA 35, 108
Pismo Coast Village 109
Pismo Dunes Natural Preserve 60, 108
Pismo State Beach **35, 40, 50,** 60, 88, **107, 108,** 109
Piute Crags 129
Piute Lake 129
Piute Pass 128, 129
Piute Pass Trail 128, 129
Placer County 24
Planet of the Apes (film) 219
Plant, Robert 254
Playboy 45
Pleasant Valley Campground 54
Pleasant Valley Reservoir 125
Pleasure Point Boat Landing 245
Plummer Park 71
Point Bennett 201
Point Conception 175, 176
Point Dume State Beach 18, 78, 230, 234, 235
Point Fermin 80
Point Loma 78, 279
Point Loma Sportsfishing 78, 280
Point Loma, CA 78
Point Mariah 24
Point Mugu State Park 16, 37, 78, **202,** 203, 204, 236, 237, 270, 303
  Ranger Office 37, 204
Point Vicente 78
Point Vicente Park **232**
Poles Trail 269
Ponderosa Lodge 163
Ponderosa, CA 18
Ponderosa, The **163**

Port Hueneme, CA 36, 37
Port San Luis Harbor 56, 110
Port San Luis Pier 110
Porterville, CA 160, 305
Pothole Lake, Little **4**
Pothole Lakes 60
Potrero Campground 177
Potwisha Campground 147, **148**
Providence Mountains Campground 256
Providence Mountains State Recreation Area **256,** 257
Pumice Flat 123
Punchbowl Creek 13
Pyramid Lake 55, **62**
Pyramid Lake Concession 62

Q

Quaking Aspen Campground **161**, 162
Quarry Cove 106

R

Rae Lakes 141
Rainbow Basin National Landmark **14**
Rainbow Falls 120, **121**
Rainbow Pack Station **69**
Rainbow Summit 118
Ramona, CA 304
Ranch of the 7th Range **70**
Rancho Bernardo, CA 304
Rancho Cuyamaca State Park 273, 293
Rancho Mirage, CA 84
Rancho Palos Verdes, CA 80, 87, 232, 233
Rancho Santa Fe, CA 280
Rancho Sierra Vista 203, 204
Red Butte Trail 282
Red Cliffs Area 171
Red Rock (on the Lower Santa Ynez River) **43,** 184, 185

INDEX

Red Rock Canyon State Park **170,** 171, 222, 223, 303
Red Rock Creek 222, 223
Redlands, CA 91, 247, 251
Redondo Beach 234, 235
Redondo Beach, CA 25, 57, 76, 233
  Pier **57,** 235
Redondo Sportsfishing 57
Reds Meadow **69,** 120, 121, 123
Reds Meadow Resort 121
Redwood Canyon **141**
Redwood Crossing **15**
Redwood Crossing Trail 155, 160
Redwood Meadows Campground **161**
Reed, Doug 278
Reef Point 80
Refugio State Beach **36,** 78
REI 19, 192, 290, 294, 299, 301, 307
Reyes Ranger Station 28
Ridge Trail (Montana de Oro State Park) 106
Ridgecrest, CA 15, 152, 306
Rim Nordic Ski Resort **22,** 23
Rim of the World Scenic Byway **93**
Rim Trail (Montana de Oro State Park) 105
Rincon Beach County Park **40**
Rincon Peak 184
Rindge Dam 220
River View Lodge 166, 170
Riverside, CA 305
Robert H. Meyer State Beach **229**
Rocco's 225
Rock Creek 4, 126, 127
Rock Creek Canyon 4, 69, 92, 126, 127, 128
Rock Creek Lake 126, 127
Rock Creek Lake Campground 127
Rock Creek Lodge 126, 128
Rock Creek Pack Station **69**
Rock Pool 219
Rockhouse Canyon 277
Rocking K Stables **70**
Rockreation 19
Rogers Lake 172
Rogers Trail 225
Rogers, Will, State Beach **40,** 225, 230, 234, 236
Ronald W. Caspers Wilderness Park 32, 43, 91, **266,** 267
Round Meadow 145, 150
Round Valley Campground 258, 259
Royal Gorge Cross-Country Ski Area **24**
Running Springs, CA 23, 94, 245, 250, 251
Rustic Canyon 224
Ryan Campground 253

S

Sabrina Campground 129
Sabrina, Lake 129, 130, 131
Sacramento, CA 303
Saddleback Butte State Park 303
Salmon Creek 157
Salmon Creek Falls 157
Salmon Creek Trail 157
Salt Creek 133
Salton City, CA 95
Salton Sea 75, 95, 253
San Andreas Fault 12, 28, 302
San Andreas Rift Zone 28
San Antonio, Lake 58, 59, **75,** **101,** 102, 103
San Antonio, Mount (*see also* Mount Baldy) 7, 47, 90, 208, **213,** 217, 218

INDEX

San Bernardino Mountains 11, 22, 26, 62, 216, 244, **245,** 246, 247, **248,** 251
San Bernardino National Forest 9, 12, 18, 98, 196, 209, 245, 247, 258, 305
   Arrowhead Ranger District 98
   Big Bear Ranger District 247, 248, 305
   Front Country Ranger District 305
   Idyllwild Ranger District 305
   Mountain Top Ranger District 305
   San Gorgonio Ranger District 9, 305
   San Jacinto Ranger District 30
   Supervisor's Office 305
San Bernardino, CA 49, 93, 244, 245, 248, 305
San Buenaventura State Beach **25**
San Clemente State Beach **38**
San Clemente, CA 38
San Diego Audubon Society 74
San Diego Bay 280
San Diego County Parks Department 65, 66
San Diego Harbor 58, 280
San Diego Hilton 283, 284, 285
San Diego Regional Bikeway Information 27
San Diego, CA 19, 27, 45, 47, 49, 57, 58, 65, 70, 76, 78, 93, 232, 273, 274, 275, 278, 279, 280, 281, 283, 284, 293, 300
   Visitor Information Center 27
San Dieguito River 280
San Dimas, CA 19, 301
San Elijo State Beach **38**
San Fernando Valley 18, 61, 71, 191, 213, 215, 216, 224, 226, 227, 239
San Fernando Valley, CA 52
San Fernando, CA 214, 304
San Francisco AIDS Foundation 32
San Gabriel Canyon 214
San Gabriel Mountains 11, 17, 26, 30, 68, 94, 208, 209, 211, 213, **215,** 216, 218, 224, 227, 234, 249
San Gabriel River 26
San Gabriel River Trail **26**
San Gabriel Valley 209, 226, 227, 300
San Gorgonio Peak **9**
San Gorgonio Wilderness 9, 16, **247,** 248
   Mill Creek Ranger District 9
   Ranger District 9, 305
San Gorgonio, Mount 7, 9, 10, 30, 47, 213, 247
San Jacinto Mountains 17, 63, 245, 253, **258,** 259, 260
San Jacinto, Mount 7, **10,** 11, 15, **21,** 22, 30, 47, 213, 259, 260
San Jacinto, Mount, State Park 11, 15, 21, 22, 258, 259, 260
   Ranger District 30
San Joaquin River **54,** 116, 120, 121, **123,** 124, 125
San Joaquin Valley 12, 62, 68, 120, 121, 122, 142, 144, 160, 162
San Juan Capistrano, CA 49, 94, 266
San Juan Trail **270,** 271
San Luis Bay 109
San Luis Obispo, CA 19, 56, 59, 92, 96, 102, 103, **106,** 107, 301
San Luis Pier **56**
San Luis Rey River 271
San Marcos Pass 29, 97, 182, 183
   Ranger Station 29
San Mateo Canyon **43, 260,** 261

INDEX

San Mateo Creek 260, 261
San Mateo Point 41
San Mateo Trail 261
San Mateo Wilderness 261
San Miguel Island 197, **200, 201,** 202
San Onofre Nuclear Power Plant 38, 41
San Onofre State Beach **38, 41,** 260
San Onofre, CA 38
San Pedro, CA 76, 78, 79, 80, 167, 234
San Rafael Mountains 181
San Rafael Wilderness **176,** 177, 178
San Simeon State Park 303
San Simeon, CA 106
San Ysidro Stables **70**
Sand Dunes (Death Valley National Park) **133**
Sandi's Rental Stables **70**
Sands, The 107
Sanford Winery 182
Santa Ana Mountains 47, 94, 260, 266, 270
Santa Ana River Trail **26**
Santa Ana, CA 19, 301
Santa Anita Creek, Big 212
Santa Barbara Channel 197
Santa Barbara County Department of Parks and Recreation 40
Santa Barbara County Vintners' Association 180, 181, 182
Santa Barbara Island 197, **200, 201,** 202
Santa Barbara Museum of Natural History 78, 79, 302
Santa Barbara Ranger District 29, 97, 185, 186, 187
Santa Barbara, CA 25, 29, 33, 35, 36, 52, 76, 78, 79, 87, 97, 104, 106, 177, 178, 180, 182, 183, 184, 185, 186, 200, 202, 268, 302, 305
Visitor Information Center 25
Santa Clara Estuary Natural Preserve 36, 37
Santa Clarita, CA 18, 61
Santa Cruz Island 86, 197, **198,** 200, 201
Santa Cruz, CA 32
Santa Lucia Mountains 104
Santa Lucia Ranger District 178, 180
Santa Lucia Wilderness 111
Santa Margarita Lake 59, 60, 301
Santa Maria, CA 32, 35, 305
Santa Monica Bait and Tackle 57
Santa Monica Bay 224
Santa Monica Mountains 31, 37, 83, 94, 177, 202, 203, 213, 218, 219, 221, 222, 223, 225, 226, 236, 290, 301
Santa Monica Mountains National Recreation Area 204, 236, 303, 304
Visitor Center 222
Santa Monica Mountains Conservancy 236
Santa Monica State Beach **231**
Santa Monica, CA 25, 32, 33, 40, 57, 230, 231, 268, 302
Municipal Pier **57,** 231, 234
Santa Paula Creek **55**
Santa Paula, CA 55
Santa Rosa Island 197, **200, 201,** 202, 282
Santa Rosa Mountains 276
Santa Rosa Plateau 84
Santa Ynez Canyon 224
Santa Ynez Falls 224
Santa Ynez Mountains 29, 60, 175, 181, 182

INDEX

Santa Ynez River 29, 43, 90, 182, 184, 185, 186
  Lower 185
  Mid, Campground 185, 186
  Upper 184, **185**
Santa Ynez Trail 224
Santa Ynez Valley 29, 179, 180, 181, 182, 183, 184, 224
Santa Ynez, CA 181
Santee, CA 65, 75
Santiago Trail 271
SC Village 44
Schatz Bakery 92
Scorpion Ranch 199
Scott's Cabin 272
Scott's Cabin Trail 272
Scotty's Castle 134, **135**
Scripps Institution of Oceanography 81
Sea Center 79, 302
Sea Cliff, CA 25
Sea Landing Sportfishing 78
Seaforth Sportfishing 78, 280
Seagal, Steven 239
Seal Beach Lifeguard Station 40
Seal Beach **40**
Seal Beach, CA 26, 40
Sentinel Campground **142**
Sepulveda Basin Bikeway **25**
Sequoia Motor Lodge 166, 170
Sequoia National Forest 13, 29, 96, 152, 153, 156, 157, 160, 164, 166, 305
  Cannell Meadow Ranger District 6, 153, 155, 157, 158, 169, 170, 305
  Greenhorn Ranger District 97, 305
  Hot Springs Ranger District 161, 305
  Hume Lake Ranger District 305
  Lake Isabella Ranger District 170

  Supervisor's Office 305
  Tule River Ranger District 162, 163, 305
Sequoia National Park 8, 11, 15, **22,** 23, **60, 70,** 92, 96, 140, 144, 145, 146, 147, **149,** 150, 151, 155, 159, 160, 161, 170, 303, 304
Sespe Canyon 195
Sespe Creek **15,** 195
Sespe Gorge 18
Sespe Hot Springs 95, **97,** 98, 194
Sespe River **55,** 58, 194, 195
Sespe Wilderness 15, 93, 97, 98, **194,** 195, 196
Shadow Lake **121,** 122, 125
Sheep Creek **142**
Sheep Mountain Wilderness 210
Sheep Pass 252
Shell Beach 33, 107, **108,** 109
Shell Beach, CA 108
Shelter Island Pier **58**
Sherman Oaks, CA 25
Sherman, Brad 236
Sherwin Creek 124, 125
Sherwin Creek Campground 124
Siberia Creek Trail 247
Sierra Club 297, 307
Sierra Club Angeles Chapter 299, 300, 302
Sierra Crest 120, 121, 126, 129
Sierra Madre Mountains 93
Sierra National Forest 128
Sierra Nevada 9, 11
Sierra Nevada Recreation Corporation 13
Sierra South Mountain Sports 29, 158, 166
Silver City Store 151
Silver City, CA 151
Silver Crest Picnic Area **43,** 272

INDEX

Silver Moccasin Trail **211**
Silver Mountain 249
Silverwood Lake **62**
Silverwood Wildlife Sanctuary **74**
Silverwood Wildlife Society 74
Simi Valley 48, 61
Sisquoc River 177
Skelton Lake **3**
Ski Green Valley (*see also* Big Air Green Valley) 250
Ski Sunrise 217, **218**
Skidoo Site **134**
Skinner, Lake 47, **64**
Skinner, Lake, County Park 64
Skydive Elsinore 47
Skyforest, CA 305
Skyline Park 30
Skyline Trail 227
Skysurfer Balloon Company 280
Slater, Kelly 39
Slide Peak 250
Smoke Tree Stables **70**
Snow Summit Ski Resort **30**, 216, 244, **248**, 249, 250, 251
Snow Valley 216, **250**
Snowcrest at Kratka Ridge **218**
Soda Springs, Upper 123
Solana Beach 38
Solana Beach, CA 19, 300
Solid Rock Gym 19
Solvang, CA 181, 182
South Bay Bike Trail **25**, 231, **234**
South Fork Campground (Sequoia National Park) **148**
South Fork Bishop Creek 130, 131
South Fork Kern River 5, 154
South Fork Kings River 140, 141, 142
South Fork Trail 9

South Lake (Bishop Creek Canyon) 130, 131, 300
Spirit Cruises 78
Split Mountain 15
Split Rock 268
Spooner's Cove **43,** 79, 105, 106
Sport and Science of Fly Fishing, The (UCLA class) 53
Sport Chalet 21, 192, 294
Sportsmart 294
Spring Valley, CA 70
Springville, CA 160, 163, 164, 305
Spyglass Inn 109
Stanfield Cutoff 26
Star Rise Trail 266
Star Trek V: The Final Frontier (film) 14
Stearns Wharf 79, 302
Steven Birch Aquarium 81
Stienstra, Tom 129
Stone Creek Campground 259
Stoney Point 18, **239**
Stovepipe Wells Campground **134**
Stovepipe Wells Inn **135**
Stovepipe Wells Motel 133
Stovepipe Wells, CA 10, 15, 132, 133, 135
  Visitor Center 136
Strauss, Peter, Ranch State Park 94
Stunt Creek 223
Stunt High Trail **222,** 223
Sturtevant Falls **212**
Suicide Peak 18
Suicide Rock 260
Sulphur Springs Trail 31
Summit Run 249
Sunrise Balloons 281
Sunset Beach 27
Sunset Ranch **70**
Sunset Ridge 211, 212
Sunset Ridge Trail 211

INDEX

Sunset Campground
  (Death Valley National Park) **134**
  (Kings Canyon National Park) **142**
Surfer's Point **40**
Surfrider Beach (*see also* Malibu Lagoon State Beach) **40**, 80
Swami's Beach **41**, 81
Sweetwater River 273
Sweetwater Trail 183
Switzer Campground 209
Switzer Falls 210
Switzer Falls Picnic Area 209
Switzer Falls Trail **209**
Sycamore Canyon **16**, **37**, 78, 203, 204, 270
Sycamore Canyon Beach 37, 203
Sycamore Canyon Campground 203, 204
Sycamore Canyon Trail 203
Sycamore Creek 203
Sycamore Mineral Springs **96**, 109
Sylmar, CA 44

T

Table Mountain Group Campground 130, 131
Taft, CA 47
Tahoe, Lake 301
Tahquitz Peak 17, 18, 30
Tahquitz Rock (*see also* Lily Rock) 260
Talken, Kirsten 256
Tamarack Cross-County Ski Area **23**
Tamarack Lakes 126, 127
Tamarack Lakes Trail 126
Tamarack Lodge and Cross-Country Ski Center 23
Tamarisk Grove 277
Tapia Park 219
Tarantula Point 175
Tarzana, CA 18, 300
Taylor Dome 18
Taylor, Neal 53, 54, 183
Tecopa Hot Springs County Park **97**
Tecopa, CA 97
Tejon Pass 191
Tejon Ranch 68
Telegraph Canyon 32
Telescope Peak 7, **9**, 10, 86, **133**, 134, 136
Temecula, CA 64, 281
Temescal Canyon 230
Tenaja Canyon 261
Tenaja Creek 261
Texas Springs **134**
The Livery Stable **69**
The Restaurant 59
Thomas Brothers Guide to Los Angeles (book) 215, 223
Thompson, Mount 131
Thoreau, Henry 306
Thorndike Campground 10, **134**
Thornhill Broome State Beach **37**
Thornhill Broome State Beach Campground 204
Thorp's Log 146
Thousand Island Lake 121, 125
Thousand Oaks, CA 31
Three Rivers, CA 22, 23, 89, 92, 141, 145, 147, 150, 151, 304
Tijuana River 75
Tijuana Slough National Wildlife Reserve **75**
Tijuana Slough State Park 75
Timber Lake 9
Timber Ridge 249
Titus Canyon **133**

INDEX

Tom Harrison Cartography (Recreation Maps)
  Cuyamaco Rancho State Park 275
  Mammoth High Country 4
  Mono Divide High Country 4, 131
  Sequoia and Kings Canyon National Parks 144, 150
  San Gabriel Mountains 209
Tony Alvis' Los Padres Wilderness Outfitters **70,** 194, 195, 196
Topanga Canyon 31, 222, 224, 225
Topanga Creek 224, 225
Topanga State Park 31, 222, **223,** 224, 225, 226, 236, 303
Topanga, CA 303
Topatopa Mountains 192, 193
Torrance Beach 233, 234
Torrey Pines Gliderport 49
Torrey Pines State Reserve **43, 51,** 78, **282,** 283
Toys-R-Us 297
Trabuco Canyon 271
Trabuco Ranger District 261, 271
Traditional Equitation School 226, 227
Trail Camp (Mount Whitney) 8
Trail of 100 Giants 161
Travelodge 103
Trestles Beach **41**
Trevore, Eric 17, 18
Tri-Peaks 203
Trippet Ranch 224
Trona Pinnacles **14**
Trout Creek 29
Trout Creek Trail 28
Trout Unlimited 307
Troy Meadows 154, 158
Truth Aquatics 202
Tucker Wildlife Sanctuary **74**

Tujunga Ranger District 214
Tulare River 164
Tule River 159, 162
  Middle Fork
  South Fork of 162
  North Fork 155, 159, 162
  Ranger District 161, 162, 163, 164
20th Century–Fox 219
22nd St. Landing 78
29 Palms Inn 254
Twentynine Falms Marine Corps Base 14 252, 254
Twentynine Falms, CA 254, 304
Twin Lakes 23, 54, 120, 123
Two Harbors, CA 237, 238

U

U.S. Highway 395 **92**
U.S. Army Corps of Engineers 221
U.S. Department of the Interior 307
U.S. Fish and Wildlife Service 307
U.S. Forest Service 3, 5, 6, 7, 8, 28, 29, 59, 111, 122, 123, 127, 128, 130, 131, 147, 152, 153, 156, 157, 158, 160, 161, 162, 164, 165, 166, 167, 168, 177, 178, 180, 185, 186, 187, 192, 194, 196, 209, 213, 247, 261, 271, 273, 294, 304, 307
  Cannell Meadow District Office 158
  Lone Pine Interagency Visitor Center 3
  Visitor Center, Bishop 3
  Visitor Center, Mammoth Lakes 3
U.S. Geological Survey 307
U.S. Hang Gliding Association 49

INDEX

Under Siege 2 (film) 239
Underwater Park 238
Union Pacific Railroad
    Depot 255
United States Fish and Wildlife
    Service 75
United States Geological
    Survey 305, 307
United States Parachute
    Association 47
Universal City, CA 302
University of California
    Irvine 269, 302
        Recreation Office 302
    Los Angeles 223
        Extension 54, 72, 302
    Riverside 302
        Extension 303
    San Diego 32, 81
University Peak 5
Upper Hilton Lake 126, 127
Upper Kern Plateau
    28, 29, 156, 158
Upper Morgan Lake 126
Upper Newport Bay 37
Upper Newport Bay
    Ecological Reserve and
    Regional Park **74**
Upper Pine Grove
    Campground 127
Upper Santa Ynez River
    184, **185**
Upper Soda Springs 123

V

Vail and Vickers
    Company 201
Vallecito Mountains 15
Van Nuys, CA 48, 49
Vandenberg Air Force
    Base 176
Vasquez Rocks County Park
    14, 18
Venice Beach 231, 235

Venice, CA 25, 26, 234, 301
Ventura County
    General Services Agency 193
    Transportation
        Commission 25
Ventura Harbor 78, 79, 198,
    200, 201
Ventura River 184
Ventura State Beach **50,** 51
Ventura, CA 25, 32, 40, 50, 52,
    56, 57, 60, 76, 104, 192, 196,
    198, 200, 202, 303
    Department of Parks and
        Recreation 40, 57
    Municipal Pier **56**
Ventura's Village Kite & Toy
    Store 50
Verdugo Mountains 213
Vertical Adventures 19, 253
Vertical Hold 19
Victoria's Secret 107
Viejail Trail 271
Village Kite & Toy Store 52
Vincent Gap 211
Vincent Tumamait 192
Virg's Fish'n 78
Virginia, Lake 125
Vivian Creek Trail 9, **16**
Vivian Creek Trail Camp 9
"Voices of the Peruvian
    Rainforest" (audiotape) 297
Von's 124

W

W.L. Gore 307
Wallace, Jim, Skydiving
    School 45, 46
Walnut Creek, CA 12
Waterman, Mount **216,** 217
Wedge, The 42
Weir Lake 131
Well Fed Backpacker, The
    (J. Fleming) 2
West Anacapa Island 197

INDEX

West End Dive and Kayak Center 237, 238
West Hollywood, CA 33, 71, 72
West Los Angeles, CA 18, 300
Western Town 221
Westridge Freestyle Park 249
Westward Beach 230
Westwood, CA 53, 302
Wet Spot Rentals 238
Whale's Tail, The 104
White Mountains 8, 9, 53, 92, 116, 120
White Mountain Ranger District 4, 128, 130, 131
Whites Point 80
Whiteside, Kelly 283
Whitney Meadow, Big 155
Whitney Portal Campground 8
Whitney, Mount **7,** 8, 9, 10, 11, 92, 133, 146, 147, 164, 167, 170
Whitney, Mount, Zone 9
Wilderness Institute, The 13, 302
Wilderness Society, The 307
Wilderness Travel Course (Sierra Club) **299,** 302
Wildlife Waystation **214,** 215
Wildrose Canyon 133
Wildrose Peak **133, 134,** 136
Wildwood Regional Park 31
Will Rogers State Beach **40,** 225, **230,** 234, 236
Williamson, Mount 17, 18
Willow Campground 131
Wilson, Mount 213
   Observatory 208
Wilson, Mount, Toll Road 30
Windcaves 15
Winding Stairs 256
WindSports Soaring Center 48, 49
Wishon Campground **162,** 163
Wofford Heights, CA 166, 170
Wolverton Meadow 22, 70
Wolverton Pack Station **70,** 150
Wolverton, CA 60
Wonderland of Rocks **43,** 252
Woodland Hills, CA 94, 225
Woodland Trail **246**
Woods Creek Trail 141
Woods Lodge 122
Wrightwood, CA 15, 87, 90, 209, 210, 211, 214, 216, 218
Wynola, CA 95

Y

Ye Alpine Tavern 212
Yosemite National Park 8, 11, 17, 18, **23,** 92, 119, 120, 141, 159, 301, 302
Yosemite Valley 23
Yuma, AZ 306

Z

Zaca Mesa Winery 181
Zacchino, Mike 281
Zehr, Nathan and Paula 285
Zuma Beach **41,** 78, **229,** 230
Zuma Beach County Park 41, 229
Zuma Canyon 236
Zumwalt Meadow **141**
Zzyzx, CA 301

ABOUT THE AUTHORS

Steve Hymon has written for *Sports Illustrated*, the *Chicago Tribune,* and the *Los Angeles Times*. He is currently pursuing a master's degree in geography at UCLA.

Julie Sheer is deputy graphics editor in the *Los Angeles Times* art department. Before moving to Southern California, she performed various editing duties at the *Chicago Tribune* for 13 years.

Julie and Steve live in Santa Monica with their chocolate Labrador retriever, Molly.

CREDITS

Editor in Chief	Kyle Morgan
Editors	Karin Mullen
	Carolyn Perkins
Production Coordinator & Assistant Editor	Jean-Vi Lenthe
Production Assistant	Mark Aver

TRIP NOTES

FOGHORN ✌ OUTDOORS

Founded in 1985, Foghorn Press has quickly become one of the country's premier publishers of outdoor recreation guidebooks. Through its unique Books Building Community program, Foghorn Press supports community environmental issues, such as park, trail, and water ecosystem preservation.

Foghorn Press books are available throughout the United States in bookstores and some outdoor retailers. If you cannot find the title you are looking for, visit Foghorn's Web site at www.foghorn.com or call 1-800-FOGHORN.

The Complete Guide Series

- *Tom Stienstra's Outdoor Getaway Guide for Northern California* (448 pp) $18.95—New 3rd Edition
- *California Camping* (768 pp) $20.95—New 10th anniversary edition
- *California Hiking* (688 pp) $20.95—3rd edition
- *California Waterfalls* (408 pp) $17.95
- *California Fishing* (768 pp) $20.95—4th edition
- *California Golf* (1056 pp) $24.95—New 8th edition
- *California Beaches* (640 pp) $19.95
- *California Boating and Water Sports* (608 pp) $19.95
- *Pacific Northwest Camping* (656 pp) $20.95—New 6th edition
- *Pacific Northwest Hiking* (648 pp) $20.95—2nd edition
- *Washington Fishing* (488 pp) $20.95—New 2nd edition
- *Tahoe* (678 pp) $20.95—New 2nd edition
- *Alaska Fishing* (448 pp) $20.95—2nd edition
- *New England Hiking* (416 pp) $18.95
- *New England Camping* (520 pp) $19.95
- *Utah and Nevada Camping* (384 pp) $18.95
- *Southwest Camping* (544 pp) $17.95
- *Baja Camping* (288 pp) $14.95—2nd edition
- *Florida Camping* (672 pp) $20.95—New!

The National Outdoors Series

- *America's Secret Recreation Areas—Your Recreation Guide to the Bureau of Land Management's Wild Lands of the West* (640 pp) $17.95
- *America's Wilderness—The Complete Guide to More Than 600 National Wilderness Areas* (592 pp) $19.95
- *The Camper's Companion—The Pack-Along Guide for Better Outdoor Trips* (464 pp) $15.95
- *Wild Places: 20 Journeys Into the North American Outdoors* (305 pp) $15.95

A book's page count and availability are subject to change.
For more information, call 1-800-FOGHORN,
e-mail: foghorn@well.com, or write to:
Foghorn Press
340 Bodega Avenue
Petaluma, CA 94952

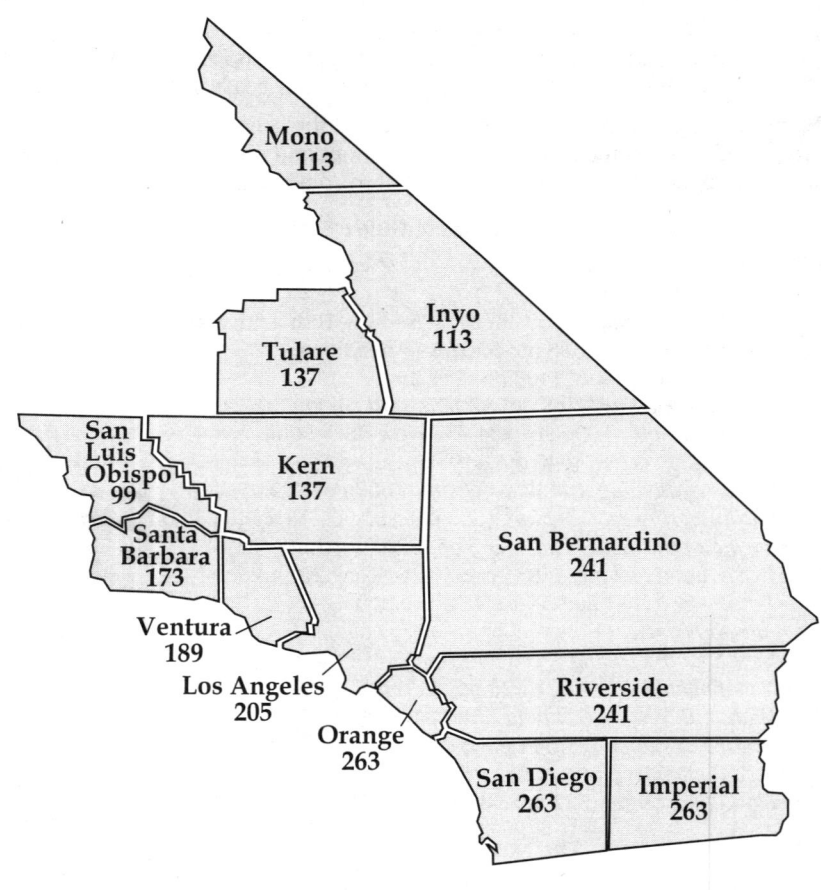

SOUTHERN CALIFORNIA